THE MODERN JEWISH CANON

A JOURNEY THROUGH LANGUAGE AND CULTURE

RUTH R. WISSE

THE FREE PRESS

NEW YORK LONDON TORONTO SYDNEY SINGAPORE

THE FREE PRESS
A Division of Simon & Schuster Inc.
1230 Avenue of the Americas
New York, NY 10020

THE FREE PRESS and colophon are trademarks
of Simon & Schuster Inc.

Part of Chapter 8 is reprinted with the permission of Cambridge University
Press from "The Classic Disinheritance" by Ruth R. Wisse in *New Essays on
"Call It Sleep*," ed. Hana Wirth-Nesher

Manufactured in the United States of America

10   9   8   7   6   5   4   3   2   1

Book design by Ellen R. Sasahara

Library of Congress Cataloging-in-Publication Data

Wisse, Ruth R.
The modern Jewish canon: a journey through language and culture/
Ruth R. Wisse.
p. cm.
Includes bibliographical references and index.
1. Jewish fiction—20th century—History and criticism. 2. Literature, Modern—Jewish authors—History and criticism. 3. Canon (Literature). I. Title.

PN842.W57 2000
809.3'0089'924—dc21   00-037656
ISBN 0-684-83075-2

FOR BILLY, JACOB, AND ABBY

CONTENTS

PREFACE

IN THE LATE 1960S, during a period of general expansion in higher education, I won permission to introduce courses on Yiddish language and literature at McGill University, where I was then teaching sections of the English literature survey. A decade earlier, when I was an undergraduate at McGill, not a single course in any department offered instruction about the Jews. McGill of the 1950s was not unusual: there were then only three full-time positions in Jewish Studies in North America—Harry Wolfson at Harvard, Salo Baron at Columbia, and Walter Fischel at the University of California at Berkeley. In proposing to teach Jewish literature, I argued that an expanded humanities curriculum would broaden the university's coverage of Western culture, legitimating the university's claim to be teaching Western, rather than Christian, civilization. Since it may prove relevant to my discussion of the works presented in this book, I might as well relate that the only member of the English department who voted against my proposal was its only other Jew, an assistant professor of English who had recently arrived from New York City.

During my undergraduate years at McGill, I had not given much thought to the exclusion of Jewish culture from the curriculum. Nevertheless, it did seem strange to me that my introductory economics course overlooked the role of Jews in trade and talked about the Rothschilds without mentioning their Jewishness, and it was painful to read certain passages in Chaucer and Celine that libeled the Jews without being invited to discuss the authors' prejudice. Although McGill had rescinded its discriminatory admissions policy in 1950 and Jews in large numbers were to be found on campus, our presence was never acknowledged, and I was occasionally troubled that the intellectual traditions and culture of the Jews went unmentioned. *"Mais sois gentille,"* my French teacher might have said had I raised the problem with her. Be grateful that you have been welcomed here despite your Jewishness, and don't expect to have your Jewishness included along with you. Why not take your place in this society as a Canadian and a Quebecer, speaking English and French and performing Shakespeare and Molière, to the point of becoming a teacher yourself should you be able to match your ability with your ambition? Why not, indeed?

But shortly after I graduated, I surprised myself rudely. The defining moment occurred during the first visit to Canada in 1959 of the Yiddish poet Abraham Sutzkever, whose speaking tour I had helped to organize. Survivor of the Vilna ghetto and witness on behalf of Russian Jewry at the Nuremberg trials, Sutzkever had become what Yiddish literary criticism calls "more than a poet"—he had become a symbol of the creative Jewish spirit after the devastation of the Second World War. His lyrics, which I read in private and heard in his public readings before Yiddish audiences, moved me to arrange a reading of a selection of his poetry for Folkways Records.[1] (I had already been introduced to Yiddish literature: it was taught in the Jewish day school I had attended, and more importantly, my parents' adoration of Yiddish culture had brought many of the leading contemporary Yiddish writers and poets into our home.) One day, when Sutzkever asked me about my professional plans, I told him I was thinking of going to graduate school to take a degree in English literature. "Why don't you study Yiddish?" he asked. I laughed aloud. "And what would I do? Teach Sholem Aleichem?"[2]

Those words changed the course of my life. The insult to Sutzkever was not as great as the shock to myself: how could I have voiced such contempt for the tradition of literature in which I had been raised? Why mock the prospect of teaching Sholem Aleichem, one of my favorite writers? Along with the education I had received at college, the eclipse of Jewish subjects in the curriculum had apparently persuaded me that Jews had no viable culture—and this in violation of the culture that had produced me! A few days later I applied to the graduate program in English and Comparative Literature at Columbia University, the only place on the continent where Yiddish then formed part of a graduate degree program. And it was after I returned to McGill to complete my graduate education and had already begun teaching there that I petitioned for and received permission to add Yiddish language and literature to that university's offerings. I hoped that the inclusion of Jewish studies in the university curriculum would allow Jews like me to do advanced study in their own sources and to invite everyone else to share in them, too.

The kind of inferiority consciousness I discovered in myself seems fairly typical of members of ethnic and religious minorities who begin to make their way into the mainstream of society. As long as we are fighting discrimination, our goal is to be treated fairly, but once we are treated fairly, we want the further respect that comes with being both tolerated and *known*. Once minority members feel sufficiently comfortable in the university, they want to incorporate their particular culture within the mainstream culture. At least, that is how it happens in democratic America, where immigrants are encouraged to become citizens, not squatters. When I tried to gain the right to include Jewish studies in the university curriculum, it never occurred to me that I might be challenging the notion of Western civilization: my conscious purpose was to strengthen that civilization by reincorporating the Jews into a framework from which they had been artificially excluded.

I even came to see the task as urgent. By the latter part of the twentieth century, no one could honestly study European philosophy or history, much less theology or politics, without tripping over the bones of the Jews. But North American society was different. It was not only an extension of Europe but also a reaction against Europe. I believed that an integrated American curriculum would reinforce an integrated society. This was more than a decade before Holocaust studies were offered at universities, and I believed then, as I still do, that it is important to teach Jewish civilization for its own sake and as a counterforce to antisemitism and that, as a matter of priority, learning about the Jews is more important for the future of humankind than learning about their extinction.

Yiddish literature seemed the perfect vehicle for this intellectual reconciliation. The vernacular language of European Jewry, Yiddish probably developed about nine hundred years ago in the small Jewish communities along the banks of the Rhine and Moselle Rivers. It then matured as it spread with its speakers throughout the continent, from Amsterdam to Omsk, arriving eventually, with their descendants, in all the other continents.[3] By 1939 there were about ten million Yiddish speakers in the world, more Jews than had ever simultaneously known a Jewish language at any time in history. Inspired by hopes of emancipation and challenged by the ideas of the Enlightenment, modern Jews had created a dynamic literature in Yiddish on a par with their European counterparts. Through the study of Yiddish poetry, fiction, and drama, I believed, students could absorb the nuanced inner experience of their writers, as opposed to the antisemitic stereotypes found in much European writing. Given how much pleasure I had derived from learning about the British, the French, the Germans, and the Russians by reading some of their best-known authors, I wanted to provide the same experience for Jewish and non-Jewish students through the reading of Yiddish works, preferably in the original but also in translation. What especially appealed to me was the normalcy of this academic arrangement: other European nations had their vernaculars, the Jews had theirs; other European nations had their literatures, the Jews had theirs. I was intent on establishing an academic symmetry so that one could study in tandem what politics had forcibly kept apart. To this end, I patterned my Yiddish courses—the Yiddish short story, the Yiddish novel in interwar Poland—on courses I had taken in other departments, making due modifications for the special properties of the literature I was teaching.

The experiment proved successful. It is exhilarating to study the coherent development of a literature with its own geneology and generative powers. Take Mendele Moykher-Sforim's *The Travels of Benjamin III* (1878), the mock adventure of a small-town Jew who sets out with his sidekick, Senderl "the housewife," to find the ten lost tribes of Israel but loses his way the minute he leaves town and ends up forcibly conscripted into the tsarist army. The book's debt to Cervantes was so obvious that his Polish translator called it *The Jewish Don Quixote,* providing name recognition for a Christian readership. But in his original Yiddish and Hebrew incarnations, Benjamin was dubbed "the Third," because he followed two earlier, historically credible, Jewish travelers (of the twelfth and the nineteenth century). Benjamin III spoofed not only the substitution of messianism for real knowledge of the world but also the attendant follies of Russian Jewry under the tsars. When Sholem Aleichem adopted the model of Benjamin for his *Menakhem-Mendl* (1892), he turned the mockery of messianism up a notch: by making Menakhem Mendl a speculator on the newly opened stock exchange, he exposed the underlying psychology of the *luftmentsh,* the Jew who begins to dream like an urban capitalist before the tsar has even granted him a residence permit. In 1924, following World War I and the Russian Revolution, Moyshe Kulbak remodeled the original pair of travelers in a rollicking narrative poem about Bunye and Bere, a couple of would-be Jewish revolutionaries who try to function like Bolshevik heroes. Thus, studying a national literature makes it possible to trace patterns of influence, the evolution of its humor, changes in its language, and the modifications that politics brings to its art.

My students took the subject of Yiddish literature in their own directions. A French Canadian anthropology student told me how frustrated he had been in his attempt to penetrate the culture of Canada's Jewish community until he progressed from a study of Bible and Jewish religion to the study of Yiddish literature, which brought to life what he had almost despaired of comprehending; he has since taught comparative courses on Yiddish and French Canadian culture. Aaron Lansky, who came to McGill as a graduate student, became so concerned about the shrinking readership of Yiddish literature that he conceived and founded the National Yiddish Book Center to protect Yiddish books and to promote Yiddish creativity. Nowadays, no one has to make a case for the inclusion of Yiddish literature in the college curriculum, for it is taught in major universities across the continent.

You might say that by integrating Yiddish literature into the curriculum, I had been obeying a version of the Zionist impulse to put Jews on an equal footing with the nations whose history they share. But then, like many Zionists, I realized that normalcy does not betoken uniformity. The symmetry I had tried to establish between Yiddish and other national literatures went only so far. Though one can hardly know the modern Jew without knowing Yiddish literature, Yiddish is not and never has been the only literature of modern Jews. Whereas Russian literature is written in Russian and includes what is written by Russian émigrées in Paris and Vermont, Jewish writing was never equivalent to writing in Yiddish. As Sholem Aleichem might have put it, all carpenters may be human but not all humans are carpenters. Hebrew had always remained the language of Jewish study, prayer, and legal correspondence, playing a far more active role in Jewish affairs than did the analogous Latin in Christian cultures. Thus, when modern Jews began to compare themselves to their European counterparts, many assumed that Hebrew, not Yiddish, was their national language, and they reclaimed it for contemporary use. The Zionist movement in particular, because it conceived of the ingathering of Jews within their ancient biblical homeland, eventually designated Hebrew as the national language of the Jewish people instead of Yiddish, the vernacular tongue of only the Ashkenazic part of the Jewish people. Most Yiddish writers born in the nineteenth century wrote in both Jewish languages before settling on one or the other, leading some critics to speak of a single literature in two languages. Indeed, my colleague Gershon Shaked was quick to point out that since Mendele Moykher-Sforim had rewritten *The Travels of Benjamin III* in Hebrew, a parallel trail of that book's influence could be traced through the Hebrew works of S. Y. Agnon and Haim Hazaz. The literature I taught had emerged out of the cultural synthesis of Yiddish and Hebrew, and doing justice to the one required studying its interaction with the other. In recognition of this interconnection, many graduate programs in modern Yiddish and Hebrew literature now require mastery of both languages and encourage comparative study of the two literatures in tandem.

But this is still only a minor part of the problem. Once, as I was reading about Franz Kafka, my eye was caught by a reproduction of a letter he had written to his Hebrew teacher Puah Bentovim. The intense effort he clearly exerted on his Hebrew penmanship touched me and reminded me that modern Jewish writers did not always have the option of writing in Jewish languages. Kafka was already a formed German writer by the time he began to hunger for Jewish language, which was too late for him to adopt one even had he wanted to. Yet surely modern Jewish literature has to include Franz Kafka. And what of Ze'ev Vladimir Jabotinsky, the founder of the Revisionist movement of Zionism, whose name is synonymous with Jewish nationalism? An amazing linguist, Jabotinsky wrote his novels in his native Russian, not in his later acquired Hebrew or Yiddish. And the most famous Jewish book of the twentieth century, *The Diary of Anne Frank*, was written in Dutch. Indeed, since the tradition of writing in the language of the land goes back to Jewish writers like Philo and Maimonides, there is no necessary correlation in ancient *or* modern Jewish literature between language and national consciousness. Defining Jewish literature with maximal inclusiveness, the first professor of Yiddish at the Hebrew University, Dov Sadan, noted that the modern Jewish writer had three choices: to address Jewish readers in one of their languages, to speak to them in a non-Jewish language, or to not write for them as Jews at all.[4] But Kafka's belated attempts to learn Hebrew is a reminder that some modern Jewish writers can choose only between the latter two.

If I had originally intended to help integrate Jewish writers into the study of Western civilization through the "traditional" avenues of Jewish national literatures in Yiddish and Hebrew, the logic of my inquiry soon led me to the opposite conclusion, namely, that modern Jewish literature cannot be circumscribed by what Hana Wirth-Nesher calls the "altogether too tidy" criterion of language alone.[5] Having wanted to normalize Jews in the curriculum by introducing courses in Yiddish literature, I realized that my approach pointed up the anomalous, not the typical, Jewish attitude toward national language and that an adequate study of modern Jewish literature would have to be as polyglot as the people who wrote it. In tandem with courses on Yiddish literature, I also began experimenting with courses on multilingual Jewish literature, analyzing how the language in which Jewishness is conceived affects the nature of the literary work.

This book tries to explain the phenomenon of a multilingual Jewish literature through a discussion of some of its greatest works of the twentieth century. There will obviously be some tension between classifying a given piece of writing as an example of Jewish literature and designating it as a work in a non-Jewish language that has a strong national tradition of its own. A multilingual Jewish literature violates, on the one hand, the concept of a national literature in a national language and, on the other, the traditional Jewish concept of a received literature that alone requires ongoing interpretation. It will satisfy neither the traditionalist who likes clean boundaries nor the postmodernist who doesn't believe in boundaries. Modern literature reflects the decline of religious faith, the disintegration of cohesive communities, the weakening of ethnic ties—a centrifugal process that is reflected most obviously in the many languages that Jews have come to speak. Yet just as there exists a modern Jewish people, so too does a modern Jewish literature exist, and I hope to show that the difficulty of defining them does not lessen their actuality.

September 2000

ACKNOWLEDGMENTS

M Y FIRST PRINCIPAL and lifelong model of a teacher, Shloime
Wiseman, loved to quote the Talmudic saying "The cow wants
to suckle more than the calf to nuzzle." Embarrassed to imagine
this imposing man as a female mammal, I was even more disturbed by the
idea that he might be as dependent on his students as we were on him. Yet
now that I am a teacher, I often recall this piece of wisdom. Therefore, I
want first and foremost to thank the students who inspired this book and
many of its ideas. Both at McGill where I taught and at Harvard, where I
now teach modern Jewish literature, I have been blessed with uncommonly bright and eager students who manifested a respect and enthusiasm
for reading that can no longer be taken for granted. I am also deeply grateful to my teaching assistants, who doubled the pleasure of introducing this
literature and who have helped to define my idea of the canon.

Over the years, I have incurred a heavy debt of gratitude to the librar-
ians of several institutions: the incomparable Widener Library at Harvard,
McLennan Library at McGill, the YIVO Institute for Jewish Research in
New York City, and the National Library at the Hebrew University in Gi-
vat Ram, Jerusalem. The presence at the Jewish Public Library of Montreal
of Eva Raby, my ever-helpful sister, makes working there a special delight.

I was helped at various points in the preparation of this manuscript by
Justin Cammy, Michal Engelman, Audrey Marcus, and Rachel Rubinstein.
Gershon Shaked and Jeremy Dauber made helpful suggestions on several
chapters. Ann Charney inspired me by the example of her discipline and
the warmth of her friendship.

The publishers Farrar, Straus & Giroux and Cambridge University
Press generously granted me permission to reprint parts of two essays I
originally wrote for other books. Small sections of this book appeared in
different form in *The New Republic* and *The Weekly Standard*. I am grateful for

fair use of this material and thank the editors, Leon Wieseltier and John Podhoretz, for the improvements they suggested. Like many of my fellow contributors to *Commentary*, I dream of some day satisfying the editorial standards of Neal Kozodoy, but in the meantime I revel in his critical interest in my work.

Over many years I have benefited from the erudition and wit of my university colleagues, who may hear echoes of our conversations in these pages. I am fortunate beyond words to have as a collaborator in the field of Yiddish and Jewish literature my brother David Roskies, than whom no one is more knowledgeable or generous. He encouraged me to write this book, and while he bears no responsibility for its failings, he contributed to whatever may be its strengths.

My association with The Free Press, which began under the stewardship of Adam Bellow and Erwin Glikes, remains more than professionally wholesome. Alys Yablon offered splendid editorial guidance and helped me pare down the manuscript without tears. I am thankful, as ever, to Glen Hartley for finding my work a home.

Some debts are too private to voice in public. How much my mother, Masha Roskies, helped to shape my idea of the Jewish people became clear only with her recent death. My husband Len's love for her was as generous and unusual as he is. The dedication of this book to our children is as much his as mine, because by now I feel his encouraging presence in everything that I do. Billy, our ebullient wordsmith, begins his latest book of poetry with the sentence "Miracles happen." I take that as my prooftext. With intelligence, patience, and love, our son Jacob saw me through the worst phase of this project, helping me face the computer revolution ("All in good time . . ."). When I told our daughter Abby that I intended to call the book *The Modern Jewish Canon*, she began singing Tchaikovsky's 1812 *Overture*, exploding the conceit and alerting me to what charges of overreaching I might expect. I am well aware how much my model of the canon resembles the dynamic of a vigorous family that fosters individuality through shared values as well as mutual love and support. I have written this book with the illusion that it will interest others, and my family has helped turn that illusion into firm hope.

THE MODERN
JEWISH CANON

INTRODUCTION

ORE THAN THE TORAH ITSELF, the written and the oral law that derives from Moses, Jewish civilization seems to depend on the *relation* of the Jewish people to its sacred teachings. The biblical canon could have vanished within a generation had it not been kept perpetually alive through habits of study. Indeed, traditional Jews refer to the calendar by the weekly portion of the Pentateuch that is read aloud in the synagogue over the course of each year. The exceptional emphasis on repetition is enshrined in the confession of faith, the Shema, which is from the Book of Deuteronomy 6:4–9:

> Hear, O Israel! The Lord is our God, the Lord alone. You shall love the Lord your God with all your heart and with all your soul, and with all your might. Take to heart these instructions with which I charge you this day. Impress them upon your children. Recite them when you stay at home and when you are away, when you lie down and when you get up. Bind them as a sign on your hand, and let them serve as frontlets on your forehead; inscribe them on the doorposts of your house and on your gates.[1]

Is this not a remarkable ratio between the content and the forms of remembrance? Begin with a declaration of the heart, by all means, because the relation to God is based on love, but then ensure that His words are engraved on the soul through every habit and limb. The human being is not a diamond that can be carved once and for all. Jewish civilization understands that words only acquire significance through constant rehearsal within a social framework that encourages—nay, that demands—repetition.

A very different approach to literary tradition is presented by Harold Bloom in *The Western Canon*, a book that appeared as I was writing this one.

An ardent reader who deplores the decline of "the art and passion of reading well and deeply," Bloom defends the idea of schooling in great books
that acquire their natural authority over time, and he issues his own list of
favorites to whet our appetites. He turns all barrels on members of what he
calls the "School of Resentment," journalists and teachers who want to
overthrow the canon in order to advance their program of social change.
Yet he distances himself equally from "right-wing defenders of the canon,
who wish to preserve it for its supposed (and non-existent) moral values":[2]

> Reading the very best writers—let us say, Homer, Dante, Shake-
> speare, Tolstoy—is not going to make us better citizens. Art is per-
> fectly useless, according to the sublime Oscar Wilde, who was
> right about everything. He also told us that all bad poetry is sin-
> cere. Had I the power to do so, I would command that these words
> be *engraved above every gate at every university*, so that each student
> might ponder the splendor of this insight.[3]

The italics are mine, of course, to indicate that Bloom is enlisting
Deuteronomy to move us from the religious domain to the secular in order
to warn *against* the Bible's moral conception of words. (The quips are
Esau's, but the voice is Jacob's.) Throughout his book on the Western
canon, Bloom is intent on getting the lesson across that the individual self
is the "only method and the whole standard for apprehending aesthetic
value." He upholds the autonomous authority of aesthetic value, "free of
history and ideology and available to whoever can be educated to read
and view it." He wants us to distinguish "the aesthetic power and authority
of the Western Canon from whatever spiritual, political, or even moral
consequences it may have fostered."[4] Whereas the rabbis inveighed
against *belles lettres* because they were not grounded in religious truth,
Bloom cautions against its opposite, against mistaking literature for an alternative form of moral education. Without wishing to be mischievous, I
think that Bloom's unwillingness to see literature used for any extra-liter-
ary purpose betrays an anxiety of Jewish influence, echoing as it does the
Jewish prohibition against misuse of God's name and against "ploughing"
with the Torah to achieve pragmatic ends. He guards the "autonomy of
the aesthetic" as jealously as the rabbis guard the sanctity of the Torah.
Using methods of inquiry that Bloom pioneered, one could demonstrate

that his kind of emphasis on reading derives from his own Jewish tradition, though he now applies it to the opposite goal of reading for individual pleasure.

Were we to accept this dichotomy at face value, we would have to abandon the identification of a Jewish canon, since both the rabbis and Harold Bloom would oppose the project on the grounds that it mixes categories they insist on keeping apart. The modern Jewish canon is not theologically reliable: literature in the secular sense of the term is, as Bloom argues, aesthetically autonomous, and may treat the sanguinary Cossacks as favorably as their Jewish victims. Of course, no book is ever going to portray the Jews in a worse light than the Bible, but modern literature does not stand in awe of God, either. From the narrowest perspective, traditionalists may well wonder in what sense modern literature can be Jewish. And from his *narrowest* perspective, Harold Bloom would agree. Literature is to him a relief from the lesser claims of society, not the collective anchor of any particular culture. Although he divides his reading list according to countries and languages, he does not consider the works in their national context. He consistently defends writers from the labeling umpires by refusing to apply any extra-aesthetic categories. "Proust," he writes, against those who protest that he did not make his narrator either a Jew or a homosexual, "is so great an artist that his aesthetic dignity deserves our seeking aesthetic motives for what were essentially aesthetic decisions."[5] I heartily concur with this statement, and on the basis of some of the very same considerations, I will presently explain why I do not include Proust in the Jewish canon. Modern literature cannot be prescriptive in dictating its terms, and literary analysis betrays only its crudeness when it judges a work by standards other than its own. The motives of a writer are in any case irrelevant to the finished work, which may not agree with his intentions. Yet coming upon the finished work, readers have every right to classify works according to diverse criteria, and finding a usable tradition for their own group or polity is one of the highest critical functions they can undertake. Oscar Wilde's admonition against the sincerity of *bad* poetry sheds no light on the Book of Isaiah, from which Jews and Christians drew their models of citizenship before the concept had even been defined.

I propose that between Bloom and the rabbis a modern Jewish canon has come into being and that in trying to describe it I am merely highlighting the line that culture has taken on its own. This modern list will probably never be as firmly redacted as the twenty-four books of the Hebrew Bible, because no contemporary community is as confident as its ancestors, and because moderns are generally warier of any process that smacks of authority. Yet should the members of any community, be it religious or ethnic, want to share in a common future, they will recognize the works that embody their collective experience and seek to ensure that they are known and transmitted. Writing may be a solitary act, and our appreciation of it may be aesthetic in the main, but reading in the Jewish tradition has always merged into a communal discipline. And that, to my mind, remains one of the greatest contributions of the Jewish people to the history of civilization. It would be odd to the point of perversity if the people best known for its preservation of the biblical canon would become so distracted or dispirited in the modern period as to ignore its newer literary harvest. A people that intends to participate meaningfully in the world would first have to know itself and be able to represent itself through a creative cultural continuum. Modern Jewish literature is the repository of modern Jewish experience. It is the most complete way of knowing the inner life of the Jews.

I see no necessary conflict between respect for the aesthetic autonomy of a work and the wish to learn from it. In the Jewish day school where I learned to read, debates over literature took up most of our class time. Once the plain meaning of the Hebrew was explained (or so we thought), we tried to figure out, for example, why Cain killed Abel and what it meant to become "a wanderer on earth." The habit of close reading was cultivated in those classes, as was the wonder at the magic that words can convey. Of course, some of our arguments and teachers may have been parochial. I was stunned to discover when I reread it as an adult that the school text of a Yiddish story about an American lynching in the South had removed the scene in which the Jewish storekeeper's son defies his father by joining the lynch mob to show solidarity with his neighbors. Our good teachers had obviously balked, like the parent in the story, at the sight of a Jewish boy harming a Black man, and they had violated the story in order to hone what they were certain was its moral point. The teachers shared the story's point of view, but whereas the author heightened the evil frenzy by showing that even a Jew could get caught up in it, the teachers could not bear to see the Jews implicated in a process that they abhorred. Still, those classes were my first introduction to textual analysis, to the *prolonged* excitement of reading when you discuss literature with others, and to the way that modern literature extends and complicates biblical plots. Even considering the dangers to the text that may accompany a moral education, I would argue that the importance it ascribes to words more than compensates for the occasional violence it does to them. Those classes made me want to study literature as an adult. This book is, in part, a wish to perpetuate the best of the education I received.

Literature may be crudely misused, turned into a gavel or a measuring stick or a ledger or even a bludgeon, and one is grateful to those, like Harold Bloom, who warn against such corruption. But the neglect of literature is more serious than its tendentious application, and it is bound to be neglected if people do not feel it belongs to them. In this book I set out some of my favorite Jewish works as a way of inviting others to continue the discussion over them. Although my criteria are largely aesthetic and personal, the works I feature derive so powerfully from a particular cultural community that they make a special claim on the members of that community to be reabsorbed by them in a cycle of creative renewal. As a start, I have limited myself to works of Ashkenazi Jews and their descendants that appeared in whole or in part in the twentieth century and, except for the years of World War II, to books of prose fiction, which more than poetry pronounces its social context and cultural affinity.

T HE MOST COMPLICATING FEATURE of modern Jewish literature as I conceive it is its relation to language. Theorists of modern nationalism, from Johann Gottfried von Herder to Benedict Anderson, place a heavy emphasis on the role of language as the basic form and medium of national consciousness. They explain how many Europeans came to regard their language and literature as guarantors of their national integrity, to the point of establishing protective language academies and sometimes even waging wars to safeguard their linguistic boundaries. Colonialism complicated these national boundaries by bringing the colonial power's language to other countries; for example, because of British rule in India much of the finest contemporary English literature is written by Indians and much of the finest Indian literature is written in English. But Jews, whose sojourn abroad endured for longer than their sovereign residence in the Land of Israel, habitually absorbed the language of their host countries, especially where they were offered civic rights and a chance for personal advancement. The Jewish religion, whose tribal nature is often maligned for its exclusivity, actually takes the international arena for granted, since Jews regard themselves as a minority by definition and can therefore never be discomfited by the presence of other peoples *per se*. Unlike Christianity, whose claims of universal salvation cannot comfortably coexist with competing religious traditions, Judaism is the way of life of a self-disciplining minority that knows it will remain a minority among the *goyim*, people of other religions and nationalities, until the end of days. As a function of living so long outside their national homeland, Jews made a virtue of adaptation, which included learning other languages and creating new Jewish languages, while perpetuating their own religious civilization. The minoritarian consciousness of Jews was reinforced by centuries in the Diaspora, and since the Jewish religious way of life can be maintained in any language (as long as one can read the Torah in Hebrew and study the Talmud in Hebrew-Aramaic), Jews routinely adapted to other tongues. Indeed, Yiddish and Ladino and Judaeo-Persian are the products of such adaptation, the unself-conscious fusion of coterritorial and older Jewish languages into new vernaculars.

No doubt many modern Jews who adopted one or more of the local languages ended by severing themselves from the Jewish people. The political liability of the Jewish condition in Europe propelled many Jews into Christianity or assimilation outright. Alternately, there were ideological Yiddishists and Hebraists from the end of the nineteenth century to the outbreak of World War II who adopted the model of other national movements and insisted that a unifying national language is the basis of modern nationhood. But these complementary forms of imitation—the non-Jewish Jew wishing to be like the Gentiles and the Jewish political nationalist wishing to be like other nationalists—did not reflect the way the Jews typically regarded themselves or the languages they spoke. Jewish language was sometimes an instrument, but never the guarantor, of Jewish nationality. Adoption of a local language could inhibit, but never determine, the development of Jewish life and culture.

The process of linguistic acculturation quickened wherever Jews assumed that Jewishness could be compatible with local civic duty. In America, for example, Anglicization was so rapid that no more than a handful of native-born children of the millions of Yiddish-speaking immigrants ever became Yiddish writers. Acculturation and linguistic adaptiveness was so energetic that Jews began to figure prominently among the writers in Gentile languages, though their writing often remained subtly—or sometimes decidedly—Jewish. In sum, the politically anomalous Jews generated a multilingual literature unlike that of any other modern nation, and in order to represent it adequately one has to span as many languages as Jews mastered—Yiddish and Hebrew, of course, but also the German of Franz Kafka and Joseph Roth, the Russian of Isaac Babel and Vasily Grossman, the French of Albert Memmi and Elie Wiesel, the English of Saul Bellow and Cynthia Ozick, and so forth.[6]

During the course of this book, we may have occasion to wonder whether the refusal of Jews to make language synonymous with national identity and their corresponding eagerness to master coterritorial cultures constitutes an admirable or a debilitating feature of their existence. At best, the refusal to be defined by language is an act of iconoclasm in obedience to the prohibition against idolatry; by and large, Jews have not substituted fealty to language for a faltering religious cohesion, as, for example, French Canadians have tried to do in the once heavily Catholic province of Quebec. On the debit side, as one consequence of their reckless disregard for national language, American Jews dropped Yiddish so precipitously that they lost the whole record of their encounter with modernity that had been forged in that language. A disturbing by-product of the Jews' attitude toward language has been the antipathy of some of its speakers, and even some of its writers, to what they considered their "inferior" tongue. The social philosopher Chaim Zhitlowsky (1865–1943) noted sardonically, "The Jewish people and the Yiddish language share almost the same fate. Both are first required to prove their legitimacy: the Jewish people, that it really is a people, and the Yiddish language, that it really is a language. . . . They must always show their passports, evincing the evidence that they are authentic, and if a single point of evidence is lacking, they are declared invalid."[7]

Jews transferred the insecurity bred by antisemitism to their mother tongue, calling into doubt their own cultural achievement. This made contacts between the German and the Yiddish language particularly thorny, since the discovery of the Enlightenment through German texts and German thinkers convinced many Yiddish speakers that theirs was the garbled version of the sublime language. Many mistook the vitality of the Jewish language—its fearless borrowings, creative fusions, and irrepressible inventiveness—for manifestations of sloppiness. One of the most tragic ironies of European history is that while Jews forged the Yiddish language as a moral alternative to German civilization, to protect their self-disciplining way of life, their modern descendants concluded that Jewish culture was inferior because their parents spoke Yiddish, not German.

Whatever the reasons, it is simply a fact that by the twentieth century ambitious Jews were raising and educating their young in local Gentile languages and keeping them ignorant of their own, thus preventing them from becoming writers in a Jewish language. Accidents of birth and upbringing proved decisive. Whereas Micah Yosef Berdichevsky (1865–1921) could write comfortably in Yiddish and Hebrew before he also began writing in German, Franz Kafka (1883–1924) was raised in German, with no access to any Jewish language until he was old enough to educate himself; that German was not wholly *his* language he knew from the moment he took up writing, and this awareness of adoption created the ontology of displacement that the name *Kafka* came to represent in literature. Every Jew felt some self-consciousness in becoming a writer in a Gentile language, each according to his situation. Nevertheless, Isaac Babel thrilled to the timing that placed him, a Russian Jew, in the eye of the Revolution, and Saul Bellow, more fortunate in his place of birth, was inspired by the opportunity afforded to the children of Jewish immigrants to make the American language their own. The examples of Babel and Bellow, each of whom was convinced that he could become the quintessential writer of his time, should disabuse us once and for all of the notion that Jewish creativity in non-Jewish languages necessarily gives rise to discomfort or a feeling of marginality. I hope this book will demonstrate that certain writers considered their Jewishness an advantage that placed them not at the edges but at the center of the universe.

The most radical description I know of the Jew's cultural dilemma occurs in the latter part of the French novel *Le sang du ciel* [Blood from the Sky], written by the Polish Jewish refugee Piotr Rawicz in Paris between 1949 and 1953. Rawicz had grown up with Yiddish and the three coterritorial languages of his native Lvov and had studied German, English, French, Sanskrit, and Hindi. In the closing pages of the novel, the autobiographical hero Boris, trying to pass himself off as a Pole, has been captured by the Gestapo and is being tortured in an attempt to establish that he is a Jew. To throw his captors off the scent he confesses that, indeed, he is not a Pole but a Ukrainian, and he challenges his captor to prove him otherwise. The Gestapo lieutenant invites the Ukrainian intellectual and collaborationist Vassili Humeniuk to help him break down the imposter, and Humeniuk begins his interrogation by asking the prisoner to name the greatest Ukrainian poet:

> It was then that the game began to amuse Boris. His brain was working as it hadn't worked for a long time. He thought: If a man wishes to prove he is an Englishman, and a well-educated English-man, he will prove nothing by answering "Shakespeare" or "Byron" to such a question. Of course not, for everyone has heard of Shake-speare and Byron, whether English or not. On the contrary, what he must do is imply, and get his interrogator to acknowledge the implication, that it is unthinkable he should be asked such a ques tion. He must immediately mention some such figure as Eliot or Edith Sitwell. [. . .] Well now, in asking me who is the greatest Ukrainian poet, our friend is expecting me to voice one name and one name only: that of their bard, Tarass Shevchenko. . . . But everybody here—not just the Ukrainians, but the Russians, Poles, and Jews living in the Ukraine—knows that this singer of the serfs' hardships and of Cossack pride is the glory of your nation. That's stale. If I were to cite Shevchenko, I'd please you, my good Hume-niuk, but I wouldn't appeal to your imagination and, most impor-tant, I wouldn't prove anything to you. [. . .] And Boris named an avant-garde poet who had died not long before, at the age of twenty-nine, an old friend of his, known and loved by perhaps two hundred readers.[8]*

The character's predicament is grotesque: were he not a Jew he would not have to prove himself a Ukrainian. But were he not a Jew trying to pass as a Pole, he probably could not have demonstrated that he was a Ukrainian.

---

*Author's note: Ellipsis points enclosed within brackets indicate my own omission of words and phrases from quoted material. Where ellipsis points in quoted material are not brack-eted, the ellipses appear in the original work.

Only Boris's acquired mastery of Ukrainian culture eventually convinces Humeniuk that he is one of them. Speaking in a language their common oppressor does not understand, Boris not only bests Humeniuk in arguments over Ukrainian culture but castigates him for betraying Ukrainian national pride by collaborating with the enemy and taunts him for his scant familiarity with the Ukrainian capital, Kiev. In order to save his life, Boris is forced to prove just what these Ukrainian and German nationalists fear, namely, that the Jew can infiltrate their culture so successfully he will usurp their very identity. Modern Jewish literature is the result of this paradox, among others: if others did not fear and hate Jews so powerfully, Jews would not have to turn cultural acquisition into a matter of life or death. Rawicz's hero is the end point, the outrageously cruel culmination of the process the Enlightenment first set into motion when it encouraged Jews to believe that rational common education would gain them admittance to society on equal terms.

Rawicz's book alone is enough to justify the concept of a multilingual Jewish literature rather than an essentialist definition based strictly on Jewish language (Hebrew, Yiddish, or Ladino). But if Boris's desperate performance foils the Ukrainians and the Nazis, it also implicitly challenges our attempt to define a meaningful Jewishness in literature. For if one were to include all the Jewish writers who succeeded in passing themselves off as Gentiles, one could easily water down the integrity of a modern Jewish canon to the point of drowning it. The sticking point of the Jews, after all, is that despite their adaptability they refuse as a people to be dissolved into Gentiles. This tends to be misunderstood nowadays in America, where the struggle against discrimination has produced an antipathy for all distinctions. We have seen called into question the very impulse to discriminate between an inferior and superior work of art, as though aesthetic worth were somehow aligned with prejudice against persons of a certain skin color or gender. Yet modern Jews have suffered from exactly the opposite kind of discrimination, from the inability of universalists to accept their choice to remain distinct. Judaism is the particularism that has been most singled out for opprobrium, precisely for the crime of wanting to remain true to itself. The concept of modern Jewish literature would have no value whatsoever if one were not prepared to respect the autonomy of Jewishness, and respect for that autonomy would have to be implicit in any work of Jewish literature. But how does one establish criteria for Jewishness in the arts when the Jews have changed so much in the twentieth century and the arts continually reinvent themselves?

With the boldness that has become her trademark, the American Jewish writer Cynthia Ozick addressed just this issue in the summer of 1970, when she called on a gathering of her literary colleagues to help bring into being a literature that was "centrally Jewish." Ozick was clearly fed up with assimilationists who wanted Judaism to stand for everything or (what amounts to the same thing) to count for nothing. She was reacting not only to the opacity of the critic George Steiner, who offered exile, geographic displacement, as a metaphor for the Jew at the very moment that the Jews had reclaimed their historic homeland, but also to the self-description of her fellow American Philip Roth: "I am not a Jewish writer; I am a writer who is a Jew." The first claim was hyperbolic, the second reductionist. "Imaginative writers are compelled to swim in the medium of culture; literature is an instrument of culture, not a summary of it," said Ozick. "Consequently there are no major works of Jewish imaginative genius written in any Gentile language, sprung out of any Gentile culture."[9] Speaking English, itself a Gentile language, Ozick seemed to be contradicting the evidence of her own writing, or else condemning her own potential to write "major works of Jewish imaginative genius." In fact, what Ozick required of herself and her fellow Jews was an imagination so suffused by Jewishness that the voice of the writer would emerge within the adopted language as "a choral voice, a communal voice, the echo of the voice of the Lord of History." She was prophesying the rise of what some have called "a minority literature," the literature of a cultural minority within a host language, except that for Ozick it was English that was to occupy the minority position within the great tradition of Jewish literature. She used Jewish religious imagery to make the point that as the Jewish religion retained its autonomous strength in many different languages, Jewish literature in Gentile languages could also include "whatever touched on the liturgical": "A liturgical literature has the configuration of the ram's horn: you give your strength to the inch-hole and the splendor spreads wide. A Jewish liturgical literature gives its strength to its peoplehood and the whole human note is heard everywhere, enlarged."[10] Everyone who has heard the struggle of the Jew who blows the *shofar* on the High Holidays in synagogue knows how difficult it is to get pure sound from that narrow mouth of the ram's horn and how satisfyingly awesome is the resonance when the job is done well. The imprecision of this metaphor was part of its power, for it invoked the concept of cultural specificity without attempting to define it. Ozick herself always strenuously resisted any attempts to constrain the literary imagination through restrictions or requirements of the kind that Judaism imposes. Here, issuing a creative manifesto rather than a set of critical guidelines, she left the "inch-hole" and the "splendor" to define themselves.

Quite the opposite approach to defining the Jewishness of culture was taken by the scholar Dov Sadan, who, in an essay on humor begins his inquiry into the cultural specificity of the Jewish joke with an example from his own university (the Hebrew University in Jerusalem) about the professor of philosophy Yehuda Leon Roth: The professor was in the habit of punctuating his lectures with ironic and sarcastic remarks, and this offended a student in his class on ethics, who wanted to know how a teacher of ethics could be so cynical. Roth asked the student, "Who else are you studying with?" The student replied, "I'm studying mathematics with Professor Abraham Halevi Fraenkel." Said Roth, "Then why don't you ask Professor Fraenkel why he is not a triangle or a trapezoid?"[11]

Sadan sets out to show that although this anecdote is about two Jews in a Jewish institution in Jerusalem, it is not a *Jewish* joke. Analyzing its form, he shows that the joke itself is constructed around the formal exchange of spheres, around the notion that what holds in one situation should hold for the other: if ethics obliges the ethicist to be an ethical person, mathematics should oblige the mathematician to be a geometric figure. That the mathematician could not do so, even with the utmost exertion, explodes the fallacy of the equivalence, incidentally reinforcing the cynicism of the lecturer, which was the original target of attack. Sadan then proceeds to show that even the philosophic language of the joke puts it outside the Jewish tradition:

> Nor is it hard to show that according to tradition (*mesorah*) it may not even come under consideration as a Jewish joke, since the school of Cynics, from *kynikos*, or dog-like, is Greek, and it is possible that those who interpret the saying from the Sages, *Haokhel bashuk domeh lekelev*, He who eats in the market is likened to a dog, are correct when they say that this actually refers to that species of philosopher.[12]

Is the reader still with me? Sadan is as dense as the Talmud and twice as mischievous, so we should not be surprised by the quick turns of his logic, but the gist of his comment is that even the content of the anecdote may be essentially non-Jewish, since it derives from Greek culture and turns on a Greek personality type, that of the cynic. The presence of such a type at the Hebrew University does not qualify his wit to be considered Jewish. What Sadan then does is to pursue an alternate trail of anecdotes involving dogs that becomes more and more irreducibly Jewish. It is worth trying to render his final example, to see Sadan's point:

This anecdote involves Joshua Heschel Schorr, the *maskil* of Brody who was known for his radicalism as the Jewish Voltaire. The cultivated Jew hearing this joke would know that a *maskil*, or exponent of the Jewish Enlightenment, is a sworn enemy of the Hasidim, enthusiasts of the religious revivalist movement that arose in the eighteenth century, about the same time as the Jewish Enlightenment. Schorr's son, appointed professor at the Sorbonne, had died an hour before his investiture. The disconsolate father used to comfort himself with a dog that he kept curled in his lap. Once he asked a visiting Hasid, pointing to his dog, "So what do you think of my *Kaddish*?" (The *Kaddish* is the prayer that sons recite in memory of their parents, and the male child was traditionally referred to by the function he would some day fulfill.) The Hasid retorted, "I think more of yours than I do of your father's." Sadan has artfully sealed his argument with a joke that circles back to the starting point of the cynic, whom the Hebrew sages liken to a dog. Like the morally offended student in the classroom, the Hasid in this joke is provoked by the Jew who mocks religious earnestness, and he outwits Schorr by comparing him invidiously to his dog. Note that here, in contrast to the first joke, it is the Jew speaking for Jewishness who gets the better of the cynic. Sadan finds that in this instance the atmosphere, surroundings, and associations of the joke *do* determine its Jewishness, because it could not be translated into a Gentile version unless every detail and aspect were to be altered—the Hasid and the *maskil*, the *Kaddish* and the Westernized son, and the uneven struggle between Jewish tradition and modernity in which the latter expects to get the upper hand.[13]

Common to both Ozick's porous concept of "liturgical" Jewish writing and Sadan's search for a texture that is Jewish through and through is the certainty that Jewish literature can be recognizable when we find it. This book shares that assumption. Ozick speaks in prophetic inspirational terms that generate creativity, and with puckish erudition Sadan defines his subject as closely as possible. My own sense of the Jewishness of a work, formed from the perspective of a reader, derives from what Lionel Trilling calls "the experience of literature." In his wonderful anthology by that title, Trilling contends that literature is coextensive with human life, that a truly adequate account of the purposes of literature would amount to nothing less than a description of the whole nature of man. He finds that the making and enjoyment of literature is "what the zoologists call a species-characteristic trait of mankind," the poet writes poetry because he is a poet, and we like to talk about his poetry because "the literary experience is communal—it asks to be shared in discourse."[14] Literature has always seemed to me the discipline that encompasses all the others. The same novel can be read for pure enjoyment and for the kind of information about life that otherwise could never be gleaned. It accommodates philosophy, history, sociology, psychology, politics, anthropology, and of course aesthetics. Literature has lately been used tendentiously to score points on class and gender but only because it has plenty to tell us about both these aspects of our existence. Literature also gives the fullest account of national experience, although the same book may sometimes belong to more than one group. The field of comparative literature was designed to address such complexities.

What I mean by Jewish experience will emerge from the works I have chosen rather than from any theoretical model that attempts to subsume the whole. Sometimes a novel plunges us into the Jewish condition, as when Isaac Bashevis Singer describes a seventeenth-century Polish town in the grip of messianic fever or when Yosef Haim Brenner situates his novel among the Jews of Palestine before World War I. Given the prominence of Jews in the twentieth century, thanks both to their own achievements and the achievements of their enemies, literature about their exploits can be expected to yield major interpretations of the modern condition. Sometimes fiction yokes us to a Jewish consciousness, as Isaac Babel does in the tales of *Red Cavalry*. The texture of prose is also part of the experience of literature, as are its imagery, allusions, and rhythms of speech. Henry Roth conveys in English the contrast between the lyrical Jewish language of the immigrant home and the coarse, defective communication of the New York street. All the layers of Jewish civilization and learning surface through quotations, allusions, and stylistic imitation in the richly intertextual Hebrew of S. Y. Agnon. Jewish writers respond to some of the same events, and occasionally to one another's work. When the hapless young soldier-protagonist of Haim Be'er's Hebrew novel *The Time of Trimming* (1987; not yet translated into English) gets sloshed with a pail of dirty water as he comes to take up his new assignment, the book he is carrying that gets soaked along with him is, appropriately, Saul Bellow's *Herzog*. Philip Roth has his artist-hero lecturing on Kafka in one novel and falling in love with the magically alive Anne Frank in another. Modern Jewish literature attests to the indissolubility of the Jews, sometimes negatively, as in Kafka, by demonstrating the consequence of deracination, but more often affirmatively, by illuminating Jewish experience from within. *Affirmative* is not used here as a synonym for *self-congratulatory*; indeed, Jewish literature suffers from far too little appreciation of Jewish worth, being the product of an exceptionally self-critical people. I mean simply that in Jewish literature the authors or characters know and let the reader know that they are Jews.

Cumulatively, modern Jewish literature tells the stories of the Jewish people in the twentieth century, and in merry defiance of those who don't like master narratives, I have tried to include in the Jewish canon the works that tell that story best. But when it comes to literature, the obvious is not always obvious. Bernard Malamud's *The Fixer* would appear to be the quintessentially Jewish novel, based as it is on the infamous 1911 trial of the Jew Mendel Beilis, who was accused of killing a Russian child to extract its blood for the baking of Passover matzos. As we shall see in the first two chapters of this book, his trial had the force of the Dreyfus case in arousing the Jews to national self-awareness. Malamud is famous for having pioneered in English a style that incorporates Yiddish grammatical structures so as to convey the flavor of Yiddish speech. Yet in turning this blood libel case into a novel, Malamud underscores its symbolic resonance at the expense of its Jewish actuality. The actual Mendel Beilis was a married man with five children. In his memoirs, which reveal that he experienced life as an unexceptional, traditional Jew, he gives the date of his arrest as the day after Tisha B'Av, "when the Jewish people mourns its great tragedy, the destruction of the Temple and being driven from its land, from Mother Zion." Arrested on a Friday, he recalls his first evening in prison as the "first desecrated Sabbath Eve of [his] life."[15] Beilis may have been crafting his story to arouse Jewish sympathies, but he clearly felt that his trial was emblematic of Jewish destiny. By contrast, Malamud makes the fictional Yakov Bok a childless loner who has been abandoned by his wife and lacks any semblance of community. He not only turns the simple Jew into a quasi-intellectual freethinker but invokes Spinoza as the proto-type for his hero as a way of universalizing his plight and distancing him from Jewish religion. Thus, when Yakov reads a history book about Peter the Great, he discovers that the Russian people is actually no less op-pressed than his own:

> The Russians make pogroms against the Russians—it went on throughout their history. What a sad country, he thought, amazed by what he had read, every possible combination of experiences, where black was white and black was black; and if the Russians, too, were massacred by their own rulers and died like flies, who were then the Chosen People? Fatigued by history, he went back to Spinoza, rereading chapters on biblical criticism, superstition, and miracles which he knew almost by heart. If there was a God, after reading Spinoza he had closed up his shop and become an idea.[16]

Bok's conflation of victim with "chosen" is characteristic of Malamud, who identifies the Jew exclusively and ideologically with the archetype of the sufferer and on this basis imagines the Jew as the ideal Christian. In his earlier and even better novel *The Assistant*, a troubled Italian boy finds his spiritual father in a Jewish shopkeeper who interprets Judaism as an ethnic form of Christianity and says to his disciple, "I suffer for you." Since Chris-tianity itself evolved out of Judaism, the literary boundary between them is never going to be absolutely firm, and portrayals of the Jew as the suf-fering Jesus are by now almost a cliché of modern Jewish art and literature. But though it is certainly no slur on Malamud to point out that he nudges his novel toward Christianity, his approach makes it less interesting as a Jewish book, and arguably less successful in aesthetic terms. We recognize the heavy-handedness of literature that tries to stir up national enthusi-asm, but the same heavy-handedness can be equally palpable in literature that tries to damp it down.

Since Lionel Trilling informs my comprehensive idea of literature, let me invoke his help to further set the limits of my subject. As a young man Trilling not only equated his consciousness with being Jewish but thought of it as a heightened form of awareness: "Being a Jew is like walking in the wind or swimming: you are touched at all points and conscious every-where."[17] Had this insight informed his fiction, he would have secured a place of honor in the modern Jewish canon. But Trilling made the protago-nist of his only novel, *Middle of the Journey* (1947), an indeterminate New York Protestant. John Laskell, recovering from a near-fatal bout with scarlet fever, realizes as a result of his brush with death that you can't "live the life of promises without yourself remaining a child."[18] A second check on his enthusiasms comes from a disaffected Communist spy who explains to him the murderous reality of the Great Experiment that most of their friends continue to identify with progress. These two conservative themes inter-sect with a third, the difficulty that liberals face in acknowledging and deal-ing with out-and-out evil. There could hardly be a more Jewish set of themes, especially in the aftermath of the Holocaust, when this book was written. Trilling's novel was a blueprint for the cultural reversal that became known as neoconservatism, but he removes his character from the Jewish milieu where this movement actually ripened, thereby depriving the book of its social substantiveness. Regardless of whether Trilling neutered John Laskell in order to make him more purely American or because he could not find an aesthetic means of integrating Jewishness into his story, its consid-eration as a Jewish book is precluded. We will not try to reinject into any work the lifeblood of a people that its author emptied out.

If it hurts to omit Trilling, it aches to leave out Proust. Some critics consider Proust a Jewish writer despite the fact that he was baptized a Catholic and received communion when he was twelve. They may do so because Proust's mother, Jeane Weil, came from a Jewish family in Metz in northeastern France, whose members he stayed in touch with all his life. Proust was deeply influenced by his mother and, through her, by his Jew-ishness. The social matrix of his work owes much to his firsthand knowl-edge of French Jewry, and when it actually came to choosing sides in the most vehement political debate of his day, Proust was with the defenders of the falsely accused Alfred Dreyfus. Obsessed by memory, Proust be-lieved that a work of art is not the creation of a single artist but is drawn from the accumulation of memories that reach far back beyond his own life: "An artist expresses not only himself, but hundreds of ancestors, the dead who find their spokesman in him."[19] Proust's Jewish ancestors assuredly formed part of that accumulated past, but ancestry is quite different from animate life. And though Proust derives from the Jews and shows sympathy with their condition, he is at pains in his writing to show that he does not share in their fate. In his famous description of Jews in "Within a Budding Grove," for example, where the narrator describes the family of his friend Bloch, it is surely not the harshness of description that excludes Proust from a Jewish canon, for one can find much harsher characterizations than this in Yiddish and Hebrew literature, but simply that his first person narrator emphasizes his own exclusion from "this Jewish colony [*cette colonie juive*]," this "solid troop, homogenous within itself [*un cortege homogène en soi*]," this "compact and closed phalanx [*une phalange compacte et close*]."[20] Though the narrator is also detached from the French majority at Balbec, he is much more sorrowfully and explicitly estranged from the Jews. Proust's familiarity and sympathies do not translate into a novel of Jewish experience, however deep and persuasive its knowledge of the subject. On the whole, I think we do well to respect the author's guidelines, instead of taking it upon ourselves to decide, as antisemites do and as the rabbis must, who is a Jew and who is not. Proust's work will continue to give pleasure from outside the Jewish canon.

A S I WAS FINISHING THIS BOOK, I was asked by a colleague what I was working on, and after I described my project, she asked, "So are you writing about Paul Celan?" I said no, my book dealt only with prose. "Bruno Schulz?" Not him either. "Who then—Gertrude Stein?" In the mounting frustration of my interlocutor I heard the exasperation of many educated readers who have formed an impression of Jewish fiction and will be disappointed that mine does not resemble theirs. To such readers I would say that while I would not expect anyone's list to exclude the books I have chosen, they are free to make a case for additional writers. I expect the greatest aversion to my project to come from those who think that globalization begins with the arts and that the denationalization of the arts must begin with the Jews. I would urge such readers to consider whether their discomfort with the category of Jewish literature does not imply discomfort with the Jewish people and to reexamine their own prejudices in tandem with this book. In sum, while the definition of Jewish literature is open to interpretation, its existence is not. Every people has a sustaining culture, and most great writers draw heavily upon their own. The receptivity of the Jews to other cultures ought to stimulate a corresponding interest in theirs, rather than a demand that since Jews are already cosmopolitan, they yield all further claim to national existence.

As for the quality of the Jewish canon, that is what this book is about. Some critics have mistaken the broad appeal of Jewish writing for proof that it belongs to no particular people, but this is to confuse universalism, which seeks to eliminate tribal categories, with universality, which is the global resonance of a tribal work. The Hebrew Bible is a tribal document that became one of the world's most influential works of literature. Modern Jewish literature, too, bears out the relation that Cynthia Ozick establishes between strength given to the inch-hole and splendor spreading wide. Much of the finest writing by Jews in the twentieth century, as in the past, gains its universal appeal from a centrally Jewish perspective.

THIS BOOK IS ARRANGED CHRONOLOGICALLY to convey my sense of literature as the repository of modern Jewish experience. Chronology, however, is everywhere complicated by considerations of language. At the beginning of the century the vast majority of Jews were Yiddish-speaking Europeans, with Yiddish the main vehicle of secularization, modernization, revolution, and reform. By the end of the century, Yiddish was in daily use only among the so-called ultraorthodox while the growing majority of Jews in Israel spoke Hebrew and the shrinking minority of Jews in America spoke English. The logic of the chapters follows this extraordinary shift of language which, in turn, derives from the manner in which Jews made and interpreted their history.

The anchoring chapter is devoted to Sholem Aleichem's *Tevye the Dairyman,* the most inexhaustible work of modern Jewish fiction that anticipates most of modernity's challenges to Jewry, albeit in somewhat milder form than they assumed. After trying his hand at any number of heroes and genres, Sholem Aleichem hit the jackpot with this traditional Ukrainian Jew who showed off the genius of Yiddish wit and humor in telling the story of himself, his wife, his horse, and his household of daughters. As Tevye confronts his rebellious daughters, Yiddish is the source of his cultural security, the expressive vehicle of his self-deprecating self-confidence; he stays morally intact through twenty years of assault. The same cannot be said for the American Tevye, who gained renown through the musical adaptation *Fiddler on the Roof.* In translating Tevye for American stage and screen, his adapters introduced certain changes into the plot that undermine his Jewish authority without even acknowledging (probably without even realizing) that they were destroying the source of his power. Tevye's transition from Yiddish to English epitomizes the difficulties Jews later run into when they try to perpetuate their culture in hospitable English.

Chapter Two traces the considerable contribution to modernism by Jewish writers of Central and Western Europe who were working in non-Jewish languages. Kafka follows so naturally after Sholem Aleichem that one might think his comic vision had derived from his older kin's. The moral and cognitive breakdown that always threatens Sholem Aleichem's characters overtakes Kafka's fiction from the very first, but whereas Tevye's Yiddish is the source of his moral self-confidence, Kafka's German heightens his anxiety the more he masters the "master tongue." The move from Yiddish to German, from Tevye's trials to Joseph K.'s Trial, turned the model of cultural security inside out. K. is the character with a truncated identity who does not understand the terms of the life that he inhabits, divulging terrifying truths about the liability of Jews in Europe. Kafka was the keenest witness to the growing chasm between the inner and the outer person. His German fiction constitutes the definitive parody of Jewish deracination.

A parallel and equally unsettling experience was being registered by fugitives from the *yeshivas* who began to write in Hebrew, trying forcibly to change the fate of Diaspora Man by reconfigurating a new Jew and a new Jewish literature in the old-new language. The Hebrew revival distinguished itself at once from assimilation (by virtue of using a Jewish language) and from Jewish populism (because the masses used Yiddish): it mitigated against the loss of tradition yet interrupted the cultural continuum whose prototype was Tevye. Yosef Haim Brenner idolized Sholem Aleichem for transmitting the voice of typical Jews, but he did not think that Sholem Aleichem spoke for *him.* At the same time that Kafka wrote *The Trial,* Brenner wrote a Hebrew novel that described the settlement of a Jew like himself in Palestine, the country to which he had just immigrated. His modernist prose is nervous and impaired, an objective correlative if there ever was one to the disconnected culture of the pioneering society. Nonetheless, Brenner's Hebrew fiction inspired the early Zionist settlers to believe that *their* story was being told (and inspired Kafka's Hebrew teacher to bring it as a gift to her ailing student). His ability to express the failings of his generation in Hebrew seemed to confirm the authenticity of the Zionist project.

One might have expected Jewish writers in Russian to be far worse off than contemporaries in other languages, because by the beginning of the twentieth century, tsarism still held out little of the promise of emancipation and Russian antisemitism had become the most violent in Europe. Yet, as I show in Chapter Three, the reactionary political atmosphere of Russia held several advantages for the Jewish writer. In a land without democratic political opposition, writers were considered the obvious counterforce to government, and Jewish as well as Russian writers were accorded the moral stature of a prophetic intelligentsia. Unlike in the West, the Jew in the atmosphere of relative backwardness felt no necessary embarrassment for his putatively inferior language and heritage. Russian Jewry produced a fervent Zionist movement, an equally fervent Jewish revolutionary movement, and a powerful literature in Yiddish, Hebrew, and Russian. Indeed, Isaac Babel started out as the boldest writer in the modern Jewish pantheon. After the Bolsheviks overturned the rotten regime, he cast the Jew of his masterpiece, *Red Cavalry* as chronicler of the Russian Revolution. The revolution guaranteed parity to its Jewish subjects, and some writers took it at its word. But it soon became clear that Jewish writers under the new regime were offered the ultimate version of Hobson's choice: either yield Judaism and take what the new order has to offer or forfeit your share in the new society. After a decade of experimental brilliance, the art of the Soviet regime began to curdle under the heat of restrictive edicts that made tsarism a paradise in retrospect. For some Soviet writers in Yiddish and Russian, Jewish consciousness was a saving grace. Although their Jewishness may have subjected the writers to greater risk, particularly as Stalin's antisemitism became overt in the mid 1930s, it protected their art by fortifying them morally.

When we think about creative centers of Judaism in the twentieth century, we might keep in mind the counterintuitive decision of young American Lucy Dawidowicz to leave New York City for Vilna in 1938 because she wanted to study Jewish history where it was being taught best.[21] Politically, the reconstituted Polish Republic of the 1930s was becoming a most unfriendly place for its three million Jews. After many centuries of by no means uniformly disagreeable interaction, Poles had begun treating the Jews as hateful intruders. But by then, the Jews had struck such deep roots in the country that their creative development continued unchecked, and was even stimulated by the need for self-reliance. Most people nowadays know Polish Jewry through the prism of the Holocaust, as a mound of ashes like the one commemorating its victims at the Maidanek death camp near Lublin. But for the student of Jewish literature in the twentieth century, interwar Poland figures (after modern Israel) as the most fertile ground of all.

Chapters Four and Five of this book are devoted to literature of and about the Poland of the 1930s. To represent Yiddish literature emanating from Poland, then the hub of Jewish literary creativity, I bring three almost contemporaneous novels of the talented Singer family—Israel Joshua, Isaac Bashevis, and their sister (Hinde) Esther Kreitman—utterly different in subject and style yet with an eerily similar conception of life that is fatally stuck between hopeless alternatives. A contrast of a different kind is manifest in the autobiographical novel of the American Yiddish writer Jacob Glatstein and of the Palestinian Hebrew writer S. Y. Agnon, each novel imaginatively based on a return visit the author paid to his native city in Poland. In the book that stands at the center of the modern Jewish canon, the epic *A Guest for the Night*, Agnon exploits the resonance of Hebrew to shape a personal myth of the modern Jewish writer who ceases to be the guest of Europe when he resettles permanently in the Jewish land. Glatstein's journey, contrarily, turns into a threnody for the Yiddish writer as well as for his native community, since he sees no home for his European Jewish tongue. In the parallel works of Agnon and Glatstein, the leading modernists in their respective languages, we can read the fate of Hebrew and Yiddish at that ominous turning point in history.

That ominous turning point was Hitler's war against the Jews. Launched under the cover of World War II, it defined Jews against their will prior to exterminating them as a people. The Jewish civilians were not only physically unarmed but unable to understand the intentions of this Nazi aggression. The Germans applied their genius to killing the Jews with methods invented and adapted precisely for this purpose, and they relied on their armed might to ensure victory. Jews fought back, mostly by trying to survive, mostly through their weapons of choice—pen, type-writer, pencil. Even the small surviving fraction of ghetto diaries and dep-ositions shows how resolutely, how religiously, Jews kept the record, determined that the truth would outlast them to condemn their destroy-ers. In the layered writing that bore witness to the Holocaust (what Yid-dish calls the *khurbn*, and what Hebrew calls the *Shoah*), the most important stratum is the first—the writing of people during the war, under the immediate pressure of events.[22] Then come the postwar memoirs and fictions of witness-survivors, at first a small stream, then swelling into a torrent as these people aged and realized that their unique experience might go undocumented. At farther remove, writers who never experi-enced the genocide began to take it for their subject—just as the Israeli Amos Oz centuries later chose to write a novel about the Crusades.[23] At the beginning of the century, expressionists and surrealists used explosive experimental forms to communicate their visions of violence and madness. The horror of the Holocaust restored the need for precision, since any ex-aggeration was bound to diminish the reality of violence and madness.

For Jews caught up in Hitler's net, language assumed existential ur-gency. The register of ghetto diaries, even when they record the same in-cident, differs, depending on whether they were kept in Yiddish or Hebrew or a non-Jewish language. In Chapter Six we see that writers who felt at home in their languages wrote differently from those who were forced to adopt a new language after the war. In her diary, Anne Frank dreams confidently in Dutch of becoming a model Dutch citizen and writer. The Italian Jew Primo Levi recognized his kinship with Dante, who likewise wrote of a descent into hell, but having come upon Yiddish speakers for the first time in Auschwitz, he later questioned his authority as a witness and tried to write a novel about the "real Jews" of the Holo-caust, the Yiddish Jews of Eastern Europe.[24] Elie Wiesel, a pious Hungarian boy whose life had been circumscribed by Jewish faith until his arrest, dis-covered Western literature in Paris after the war and wrote his memoir un-der its formative influence ten years later; he began his literary odyssey as a Yiddish and Hebrew writer but then turned his first book into French and wrote thereafter in his adopted language, largely about his native Yid-dish and Hebrew culture. In his writings, Henryk Grynberg fights back in Polish against those who drove him from his country. Some critics believe that the historical force of the *Shoah* created a new body of testimony, like the Christian Gospels. But the literature of the war attests just as forcibly to the power of language in determining the nature of that testimony.

What a relief it is to come, in Chapter Seven, to English along the continuum of Jewish literature! And after so much literature of destruction, how welcome the theme of the return to the Land of Israel and the resumption of effective Jewish self-defense! The intersection of English with the rebirth of Israel marks the most cheerful point of Jewish culture in the quarter century after the war. The English-speaking world deserved the lion's share of credit for the defeat of Hitler, and its (albeit grudging) help was critical to the flourishing of Israel. Moreover, despite punitive British policies toward the Jews in Palestine, the *spirit* of English liberalism seemed to reassure the *yishuv*, the Jewish community of Palestine, that it could effect British withdrawal from the country and perhaps even win endorsement from the British as well as the Americans. Having suffered such deep humiliation and loss in full view of the world, the Jews wanted to be reassured of the respect of the world, and they expressed that claim to dignity in the English language. The best-selling *Exodus* and the modernist Canadian Jewish classic *The Second Scroll* invoke biblical parallels to dramatize the heroic rise of the Jewish state. But George Eliot had foreseen long ago that insofar as British liberalism was an outgrowth of Christianity, it would have difficulty accepting the particularism of the Jews. She recognized that English civilization might generously wish to embrace all the world yet stop short at the point of accepting a people that does not want to be embraced. *Daniel Deronda*, the best Zionist novel (though not a Jewish book), foretells just how difficult it would be to uphold the idea of Jewish peoplehood in English literature. Taking its cue from George Eliot, Chapter Seven asks how well the Jewish story can be told in English.

One thing English assuredly did do for Jewish fiction was to allow authors to worry less about the Jews and concentrate on themselves. America became a safe haven for Jews during the decades at the turn of the century, when political antisemitism was gaining momentum in Europe, and a haven, too, for writers, journalists, artists, and playwrights. Chapter Eight traces the way the immigrant masses from Europe switched from Yiddish to English, the verb *switch* signifying the speed and finality of the changeover. The products of American public schools began telling the story of how they had adapted to the urban frontier. Soon the Jewish immigrant story joined the classics of America. Mary Antin gave one of the brightest accounts of reaching and penetrating the promised land. The master broker of the marriage between the Yiddish-speaking Jews and English America, Abraham Cahan, editor of the Yiddish daily *Forward*, implied in his novel *The Rise of David Levinsky* that the Jew may best prove himself American by remaining suspicious of his own success. Henry Roth was inspired by the modernism of James Joyce and T. S. Eliot to invent a new polyphony of English in *Call It Sleep* for telling how an immigrant boy harnessed the power of the streets against the confining force of his family. A subgenre of the American Jewish novel exposed the Jewish hustler, including the sexual hustler, who *doesn't* share Levinsky's conscience about succeeding in America. The energy of American Jewish writers was so charged, so buoyant, that for a time they appeared to dominate American fiction. But there was so little *Jewish* energy in this art that one could invent parlor games over the ethnic or religious identity of its authors: Edna Ferber? Waldo Frank? Lillian Hellman? Nathanael West? Norman Mailer? E. L. Doctorow?

For most of the twentieth century, American Jewish fiction maintained the perspective of the child or adolescent passing from home, starting out in the thirties, casting a new life, making it.[25] Writing about an autobiographical character who at age forty-two is still locked in battle with his eighty-year-old father, Herbert Gold says wryly, "only in this odd century can I still be considered young" (and he might have added, "only in America").[26] John Updike's character Henry Bech (b. 1965) was a delightfully good-natured compliment to the centrality of the Jewish writer in America, but the author's impression of his literary contemporaries is conveyed by Bech's bachelor status and absence of any Jewish affiliation. To my knowledge, the first time an American Jewish writer publicly assumed the role of a Jewish parent rather than a Jewish child was when Norman Podhoretz, then thirty-one, framed the questions for the 1961 symposium Jewishness and the Younger Intellectuals in *Commentary*, the magazine he had just begun to edit. Addressed to American-born Jews under forty, the questions gave respondents the "absolute right" to choose their loyalties, but asked, inter alia, whether they felt any obligation to extend the values inherent in Jewish tradition to the next generation, how they regarded the possibility of their children's conversion to another religion, and what loyalty, if any, they felt to Israel, the new Jewish polity.[27] The gingerliness of these questions attests to the irresponsibility that most aspiring Jewish writers cultivated toward their own people as some of them rushed to prove their tender feelings for other disadvantaged cultures and groups. But since then, the situation has changed somewhat. As the culture of the sixties came into ever-greater conflict with traditional Jewish values, the American Jewish literary world became divided as never before over political, cultural, and even theological issues. It was in this atmosphere that Saul Bellow summoned up a refugee from Hitler's Germany to provide the point of view for *Mr. Sammler's Planet*, and Cynthia Ozick declared herself an avowedly Jewish writer. Toward the end of the century, as portrayed in Chapter Nine, a trickle of American Jewish writers took up the perspective of parents rather than children and, seeing the world as Tevye saw it, asked what kind of world they had wrought.

This book ends, inevitably, with a chapter on the revitalization of Hebrew as the Jewish national language—revitalizing a language is a feat unparalleled in the history of nations—and on the singular impact this has had on the literature of the Jews. In A. M. Klein's 1951 novel *The Second Scroll*, a Canadian Jewish poet is sent to Israel by his publisher shortly after the War of Independence to prepare an anthology of translated modern Hebrew verse. He dutifully hunts down poems by Rachel, Natan Alterman, Uri Zvi Greenberg, and the school of Canaanite poets but then realizes that the "fashioning folk" had been creating "the total work that when completed would stand as epic revealed!":

> They were not members of literary societies, the men who were giving new life to the antique speech, but merchants, tradesmen, day laborers. In their daily activity, and without pose of flourish, they showed it to be alive again, the shaping Hebrew imagination. An insurance company, I observed as I lingered in Tel Aviv's commercial center, called itself *Sneh*—after Moses' burning bush, which had burned and burned but had not been consumed. Inspired metaphor, born not of the honored laureate, but of some actuary, a man of prose! A well-known brand of Israeli sausage was being advertised, it gladdened my heart to see, as Bashan—just tribute to its magnum size, royal compliment descended from Og, Bashan's giant king. [. . .] In my student days I had been fascinated always by that word which put an end to the irreconcilable controversies of the House of Hillel and the House of Shammai: this House would

maintain *Permitted,* that House would insist *Prohibited;* a deadlock would ensue. Came then the Talmud editor and wrote *taiku,* stet, the question abides. My teacher would then go on to explain that *taiku* was really a series of initials that stood for *Tishbi yetaraitz kushioth v'abayoth,* the Tishbite would resolve all problems and difficulties. Now the magic cataleptic word was before me again, in a new context, in a newspaper, the report of a football game where the score had been tied. *Taiku!*[28]

I will forego discussion of such ironies as Klein's unself-conscious assumption of masculinity in this claim for inclusiveness, and the heavy exertion that is required in English to describe the spontaneous creativity of Hebrew. Let us only register the excitement felt by a poet for the "nameless authorship" that flourished in the streets over and above the formal work of his fellow poets. The narrator is educated enough, and at the same time distant enough, to appreciate every turn of wit, every innovative appropriation of the Israeli neologians. "It was as if I was spectator to the healing of torn flesh, or *heard* a broken bone come together, set, and grow again." Klein, who appreciates the difficulty of writing Jewish poetry and prose in English, subordinates the individual talent to the miracle of Hebrew reborn.

To be sure, it is hard to hold on to the freshness of a miracle once it turns everyday. At first, Hebrew writers may have felt that they were breathing new life into the dry bones of the language, but why else go to the trouble of revitalizing a language unless you want to express yourself more truthfully? As the difficulties and contradictions of modern Jewish existence multiplied, these became the mainstay of Hebrew literature. At the same time, many Hebrew writers felt that they served Hebrew best by "serving" it least, by freeing it from national imperatives and from collective duties. After all, if Hebrew really were just the national language of a sovereign people like any other, why should national consciousness figure in its literature at all? Thus, after a lifetime of trying to inspire his students with love of Zionism, Pinness, the teacher of the pioneering village in Meir Shalev's comic saga *The Blue Mountain,* is struck in old age by the heretical desire to escape the ideological fervor he had tried to instill in his students:

Pinness envied the caveman, who had wandered to this guileless land without biblical get-thee-outs to find it unpossessed and unscarred by the petty footprints of human loyalty and love, "driven only by his own hunger and thirst and an innocent appetite, retained by every living cell to this day, for that warm, moist thing we call life."[29]

Pinness has all the sympathy of the author (and of the narrator who is here quoting his words) in evading the fateful consciousness of Abraham's heirs. Poor Jew, saddled with a history so very long and so very edifying that he has to go back to the caveman for his model of natural innocence. Shalev and his translator resort to the language of undoing—"guileless," "without biblical get-thee outs," "unpossessed and unscarred"—to free the "folk teacher" of his yoke so that he can enjoy unmediated contact with his land.

Hebrew literature is just beginning to appreciate the irony that having helped to normalize the political and cultural status of the Jewish people, it may not want to be the voice of their Jewishness. Indifference and outright hostility to Judaism is expressed in Israeli fiction not only by Israeli Arabs who may be hostile to the intentions of the Jewish state but also by Israelis who resent their Jewish birth. Being born Jewish is the greatest imaginable boon to some writers, but for others it is a nightmare from which they struggle to awaken. In Gentile America, it matters less when Jewish writers pass into the mainstream. So what if Arthur Miller deracinated Willie Loman or if Joseph Heller made Yossarian an Armenian instead of a Jew? And what difference does it make, except to a small group of their Jewish admirers, that both men later acknowledged the Jewish roots of their characters? Pressures are very different inside a Jewish state that carries not only the collective historical legacy of the Jewish people but also responsibility for its future. The Arab war against Israel re-created the mentality of siege in the very country that was created to escape it, and how can Israelis fail to feel some bitterness at still being singled out for hatred when they did everything imaginable to save the Jews from its taint? As political antisemitism moved from Europe to the Middle East, it infected Israelis as well, and overt anti-Jewishness penetrated Hebrew literature just as it had done in the work of Jewish writers in Europe a century earlier. The pressure of identity within a Jewish language is reconnecting modern Hebrew with the beginnings of modern Yiddish literature, although the resemblance has yet to be acknowledged or explored.

I call my last chapter "A Chapter in the Making," because it would require another book to contain the subject of Israeli literature. Hebrew has begun to dominate Jewish literature, just as Israel now largely determines the future of the Jewish people. The Jews are not becoming monolingual; they continue to write in the languages into which they are born, as they have been doing with surprising new confidence in parts of Europe and South America. But neither are there likely to be many great Jewish writers of the next century who are uninformed and uninspired by the spirit of Hebrew. Hebrew today is not only the language of Bible and liturgy, it is now also the language of the Jewish state where an increasing majority of the Jewish people resides. Hence, it is the crucible of the national fate. Individual genius may come wherever it comes and do whatever it does, but the Jew who has no access to the heart of the Jewish polity is ever less likely to generate a valuable literature of Jewish experience.

THE STUDY OF COMPARATIVE LITERATURE subsumes Jewish literature in all its languages. Indeed, the Western canon at large includes some of the great books that are discussed here. But Judaism is also a competitive civilization whose literature follows patterns of its own. The fact that cultural traditions can be studied in tandem does not mean that they coincide, and even when they seem perfectly compatible, as they do in America, the perpetuation of each requires some independence from the other. Modern Jewish literature contains a record of national experience unlike any other, which makes it all the worthier of study, but it promises no happy merger into universalism at the end of the day. The odd thing about the multilingual literature of the modern Jewish canon is that although its reality can easily remain obscured, once it is revealed it appears to have been there all along.

1

THE COMEDY OF ENDURANCE

SHOLEM ALEICHEM

Such a one is a natural philosopher.

SHAKESPEARE, *As You Like It*

L ITERARY HEROISM IMPLIES the possibility of meaningful action,
action that can determine the outcome of personal or national destiny. Nineteenth-century European literature had already pronounced its skepticism about such possibilities when Jewish literature was
just beginning its search for them: as Fabrice del Dongo roams the
Napoleonic battlefield in *Charterhouse of Parma* (1839) determined to prove
himself a real soldier, the narrator lets us know that he "could not understand in the least what was happening." Raskolnikov (1867) decides to test
his philosophy of exceptionalism by murdering a useless old woman and
ends by confessing his crime to the police and to God. Yet creators of the
failed or anti-hero still enjoy the benefits of the tradition they depose.
These bids for heroism may be unmasked by their authors as comically
and tragically misguided, but the young men still go into battle, still wield
their axes. The narratives remain charged with tension and dramatic action that feed off the inherited models of heroism.

Writers of the Yiddish and Hebrew renaissance at the end of the nineteenth century inherited no such tradition of literature. The politically dependent Jews found it difficult to acclaim the man of action as their
authentic Jewish hero. Most Jewish writers had not spent their youth in political action like Stendhal or in the political opposition like Dostoyevsky
but rather breaking out of *yeshivas* to gain a secular education. The man of
learning, who defined the Jewish image of masculinity, was not the best
candidate for literary heroism. There were Jews who mastered the culture

31

of the Gentiles and made their mark as intellectuals in Western Europe. But here language and cultural orientation became a problem: what kind of hero could Moses Mendelssohn or Heinrich Heine be to the writer in a *Jewish* language, whose culture was predicated on the perpetuation of *Jewish* civilization? Writers of Jewish pulp fiction created improbable saviors of damsels in danger, but their adventures and even their costumes lacked credibility. It seemed that the more Jewish the main character was, the less heroic he appeared to be and the more heroic, the less Jewish.

Sholem Aleichem was the first to break through this impasse. The anchoring work of the modern Jewish canon—*Tevye the Dairyman*—is the transcribed repertoire of the first Jewish stand-up comedian who was also in the process of creating his audience. The comic hero is something of a compromise, to be sure: his words speak louder than his actions. Still, let us not fail to note that he manages to assist women in distress.

Tevye the Dairyman: The Making of a Comic Hero

In 1894, when he was thirty-five years old, Sholem Aleichem created a character named Tevye, a village Jew with a number of unmarried daughters, as in the Yiddish proverb *"Zibn tekhter iz nisht kayn gelekhter* [seven daughters are no laughing matter]." The maxim makes fun of what it says is no laughing matter, and on that same contradictory premise Tevye would turn the problems of his life into humor. Sholem Aleichem had just returned to Kiev from his customary summer vacation in nearby Boyarka, and as he wrote to his good friend Mordecai Spector, he intended to convey some of that holiday experience in the forthcoming volume of Spector's *Hoyzfraynd* [Home Companion]:

> The story will be called *Tevye der milkhiker,* composed in Boyarka, that is to say, I heard the story from Tevye himself as he stood in front of my *dacha* with his horse and cart, weighing out our butter and cheese. The story is interesting, but Tevye himself a thousand times more interesting! I convey the story in his own words, and am spared the effort of describing him since he describes himself.[1]

Like an impresario who knows that he has just landed his meal ticket, Sholem Aleichem negotiated with Spector over every detail of spelling, layout, typeset, and the quality of paper on which the Tevye story was to be printed.[2] Before long, everyone was in on the game. Members of Sholem Aleichem's family and critics familiar with the region confirmed that there was, indeed, such a Jew named Tevye, and when a local dairy-man protested that he did not have any daughters, it seemed only to rein-force the notion that a new literary talent had been discovered.[3]

YIDDISH LITERATURE was still young and untried when Sholem Ale-ichem began writing. Just as Samuel Richardson and Daniel Defoe used "discovered" diaries and letters, pseudobiography, editorial footnotes, and other such authenticating artifices to win the trust of new English readers by insisting that their books delivered other people's words, so too did Sholem Aleichem often present himself as the intermediary between his characters and his readers to attest to the actuality of his creations. A decade earlier, after he had begun to publish in the *Di yidishe folksblat* [The Jewish People's Paper], then the only Yiddish newspaper in the Russian empire, he had turned his name into the most common greeting in the lan-guage. That is, by keeping his first name, Sholem, and changing his patronymic, Rabinovitch, he formed the phrase one might address to an old friend when meeting him in the street: "Sholem Aleichem [how are you doing]?" Behind this friendly pseudonym—really only half a disguise, since the fictive author shared the vital statistics of his creator—Sholem Aleichem gave the impression of being one of the people, intermingling with his fellow Jews wherever they happened to be.[4]

In this he had adapted the practice of the man he called *zeyde*, the "grandfather" or shaping genius of modern Yiddish and Hebrew literature, Sholem Yankev Abramovitch, who assumed the literary disguise of Mendele Moykher-Sforim (Mendele the book peddler) when he began to write Yiddish fiction in 1864. Mendele Moykher-Sforim took on such an independent reality as the agent and publisher of the stories he brought to the public that he eclipsed his creator and became known as the author of his works. The Mendele narrator seemed not only to unite but virtually to create a community of readers as he traveled through the Jewish Pale of Settlement, between cities, towns, and villages, among the learned and the simple Jews, bringing fresh reading material to men and women, old and young. By carrying both religious and secular material—amulets to ward off the evil eye and the new kind of novels—he implicitly appealed to a modern audience that included old-fashioned Jews. Rabinovitch's Sholem Aleichem was even more peripatetic and democratic than Mendele in that he figured as the listener or the amanuensis of a people, providing what many assumed was "the life of the people in its authentic form."[5] Tevye, whom the critic Meir Viner called Mendele's younger brother, was homier still. Both characters enjoy quoting Jewish sources, but undereducated Tevye feels freer to play around with them, inviting perpetual uncertainty over how much of his humor is involuntary and how much is willed. Both peddlers offer merchandise to the public, but Mendele retains the rights to everything he brings to market and has to persuade his potential customers of the value of each new book. A creature of the Jewish Enlightenment, Mendele assumes that literature must prove its worth by bettering the life of its readers. Tevye offers food and entertainment, and according to Sholem Aleichem, the very best of both. His merchandise purports to be just good, not good *for* you. And unlike Mendele, who kept mum about his private life, Tevye enjoys sharing confidences about himself and the family.

At first Sholem Aleichem went to elaborate lengths to establish the distance between Tevye and himself, the implied author of the work. In the first installment that appeared in *Hoyzfraynd* he describes a big-boned, hirsute Jew, one of those healthy village specimens who eats dumplings with cheese "and spends his ninety years on earth without the help of glasses, false teeth, hemorrhoids, and other such Jewish pains and troubles."[6] In a letter to the author, Tevye declares himself flattered by the attention of the author from Yehupetz (Sholem Aleichem's fictional rendition of Kiev) who now promises to bring *his* story to the reading public. Citing Genesis 32:11, Tevye protests, "*Kotoynti [I am not worthy]!*"—echoing Jacob's exclamation ("I am not worthy of all the mercies and of all the truth, which Thou has shown Thy servant") as he flees his vengeful brother Esau.* Jacob is reminding God of their special relationship while admitting that he does not deserve His help, and with the same mixture of humility and *chutzpa* Tevye tells Sholem Aleichem where to send the money he is owed,

---

*Author's note: Transliterated Hebrew phrases with translations are in italics within quotation marks. That part of the phrase that appears in roman type and square brackets is the fuller expansion of the text in which the translated phrase is embedded.

presumably for royalties. But by the time Tevye reappeared in a second chapter a few years later, he was brought on stage without preamble, like a performer so famous he needs no introduction.[7] Sholem Aleichem realized that he had discovered in Tevye the Jew through whom he could tell the story of his time, and he brought him back again and again over the next twenty years at critical moments in his own and the nation's life.

The first monologue, "Tevye Strikes It Rich," is exceptionally cheerful. Nine or ten years after the events in question (time enough for the narrative to have ripened), he recalls how once on his way home from Boiberik (the fictional Boyarka) after a long day of hauling logs, having earned not nearly enough to feed his abundant family, he was startled out of his late afternoon prayers by the sudden appearance of two creatures in the woods. First he fears robbers, then, seeing that they are female, demons. They turn out to be simply a Jewish mother and daughter who had lost their way in the woods that morning. Tevye is slow to understand his heroic potential in guiding these women out of the forest, and they are mildly contemptuous of the *schlimazl*, the hapless bumbler, who has to serve as their savior. But at their urging, he agrees to turn his horse and wagon around and to transport them back to their dacha in Boiberik. There he is rewarded beyond his wildest fantasies. For bringing the women home, the head of the family, a traditional Jew like himself, showers Tevye with more money than he has the temerity to ask for and invites all the other members of the family to contribute something from their own pockets as well. The bounty Tevye receives that day allows him and his wife to set up a home dairy, producing cheese and butter products they had never before been able to afford.

Tevye tells this story at his leisure in Boiberik, the charming summer retreat. The literary scholar Frank Kermode argues that Ben Jonson and William Shakespeare were attracted by the pastoral genre at a time of exceptionally poignant social transformation in England: when London was developing a "distinctively metropolitan ethos" and traditionally rural citizens had to adjust to the new social standing of the commercial classes and the growth of wealth based on new values.[8] Using Nature as its background, Elizabethan drama reestablished a common humanity among people otherwise estranged. Similarly, Sholem Aleichem conjured up the perpetually summery Boiberik-Boyarka in a period of significant upheaval among Russian Jews. The infamous May Laws, imposed after the assassi-

nation of Alexander II in 1881, had prohibited Jews from settling or buying property outside their towns, or *shtetlakh*, and forbade them to open
their markets to peasants on Sundays and Christian holidays. "Poor!" I. L.
Peretz had exclaimed in a story of the previous year. "It's hard to imagine
how poor! Ten grain dealers throw themselves on every measure of rye
that a peasant brings . . . one hundred tailors for one pair of overalls, fifty
shoemakers for one small repair."[9]

The government not only failed to protect its Jewish subjects from the
violence of pogroms but conducted what the historian Simon Dubnow
called "legislative pogroms" through its policies of economic harassment.[10]
Such solidarity as might have been created among Jews in reaction to
these punitive measures was undermined by a policy of exceptions that allowed certain categories of Jewish merchants, professionals, artists, students, and craftsmen to live in cities outside the Pale. By distinguishing
between wealthy and poor Jews, educated and ignorant Jews, the Russian
government drove a wedge into the Jewish body politic, rewarding those
who were able to distance themselves from the masses. Sholem Aleichem's
readers would have known that while the summer vacationers enjoyed the
privilege of residence in Yehupetz, a Jew like Tevye could not legally stay
in the city overnight.

Anti-tsarism contributed to the problem. Opposed to the government's
oppressive policies in all other respects, Jewish nihilists shared the tsar's
interest in exacerbating the tension between richer and poorer Jews in order to replace Jewish loyalties by loyalties to class. Already in the 1870s,
Jews in the revolutionary movement had repudiated national allegiance in
favor of class solidarity. "You know very well that I detest Judaism just as I
hate all other . . . isms," wrote Aaron Lieberman, the founder of the first
Jewish socialist organization, who claimed to fight only for the oppressed
Jews, "the suffering masses among them and those who intend to join us."[11]
While only a minority of revolutionaries actually welcomed the anti-Jewish pogroms of 1881 as a preparatory stage for the revolt of the masses, socialism substituted the brotherhood of class for the communal discipline
of the Jews and encouraged Jews to express the kind of hostility toward
the rich that could never be openly voiced against the *goyim* (people of
other religions and nationalities).

Against this background of repression and divisiveness, Tevye tells of bridging the extremes of poverty and wealth. The chapter title "Dos groyse gevins [The Big Win]" refers literally to winning the lottery, but had Tevye won such a jackpot, the miracle would have been his alone, insulating one more Jew from his impoverished coreligionists. Instead, Tevye's windfall is the result of a Jewish exchange of services very much like the interaction between him and the author in the frame of the story. Just as Tevye makes a living off Sholem Aleichem, so the vacationing author intends to milk the milkman, turning Tevye's stories into literature and then bringing them to market. Neither commercial exploitation nor charity, theirs is a mutually beneficial transaction. As such, Tevye *earns* his reward from the rich man's family through his own generous act, just as he earns his author's gratitude for his humor and his cheese.

Tevye's narrative is set at the beginning of summer—the high season of literary comedy. He is returning from a long day's work and, in the way that an epic narrator might call upon his muse, is reciting the *shimenesre* (Eighteen Benedictions of the afternoon service) when his horse suddenly breaks away on a "pleasure jaunt":

> In a word, there I was running behind the wagon and singing the *shimenesre*, forgive the comparison, like a cantor at the pulpit: *Mekhalkeyl khayim bekhesed,* Who provideth life with His bounty, *Umekayeym emunosoy lisheyney ofor,* Who keepeth faith with them who slumber in earth—even with those who already lie in the ground baking bagels. With my troubles I was six feet underground already! Oh, do we suffer! Not like those rich Yehupetz Jews sitting all summer long in their dachas in Boiberik, eating and drinking and swimming in luxury! Master of the Universe, what have I done to deserve all this? Am I or am I not a Jew like any other? Help! . . . *Re'ey-no be'onyeynu,* See us in our affliction—take a good look at us poor folk slaving away and do something about it, because if You don't, just who do You think will?[12]

Running away with texts is as much a part of Jewish tradition as prayer itself, but the dialectical tension of Tevye's argument is new. The reader trained in paradox may note that Tevye's prayer triggers the revolt against it: praising the Lord for His bounty reminds him of his want, the Hebrew

affirmation prompting his Yiddish commentary in perpetual point counterpoint. What the verbs promise—a God "Who provideth" and "keepeth
faith"—Tevye desires for himself. Remove the liturgical text, and you have
the slogans of the emerging revolution. The then–Marxist critic I. I. Trunk
took this theological independence to mean that "for all his Jewish belief,
Tevye doesn't have the least confidence in God."[13] But one can as readily
cite Tevye's interpolations as proofs of his investment in God. After all,
who but Tevye out there in Nature cared whether or not he recited his
prayers? Without the liturgy's repeated promises of justice Tevye would
have no occasion to take his human lot so seriously, no context for expecting any more than he has. The Covenant is the source of his self-confidence, inviting him to expect fair judgment and to appreciate his worth.

Tevye's eagerness to show off prompted some critics to accuse him of
overreaching, as though he were the Mrs. Malaprop of Yiddish letters.
Richard Sheridan's memorable character says things like "Forget this fellow: illiterate him from your memory" and "I'm sorry my affluence over my
niece is very small," mistakes that expose her ignorance at the very moment that she is trying to impress us with her expanded vocabulary.
Sholem Aleichem's translator Frances Butwin thought that Tevye's interpolations were similarly "completely cockeyed": "The juxtaposition of a lofty
phrase in Hebrew or Aramaic with a homely Yiddish phrase which is supposed to explain it but has no bearing on it whatever—that is the gist of
Tevye's humor. Tevye, of course, has no idea that he is funny."[14] But this is
like saying that Sholem Aleichem himself has no idea that he is being
funny. Tevye's delight in mangling and appropriating quotations is the en-
tertainer's delight in amusing his public. Not only does his play with the
Hebrew sources confirm his psychological adaptiveness, but it also shows
off the culture's strategy for coping with adversity, since much of his routine was already drawn from the Yiddish idiom. By making Tevye a more
traditional Jew than himself, Sholem Aleichem could turn him into an exegetical humorist, a comical Rashi,[15] rewarding those readers who were familiar with the sources by inviting them to enjoy his distortions.

Tevye's comedy accepts the ontological disparity between what is possible and what is necessary, refusing to homogenize the competing claims
of hope and skepticism. Tevye stood Hegelian ambition on its head, in the
sense of denying that there can be any *development* in the tension between
thesis and antithesis, since the finite human being can never attain what he

must continue to struggle for. Tevye's humor follows the pattern of those Yiddish proverbs that simultaneously credit and subvert the quotations from which they derive: "*Ato bokhartonu [Thou has chosen us* from among the nations]: why did you have to pick on the Jews?" "*Avodim boyinu [we were slaves* in the land of Egypt]: that's reason enough for being Jews in the world!" (How, you may ask, can slavery make it worth being a Jew? Because the preeminence of the Jew is rooted in this history of slavery, which also became the basis for Jewish moral imperatives ["because you were slaves in the land of Egypt"]. The heights of Jewish national fortunes—the Exodus and the granting of the Law at Sinai—begin at the lowest point of Jewish degradation in Egypt; that is, the history of Jewish humiliation is also the ground of Jewish pride.)

It is legitimate to place Tevye, as Hillel Halkin does, in the long tradition of God-arguers that "starts with Abraham and runs prominently on through Moses, through Job . . . [to] Levi Yitzchak of Berdichev, the saintly Hasidic master who is said to have held a trial at which God was the absentee defendant, accused of having inflicted undeserved suffering on His people."[16] Yet in realistic fiction, justice can only be effected through human agency. While most intellectuals and writers of his day expected a kindlier solidarity to replace a society founded on religion, Sholem Aleichem recognized the likelier possibility that without fealty to a common God, Jews would have no further claim on one another's loyalty. Hence, Tevye's negotiations with the *gvir* (the wealthy Jew) are a testier version of his exchange with the Almighty:

> "A little brandy?" I say. "Who can refuse a little brandy? What does it say in the books: *Eyze 'lekhayim' ve'eyze lemoves,* who shall live and who shall die, or as Rashi comments, God is God and brandy is brandy. *Lekhayim!*" And I emptied the glass in one gulp. "God should only help you to stay rich and happy," I said, "and may Jews always remain Jews; God give them health and strength to overcome their troubles."
>
> "What name do you go by?" asked the man of the house, a fine-looking Jew with a skullcap. "Where do you hail from? Where do you live now? What's your work? Do you have a wife? Children? How many?"
>
> "Children?" I say. "I cannot complain. If each child of mine were

worth a million rubles, as my Golde tries convincing me they are, I'd be richer than anyone in Yehupetz. The only trouble is that poor isn't rich and a mountain's no ditch. As it says in the prayer book, *Hamavdil beyn koydesh lekhoyl*—some make hay while others toil. The Brodskys have money and I have daughters. . . . But you'll have to excuse me for carrying on like this. There is nothing straighter than a crooked ladder and nothing as crooked as an honest word, especially as I've gone and made the blessing over brandy on an empty stomach."[17]

Nervous and nervy, Tevye tells the rich Jew what he told the Almighty, that even the greatest spiritual inheritance is no substitute for a square meal. Offered a drink, Tevye tucks his toast "to life [*Lekhayim*]!" into the liturgy's ominous forecast of "who shall live and who shall die." Hence, the blessing he proffers ("God should only help you to stay rich and happy") hints broadly at the alternative. Comparing himself to the Brodskys, the Jewish sugar magnates who were Russia's version of the Rothschilds, Tevye both accepts God's arrangement and objects to having another Jew arranged on top of him. He is not quite as aggressive as that beggar of the Jewish joke who protests when informed that his benefactor has gone bankrupt, "So if his business is bad, why should I suffer?" That wit risks everything on a strategy of confrontation, claiming his right *ahead* of his benefactor's. Tevye merely confirms that Jews are responsible for one another; hence his wish that Jews may remain Jews so that he can tap into that obligation. Similarly, Sholem Aleichem knew that his career, like Tevye's reward, depended materially and morally on Jews who still felt bound by the traditions in which they had been raised.

In the humor anthology edited by Sholem Aleichem's close friend Y. Kh. Ravnitski, we find the following joke: A group of Jewish merchants in a restaurant are being harassed by a peddler who will not take no for an answer. Time and again he invites them to buy his handkerchiefs, wallets, haberdashery. Finally, one of the merchants says, "Watch me. I'll play a trick on him that he won't soon forget." The next time the peddler comes over to their table, he asks, "How much for these suspenders?" The peddler, still praising his merchandise to the skies, quotes a price of two rubles. Without a word, the merchant hands over the sum, and the peddler walks off in confusion. "How do you like the trick I played on him?" asked the merchant. "Now he'll be kicking himself all day for not having asked three rubles."[18]

When Tevye is asked how much he is owed for having brought the women home, each party wants the other to name his price:

> "No," they say, "we want you to tell us, Reb Tevye. You needn't be afraid. We won't chop your head off."
>
> Now what? I asked myself. I was really in a pretty pickle. It would be a crime to ask for one ruble when they might agree to two. On the other hand, if I asked for two they might think I was mad. *Two* rubles for one little wagon ride?
>
> "Three rubles!" The words were out of my mouth before I could stop them.
>
> Everyone began to laugh so hard that I could have crawled into a hole in the ground.[19]

While Ravnitski's version perfectly illustrates Freud's interpretation of tendentious jokes as instruments of aggression, Tevye invites us to experience the disjunction between dreams of profit and fears of loss. The sum he is embarrassed to ask for amuses his benefactors by its modesty. The merchant springs the surprise of the joke by subordinating his economic interests to his pychological victory, drawing attention to the competitive element in buying and selling that goes far beyond the incentive for profit. As the joke's point of view shifts from merchant to peddler, it reveals the human cost that the joke was designed to mask. The host in the Tevye version intervenes to put a stop to the merriment, chiding the insensitivity of those newly raised in wealth. The humorist wins his reward by making himself the *sentient* target rather than the butt of the joke.

Often mistaken for a typical *shtetl* Jew,[20] Tevye is actually distinguished by the fact that he is a villager, the antithesis of those *"kleyne mentshelekh mit kleyne hasoges* [little people with little ideas]," the far too many salesfolk and tradesfolk chasing after too few potential customers in Sholem Aleichem's stories about the *shtetl*. Not unlike his author, Tevye manages both the means of production and the distribution of his wares, standing somewhat apart from the Jewish society he serves. He only visits Anatevka, the local Jewish market town, twice a year, when he needs a *minyan* (the quorum of ten Jews required for communal worship) to say *Kaddish*, the memorial prayer on the anniversary of his parents' deaths. To emphasize this independence of the *shtetl* is no mere quibble. For although it has been noted that Sholem Aleichem creates a Jewish "quasi territory" in his writing—a network of fictional Jewish towns, villages, and cities with nary a church steeple in sight—the virtual island of discourse inhabited by Tevye and Sholem Aleichem is the first genuinely autonomous Jewish territory to appear in modern Yiddish literature, not coincidentally at the very moment that Zionism became a mass movement. Though obviously rooted in Ukrainian soil and still negotiating a generally hostile Christian world, Tevye and Sholem Aleichem are culturally autonomous and economically interdependent, serving their Christian neighbors out of superfluity, not necessity. As arguments began to appear in the Jewish press over the prospects of Jewish agricultural initiatives in Palestine, Sholem Aleichem, who was in sympathy with these efforts, created an adumbrated, comically miniature land of *milk* and honey in this opening episode of the Tevye saga.[21]

Sholem Aleichem: The Author Behind the Character

Autobiography, the most popular form of Jewish literature in the nineteenth century, usually claims that the first-person singular guarantees the truthfulness of the disclosure. But Tevye is a character twice removed from the author by the presence of the fictional Sholem Aleichem. Sholem Rabinovitch was a sophisticated literary man who spoke Russian to his children. How could the Kiev householder with the golden watch chain across his vest be mistaken for a dairyman who thinks two cows constitute a fortune? Yet, differences notwithstanding, Sholem Rabinovitch consigned to Tevye the most significant aspects of his life, beginning with the all-important matter of his talent and extending to the size of his household. Twice before, Rabinovitch had tried to compose a novel about an artist—the eponymous Stempenyu, a gifted fiddler, and Yosele Solovey, a golden-voiced cantor—who must either realize his ambitions by going out into the world or suffer the tragic consequence of staying home among the Jews.[22] But in Tevye he had a performer whose skill actually depended on a Jewish audience.

The humorist's instrument is his language. Sholem Rabinovitch's creative pleasure and anxieties as a Yiddish writer are transposed into Tevye's delight in racontage and fear of a breakdown in communication with his children. Among artists, the humorist was destined not to be taken with ultimate seriousness because of his delight in disinhibition, his ability to be "unashamedly childish."[23] Hence, *kotoynti*, Tevye's artful modesty, embodies his creator's admission that he excels at the disdained literary form of humor rather than the epic novel to which he aspired. Tevye *der milkhiker* meant not simply Tevye the dairyman but a man of milky disposition.[24] In Russian, milquetoasts were sometimes called *molokanye*, or milk-drinkers, after the sect of Russian pacifists who abjured meat, and, of course, the Jewish dietary laws that proscribe the mixing of dairy with meat had produced a typology of *milkhik* (milky) and *fleyshik* (meaty) personalities. Sholem Rabinovitch endowed Tevye with his own sweet male temper that used humor to parry aggression it could not oppose in kind.

The author's life had been transformed by a lucky break very much like Tevye's.[25] He was born in 1859 in Pereyaslav, Ukraine, and spent his childhood in the smaller Voronkov, where he attended a traditional *cheder* until a sudden business reversal forced his father to bring the family back to his native city under reduced circumstances, and with a sense of having come down in the world. His mother's early death further unsettled the boy and saddled him with a punitive, unfriendly stepmother. His father, who was interested in the new Hebrew literature and the Jewish Enlightenment, supervised his son's Hebrew education and, recognizing his intellectual gifts, sent him to the local Russian *gymnasium*, from which he graduated with distinction. Then, at seventeen, like hundreds of other young men without economic prospects, Sholem tried to support himself by tutoring. He left home, hoping to find a job as secretary or bookkeeper to one of the newly minted Russian Jewish entrepreneurs. Through a serendipitous encounter, he was hired by Elimelekh Loyev, a rich Jewish landowner in the Kiev province, to become the tutor of his only daughter. The Cinderella romance that developed between teacher and pupil angered Loyev when he first discovered it, more out of pique at the secrecy of the young couple than because he objected to his future son-in-law, but he was reconciled to their marriage, which occurred in 1883. Two years later Loyev died, leaving Sholem Rabinovitch in charge of a household of females that included his wife, her younger cousin, and his mother-in-law, who lived with them thereafter. The atmosphere of Loyev's welcoming wealth permeates the opening monologue of *Tevye the Dairyman*.

Rabinovitch's most productive years were 1883–1890, when he lived in Kiev as a speculator in the double sense, investing on the newly opened stock exchange and in a new high-level Yiddish literature, paying the highest royalties ever for Yiddish writing. He adopted the Yiddish pen name Sholem Aleichem so as "not to embarrass [his] father," who expected him to write in Hebrew, and waged literary battles against the trashy romances that he felt were corrupting Yiddish literature. But he overreached and went bankrupt, and until his family paid off his debts he was forced to wander for several years to Odessa, Paris, Vienna, and Czernowitz.

The second Tevye monologue, "The Bubble Bursts" (1899), is all about overreaching. Here it is as if Shakespeare had brought together Hamlet and Othello in a single work, pitting the hesitancy of the first against the impulsiveness of the second, for Tevye encounters Menakhem-Mendl, the frenetic speculator whom Sholem Aleichem had introduced to readers in 1892. Menakhem-Mendl figured in his own comic series as the male half of an epistolary exchange with his *shtetl*-bound wife Sheyne-Sheyndl.[26] Having left his small-town family to seek his fortune in the big city, he is the prototype of the *luftmentsh*, the man who lives on air, and of the philosophic optimist, the Jew who lives on faith. Each series of letters is organized around another of Menakhem-Mendl's ventures—into stocks, bonds, brokerage, and so forth—and each sequence repeats the same pattern: the husband writes home to his wife about the new investments that are bound to bring him a fortune, he enjoys the first dizzying returns, the market crashes, he rebounds. Sheyne-Sheyndl's (losing) argument is also the same, reinforced by her mother's proverbs, such as "*Kreplakh* [dumplings] in a dream are not *kreplakh* but a dream." "The worm lies in horseradish and finds it sweet." Her barbs puncture her son-in-law's airy schemes, but the longer the comedy continues, the more certain it is that Menakhem-Mendl will never return to the *shtetl*.

If Tevye's first monologue fulfilled the promise of Psalm 113—"He lifts the poor man from the dust, from dirt he raises the beggar"—his metamorphosis into a small entrepreneur now situates him among the potential benefactors rather than the petitioners, with a corresponding shift of economic and social responsibility. Having previously demonstrated the benefit that Jews could bring one another through a minor redistribution of resources, this late-autumn episode explores the opposite proposition, the destabilizing effect of economic temptation. Inevitably, it is in the big city

Yehupetz that Tevye falls prey to temptation. Looking at a shopwindow display of silver, gold, and banknotes and dreaming of the things he could do with but a tithe of that money, Tevye is tapped on the shoulder by a bedraggled Menakhem-Mendl, who introduces himself as a relative by marriage twice removed and explains that he is slinking around the city without a residence permit, eluding the police. Tevye invites the hungry man to join him for a day in the country. There Golde fills Menakhem-Mendl's stomach, and Menakhem-Mendl fills Tevye's head with get-rich-quick schemes. Neither man can resist what the other offers.

In this fateful encounter between his two major protagonists and the two sides of his own personality, the dependable father and the irresponsible child, Sholem Aleichem gives Tevye pride of place. Menakhem-Mendl figures in Tevye's monologue—not vice versa—as the *schlimazl* who gave him "the itch to be rich."[27] To be sure, Menakhem-Mendl may well signify Sholem Aleichem's unfettered creative impulse, the necessary condition for art. But nothing is as characteristic of Sholem Aleichem's opus as the regretful subordination of the messianist to the qualified optimist, and the contrast between the two men as husbands may clarify what is at stake. Menakhem-Mendl resists domestication with near-fatal abandon; no matter how desperate the news from his wife, neither duty nor practical self-interest can lure him home. Even as he enjoys his relatives' bounty, he does not hesitate to put it at risk. For his part, Tevye will not celebrate striking it rich until he has first fed his horse. He cries when he sees his daughters wolfing down their first abundant meal, and he cannot live without the approval of the wife whom he mocks as his inferior.

And so after losing all his savings on what came to be known in Yiddish parlance as a Menakhem-Mendl scheme, Tevye seesaws to equilibrium:

> And that, Pani Sholem Aleichem, is how I blew all my money. But if you think I've been eating my heart out about it, you have another guess coming. You know the Bible's opinion: *li bakesef veli hazohov*—money is muck! What matters is the man who has it—I mean, what matters is for a man to be a man. Do you know what I still can't get over though? Losing my dream! If only you knew how badly, oh Lord, how really badly I wanted to be a rich Jew, if only for a while! But go be smarter than life. Doesn't it say *be'al korkhekho atoh khai*—nobody asks if you want to be born or if you want your

last pair of boots to be torn. "Instead of dreaming, Tevye," God was trying to tell me, "you should have stuck to your cheese and butter." Does that mean I've lost faith and stopped hoping for better times? Don't you believe it! The more troubles, the more faith, the bigger the beggar, the greater his hopes.[28]

The supportive quotation from the prophet Haggai (2:18), "*The silver is mine and the gold is mine,* saith the Lord of Hosts," delivers God's promise to Israel that the glory of the rebuilt Temple will surpass the one that was destroyed. Tevye rebounds with gratitude to the challenge of his loss the way the Jews have been doing since at least the Babylonian exile, with an appreciation of paradox grown suppler over the centuries. Acknowledging God's grandeur, Tevye briefly downplays the importance of his own material assets, but then, having recovered his optimism, he regrets not having the money after all. The cycle starts again with Tevye's favorite quotation from *Ethics of the Fathers*: "Regardless of thy will thou art conceived, and regardless of thy will thou art born, and *regardless of thy will thou livest*, and regardless of thy will thou diest." No sooner does he reconcile himself to mortal finitude than he begins to hope for better times. Tevye never simply quotes but rather subjects all authority to his own interpretation, so that even God seems merely to confirm a conclusion he has reached on his own.[29] Resignation is no sooner denied than readmitted: the expulsion from Eden triggers the yearning for redemption; the authority of texts can only be demonstrated when individuals freely adapt them; the Covenant with God invites man to stand up against Him; in the surrender to nature is born the instinct for life. Chastened by the blowout that follows hitting the jackpot, Tevye henceforth tries to hold on to what he has.

The Daughters

How many daughters had Tevye? In asking this question, the literary scholar Chone Shmeruk highlights a discrepancy that emerged in Sholem Aleichem's masterpiece as a result of its having been written in real time, over a span of twenty years.[30] In the opening monologue (1895) Tevye is worried about having to feed seven hungry daughters; by the sixth chapter (1907) he mentions only six girls, and by the seventh (1909) he is left with five. Clearly, the author did not know when he wrote his first Tevye monologue that he would go on to develop a family saga, but as he himself had four daughters of six children, superabundant paternity was one of his biographical connections with Tevye. He developed the stories of the daughters—Tsaytl, Hodl, Chava, Shprintse, and Beilke—one at a time, never knowing from one episode to the next when or how he would continue. But why, then, didn't Sholem Aleichem redact his text to provide internal consistency? Did he balk at retroactively "killing off" the excess children out of some sense that they had been his own? Was he still hoping to continue the series when death cut it short?

More intriguing than the number of his daughters is that in contradistinction to most contemporary European literature, Sholem Aleichem wrote his masterwork about generational conflict from the *parent's* point of view. From the moment that Bazarov appeared in Turgenev's *Fathers and Sons*, he involved all literate Russia in an argument over whether he was the villain or hero of the emerging new age. Dostoyevsky created a rogues' gallery of revolutionaries that warned Russia long before the Bolsheviks took power of the social threat posed by young people who stood free of God. Leo Tolstoy cast Levin and Anna Karenina as the happy and the unhappy face of Russia, as the psychological and moral alternatives in a land where the educated young were forcing a new society into being. From Samuel Butler's *The Way of All Flesh* to D. H. Lawrence's *Sons and Lovers* and throughout most Yiddish and Hebrew literature, authors presented the clash between parents and children from the dynamic perspective of the rebels, and in his formal novels Sholem Aleichem did exactly the same.

Yet Sholem Aleichem had an overriding artistic reason for creating a Yiddish narrator of the older generation. By the late nineteenth century, Yiddish may have been as fully formed and culturally productive as most other European languages, but every youngster who quit his or her traditional home to attend *gymnasium* or to foment revolution or to move to America or to a settlement in Palestine felt the need to adopt a language other than Yiddish as a consequence of the change. Yiddish may have been spoken by the vast majority of Jews in the Russian Empire—indeed, by more Jews than had ever before simultaneously spoken a common language—but as the repository of Jewish religious civilization, Yiddish would not suffice for Jews who no longer wanted to remain exclusively within its bounds. Sholem Aleichem had often alluded to this problem:

Once, about ten years ago, Morris Silverman was called "Meir," and his mother Golde Reb Meir's still calls him "Meir'l" to this day. But since civilization began to appear among our brethren, we bolted in fear of her, and quickly began to adjust our clothing and our names: the satin *kapote* and the round *shtreiml* were traded in for a short jacket and top hat, and yesterday's Meir Berl's, Zerakh Naphtali's, and Kalman Reb Velvele's suddenly became Morris Borisovitch, Zachary Pantelemonovitch, and Clementi Vladimir-ovitch . . .[31]

Morris Silverman in *Taybele*, this early work of Sholem Aleichem's, antici-pates Ahronchik, the mama's boy who will break Shprintse's heart in the sixth chapter of *Tevye the Dairyman*. But the broken heart at issue here was the author's: Sholem Aleichem knew that he could not hope to satisfy the new Morrises and Zacharys and Clementis, because he himself was speak-ing and writing Russian to his children. So that they might have access to everything emancipation had to offer, he weaned them from the language to which he was devoting his creative genius. Tevye is the expression of this tragic paradox. The father knows that in addition to letting his chil-dren go, he will abet their defection so that they might enjoy a better life.

Sholem Aleichem may have absorbed a great deal from his beloved Nikolai Gogol, but there is nothing in his writing remotely like *Taras Bulba*, the all-out struggle between the dashing Andrey, who abandons his people for the love of a woman, and the Cossack father who is obliged to kill his renegade son. In the oedipal conflicts of the "Jewish Gogol," the prepubes-cent child already assumes responsibility for what his father is too weak to protect: a boy in Sholem Aleichem's maiden story, "The Penknife," sacri-fices his desire to own a penknife in deference to his sickly father.[32] The nar-rator renounces the forbidden temptation and redirects his libidinous energy into telling the story of his parentification. Should the long-overdue critical biography of Sholem Rabinovitch ever be written, it may connect this theme of renunciation with his becoming "merely" a humorist, whose measure of the human is the capacity for accommodation.

Freud might have had Sholem Aleichem in mind when he wrote, "Is there any sense in saying that [the humorist] is treating himself like a child and is at the same time playing the part of the superior adult in relation to this child?" Freud suggested that through the agency of humor, the super-ego tries to comfort the ego and to protect it from suffering, as if saying, "Look here! This is all that this seemingly dangerous world amounts to. Child's play—the very thing to jest about!"[33] Tevye was this mature child. Whether Sholem Aleichem kept his characters within bonds because the nature of Yiddish seemed to require it or adored Yiddish because it flourished within filial bonds, he recognized an uncanny congruence between his natural talent and the fate of his language.

Tsaytl

Tevye's attempt to arrange a proper match for his eldest daughter, Tsaytl, in the "Modern Children" episode begins in the slapstick tradition. Tevye's encounter with the butcher Leyzer Wolf turns on the classic misunderstanding over what the two men have come to barter—here, daughter or cow—and from behind the hilarity of their confusion emerges criticism of arranged marriages in which women may be treated like *beheymes* (domestic animals). According to the East European concept of *yikhes*, the hierarchy of Jewish social standing, no one was lower than the artisan. Tsaytl's preference for the lowly patchwork tailor Motl Kamzoyl over a wealthy butcher signals the protest that was common to positivists and revolutionaries against a system that undervalued productivity and equal rights. The seed of revolt is sown by the daughter who follows her heart into marriage.

Today, with feminism once again in ascendance, one can appreciate how the rebellion of daughters rather than sons both softened and sharpened the theme of generational conflict. While the absence of overt competition cushioned the force of female rebellion, Jewish women could attack the tradition more forcefully since they had no stake in its intellectual heritage. Tevye's pride in his ability to quote from the traditional sources does nothing to shore up his authority among the womenfolk. "Spare us your Bible!" says Golde, impatient with the impractical drift of Tevye's thought. Her sarcasm grows heavier with the years: "My *milkhik* borsht is more fundamental than all your fundamentals!"[34] Hodl and Chava have no trouble outarguing their father—precisely because they talk right to the point without any need for prooftexts. Tevye knows that his power is invested in his speech and that it, like Samson's hair, can be cut off by women. The decline of his authority is manifest in the collapse of communication from one daughter to the next.

From Tsaytl's 1899 romance Tevye still emerges unscathed. Having betrothed her to the wrong man, he not only undoes the damage and accepts the proposal of the tailor Motl Kamzoyl, but dreams up a scheme to reconcile his wife to the inferior match: "'You know what, Motl?' I said to my future son-in-law. 'You go home and leave the rest of it to me. . . . As it says in the Book of Esther, *vehashtiyah kedos*—everything has to be thought through.'"[35] Minutes after yielding to the boy, Tevye casts himself majestically as King Ahasuerus through the quotation "And the king [Ahasuerus] made a feast . . . *and the drinking was according to custom*," thus assuring the couple by means of a pun on the word *kedos* that they will be married *kedos moshe veyisroel*, that is, according to the laws of Moses and Israel (part of the marriage vow), and that they can count on him to do right by them with a merry celebration. At the end of this episode Tevye is shaking with laughter.

Hodl

By contrast, Tevye's communication with his second daughter and Perchik in the next episode, "Hodl" (1904), is frayed by dramatic irony. On some level, Tevye must have wanted this Marxist firebrand for a son-in-law, since the very first time he meets him on the road, he parodies a bridegroom being called up to the reading of the Torah: "*Yaamoyd hakhosn reb yokl ben flekl* [Let the bridegroom Yokel son of Jokel rise]!" He brings him into his household of daughters: "We crowned him with the name 'Feferl' [Peppercorn], transposing Perchik into Yiddish, and you could say that we began to love him as one of our own."[36] But whereas Tevye's meager investment in the social hierarchy had made it relatively easy for him to accept a tailor for a son-in-law, he knows that the revolutionary's plotting against tsarist authority is also directed in some measure against himself. Feferl and Hodl are secretive by design, and assuming that Tevye cannot grasp their ideas, they don't bother to explain their conspiratorial work. "I can't tell you that, it's confidential," says Feferl when Tevye asks him why he must leave his new wife so soon after their marriage. "The trouble is, you don't understand," says Hodl when Tevye asks what the young couple is up to. The phrase from the Book of Esther that Tevye repeatedly associates with her—"*Eyn ester magedes*," from "*And Esther spoke not of her nativity or her people*"—refers to the way Esther concealed her Jewishness from the other girls when she was in the harem of Ahasuerus, hence to the way

Hodl conceals her *non-Jewish* behavior from her father here. The correspondence between Esther, who is ordered by her cousin Mordecai to say nothing (in order that she might benefit the Jews in the long run), and Hodl, who is told by Perchik to say nothing (in order that they might advance the Russian Revolution), casts Tevye once again as King Ahasuerus, only here as the foolish authority who is duped into compliance.

Sholem Aleichem compressed his contradictory feelings about the revolutionary movement in this, Tevye's most ambivalent story. Perchik the revolutionary is attractive and lethal in just the way Menakhem-Mendl was, promising great things but stealing away a treasure. Perchik steals a beloved daughter, just as Menakhem-Mendl stole Tevye's accumulated fortune. Had Sholem Aleichem wanted to promote Marxism among Jews, he could have cast Perchik as a member of the Jewish Socialist Bund, which was organizing Jewish workers in Yiddish. Instead, Perchik's fellow revolutionary is "dressed like a *sheygetz* [Gentile], if you will forgive me," and the gang goes off to propagandize among the "real" Russians in the north. The socialist sympathies of this story, so admired by like-minded critics, are greatly complicated by the mutual distrust between the skeptical father and the children who think they know ever so much more than he does. Tevye suspects when he says good-bye to Hodl that he will never see her again. He ends his wrenching monologue with what was to become his most famous tag line: "You know what, Pani Sholem Aleichem? Let's talk about something more cheerful: Have you heard any news of the cholera in Odessa?"[37] "More cheerful" is Tevye's theory of relativity.

Chava

"Chava goes beyond Hodl, but is not simply a repetition," Sholem Aleichem wrote to his friend Y. Kh. Ravnitski when he was on the point of finishing the story "Chava" in 1906.[38] This was an understatement, for although this episode follows almost exactly the narrative pattern of its predecessors, Tevye's third daughter takes the romantic impulse to its logical conclusion: if a girl may follow her heart into marriage, why should she be prevented from marrying a Christian? In tsarist Russia, unlike America, exogamy required conversion to the dominant religion. The implications of love as the arbiter of destiny are made explicit as Chava converts to Christianity to marry Chvedka Galagan, the Ukrainian village scribe whom she considers "a second Gorky." Her romance therefore involves Tevye in negotiations with the local priest and marks the first time that his rhetorical strategies come up against the religion of the state. What begins as a friendly discussion between Tevye and the village priest about "your God and my God" escalates into the priest's insistence "that his God had it over on mine." Tevye trades quotations with his usual flair, but just as he is giving his adversary a piece of his mind, he notices the priest laughing and combing out his beard. "I tell you, there's nothing more aggravating in all the world than being treated to silence by the person you've just reduced to dirt."[39] The priest can afford his smug silence, knowing that Tevye's daughter Chava is in love with a Christian and that standing behind *his* religion is the power of the tsar.

Chava is the first of Tevye's daughters to present her own case to her father without the mediation of a boyfriend:

"It's beyond belief," she says, "how you have a verse from the Bible for everything! Maybe you also have one that explains why human beings have to be divided into Jews and Christians, masters and slaves, beggars and millionaires. . . ."

"Why, bless my soul," I say, "if you don't seem to think, my daughter, that the millennium has arrived." And I tried explaining to her that the way things are now is the way they've been since Day One.

"But why are they that way?" she asks.

"Because that's how God made them," I say.

"Well, why did He make them like that?"

"Look here," I say, "if you're going to ask why, why, why all the time, we'll just keep going around in circles."

"But what did God give us brains for if we're not supposed to use them?" she asks.

"You know," I say, "we Jews have an old custom that when a hen begins to crow like a rooster, off to the slaughterer she goes. That's why we say in the morning prayer, *hanoyseyn lasekhvi binoh*—not only did God give us brains, He gave some of us more of them than others."[40]

Rescued from this losing argument by Golde's call to supper, Tevye offers not a single reason for why Jews should remain a people apart. Never mind that he cannot quote Maimonides; he does not even quote some Hasidic master or express appreciation for Jewish practices such as the Sabbath, which is said to preserve the Jews more than the Jews preserve it. Tevye's traditionalism obscures the fact that, apart from his contentious praying, he is never seen observing any Jewish ritual, unless eating blintzes on Shavuos can be termed a religious act. For all his implicit observance, he resembles, in what we see of him, many another modern Jew who wants to keep his child Jewish just because she *is* his child. The verse that he cites from the morning prayers to clinch the debate with Chava—"Blessed are Thou, O Lord God, King of the Universe, *Who giveth the rooster knowledge* to tell the dawn from the night"—exposes his desperation, for had he been better able to parry her universalist ideals, he would not have had to threaten his errant daughter with the example of the hen that is slaughtered for imagining herself a rooster. Unable to win the argument, he tries to resort to the priest's strategy of flaunting his power. But this merely betrays his helplessness, for the priest's power is precisely what he lacks.

The reader should not be surprised by how much intelligent sympathy is invested in Chava's passion for the "second Gorky." Following the Kishinev pogrom of 1903, Sholem Aleichem himself paid a call on the actual Maxim Gorky to enlist his support for the victims and the families of the dead. In letters to his children he gushed over the warmth of the reception he had received at the hands of the man he called "the icon of our age."[41] It is this naive hope of his own for Jewish rapprochement with the Russian intelligentsia that Sholem Aleichem here imaginatively ascribes to Tevye's third daughter, deputizing her to speak for the humanism of his day.

To remain a Jew, Tevye has to play the tyrant, repudiating not just his daughter but his own *milkhik* nature. The metaphoric hen that he brings to the slaughterer is the tender part of his soul. Ultimately, however, he gains the moral advantage. Once the priest has Chava in his house, preparing her for conversion, Tevye is not even allowed to see his daughter, lest he persuade her to change her mind! The juxtaposition of Tevye's discussions with his daughter and with the priest shows up the cruelty of what is supposed to be the "religion of love." Chava's high-minded humanism translates into a victory of the priest over her father and not, as she would have it, into a kindlier tolerance. Tevye reaches the limits of accommodation when on the day after her defection Chava tries to intercept her father at nearly the same spot on the road where he had given in to Tsaytl and Motl Kamzoyl in Episode Three and picked up the revolutionary Perchik in Episode Four. In narrative terms, Chava appeals to her father's tenderness at the very place where he has so often proven it. But Tevye is transformed from a passive into an active hero when he refuses to speak to his Christian daughter on the forest road. He commands his family to sit *shiva*, that is, to repudiate Chava's apostasy by mourning her as dead.

Tevye understands—even if his daughter pretends not to—the essential weakness of the Jew in Christian society, and he is furious with Chava for exposing his impotence. But he also admits that her argument emanates from his own enlarged sympathies, for he, too, wonders why being or not being a Jew should matter. "Why did God have to create both? And if He did, why put such walls between them, so that neither would look at the other even though both were His creatures?"[42] Ultimately, he is humbled by one of his favorite quotations from Psalms: *kerakheym ov al bonim, "Like as a father pitieth his children"* [so the Lord pitieth them that fear Him]. Just a few pages earlier he had tweaked a phrase from this quotation to his own male advantage: "Why doesn't it also say *kerakheym eym al bonim*—as a mother loves her own child—too? Because a mother isn't a father. A father speaks to his children differently."[43] But now he is haunted by quite another image of paternity: "Could there be anywhere a child so bad that a father couldn't still love it?"[44] Far from denying his love for Chava to make his task easier, Tevye admits that she is the most deeply "baked into his heart," having been sickly in childhood and exceptionally sweet as a girl. In Sholem Aleichem's version, the Jew who so often stands accused of authoritarian rectitude is just the opposite—a father who barely has it in him to defend his Jewishness.[45]

As Tevye describes to Sholem Aleichem an imaginary visit to Chava, a strange thing happens in the text: Tevye is told by the station agent when he tries to buy a ticket for Yehupetz that he has never heard of such a place, reminding readers that Tevye has been inhabiting an imaginary Jewish location within a Gentile society that has no objective correspondence on the Russian map. Simultaneously, Tevye worries for the first time about having become the butt rather than the purveyor of his humor. The priest's derision can now be heard reverberating inside himself. The conversion of Chava has pushed the humor over the edge, and whenever Sholem Aleichem reaches such a point, he is in the habit of exploding the fiction he has hitherto presented as real.[46] Tevye asks for anonymity when he takes his leave from Sholem Aleichem in this episode, putting a reverse twist on the biblical reference to Joseph, *"Vayishkokheyhu"* [And the Chief Butler did not remember Joseph] *and he forgot him* (Gen. 40:23). As a result of the Chief Butler's neglect, Joseph languishes unjustly in prison, but Tevye *asks* to be ignored, at least for the moment, because the humorist-hero doesn't want to be seen stripped of his daughter and his art.

Shprintse and Beilke

Sholem Aleichem would celebrate the completion of each new Tevye episode by gathering his family for a preview performance. They knew that Tevye best expressed their father's "philosophy of life, his attitudes toward God and other human beings."[47] The family custom must have acquired new urgency following the abortive Russian Revolution of 1905. During the Easter pogrom in Kiev, the Rabinovitch household was forced into hiding for three days while their housekeeper protected their apartment by convincing the pogromists that she was in the service of Christians. As the tsar's long-awaited constitution became the catalyst for unprecedented violence against the Jews, Sholem Aleichem saw no further point in pretending that Russia could be his home. Along with hundreds of thousands of his fellow Jews, he made plans to leave his native land, and by the time he wrote "Chava," in the spring of 1906, he was already in Lemberg en route to America. The mourning period for Chava expressed Sholem Aleichem's grieving for the liberal illusion of Russian–Jewish brotherhood.

Coming as they do after the dramatic climax of Chava, Tevye's stories about his fourth and fifth daughters almost sink under their historical weight. When Tevye meets Sholem Aleichem at the beginning of "Shprintse" (1907), he notes how much has happened since their last encounter—"Kishinev, a Constantution, pogroms, riots, and troubles" —dating their previous meeting about 1902, before the Kishinev pogroms, or, in terms of the narrative, before the fatal downturn in Jewish political fortunes. Although he had written the Chava episode only one year earlier, Sholem Aleichem situated it retroactively during the high tide of idealism, while setting the story of Shprintse in the dark days that followed. From this point onward, the narrative darkens, too. Writing from "exile" in western Europe and America, Sholem Aleichem confronted

Tevye with a collapsing world as if to test how much adversity his humor could absorb.

Shprintse's story reverses Tevye's lucky break. As he had once rescued the Jewish women in the forest, Tevye tries to help out one of his customers, a wealthy widow, whose only son, Ahronchik, is itching for a father's authority. He invites the young man into his home as he had done with Perchik, and once Ahronchik begins showing an interest in Shprintse, Tevye dreams that a union may result in another mutually beneficial exchange between the Jewish haves and have-nots. Instead, having insisted that he wanted to marry Shprintse, Ahronchik abandons her without a word, and his uncle comes down from St. Petersburg to extricate his nephew from the affair. The uncle accuses Tevye of being a shadier kind of "uncle," of having set up his daughter, "assuming that that really is your daughter," in order to ensnare a wealthy boy. Tevye is rendered speechless by this cynicism of a fellow Jew, and is reduced to tears once he is safely out of sight. "What did poor Job ever do to You, dear Lord, to make You hound him day and night?"[48] Shprintse takes her cue from her father. She voices no protest either but drowns herself, "like a candle flickering out."

The succeeding episode is an even more stunning parody of Tevye's dreams. Tevye meets Sholem Aleichem on a train looking very prosperous in new clothes. He explains that following the death of Golde, his youngest daughter Beilke had married a rich man, playing out at last his fantasy of the ideal match. But the social climbing son-in-law was so embarrassed to have a Jewish dairyman for a father-in-law that he determined to ship him out of the country! When he suggested America, Tevye held out for Palestine ("Isn't that where all the old Jews go?"), acceding to the proposal because his daughter's marriage had anyhow failed to provide him with a home. Whereas Tevye wanted to be rich so that he could be a better Jew, his son-in-law Podhotsur (a biblical name here hinting of *putz*, Yiddish for penis) wants to be rich so that he can cease being a Jew. Thus, Tevye takes "never judge by appearances" for his parting theme: "*Al tistakeyl bakankan*" [Rabbi Yehuda Hanasi said, *Look not at the storage jar* but at what it stores]. Now that Teyve looks like the man he thought he wanted to be, he feels he is being driven through the gauntlet.

The title of this seventh episode, "Tevye Leaves for the Land of Israel" (1909), hints at historical changes on a larger scale. Sholem Aleichem's son-in-law I. D. Berkowitz says that when some of the author's admirers promised to set him up in Eretz Israel, he thought of shipping Tevye off there in advance of his own departure.[49] Under doctors' care at the time in Nervi, Italy, Sholem Aleichem wept tears of joy when he read of the ovations that greeted Haim Nahman Bialik upon his arrival for a visit in Palestine, envying him not the reception itself but "the honor" of having reached the Land of Israel.[50] But since Sholem Aleichem did not make it to Palestine, the title of the story remained a tease. Once again, he expressed through Tevye his unfulfilled longings, his disappointed dreams.

Idealism in the early episodes was conveyed by the notion that love conquers all, so when Tevye yields to the wishes of his daughters, he feels his sympathies are enlarged by their ideas of progress. Shprintse and Beilke are the victims of a morally altered atmosphere of crude material striving. "Don't go comparing me to Hodl," says Beilke whenever her father invokes the sister who went off to Siberia. "In Hodl's day the world was on the brink. There was going to be a revolution and everyone cared about everyone. Now the world is its own self again, and it's everyone for his own self again, too."[51] Indeed, Tevye's lingering and unresolved admiration for Russian radicalism makes it that much harder for his youngest daughter to adjust to what she considers her duty. But in Tevye's telling, her pragmatism threatens his poised faith no less than, and perhaps even more than, the rebellions of his other children, which had at least some aspiration, some goal, in common with Tevye's reach for godliness. Beilke's well-intentioned material calculations destroy the home they were intended to protect.

"Get Thee Out": Turning History into Humor

After the Beilke chapter, five years elapsed before Sholem Aleichem returned to his favorite character, the longest time that had ever passed between episodes. The impulse for revisiting Tevye seems to have been the worsening situation of Jews in Russia.[52] The incredible 1911 case of Mendel Beilis, charged in Kiev with murdering a Christian boy to secure ritual blood for Passover matzos, heralded a new and more lethal government-sponsored antisemitism. Using the potential for Jewish disloyalty as its excuse, the tsarist government forced evictions of Jews from border villages and gave local authorities the right to change the status of town to village for that express purpose. An eviction of this kind is precisely what sends Tevye packing in "Get Thee Out," the eighth Tevye episode, which captures the full anxiety of the time in which it was written.

Greeting his old friend Sholem Aleichem after their long separation, Tevye for the first time attributes his deteriorated appearance only partly to his private sorrows—"God forgive me for putting myself first!"—and the rest to the collective sorrows of the Jewish people. Having given up his dairy business, Tevye says he has become "just a Jew, a plain ordinary Jew," about to be evicted from his home. His wife is dead, Hodl lost to the Revolution, Chava to Christianity, Shprintse to the river. Beilke and her husband have escaped their creditors by fleeing to America—which explains why Tevye can no longer be supported by his son-in-law in Eretz Israel and must instead return to his homestead. But although the last chapter recounts Tevye's expulsion from what had for so long been the land of his fathers, nothing about his narrative is ever linear or final. Since Tsaytl and her children became Tevye's charges when Motl died, Tevye is once again responsible for sustaining a family. And at the point of his leaving, Chava comes home. The exodus from Russia is the beginning of national reunification.

Sholem Aleichem was not quite accurate when he once wrote that Tevye remained unchanged throughout his cycle of stories. The man who gave us his first running commentary on prayers as he was chasing his horse now takes possession of the biblical text with the authority of a *darshan*, a homespun preacher.

> In a word, what Bible reading are you up to in the synagogue this week, the first chapter of Leviticus? [This would situate the monologue about the end of March, a couple of weeks before Passover.] Well, I'm on another chapter, on *Lekh lekho. Lekh lekho*—get thee out, Tevye, I was told—*meyartsekho*—from your land—*umimoyladitkho*—and from the village you were born in and lived your whole life—*el ha'orets asher arekho*—to wherever your legs will carry you! . . . And when did it occur to the authorities to read Tevye that passage? At the very moment when he is old and weak and lonely, as we say in the Rosh Hashanah prayers: *al tashlikheynu le'eys ziknoh!* [*Cast us not away, O Lord, in our old age.*][53]

If we think of the English expression "to pull out all the stops," having in mind the organist who releases the foreshortening hammers, we may appreciate Tevye's gloss on the emergence of the modern Jewish people. Just as God told Abraham to leave everything behind (at the beginning of Genesis 12), so too do the Russian authorities tell this to the Jews, but though God promised Abraham that He would show him a new land, "make of thee a mighty nation," "bless thee, and make thy name great," Tevye hears himself being told to "go wherever your legs will carry you." The irony doesn't make him feel Abraham is inferior or threaten the terms of the ancient Covenant. Tevye's helplessness at the hands of the political powers-that-be may call into question God's ability to secure him, but his intimacy with God calls into question the ultimate authority over him of the powers-that-be. Moreover, as he conflates Abraham's situation with the heart-stopping plea of the penitential prayers (don't cast us out in our old age), he domesticates the image of the solitary Abraham and takes the patriarch under his wing as a fellow aging Jew. All the while that Tevye adds his Yiddish gloss to the Hebrew quotation, he is slipping from the domain of sanctity into the profane, undercutting the biblical promise with evidence that it has not been fulfilled. This legacy of eternal postponement reconnects him to his biblical ancestors, who were promised a security that still eludes their descendants.

There are two main events in this chapter, the expulsion order and the return of Chava, and Tevye asks us to attend carefully to the order in which they occur.

> But before we get to *Lekh-lekho*, suppose we have a look, if you don't mind, at the chapter on Balak [Numbers 22–25]. I know that the way things have always been done in this world, *Lekh-lekho* comes before Balak, but in my case the lesson of Balak came first and *Lekh-lekho* after. And I suggest that you listen to the lesson they taught me, because it may come in useful some day.[54]

The Yiddish idiom *lernen Balak*, meaning to teach someone a harsh lesson, suits Tevye's context particularly well, since it invokes the attempt of the Moabite king to frighten the Jews with a false prophecy. When his Ukrainian neighbors, from the village elder to the shepherd, come to perpetrate a pogrom against him, Tevye asks them (as if teaching *them* the chapter of Balak) whether they are certain that the God who stands above the tsar is on their side or his. The concession he wins from them is that instead of roughing him up and destroying his house, they merely break his windows.

In a second, weaker, version of the expulsion story that Sholem Aleichem wrote two years later, Tevye challenges the Ukrainians to repeat a Hebrew word that he will "randomly" choose at the place where his psalter opens. The book opens at Psalm 35, the prayer of a virtuous man under oppression who asks God to confound those who would plot his downfall, to make their way dark and slippery (*vekhalaklakoys*). Of course, the Ukrainians slip up on this word, just as Tevye intended, and he concludes from this sport that at least in verbal matters "there's no getting around the fact that we Jews are the best and smartest people." Twice before in his monologues, Tevye had manufactured quotations to expose the ignorance of Leyzer Wolf the butcher and Podhotsur the purveyor, but here his life is at stake. The humor that has always been Tevye's salvation is now his only protection.

Yet Sholem Aleichem holds out at least one consolation for Tevye. The trajectory of loss that cuts through the monologues—from the debacle of Menakhem-Mendl's scheme, through the rebellions of the daughters, to his humiliations at the hands of his fellow Jews—stops when Chava returns to her father at the very moment that he is driven from his home. Sholem Aleichem may have regretted letting Chava convert in the first place (the only such instance of intermarriage in his oeuvre) and was now trying to reverse the deed. Chone Shmeruk wonders "whether the expulsion from the village is the crux of the issue, or merely the rationale and background for Chava's penitent return (*khazara bitshuvah*)."[55] Since Chava does not figure at all in the second expulsion story, it might be more accurate to say that Sholem Aleichem provided Tevye with not one but two psychological–rhetorical rejoinders to the humiliations heaped upon him—an outlet for his anger in the *vekhalaklakoys* monologue and recompense for his steadfastness with Chava's return. In trying to eliminate the Jewish presence, the Christians inadvertently return some Jews to their people. Chava's homecoming rewards Tevye for his earlier resistance to her intermarriage by a belated expression of the loyalty that his own Jewish loyalties have bred in her.[56]

Political Opposition to Tevye

Sholem Aleichem paid a price for telling the story of "progress" from a conservative perspective. Between his two comic heroes, Tevye and Menakhem-Mendl, almost the entire Jewish intelligentsia preferred the radical over the balanced ironist. The Marxist literary historian Max Erik, writing in Moscow in the mid-1930s, cherished Mehakhem-Mendl, as the caricature of capitalism run amok, over Tevye, the sorry embodiment of the falsely idealized petit bourgeoisie.[57] With subtler appreciation for the psychology of these two archetypes, I. I. Trunk in Warsaw interpreted Menakhem-Mendl and Tevye as the vying forces of messianism and ironic resignation that govern Jewish history. But in 1939 when Trunk had to flee the Nazis, the very sanity he had admired in Tevye proved insufficient to counteract the madness of Europe, while Menakhem-Mendl's credulity seemed reliable precisely because it was not subject to rational or experiential disproof.[58] Even the American Yiddish modernist Jacob Glatstein, who was untouched by Marxist influence, singled out Menakhem-Mendl from among Sholem Aleichem's characters for the *poetry* of his Yiddish.[59] Glatstein explained that his generation had considered Sholem Aleichem too old-fashioned for its taste and had to pass through a chastening lifetime before it "did penance" for its artistic oversight. Tevye was to Menakhem-Mendl as Sholem Aleichem was to the Jewish intelligenstia— the conservative impulse in a time of revolution.

The Yiddish literary elites disdained the "harmonious nature" of Tevye, because they understood the conservative roots of his humor. The team that adapted Tevye to the American stage and screen in *Fiddler on the Roof*— lyricist Sheldon Harnick, composer Jerry Bock, and writer Joseph Stein— simply changed Tevye into the character they wanted without acknowledging that they had done him any violence at all. In two interpolated scenes, they recast the Ukrainian who marries Chava as a liberal savior of the Jews while presenting Tevye's desire to remain Jewish as a form of prejudice. Fyedka (their version of Chvedka) is first seen protecting Chava from some of his friends, who have ambushed her, and when she still refuses his advances after he has saved her, he asks, "Do you feel about me the way they feel about you?" This parity between aggression against the Jew and Jewish self-affirmation is reinforced in the closing sequence when the Jews are expelled from their villages and Tevye is packing up to leave. The film shows Chava and her husband Fyedka passing by his house as part of the stream of refugees.

> CHAVA: Papa, we came to say good-bye. We are also leaving this place. We're going to Cracow.
> FYEDKA: We cannot stay among people who could do such things to others.
> CHAVA: We wanted you to know that.[60]

Leaving aside the historical improbability that a Ukrainian writer would join his wife in Polish exile, this resolution means that Chava can never come home to her father or to her people, because she would be betraying the assimilationism that has become—and here remains—her creed. Seth Wolitz claims that the writers of *Fiddler* created a paradox in their Americanization of Tevye, maintaining Tevye's wavering ambivalence toward Chava yet legitimizing her mixed marriage.[61] But the American version is not ambivalent at all. When Tevye continues to ignore the couple, Fyedka chides, "Some are driven away by edicts; others by silence." According to the stage directions, Tevye, who has been trying to ignore the couple as he packs his wagon, now says under his breath, "And God be with you," thereby invoking the Almighty's blessing on the daughter who has converted. The Ukrainian son-in-law has become Tevye's moral instructor! Drawing a parallel between the tsar's edict of expulsion and Tevye's wish to have his daughter remain a Jew, Fyedka accuses the Jew of bigotry for wishing to remain a people apart. Tevye is made to apologize for holding firm as a Jew by the Ukrainian who appears as the spokesman for tolerance.

It should be said that the interpretation of Chvedka or Fedya-Fyedka, was always the most changeable feature of the dramatic version of the Tevye stories. In one of Sholem Aleichem's unpublished drafts of the play, Chava says she left her husband because he joked about Jews needing Christian blood for Passover. Berkowitz, who reworked the play after Sholem Aleichem's death (and after an estimated one hundred thousand Jews had been killed in the Ukrainian massacres of 1918–19), "dipped Fedya into hot tar" and turned him into an overt antisemite.[62] More usually, Yiddish and Hebrew productions did not attribute antisemitism to Fedya, if for no other reason than it would have undermined Chava's credibility as a character to have married a Jew-hating Gentile. In Sholem Aleichem's own final version of the play, Chvedka's only fault is that he failed to tell Chava about the impending expulsion of Jews from the village. All these modifications to the character of the husband did not affect, however, the basic action of Chava's return to her father. The American version was the first to champion mixed marriage and the liberal ideal of an undifferentiated humankind.

Adaptation is part of the tradition of theater, and *Fiddler* is in many respects an adaptation of genius, perfectly attuned to the liberal ethos of America and the integrationist theme that was then at its height. The production was mounted in 1964, when second and third generations of American Jews were enjoying as never before the benefits of a genuinely democratic society, and popular culture was touting the advantages of youth, individual self-expression, and choices of the heart. The American civil rights movement was on the march, with rabbis joining Black leaders to enfranchise Americans "irrespective of color, race, or creed." While the promise of emancipation on the European continent was always being discredited by thuggish antisemitism, just the way Chava's humanism is mocked by the pogromists who chase her family off its land, America had never reneged on its promise to respect religious pluralism. It must have felt perfectly innocent to change a Jewish classic into a liberal classic, making the team of Chava and Fyedka, rather than Tevye, the moral anchors of the play. But if a Jewish work can only enter American culture by forfeiting its moral authority and its commitment to group survival, one has to wonder about the bargain that destroys the Jews with its applause.

The transformation of Sholem Aleichem's *Tevye the Dairyman* into *Fiddler on the Roof* goes to the very heart of this book about the Jewish canon. Part of the impulse of modernity that gave birth to modern Jewish literature was the need to interact with the world at large. The end result of such interaction was often the wish to join that world as an undifferentiated member. Writers starting down that open road did not always see where it led, but none could pretend to ignore the fork when they reached it. Liberalism may take the sting out of conversion by seeming to ignore the relevance of distinctions among peoples and religions in favor of the human sympathies that draw them together. But when liberalism *requires* merging as the price of its tolerance, it denies the pluralism it pretends to uphold. No artistic creation that ignores this immanent conflict can qualify as a Jewish work, or as a great and truthful work.

What was King Lear's expectation of Cordelia as compared with Tevye's of Chava? Lear's whim was no more than a matter of pride, yet Shakespeare builds his greatest tragedy on a daughter's refusal to give exaggerated protestations of her love. By contrast, Chava's conversion assaults Tevye's very being: his God, his way of life, his idea of family, the source of his language, not to mention his *Jewish* pride before the antisemitic representative of the Church. In effect, she is substituting the "religion of Love" for Judaism and asking him to dissolve his religious civilization in her favor. Tevye's nature is so contrary to Lear's that he is tempted to sacrifice all this for the sake of his daughter. He is therefore faced with the opposite set of challenges—to stand firm where Lear should yield, to insist on his Jewish integrity where Lear should acknowledge the limits of his power.

Tevye became the first hero of modern Jewish literature when he contained his impulse of leniency, the milkiness of his nature. His humor knew better than to leave its Jewish sources, because it would have failed him at the point of letting go. His trilingual play with the Hebrew sources, Gentile folk sayings, and his Yiddish vernacular gives the impression of being impossible to translate, yet when students are asked to describe an incident in their lives "in the style of Tevye," the daughter of Korean immigrants and the Puerto Rican freshman know just how to approximate his irony with folk quotations from their native languages. In Sholem Aleichem's comedy the father tries to realize his freedom and to grant his children freedom without sacrificing the model of peoplehood that created his model of freedom. At the same historical moment that Theodor Herzl created *Altneuland* (Old-New Land), the utopian fantasy of a people trying to regain its sovereignty, Tevye provided one man's comic experience of auto-emancipation.

2

THE LOGIC OF LANGUAGE AND
THE TRIALS OF THE JEWS

Franz Kafka and
Yosef Haim Brenner

> In the organism of humanity there are no two peoples
> which attract and repel each other more than the Germans
> and the Jews.
>
> Moses Hess, 1862[1]

TEVYE'S COMEDY EXEMPLIFIES the paradox of the Jewish diaspora: perpetual adaptation is required in order to preserve the Jewish way of life. The adaptiveness remained subordinate to the tradition until the idea of progress inverted cause and effect. Once Jews no longer obeyed the imperatives of their religion, they were virtually obliged to create new forms of identity, turning accommodation from means to end. Literature was a proving ground for the reinvention of the self. One-tenth of the Nobel Prize winners for literature in the twentieth century were born Jews, but only two of them—Shmuel Yosef Agnon (1966) and Isaac Bashevis Singer (1978)—wrote in a Jewish language and only about half thought of themselves as Jews. Paul Heyse (1910), Nellie Sachs (1966), and Elias Canetti (1981) wrote in German; Henri Bergson (1927) in French; Boris Pasternak (1958) and Joseph Brodsky (1987) in Russian; and Saul Bellow (1976) and Nadine Gordimer (1991) in English. Jews had always prided themselves on their literacy, and as they began plying their talents in their adopted tongues, they tried to make sense of their situation and themselves as the subjects and objects of history.

But since every language is the cultural repository of a distinct people, the literary prospects of a Jewish writer in a non-Jewish language are affected by the attitude of that language toward the Jews. What then happens to the Jew who is writing in a language inhospitable to the people from whom he or she derives? This chapter explores the effects of language on literature by looking at the works of near contemporaries who were subject to opposite cultural constraints.

The Transition from Yiddish to German

Kafka's *The Trial* begins just where *Tevye the Dairyman* leaves off: with the inexplicable arrest of a man who has been minding his own business. Sholem Aleichem wrote "Get Thee Out" in the spring of 1914, and Kafka began his novel in late summer of that year, just before the outbreak of World War I. Sholem Aleichem was recovering in Nervi, Italy, from a series of ailments so severe he thought he had already "descended to the grave." Since fleeing Russia with his family after the Kiev pogrom of 1905, he had not found a permanent home, and at the time of writing he was planning yet another emigration, to America, where he thought he could better support his family. Kafka had just broken off his engagement with his fiancée, Felice Bauer, and had moved out of his parents' home for the first time. The war stoked his private anxieties. "The thoughts provoked in me by the war resemble my old worries over F[elice] in the tormenting way in which they devour me from every direction."[2]

Both men had followed from afar the notorious Beilis case in Russia. Sholem Aleichem wove this affair into his novel *The Bloody Hoax*, about a young Russian student who trades identities with his Jewish friend and then becomes a suspect in a case of blood libel. Tevye's concluding monologue is actually situated the days "when Mendel Beilis was atoning for all our sins by going through the torments of hell and the whole world was talking of nothing else."[3] Kafka read about the case in the Prague Zionist weekly *Selbstwehr* (Self-Defense), which ran so many stories on the Beilis trial that it referred to the event simply as *Der Prozess* (the trial).[4] Russia figures as a prison house in Kafka's 1912 story "The Judgment," as background and parallel to the family struggle being waged between Georg Bendemann and his father. Georg's unnamed Russian friend had been a witness in 1905 to the Kiev pogrom (the same pogrom that drove Sholem Aleichem from his home); now he is imagined by George "[at] the door of an empty, plundered warehouse. Among the wreckage of his showcases, the slashed remnants of his wares, the falling gas brackets, he was just standing up."[5] The Beilis blood libel was the first such accusation to be sponsored by a national government, and the violence that it unleashed in Russia shocked even Vladimir Ilich (Ulyanov) Lenin with its intensity.[6] Small wonder that a Jewish writer should have chosen this moment to write about a man arbitrarily accused.

The surprise lies rather in the contrast of treatment. Tevye just happens to be sitting on his front stoop one hot summer's day when the local police officer gallops up with the news that he is about to be expelled from his village. "And what good deeds have I done you to deserve such an honor?" he asks.[7] Tevye is relieved to learn that the expulsion decree was issued not against him personally but against a category of persons, namely, the Jews, who are to be removed from all villages—and from towns that may designate themselves villages for the purpose of legally expelling their Jews. He is relieved not only because, as he says, *"tsores rabim khatsi nekhomoh* [misery never minds a bit of company]" but because reference to the Jews seems to explain what would otherwise seem arbitrary and lunatic. Never mind that the explusion decree against Jews is far more threatening than some private vendetta. Tevye recalls that the patriarch Abraham was "similarly" sent packing by God from the land of Ur, and his moral security as a Jew, rooted in his language, is, if anything, reinforced by his realization that he is being expelled from what turns out to have been, after centuries of settlement, an alien land. "Say hello for me to all our Jews," he says to Sholem Aleichem in parting, "and tell them wherever they are, not to worry: the old God of Israel still lives!"[8]

The historical and theological security of the Yiddish text was forfeited once its covenantal assumptions were called into doubt. Hannah Arendt makes an analogous point at the beginning of her book *The Origins of Totalitarianism,* quoting a joke that circulated after the First World War: An antisemite declares that the war was the fault of the Jews. Yes, agrees his listener, of the Jews and bicyclists. Why the bicyclists? asks the one. Why the Jews? asks the other.[9] The joke uncovers the absurdity of Jew hatred that has gone on for so long it offers the advantage of apparent rationality. But antisemitism also exposed the absurdity of Jewish victimhood once God no longer guarantees ultimate justice. Without Tevye's metaphysical trust, Jewish experience in Europe becomes a meaningless punishment.

* * *

THE OPENING SENTENCE OF *The Trial* is one of the most famous in modern literature: "Jemand muste Josef K. verleumdet haben, denn ohne dass er etwas Boses getan hatte, wurde er eines Morgens verhaftet. ["Someone must have been telling lies about Joseph K., for without having done anything wrong he was arrested one fine morning."][10] The sentence is disturbing for more than the information it conveys. Why, for instance, does this Joseph have a truncated last name? Had the arrested man remained anonymous, we might have expected to learn more about his identity as the story unfolded. Or, say, had a certain Joseph Katz been arrested, we could have assumed some connection between the offender and his identity, in this case, his being a Jew. Instead, the initial in place of a surname makes the character suspect of more than his putative crime, because it is not clear who is obscuring his identity—the character or the author who shares his initial. The accusation of guilt exposes the problem of identity, anticipating that K.'s difficulties go beyond problems with the law.

Even more unsettling is the presumptive subjunctive form of the verb: "*Jemand muste Josef K. verleumdet haben* ["Someone *must have been* slandering Joseph K]." Well, yes or no? Who else but the narrator ought to know whether rumor had anything to do with the man's arrest? Troubling as it is in the Book of Job that God allows Satan to raise suspicions about the morality of an innocent man, at least the biblical narrator identifies the subversive source and nature of evil. But here the narrator seems not to possess the relevant facts. The verb offers us no way of knowing whether our guide to the action knows what he has chosen to withhold or is as much in the dark as the apparently falsely accused.

Breon Mitchell, a new English translator of Kafka, describes the difficulty of rendering the moral ambiguities of this opening sentence, particularly of *Boses*, "a word which, when applied to the actions of an adult, reverberates with moral and philosophical overtones ranging from the story of the Fall in the Garden of Eden to Nietzsche's discussion of the origins of morality in *Jenseits von Gut und Bose* [Beyond Good and Evil]".[11] He translates *Boses* as "truly wrong" in order to push the word toward the province of the criminally malicious and "to introduce, on a level corresponding to the almost subliminal use of the subjunctive in German, the question of truth." But "truly wrong" is much more explicit than the original, which is unclear about whether K. committed any wrong at all.

THE GERMAN–JEWISH SYMBIOSIS had seemed altogether natural to the generation of Kafka's parents, the last restrictions against whom were lifted in 1867 when all Jewish subjects of the Habsburg empire became equal citizens. Since the adoption of German coincided with the expansion of political rights and economic opportunities, acculturation was almost universally perceived as an improvement. Kafka's father was proud that he had worked his way up from a poor village boy into a prosperous Prague shopkeeper, exchanging Czech and Yiddish for German in the process of advancement. But the rapid influx of Jews into German culture as a result of this emancipatory process had unanticipated consequences, such as fear among Germans of Jewish usurpation, and guilt among Jews of having traduced their heritage. Moses Hess observed that the Germans first convinced the Jews that their nationality was an obstacle to their inner emancipation, then suspected them of treachery for trying to pass themselves off as Gentiles.[12] In Prague it also angered some of the Czech majority, just beginning to define its own national ambitions, that Jews should join the German ranks instead of theirs.

Franz Kafka's generation was ill equipped to handle antisemitism, a term coined four years before his birth to define a politics of resentment. Whereas the parents had gained confidence in themselves and in their society through accommodation to the dominant culture, their children witnessed anti-Jewish riots in Prague at the end of the century without understanding what it meant to be Jews. Their proficiency in German epitomized this dilemma. Unlike his parents, who ran a haberdashery store, Franz did not have to content himself with supervising Czech salesclerks and accommodating customers in order to sell his finery to the public. Having received the finest German education, he could become a German writer, a purveyor of German culture. But while a man does not have to reveal his identity to sell buttons and bows, the Jew who wanted to become a great writer would have to bare his soul in the language of Martin Luther and Wilhelm Marr and to compete with von Kleist and Goethe in a language that increasingly mocked and maligned him. The name *Kafka*, Czech for jackdaw, might not betray the origins of the shopkeeper who hung out this name on his store, but if a Jew wrote in German, he would have to face the question of his Jewishness, whether through affirmation, denial, irony, or some other strategy of revelation or concealment.

In some ways, Prague's Jewish writers and intellectuals considered themselves better off than their German or Austrian counterparts, enjoying what the historian Ezra Mendelsohn calls the "ideal environment for modern Jewish nationalism"—a binational or multinational region inhabited by two or more well-defined national groups rather than a mononational country with an all-powerful and exclusivist national language.[13] Czech national consciousness helped to stem the automatic self-identification of Prague's Jews with German culture, even as it created a social climate less favorable to their integration. Thus, the Bar Kokhba Association, founded in 1899 and named for the leader of the last Jewish military uprising against Rome, encouraged local Jewish university youth to study their own sources and to take the lead in reclaiming their national independence. Many of Kafka's friends in the club were inspired by Martin Buber to rediscover in Jewish religion, particularly in Hasidism, "a remarkable spiritual universe of mystical profundity" that allowed them to reidentify with the Jewish people while expressing their opposition to the embourgeoisement of their parents.[14]

Kafka's good friend Felix Weltsch explained how their need for a meaningful personal life inspired the search for Jewish unity: the ego tries to transcend the limited life-span by integrating itself into a larger historical cohesion, with a consciousness of past and future that gives it origin and aim, "a home and a hope."[15] The three main orders of this transcendent unity were thought to be language, ancestry, and religion (in that order). Membership in a linguistic commmunity locates the individual within a cultural tradition that is also the font of new creative consciousness; ancestry or ethnic origin is a natural principle that rests on biological foundations, like an expanded sense of family; a common faith is the origin and the presupposition of the community's historical consciousness. But, oddly enough, in borrowing these categories from contemporary discussions of nationalism, Weltsch did not ask how Jewish national identity was supposed to realize itself in the German national language. Though he and Max Brod began studying Hebrew with the aim of moving to Palestine, they continued to forge a strong Zionism in German without belaboring the apparent contradiction. (The youthfulness of Zionism was a help in this, since Hebrew was not yet fixed as the language of the Jewish state and since Herzl himself, the architect of political Zionism, had imagined and promoted it in German.) Kafka alone among his friends seems to have felt the organic fusion of a writer with his language and hence the permanently inhibiting effect of German on the Jew's ability to be at home in it.

Kafka was only a lukewarm member of the Bar Kokhba Association, and he remained unpersuaded by Buber's mystical project for Jewish redemption.[16] But the unity of consciousness that Weltsch described was just what Kafka encountered—with the force of a revelation—in the Yiddish theater in 1911. Attending the performances of a visiting troupe that had taken over the local Cafe Savoy, Kafka fell under the spell of an experience rather than a set of ideas. The forced intimacy of the Yiddish theater, with its unfamiliar repertoire of historical operettas about ancient Judaea and familial melodramas about lust and greed, released in him a rush of identification: "The sympathy we have for these actors who are so good, who earn nothing and who do not get nearly enough gratitude and fame, is really only sympathy for the sad fate of many noble strivings, above all our own. Therefore, too, it is so immoderately strong, because on the surface it is attached to strangers and in reality it belongs to us."[17] As if he were watching psychodrama—distorted, externalized versions of his inner experience—Kafka tried to decipher the gestures and costumes and expressions of what he took to be his own story.

The normally guarded Kafka let himself feel for this company the passions of a schoolboy—extravagant fondness for the leading lady, Mrs. Mania Tschissik, and for the actor Yitzhak Lowy—as if he had discovered the Jewish family that might have been his. For the first time, he was in a Jewish atmosphere, where the demographic proportions were reversed, with the Jews bathed in the collective security of their own language and the solitary Christian standing nervously apart.

Kafka, who did nothing by half measures, began exploring the cultural roots of this artistic stimulus. "Eagerly and happily," he took up *The History of the Jews* by Heinrich Graetz,[18] and, several months later, Pines's *History of Judeo-German Literature* "with such thoroughness, haste and joy as I have never yet shown in the case of similar books."[19] Yiddish literature seemed "obviously characterized by an uninterrupted tradition of national struggle that determines every work."[20] From Lowy he heard what it had felt like to grow up in an observant religious household, go off to a *yeshiva* to study, share the poverty of most of his coreligionists, and then recognize some of his own experiences in the emerging Yiddish and Hebrew literature. Kafka's passion for Yiddish culture was kindled at a safe remove from its source. When Heinrich Heine had first caught sight of a Jewish village on his trip to Poland in 1821, he experienced a shudder of disgust at the poverty and the jabber (*mauscheln*) of the Polish Jews, "a kind of German shot through with Hebrew and decked out with Polish."[21] A few years later, Kafka was to experience something similar when his friend George Langer introduced him to the entourage of the Hasidic rebbe of Belz during a visit to Marienbad: "Langer tries to find or thinks he finds a deeper meaning in all this; I think that the deeper meaning is that there is none, and in my opinion this is quite enough."[22] Kafka was brutally honest about the limits of his attraction to the Yiddish-speaking religious community, admitting that the Judaism he hoped would enlighten him and carry him farther instead "moves farther away from me the more I hear of it."[23] He had merely found enough in Yiddish theater to help him define what he lacked.

Yet this disadvantaged culture roused Kafka to a brand-new sense of protectiveness. At a benefit evening for the indigent Lowy, he challenged an audience of Jews to reconsider their attitude to their native and adopted cultures:

> I am not really worried about the impact this evening holds in store for each of you, but I should like it to be universally comprehensible, if it merits it. Yet this cannot happen as long as many of you are so frightened of Yiddish that one can almost see it in your faces. Of those who take an arrogant attitude to Yiddish I do not even speak. But dread of Yiddish [*Angst vor dem Jargon*], dread mingled with a certain fundamental distaste, is ultimately understandable if one wishes to understand it.[24]

The dread that Kafka refers to is the view of oneself through the eyes of the antisemitic Gentile who is emancipating the Jew on condition that he cease to be one. The Jew is afraid that his good bourgeois standing, so painstakingly acquired, may be revoked if he betrays his telltale ghetto origins.[25] Kafka himself sounds in this speech like an analysand turned analyst, much less the patient suffering from angst than the therapist about to effect a cure. Many a German critic has spoken of the *Sprakhkrise* or *Sprachskepsis*, the crisis of faith in language that was prevalent in German and Austrian letters at the turn of the century, as the crucible of Kafka's art.[26] The most striking feature of this talk on Yiddish is its repeated emphasis on what it is to understand, on what is understandable, and on the art of understanding (*verstehen*, *verstandlich*, and *Verstandnis*), the kind of comprehension that invites individuals to know themselves as a prerequisite for knowing the world.

The encounter with Yiddish first alerted Kafka to the special danger that language posed for the German-speaking Jew, precisely because of the semantic kinship between German and Yiddish.

> [Seen] from a distance, though of course only from a great distance, the superficial comprehensibility of Yiddish is a product of the German language; this is an advantage it has over all the other languages in the world. To make up for that, it is only fair that it should also have a disadvantage in comparison with all others. The fact is, Yiddish cannot be translated into German. The links between Yiddish and German are too delicate and significant not to be torn to shreds the instant Yiddish is transformed back into German, that is to say, it is no longer Yiddish that is transformed, but something that has utterly lost its essential character. If it is translated into French, for instance, Yiddish can be conveyed to the French, but if it is translated into German it is destroyed. *Toit*, for instance, is not the same thing as *tot* [death], and *blut* is far from being *blut* [blood].[27]

Kafka's choice of examples follows Moses Hess in pointing out the *lethal* potential in the encounter of German and Jew. The acculturating Jew in Moscow, Paris, or New York, eager to learn the local language, might have become anxious about the telltale accent or constructions that marked him as an immigrant, but there was nothing about his native tongue as opposed to Russian, French, or English that singled him out for opprobrium. Only in German may speakers take the proximity between the Gentile and Jewish languages as proof that the first is the perfect version of the garbled other.[28]

Kafka's image of how the language links are "torn to shreds" when Yiddish passes into German suggests that Germans interpreted the strengths of Jewish nationality as threats: Jews had developed a genius for linguistic adaptation honed through centuries of migration and political adjustment; their ongoing commitment to universal literacy in the Hebrew-Aramaic alphabet encouraged the development of a bilingual or multilingual population; the Jewish love of wit and paradox and language-play enjoyed all that was mixed, piebald, and impure in the language as opposed to its perfect uniformity. Such features of Yiddish as its own writers exploited, which included openness to coterritorial influence, dialectical variation, ironic self-consciousness, emotive intensity, and experimental play with the fused elements in the language, were perceived by Germans as signs of deficiency in the Jew. It did not help that Yiddish was known as "Jargon," this being the word that Kafka uses for it throughout his speech.

In a much-quoted passage of his diaries, Kafka went so far as to accuse German of destroying the inner life of the Jew who adopted it:

> "Mutter" is peculiarly German for the Jew, it unconsciously contains, together with Christian splendor Christian coldness also, the Jewish woman who is called "Mutter" therefore becomes not only comic but strange. Mama would be a better name if only one didn't imagine "Mutter" behind it. I believe that it is only the memories of the ghetto that still preserve the Jewish family, for the word "Vater" too is far from meaning the Jewish father.[29]

Kafka grasped that his parents' flight from Yiddish was an attempt to win the approval of authority by denying the rejected part of themselves. He felt that if only he could persuade them to confront the source of their anxiety, he would win his father's appreciation and his mother's love. "You begin to come quite close to Yiddish if you bear in mind that apart from what you know there are active in yourselves forces and associations with forces that enable you to understand Yiddish intuitively." The insightful Marthe Robert points out that nowhere else in his diaries is Kafka "so confident of his talent, so proud of his ease of movement and action," as on that day he interpreted modern Jews to themselves.[30]

Kafka's therapeutic approach to Yiddish was very different from other attempts to offset feelings of Jewish inferiority with proofs of Jewish cultural and moral accomplishment. Rather than prove the achievements of

Yiddish, as Pines does in his *History*, or the grandeur of Judaism, as Buber did in his interpretation of Hasidism, or the potency of Jewish nation-hood, as Max Brod and Felix Weltsch were to do in their studies of Jewish history, Kafka wanted his fellow Jews to acknowledge their affinity with their own European language, despite its evident frailties, just because it was theirs. The moral advantage that Moses Mendelssohn and his follow-ers purported to have found by exchanging the impure Yiddish for elegant German was identified by Kafka as abject self-surrender.

But Kafka's insight condemned him as a writer. The corollary of this confidence in Yiddish was the permanent anxiety of the Jew writing in Ger-man. Doubly accused—by the dominant language for the act of usurpation and by Yiddish and Hebrew for having abandoned his hereditary alpha-bet—such a Jew could only penetrate his selfhood negatively, as the sus-pect subject of his own art. Critics from within Kafka's European Jewish milieu recognized that "again and again Kafka is tempted to side with the world against himself"[31]—and we may identify the ontology of this negativ-ity in language. Whereas Yiddish could bring about "the unity and solidar-ity of national consciousness,"[32] the *Einheit*, the unity, of German would keep the non-German Jewish writer forever on trial. Kafka's exposure to Yiddish had provided an apprehension of language as destiny. Joseph K. in *The Trial* is condemned by the universal language in which he lives.

Franz Kafka: *The Trial*

The plot of *The Trial* is notoriously difficult to summarize, since puzzle-ment is its subject and theme. Upon waking one morning, Joseph K., a re-spectable bank employee, is arrested on an unspecified charge by an unspecified authority that follows unspecified procedures. In the course of trying to exonerate himself while trying to establish his offense, K. shows up in court; seeks help from a lawyer; consults an array of citizens, includ-ing a manufacturer, a painter, and fellow defendants; and visits a cathedral, but in the end he accepts the penalty of death without having established either his guilt or his innocence or the source of the charge against him. The term *Kafkaesque* testifies to the originality of this fiction that could not be compared to anything but itself yet became an indispensable descrip-tion of reality the moment it was apprehended.

Joseph K. inhabits German at the cost of everything else. He lives in a boardinghouse among strangers, without friends, and passes off as his sweetheart the prostitute whom he visits once a week. He bears no traces of a national, ethnic, or religious identity. He reads no books that would tell us about his interests and engages in no team sports or activities; the only group he had ever joined, and then "purely for business reasons," is the Society for the Preservation of Municipal Monuments of Art.[33] Both the bloodless nature of this Society and K.'s reasons for joining it underscore the absence of such genuine attachment as would normally inspire membership in a group.

K.'s missing surname obscures any hint of his origins. A month after his arrest, his uncle rushes in from the country, because his nephew has become a potential source of embarrassment. Though K. is his uncle's ward, he had not thought to involve this "ghost from the country" in his case, either to inform him of the situation or to ask for advice. His uncle learned of the problem from his daughter Erna, who had only heard about it through gossip. "Joseph, dear Joseph," the uncle cries upon hearing about K.'s predicament, "think of yourself, think of your relatives, of our good name. You've always been our pride and joy, you mustn't disgrace us now. Your attitude . . . doesn't please me at all, that's not how an innocent man acts who still has his strength."[34] Compare relations between K.'s family members with Tevye's response to Menakhem-Mendl, his wife's cousin twice removed, whom he just happens to bump into on the street in Yehupetz! Confirming his isolation from his own past as well as from other people, K.'s only spontaneous memory in this novel, at the point of visiting the Cathedral, is of "how even as a small child he'd been struck by the fact that the houses on this narrow square always had their window blinds drawn down."[35] Everything that follows from K.'s truncated name draws attention to cultural dearth, human deficiency, the absence of an individuated identity. He is a caricature of deracination.

Although K.'s emptiness is incontestible—like the two-dimensional black figures with which Kafka illustrated his text—the function of this anonymity in the novel is open to antithetical interpretations. Is Joseph K. the nondescript modern who gets lost in the machinery of an uncaring court, the pitiable "little man" of an oppressive system? Or is this a novel about moral accountability? Among Kafka's interpreters, Eric Marson builds the most radical case against Josef K.'s "ethical deformity," while Ritchie Robertson offers a more nuanced argument that Joseph K., "far

from being victimized, is morally at fault."[36] Robertson finds Joseph so calculating in his interaction with people, so neglectful of his family and social duties, and so spiritually stunted that he deserves to be put on trial as
part of his moral education. These interpretations follow the example of
the book in not sentimentalizing the victim. But even granted that K. may
be morally at fault, Marson and Robertson do not explain why the punishment meted out to him should be so wildly out of proportion to his failings. K. is no brute aggressor. If his sins are of omission, why should his
end be so violent?

K.'s arrest triggers two related yet separate sets of problems. The sim-
pler involves establishing his innocence or guilt as if this were a detective
novel where the reader is enjoined to help the suspect figure things out.
K's intelligence ought to make it possible for him to exonerate himself.
Closely attentive to detail, he notices the way people interact with one
another and who wields power over whom. When the warders appropriate
his belongings, he is undistracted by the loss of his things, "being much
more interested in gaining some clarity about his situation."[37] His powers
of observation are complemented by a good analytical mind. He argues
his case in open court, outperforms his lawyer in legal gymnastics, and
demonstrates his mastery of logic with any number of interlocutors. He
wants "to slip into his guards' thoughts somehow and turn them to his own
advantage or accustom himself to them," believing that this is just the way
lawyers go about handling their witnesses and the way detectives try to
penetrate the criminal mind.[38] K. thinks himself equal to or smarter than
everyone he meets, and he assumes that his intellectual superiority will
prove advantageous.

K.'s confidence recalls the description that Franz Kafka offered his audience at the lecture on Yiddish about living "in positively cheerful con-
cord, understanding each other whenever necessary, getting along
without each other whenever it suits us, and understanding each other
even then." The novel is situated in identical terms: "After all, K. lived in a
state governed by law, there was universal peace, all statutes were in force;
who dared assault him in his own lodgings? He'd always tended to take
things lightly, to believe the worst only when it arrived, making no provi-
sion for the future, even when things looked bad."[39] Based on these assumptions, Joseph K. should have had nothing to fear.

Yet K.'s second set of problems are cognitive. The arrest requires that he establish his innocence, but logic proves ineffectual because his language no longer supports his assumptions. His legal predicament is subsumed by an epistemological crisis: K. is quick, even eager, to obey the summons of the Inspector, thinking that now at last he will confront someone at his own level, someone who will explain the nature of the Court and of the accusation. Instead, the "plainly stupid" warders reprimand him for thinking that he can appear in his nightshirt. K. protests: "If you assault me in bed, you can hardly expect to find me in formal dress." He is the more upset when they insist that he wear a black coat. "K. threw the coat on the floor in response and said—without knowing himself in what sense he meant it—'But this isn't the main hearing yet.'"[40] Here he is, still at the earliest stage of his case, saying something he himself doesn't understand! The logic that served him so well as long as nothing ruffled his tenuous arrangements turns useless once the premise of his security is disturbed. The sudden violation of his privacy awakens a suppressed fear that there may be no safe boundary between sleeping and waking, between the public and the private spheres. K., the optimistic creature of the Enlightenment, believed until the moment of his arrest that innocence consisted of not breaking the rules. But K's intellect only sustains him within the illusion of rationality, and once that is challenged, he cannot even be sure of himself.

Still, if this were merely an epistemological crisis, K. would only have to fear for his mind, not for his life. In the worst case, he would go insane. Alice in Wonderland, who crosses the boundary between wakefulness and dream, tries similarly to figure out the causal connections between arbitrary and changeable experiences, but not until the very end of her dream does she face so much as a paper threat from the Queen of Hearts. K., on the other hand, is immediately under arrest, with no way of assessing what kind of muscle lies behind the charge. Max Brod describes how Kafka joined in the laughter when he read his friends this first chapter of the novel. K., too, is tempted to laugh when he asks how he could be under arrest, and particularly in such a ridiculous fashion. But something tells him that he cannot afford to treat the thing as a joke. This novel inverts the causal link between Enlightenment and Emancipation. It had been assumed that with the eclipse of Divine Authority would come increased personal freedom and progress toward democratic harmony. Man feels himself becoming sovereign as control over Nature and Law passes into his hands. But once Reason begins to prove fallible (a process that starts almost as soon as it has unseated the moral certainties of Religion), Man finds himself at the mercy of other powers, each of which declares reasonable its own demonstration of power. Most endangered by the crisis were people like liberal Jews, who, having come to trust that reason *was* power, had forfeited the protection of God without shoring up any political alternative.

It is hard to resist the aura of political prophecy that retroactively enfolds this novel. Aleksandr Solzhenitsyn's *Gulag Archipelago*, based on reports, memoirs, and letters of 227 witnesses, opens with the following description of the Soviet experience:

> Arrest! Need it be said that it is a breaking point in your life, a bolt of lightning which has scored a direct hit on you? That it is an unassailable spiritual earthquake not every person can cope with, as a result of which people often slip into insanity?
>
> The Universe has as many different centers as there are living beings in it. Each of us is a center of the Universe, and that Universe is shattered when they hiss at you: *"You are under arrest."*
>
> If *you* are arrested, can anything else remain unshattered by this cataclysm?[41]

The anonymous knock at the door is the definitive assault on cognitive confidence. Uninformed of his crime, the culprit has no way of understanding social cause and effect and no way of arguing his innocence.

Kafka's *Trial* may appear to anticipate totalitarian politics, but the text implicates K. no less than his unseen accusers. K. is not stripped of his individuality the way Soviet and, later, Nazi prisoners were in the camps: vacancy is the sufficient condition of his life. Whereas Solzhenitsyn describes the violence done by an evil system to its innocent victims, the arrest of K. exposes weaknesses in himself that the defendant might never have recognized had it not been for this interruption of his routine.

Neither is the function of Authority in this book identical with that of the despotic State. K. is not physically coerced into participating in his trial. When summoned for his first interrogation, he correctly intuits the time he is expected to show up, or else the court materializes *because* he shows up, and his involvement in the process is that of a participant, not a victim. The reader cannot help feeling as K. looks for the court among the kitchens and bedrooms of the suburb to which he has been sent that he was due for some initiation into these domestic tableaux just because he had arranged his life to avoid them. K. has assumed that spheres of experience are separate, along the lines of Judah Leib Gordon's famous dichotomy: "Be a Jew at home and a man in the street." (Kafka had copied this dictum into his diary.) But unlike the political novel where tyranny invades private life, this book proves that the system of justice cuts through the bedroom, that the intrinsic and extrinsic are fused. K. thinks he needs a ruse to justify his search, so he pretends to be looking for a carpenter named Lanz, but what use is subterfuge when you are ignorant of what you are trying to elude?

The episode of "The Whipper" goes farthest in implicating K. in the violence being done to him. One of the last to leave the Bank one evening, K. discovers his warders (in what he had thought was a junk room) being whipped because of his, K.'s, complaint to the Examining Magistrate that they had taken his clothes. The scene he comes upon is obviously his projection, appearing and disappearing as he opens and shuts the door, like a world of eternal sin and damnation that he had tried to ignore. The orders he barks to the bank attendants—"Clear out that junk-room, once and for all. . . . We're drowning in filth!"—shows how ill prepared he is to deal with what he doesn't want to acknowledge.[42] Thus, K. learns that he will never be offered the kind of rational explanation he seeks, not because Authority is deceiving him but because he is part of whatever system is putting him on trial. Kafka grants K. no immunity from the system that condemns him: K.'s guilt is never established, but neither is his innocence.

DURING THE YEAR of the novel, between K.'s thirtieth birthday and the eve of his thirty-first, K. moves through different spheres of life, implicating them all in his trial as he attempts to gain the understanding that will allow him to remain at large. The boarding house is a parody of the family: in place of the mother, a landlady who provides meals and favors the boarder who provides the steadiest rent; in place of the father, the landlady's male relative, a certain "captain" whose unspoken wishes must be accommodated; in place of sister or wife, two female boarders who form a kind of gender alliance against K. once it is clear that he is either in trouble or likely to cause it. In this surrogate family life he is both predatory and helpless, one moment aggressive and the next ingratiating, without intimacy or trust.

So, too, in the parodic Court. K. tries to present himself as a classic victim of injustice and spokesman for all the falsely accused. However, whereas Alfred Dreyfus or Mendel Beilis could win belated exoneration from a nominally autonomous judiciary, the more K. exposes the underlying conditions that govern the legal system, such as the dirty pictures he finds in the magistrate's notebook and the identical badges he discovers on the magistrates and people in the galleries, the less he can hope to prove his innocence according to some objective standard of laws. Man cannot eat the apple of knowledge and have it, too. K. may congratulate himself for exposing the "underlying" basis of human behavior, but if the human being is truly governed by the subjective and the irrational, each new discovery of "filth" can only doom him the more.

Of several targets that include family, commerce, and art, the novel aims its most damaging satire at the legal system in which Franz Kafka had trained. And in defiance of all liberal expectations, the most debased creature in this system is the defendant Rudi Block, one of the few identifiably Jewish characters in Kafka's fiction. Block tries to impress on K. the importance of obedience, "wagging his tongue far too much," cocking his head "as if listening for a summons," sitting and standing on command.[43] The lawyer Huld miscalculates when he tries to impress K. with his client's devotion: "He was no longer a client, he was the lawyer's dog. If the lawyer had ordered him to crawl under the bed, as into a kennel, and bark, he would have done so gladly."[44] The caricature of Rudi Block the tradesman sets this book in opposition to the victim literature with which it is often confused. The creature that tries to satisfy a system without an autonomous set of values will soon be on his hands and knees as a condition of his existence. Kafka never concluded the episode of Rudi Block, abandoning him in that pose of humiliating obsequiousness. "Fortunately," K., who had "not been long enough exposed" to the pressures of the trial, fires Huld and is spared the next few steps of degradation. He faces the rest of his trial "like" a dog but without yet having become one.

K APPROACHES THE CLIMAX of his quest for exoneration and/or comprehension in a parodic visit to the Cathedral. Even less than a tourist, he has been delegated by his employer to accompany a visiting Italian client of the Bank, and having prepared for his visit the night before by boning up on an Italian phrase book, he brings along a guidebook—his version of the book of prayer. Stripped of religious training, rational man experiences his uttermost deprivation in the great houses of worship that were designed to inspire and calm him. Nowhere else, not even as he approaches his execution, is K. more genuinely needy. "Won't you come down now?" he implores the priest. "Have you a little time for me?" Instead of comfort, the priest gives him the "Parable of the law," a set piece that is situated in the novel, surrounded by commentary, like a quotation from the Mishnah on a page of the Talmud: The "man from the country" waits a lifetime for admission to the Law. Before he dies, he puts a single question to the doorkeeper whom he has been petitioning for admittance. "Everyone strives to reach the Law. How does it happen, then, that in all these years no one but me has requested admittance?" By this time the petitioner is so ancient that the doorkeeper has to bellow into his ear: "No one else could gain admittance here, because this entrance was meant solely for you. I'm going to go and shut it now."[45]

The parable, which invites direct and universal apprehension, has always been the preferred instrument of religious instruction. Jesus praises its powers of healing in the Gospel of Matthew: "The reason I talk to them in parables is that they look without seeing and listen without hearing or understanding." What a sadistic perversion, then, is the parable told to K.! The individuality that was supposed to enfranchise the *amorets* (literally, "people of the country," Hebrew and Yiddish idiom for ignoramus or boor) has instead left him isolated, excluded, uninformed, and the trust that he placed in his own intelligence has kept him from grasping what he most needed to know. The rabbis always worried lest explication of the Law turn into mere *pilpul*, casuistry. Here, the casuistic debate between the priest and K. over religion (instead of within it) excludes both participants from the possibility of religious experience. The coldest of verdicts ends this chapter: "[The Court] receives you when you come and dismisses you when you go." We need not be surprised, then, that after the scene in the Cathedral, with the door to divine justice shut in his face, K. is reconciled to his execution. He has been dispossessed of grace, as though the function of religious residue were now to mock the modern seeker.

During the trial, which is the course of the novel, K. neither discovers his crime nor establishes his innocence, but he does acquire the negative knowledge that his life was not what it had seemed to be. In consequence of that insight, he receives his executioners in a reversal of the opening scene. "Without having been informed of their visit, K., also dressed in black, was sitting in an armchair near the door, slowly pulling on new gloves that stretched tightly over his fingers, with the look of someone expecting guests." If we had any hopes all along that K. would break through the "all-encompassing ambiguity," we now witness his resignation as his logic shuts down.[46] Indeed, as he grasps the symmetry between his arrest a year earlier and his impending execution, K. spurns suicide, never even considers flight, and wonders only how he should play his final scene. Whereas Tevye's narrative reinforces his confidence, K.'s reduces him to the culprit who is beyond redemption.

Once impatient with the neighbors who peered into his private life, K. spends his final hours seeking out responsive witnesses. His hopes of locating a friend, a good person, someone who cares, someone who wants to help, controvert the logical self-sufficiency that characterized K. when he was first awakened to his trial.

> Were there pleas in his defense that had been forgotten? Of course there were. Logic is no doubt unshakable, but it can't withstand a person who wants to live. Where was the judge he'd never seen? Where was the high court he'd never reached? He raised his hands and spread out all his fingers.
>
> But the hands of one man were right at K.'s throat, while the other thrust the knife into his heart and turned it there twice. With failing sight K. saw how the men drew near his face, leaning cheek-to-cheek to observe the verdict. "Like a dog!" he said; it seemed as though the shame were meant to outlive him.[47]

K.'s final appeal for grace is also his first. He has let go of merciless logic at the penultimate moment, too late to escape the final syllogism of his death. We see a ballet of gestures, the victim spreading out his fingers in appeal, or demonstrating that he is unarmed, while mute hands choke and knife him to death. The danger to K. has come not in the form of hatred but, just as he had once explained it to his Jewish audience, from a trust that has become the more groundless the more it trusts. He has no one to blame but himself, and no one to come to his rescue. K.'s punishment fits the crime in the sense that the impersonality he cultivated became the theater of his execution.

Why couldn't Kafka leave K. with the possibility of grace that Dostoyevsky insists on? Why did Kafka differ from his Jewish literary cohort for whom the rediscovery of Jewish sources held out a redemptive promise? Kafka has been called "the reluctant pessimist," but why did he so cruelly deny his characters the opportunities of self-affirmation that he witnessed all around him? As a writer, Kafka resembled less the intellectual or the plastic artist than the dancer whose performance can never outstrip the potential of his body. He had been born into the German language—and to this body he felt himself condemned irrespective of how much he exercised it and what repertoire he performed. Kafka's adversarial relation to his body is the organic source of his adversarial relation to his language—or perhaps it is the other way around, with the poisoned language affecting the body's health. In Kafka's time, German was the most powerful and prestigious language in Europe, and certainly among Western Jews it enjoyed the highest reputation. K. inhabited German the way he lived in his father's house, enjoying a bounty he was made to feel he did not merit. It might not have mattered so much had Kafka wanted to be merely a writer, or even a good writer. It was the absolutism of his ambition to be a perfect writer (and perhaps also the perfect son) that imperiled him. In an extraordinary letter to Max Brod, Kafka described the literature of Jews writing in German as "a literature impossible in all respects, a gypsy literature which had stolen the German child out of its cradle and in great haste put it through some kind of training, for someone has to dance on the tightrope. (But it wasn't even a German child, it was nothing; people merely said that somebody was dancing)."[48] The illegitimate possession engenders their guilt, but it is the act of precarious showmanship that constitutes the danger. The tightrope dancer must turn in perfect performances or face certain death. Kafka's writing does both: death is the price that Joseph K. pays for living in German, and the shame will outlive him because he had acquiesced to its terms.

"Major" and "Minor" Literatures

Kafka's emptied-out fiction induces readers to try to fill in what he left out. Disquieted and moved by the fate of his protagonists, perhaps like those good people K. reaches out to before his death, readers often feel called upon to supply from the biography and from the author's personal writings what is missing in the text. Given its obliteration of the boundary between natural and preternatural phenomena, many readers have interpreted The Trial as a psychological document about the author in conflict with himself. Michel Carrouges finds "a dark pyramid of involved trials that Kafka instigated in secret" to dramatize his tortured relations with his father: the trial of the son, Joseph K., by the father for not having had the strength to marry; the same trial turned against the father who sapped his son of the strength to marry; and trial of the son by the son, with the warder named Franz arresting the provocative K.[49] Elias Cannetti was moved by his reading of Kafka's letters to Felice Bauer to interpret the The Trial as Kafka's imaginative re-creation of that relationship, complete with the negative judgment on his manhood.

More recently, the critics Gilles Deleuze and Félix Guattari have not merely interpreted Kafka but conscripted him as the prooftext of a new theory of inversion that they call a "minor literature." The term itself comes from Kafka, who used it quite precisely to designate the achievements of Yiddish and Czech writers, that is, writers in the language of a political minority. He acknowledged "the pride which a nation gains from a literature of its own and the support it is afforded in the face of the hostile surrounding world."[50] But he also recognized the political and artistic handicap of writers who are born into the language of a relatively small and powerless people (hence, a minor literature) as opposed to himself, who wrote in the language of a dominant power. Deleuze and Guattari reverse this plain meaning: "A minor literature doesn't come from a minor language; it is rather that which a minority constructs within a major language."[51] The three characteristics of this minor literature are said to be the "deterritorialization of language," the connection of the individual to political immediacy, and the collective value it assumes. This would presumably make Kafka a Jewish writer bearing the consciousness of the Jewish collectivity. But nowhere do these theorists consider the properties of a Jewish literature, or even pause to consider what being a Jewish writer might mean. Just as an earlier generation of Marxists used the "deterritorialized" Jews as their model for a historically determined stateless egalitarianism, Deleuze and Guattari interpret the German of the Prague Jewish circle as a "linguistic Third World zone" where a language can escape colonializing domination.[52] Kafka is their prototype of the "deterritorialized" writer, a literary Trotsky who subverts from within the imperial language that oppresses him and becomes the cultural equivalent of a socialist revolutionary.[53]

But this was precisely the sort of moral mystique that Kafka denied his art. Leaving aside the larger problems of the Deleuze–Guattari theory of a "minor literature," they turn Kafka's exact term into a metaphor, and while explaining that Kafka deliberately "kills" all metaphor (citing his diary entry "Metaphors are one of the things that make me despair of literature"), they themselves substitute imaginary political categories for those that Kafka knew to be actual and real.[54] Kafka's anxiety as a writer arose from the knowledge that he was privileged to be writing in a *major* literature, what many considered to be the major literature of the continent. In his respect for finitude, he may have been the most conservative Jew in central Europe, recognizing his fatally suspect situation as a Jewish writer of German literature and even exaggerating, as it seems to many readers, the burden of proof an artist was expected to bear. His unfinished novels that were brought to near—but only to near—completion corroborate his precarious position in German literature, a verdict he never allowed German to pronounce on him by pronouncing it first on himself.

By defining a Jewish canon across linguistic lines, I, too, challenge the automatic association of language with the works that are produced in it. Without question, Jews who wrote in the languages of their countries of residence helped to redefine the relation between language and nationality in ways that became ever more common and complicated as colonialization and migration transformed patterns of culture. But I would not call Jewish literature a "minor" literature despite the fact that it is generated by a political minority, no more than I would call the Jews a "minor" people despite their small numbers and political vulnerability. Those writers who knowingly straddled two cultures belong to two literary traditions, each of which accords them a place according to its judgment. Even when these cultures are as antithetical as Yiddish and German, the writer may find a way, as Kafka did, of telling the truth in both.

By now in the history of culture and politics, a warning bell should toll whenever a social scientist, cultural critic, or politician exploits the word *Jew* to mean the man without a country and turns him into the standard-bearer of yet another theory of "deterritorialization"—"internationalism" or evaporation by a subtler name. Kafka, in particular, who was starved for the security of language and culture, should not be turned into an ideological weapon against such longing.[55]

Yosef Haim Brenner: Breakdown and Bereavement

In the last months before his death in 1924 in the sanatorium at Steglitz, Kafka was struggling through a Hebrew novel, Yosef Haim Brenner's *Shekol vekishalon*, written in Palestine in 1913–14 and, like *The Trial*, left unpublished for several years because the author was dissatisfied with it. Brenner finally published the book in 1920, and Kafka's Hebrew teacher Puah Bentovim brought him a copy after Brenner's murder the following year. Kafka admitted to Robert Klopstock, his fellow Hebrew student and a former tuberculosis patient, that he did not fully understand the two nouns of the title: "At any rate they are an attempt to set down the quintessence of misfortune. *Shekol* means literally childlessness, so perhaps unfruitfulness, fruitlessness, pointless effort; and *kishalon* means literally stumble, fall."[56] The English translator Hillel Halkin inverted the nouns as *Breakdown and Bereavement*.[57] Kafka expressed a "certain awe" for Brenner, but since he had been studying Hebrew with the thought of *escaping* the condition of the Hunger Artist by emigrating to Palestine, he did not appreciate the bleakness of the novel or its author. "Imagination and things I have heard were mingled in my feeling about him," Kafka wrote to Max Brod. "There has always been talk of his sadness. And 'sadness in Palestine?'"[58]

Brenner was born in the small Ukrainian Jewish town of Novy Mlini, in the historically charged year 1881, when the assassination of Alexander II unleashed a series of pogroms and repressive laws that changed the course of East European Jewry. A gifted *yeshiva* student, he underwent the obligatory intellectual and spiritual crisis when he began to teach himself Russian and to read modern literature and philosophy, but unlike those of his contemporaries who found alternatives to the religious way of life in political action or ideological conviction, Brenner exemplified the crisis itself. It began with his choice of language. On abandoning his studies he briefly joined the Jewish Socialist Bund and edited its underground Yiddish paper, *Der kamf* [Combat], in Gomel, White Russia. Yiddish literature and socialist politics were in lively ascendance in the early decades of the century. Brenner quickly became such a hero of the Bund that when he was imprisoned as a deserter from the Russian army—having first insisted on serving lest another Jew be drafted in his stead—a band of sympathizers snatched him from the police convoy and spirited him out of the country. He found temporary haven in London and work in the local Yiddish press. But by this time Brenner had chosen the lonelier path of Hebrew—perhaps, in no small part, because it *was* the lonelier. His novellas conveyed the experience of those, like himself, who set up a modern secular library in place of the traditional house of study, with all their concomitant spiritual and intellectual hardships. In the aftermath of the failed revolution of 1905, the Hebrew press almost completely shut down in Russia as a result of tsarist censorship and a faltering cultural base. Brenner founded in London a Hebrew-Zionist periodical, called *Hame'orer* [The Awakener] (1906), that seemed to sustain the Hebrew revival almost single-handedly by soliciting and encouraging contributions from writers across Europe, who confessed that they might otherwise have ceased to write. Yet his attitude had nothing in common with such other Hebrew loyalists as Ahad Ha'am and Joseph Klausner, who vilified Yiddish as the debilitating symbol of Jewish exile. A heavy current of Yiddish runs through Brenner's Hebrew prose, like a vein of accumulated Diaspora experience that cannot be expunged. Hebrew literature was for him the truthful record of tortured reality, not the vehicle of a futuristic dream.

The same held true for Brenner's Zionism. Upon arrival in Jaffa in February 1909, he became one of the leading figures of the Second Aliyah, the ideologically driven wave of Jewish immigration to Palestine in 1904–14 that laid the groundwork for its socialist and many of its national institutions. His early dreams of founding a Tolstoyan agricultural community and the regnant Labor–Zionist ideal of economic self-sufficiency made him eager to work the land. But he was as physically and temperamentally unsuited as Kafka was to realize the healthful and positive ambitions that he harbored. Brenner shared Otto Weininger's fevered convictions that there was something characterologically deficient in the Jews that would resist geographic and political transformation. He feared that though Jews *must* extricate themselves from the Diaspora to found a modern nation, the Jewish neuroses of his generation could only be solved individually, by a kind of psychoanalytic self-purgation. Writing honestly about this condition was his only hope of expelling it from the body and the body politic. Although Brenner married in Palestine in 1913 and fathered a son, he could no more live within a family than in a kibbutz, and he soon returned to his solitary regimen in a bare rented room. His Hebrew colleagues considered him their "literary conscience," the man who transforms the experience of life into the experience of letters.[59]

Brenner's legend as "a secular servant of God, a stricken saint, who carries on his shoulders the burden of Judaism and Humanism," was sealed when he was killed by Arab marauders in the first widespread anti-Zionist rampages of 1921, having refused to heed the warnings of friends to return from his room on the outskirts of Jaffa to the safety of the city.[60] Given that Brenner's life was one of ideological asceticism and that he had just published an appeal for Arab-Jewish understanding, his was considered "a desired martyrdom, not unsought by himself."[61] The crux of the artistic legend, however, was the writer's uncompromising dedication to the honesty of literary work. The "sadness" that Kafka regretted in Brenner was the same haunting truthfulness that other readers found in his work.

Without knowing that Kafka had ever read Brenner, the Hebrew critic Barukh Kurzweil called *Breakdown and Bereavement* the terrifying Hebrew counterpart of Kafka's *Trial*, terrifying precisely because it undercut Zionist hopes for a clean historical start. Among the many parallels: Brenner's novel exposes lying as a universal principle—which is K.'s final comment on the parable of the Law. It constitutes the most brutal self-flagellation in Hebrew literature; having followed Nietzsche in removing man from before the Seat of Judgment, it records man's inability to liberate himself from the self. Like the petitioner in the parable, Brenner's hero waits to be admitted into the happiness of Palestine even as his weakness prevents him from entering its door. Kurzweil calls this novel the last station in the existence of "Jew the Absurd."[62] What Kurzweil fails to note, however, is the inverted nature of the problem of Brenner's hero, who suffers from a surfeit rather than a dearth of historical memory that is embedded in *his* language, burdening *his* soul.

Brenner's "trial" is situated in a precise time and place—Palestine of the Second Aliyah—and follows the life of a named protagonist with closely observed particulars about the new settlement and members of his family who have also settled in the country. The narrator-editor explains that he cobbled together this clumsy fiction from notebooks left behind by "a certain homely and unfortunate" fellow passenger whom he had encountered on a ship sailing away from Palestine and who had to be taken ashore for hospitalization when he suffered a nervous breakdown. He even shares with the reader his misgivings about the artistic value of his project and also about its timing, "which is neither suitable nor conducive to the consumption of such tales."[63] The preface anticipates Kafka's discomfort about a pessimistic novel set in Palestine. Since the Jews are experiencing a national emergency—and no one disputed that the exodus from Russia had created a Jewish crisis—why tell of collapse and failure in the designated place of Jewish refuge and reconstruction?

The story begins with an arresting misfortune: "It was an afternoon in the middle of April when the accident occurred." Yehezkel Hefetz, until then a "regular member of the commune, zealously straining every muscle, as had always been his way," suffers an injury in the groin while harvesting hay. The theme of impotence is thus introduced as both a private and public matter, threatening not only the individual but also the group's reliance on him. Members of the commune, one of those brand-new *kibbutzim* founded on rational principles of collectivism, egalitarianism, and productivity, recall that Hefetz had already left their company once before to return to Europe, "overcome by inner desire" (*hefetz* means desire). This accident during the critical harvest now requires that he be sent for treatment to Jerusalem. K.'s arrest at the beginning of *The Trial* exposes his false self-sufficiency. The Jew-in-Palestine's inability to control his desire or to surmount his weakness augurs badly for the collectivity of which he forms a part. Accompanied to Jerusalem by a hired hand appropriately named Menahem (consoler), Hefetz lacks the strength to accomplish the self-transformation that he considers necessary to regain his health, and the book becomes the record of that failure.

Brenner, who was translating Dostoyevsky's *Crime and Punishment* about the time he began this novel, was obviously alerted to the similarities between Russian students like Raskolnikov and Jewish students like himself, students who lose their moral and intellectual equilibrium when they are exposed to the new explanations and expectations of man. Hefetz's injury is not the kind that can be cured with a truss: "[It] was as though some horror of life had taken hold of him, a revulsion toward everything around him. Food disgusted him; he grew thinner every day, and the less he ate, the more he dreamed and talked, as if to escape his inner fears. And he had not been much of a talker before."[64] Recuperating at his uncle's house in Jerusalem, Hefetz blames himself for his superfluity and fancies himself such a great sinner that, without naming the corrupting deed, he wonders what would happen if he should suddenly be discovered as the "one who did it." He is seized by a queer impulse to confess, although no one has yet caused, or accused him of having caused, any harm that we can see.[65] Hefetz does not suffer from K.'s eclipse of identity nor from Raskolnikov's need to prove his singularity. Sensibility itself is the crime of the Jew who cannot contribute to the improvement of his people because he is the manifestation of its disease.

Hefetz discovers a country almost as dysfunctional as he is. Jerusalem is "a large city completely dependent on the whims of philanthropy! A city which if you deprived it of the handouts it gets from all over the world— would die of starvation!"[66] His uncle by marriage, Reb Yosef Hefetz, is part of this unhealthy system of sentimental charity. The guest house where the family resides is sustained by money from the Diaspora. The house- hold includes two unmarried daughters, Esther and Miriam, and Uncle Yosef's brother Haim, all trying to establish themselves in the emerging society. Haim, trained as a mason, is the only one with useful skills. Some- where at a mill in the Galilee is Haim's son Hanoch, stubbornly pioneer- ing the long-neglected land. In Brenner's representation of Jerusalem, only the unscrupulous succeed: Goldmann, the landlord, who exploits the reli- gious sentiment of donors to enrich himself and his family, and Hamilin, an unlicensed doctor and sexual glad-hander, whom Hefetz had encoun- tered abroad as the seducer of the girl he was courting. By the end of the novel, Goldmann's daughter, who had divorced Haim's son because she could not bear his pioneering zeal, marries Hamilin and goes off with him to Beirut. Hanoch dies cultivating the land that others exploit and aban- don.

In this familial–national compound, one man's failings condemn every- one else. Hefetz's unmanliness helps to seal the doom of his female cousins, both the elder Esther, who craves some outlet for her romantic and maternal longings, and the younger Miriam, eager to experience love, adventure, life. The entanglement with Esther, who feels she has some claim on her cousin's affections after she tries to nurse him back to health and then takes a job as nurse in the mental hospital to which he is confined for half a year, precipitates a scene of peerless humiliation: offended by the amalgam of pity and obligation that Hefetz first extends to her and then withdraws, Esther, feigning ignorance of his presence, empties her slop pail on his head from her balcony. His failure to rescue Miriam has more tragic implications, since his desire for her might have resulted in their union and prevented her death. Instead, like the princess in an inverted fairy tale, Miriam stabs her finger with a hairpin in desperation over her floundering life and expires of blood poisoning. Hefetz would appear to be a villain through acts of omission whose causes may be indeterminate but whose consequences are all too finite.

Yet because Hefetz has assembled these notes about himself as an act of self-analysis, the misgivings of the fictional editor are turned inside out: by foregrounding this severely damaged product of the Jewish Diaspora, the novel discloses the paralyzing insecurities that are being overcome under the brave camouflage of the Zionist movement. Here is a community of East European Jews, displaced in a land that is always at some extreme of temperature, who are able to express their sense of inadequacy, to talk about their unhappiness, and even to collapse under the strain of the life they have undertaken. *"We're all so pathetic, pathetic,"* Hefetz murmurs during one of his futile entanglements with Esther. *"We all deserve to be pitied. Who dares to be angry! Who dares to look down! To mock? Ay, let the mockers mock if they can."*[67] True emancipation confers the right to admit weakness without having to worry about reputation or the dangers of a hostile environment. Thus, when Esther empties her chamber pot over his head, the filth makes Hefetz realize the filthy lies he has been living: he had considered marrying Esther out of pity, and out of the same twisted self-aggrandizement he had concocted a plan to keep Haim ignorant of his son Hanoch's death by sending letters from the Galilee in his stead. It takes the shower of excrement to wash away the phony martyrdom. If he cannot love his cousin or perform as a pioneer, he can at least, like Nietzsche on a Jewish scale, clear away the detritus of sickly guilt.

A Language of Negative Experience

One of the major challenges facing modern Hebrew writers was to break away from classical Hebrew prose into what Robert Alter calls "a language of experience," which can be "a means for implicating the reader in the processes of the character's thoughts and feeling."[68] While the purposeful members of emerging Zionism forged a Hebrew that could carry the mission of statehood, including a repertoire of poems and hymns and national manifestos, Brenner voiced the thought and feeling that could not make the grade. This admission of breakdown and bereavement at the heart of the "national project" is what made Brenner's work, "without a doubt, among the most important novels in the history of Hebrew literature."[69]

If Kafka's K. suffers from an eclipsed inheritance that we call deracination, Yehezkel Hefetz snaps under an excessive cultural load. On first acquiring his truss, he thinks:

> What an ugly way to suffer. . . . In the book of Job the Leper it is written: "And he took a potsherd to scrape himself with." . . . Only I am not Job: I have no complaints against God. In fact, I have no God. . . . I'm not Job. And I don't sit in ashes either, but in refuse, in the refuse of my own ugly suffering. Only I don't let go of the potsherd. I can't stop scratching. Yes, a potsherd is probably the one thing I cannot do without.[70]

The vocabulary of Jewish misery has so overtaken its constituents that Hefetz cannot suffer a minor injury without imagining himself the scabby Job. Hefetz's potsherd is like Brenner's pen, the substitute for lost potency that expresses his sentient pain. At other moments, Hefetz feels an equally suggestive and tortured kinship with the prophet Ezekiel (Yehezkel), whose name he bears, and with Jesus, the favored self-image of Yiddish and Hebrew writers who wanted to both subvert and appropriate the theme of martyrdom. Hefetz does not handle these allusions for mock-epic effect, as Tevye does when he moves from the high Hebrew source-language to his vernacular Yiddish. Unlike the confident dairyman, Hefetz is trying to express a very modern and complex self in a language at once too old and too new, burdened by national memory yet without a mother or a wife's reassuring voice.

All the handicaps of Jewish national revival are represented in *Breakdown and Bereavement* by disfigurements of speech. Herr Kauffmann, a businessman, "for whom there was no language too extravagant in the guesthouse chapel with which to describe the future of trade in

Jerusalem . . . was at a complete loss for words when actually obliged to approach someone on a matter of business."[71] Schneirson, an ideological Zionist, is undone by his rhetoric: "Tired or not . . . the Bible is eternal for everyone, even . . . even for the tired! Let the weary read it and take strength. 'Ponder it and ponder it for it is all in all.' And you don't have to be a religious man to believe that. On the contrary!"[72] The propagandist drums without melody, offering no evidence for his enthusiasm save his enthusiasm itself. At the other extreme of the referential talkers is Hefetz's uncle Reb Yosef, the Maskil, or enlightened Jew, or "who held on to both ends of the rope" of traditional practice and modern thought. Yosef has earned his quotations the way he accumulated the books of his precious library, one at a time. Yet he realizes that his treasure cannot be sustained in Palestine. He forfeits his library because he lacks the paltry sum necessary to get the books out of storage, and correspondingly, he becomes aware of "a great impairment in his own mind, a drying up of inspiration."[73] The physical challenges of the new land render useless the kind of accumulated learning that characterized Jews in the Diaspora and that helped them maintain their intellectual and psychological advantage over the Gentiles. "It was clear enough that the words that had once been of value to him were no longer any use."[74] Greatly humbled during the course of the novel by the loss of his daughter Miriam, Yosef moves from the hilltop Jerusalem down to Tiberias, physically and metaphorically one of the lowest places in the land.

Brenner conveys the comedy as well the tragedy underlying such concepts as "the national revival." When Schneirson courts a Sephardic girl, he insists on speaking Hebrew, fulfilling one of the aims of the Hebrew renaissance, which was to unite Jews from the East and the West in a common tongue. Except that as a native Jerusalemite and like all the Jews from the Levant who had dealings with the Ashkenazim from eastern Europe, the girl knows Yiddish as well as he does.

> Yet despite the fact that she knew, and that Schneirson knew that she knew, and that she knew that Schneirson knew that she knew, and that Schneirson knew that she knew that he knew that she knew—nevertheless, he, Schneirson, and she, the exotic type of his dreams, pretended that . . . *What? They speak that jargon called Yiddish? The idea!* That is, they made believe that as representatives

of the two halves of the Jewish people in the Holy Land they could communicate only in Hebrew.[75]

Their courtship "in the Holy Tongue" barely suffices for nibbling chocolate, let alone sexual flirtation.

When Kafka's narrator describes K.'s uncertainty, the prose never falters or adapts to his fatigue:

> At long last K. had decided to withdraw his case from the lawyer. Doubts as to whether it was the right thing to do could not be totally rooted out, but the firm conviction of its necessity outweighed them. This resolution drained K. of a great deal of energy the day he planned to visit the lawyer; he worked at an unusually slow pace, stayed late at the office, and it was past ten before he finally stood at the lawyer's door.[76]

K.'s doubts, charted through several *dochs* and *abers*, the yets and buts of a hyperlogical mind, are rendered through an uninflected prose that, however approximate to his, is not actually his and that remains, however wavering in its content, perfectly firm in grammar and tone. The emotional indifference of the narrative is the key to the novel that abandons K. to his fate. By comparison, Brenner's narrator, presumably drawing from Hefetz's notebooks, replicates his fumbling style:

> Yes, Hefetz could talk on about being a wreck of a man—but did she follow him? Did she understand? And no sooner had he finished, than full of contempt for his own fear of telling the truth, of the final humiliation of calling each thing by name, he would stammer almost involuntarily: *a wreck . . . malarial . . . up in the air . . . without a thing to fall back on . . .* did she understand?[77]

Hefetz may envy the smooth-talking Hamilin for the way that man happily follows his instincts, but given that he cannot do the same, neither does he talk the same. Modern Hebrew is in the position of Hefetz, eager to experience healthful sex and satisfied living but meanwhile nervously circumlocutory as it gropes its way out of the burdened past. Authenticity and truthfulness are represented in Brenner by clumsy rhetoric, circling around the point, fractured thoughts, and groping phrases while the predatory Hamilin and the greedy Goldmann talk as glibly as they live.

YIDDISH REPRESENTED TO BRENNER, as it did to Kafka, a more cohesive Jewry than he could feel a part of. He felt it had the integrity of premodern culture, and he eulogized Sholem Aleichem as "the living essence of the folk itself."

> Is there such a thing as a Jewish people? Do these caravans wandering to and fro over the globe share any particular characteristic or a unique approach to the world? Do the vicissitudes of life evoke in them a unique form of laughter and tears? Are there certain life-giving forces in their midst, any special talents in life's enterprise? Why yes, of course! Sholem Aleichem![78]

Collapsing distinctions between writer, work, and audience in a way that belies his own literary experience—and obviously misrepresents Sholem Aleichem's—Brenner ignores the prevalent view of Yiddish as the insecure jargon and of Hebrew as the solid national tongue, focusing on the artistic potential of each language rather than on its sociological status. The very notion of Yiddish as a folk language precluded his use of it, since the language of continuities would not suit the literature of modern truths. Brenner grasped, or rather he forged, the evident fact that Hebrew, the original language of the Jews, could only succeed in reuniting them in Zion if it were prepared to take the risks of breaking radically with the culture of the Diaspora. No matter how silly Schneirson and his Levantine bride sound spooning in a language neither of them knows, theirs is the clumsy instrument of transition.

Brenner released in Hebrew the vomit, depression, and madness of the sexually crippled, culturally overdetermined, politically hounded Jewish immigrants to Palestine. He developed a poetics of "negative principle," whereby only the broken, faltering style of "nerves" and neuroses could be a trustworthy vehicle of Jewish national recovery.[79] The aesthetic-moral connection between stammering and authenticity is made explicit in the figure of Hanoch, who dies in solitude tending a mill in the Galilee:

"I'm saying," Hanoch stammered, "I'm saying . . . that if God made all this . . . and if He made it so that I shouldn't know about Him—f-fine, then I don't know. B-b-but why did He make it so I sh-shouldn't know? And how d-do I know it was Him? And what difference does it make whether I say that He did or didn't? I'm asking you what difference . . . what difference does it make whether I pray to Him or not . . . will He listen to me if I do? Life is hard for those who b-b-believe and h-hard for those who don't . . . s-so why b-bother? If t-times are hard . . . I'll get by . . . I'll get by without Him. Wh-what? You want me to open the Holy Ark and cry m-mercy? It would be out of place (*Lo zeh hama-ma-makom!*)."[80]

Hanoch's stammer evokes the humility of Moses, the true leader of the Jews. The hardships he faces are conveyed through the difficulty he has describing them. The Talmud asks, "Why do we call God *Hamakom*? Because He is the place (*mekomo*) of the world but the world is not His place (*eyn olamo mekomo*)." Hanoch puns on this concept in explaining his emphasis on physical rather than metaphysical existence, letting the language retain ambiguity even as it determines to do God's work without Him. The pioneer's thoughts are conveyed indirectly by his father Haim, since Hanoch himself never appears before us in the novel. In the same way, the abandoned notebooks of Hefetz and, by inference, the imperfect writings of Brenner are examples of modern Hebrew's "inspirational" texts that are being brought to the reader at second hand.

Such tenuous hope as the novel does hold out at the end comes from Yosef and his brother Haim (yoking the author's two names), brothers of the older, devout generation, who are going to retrieve Haim's grandson, Hanoch's only child, from Beirut, where his mother has taken him, and bring him to live with them in Tiberias. Haim has lost his son Hanoch and Yosef his daughter Miriam. Yosef realizes that his judgments of other people have been too harsh and his values unrealistic. "*And after all these things,* Reb Yosef suddenly found himself humming to the melody of the Book of Esther, *when the wrath of the king had abated.*"[81] In the Book of Esther 2:1, King Ahasuerus is humiliated by the refusal of Queen Vashti to accept his summons, and only after his wrath has abated does he initiate the search for the new queen. The quotation reconciles Yosef to *his* Esther, the remaining spinster daughter who is left to him after the death of Miriam. Brenner does not play off the Hebrew original against the Yiddish reality, as Sholem Aleichem does when Tevye balances inheritance against experience. Through his hummed melody, Yosef creates the language of what Herzl called the "old-new land," but registers the full cost, the agonizing effort that goes into actualizing that phrase.

THE LOGIC OF LANGUAGE imposed itself on the kindred writers, Kafka and Brenner, to spectacularly different ends. Brenner's hero Hefetz went mad within the security of Hebrew while his author was murdered by Arab assailants who imported the pogrom politics of Europe into the Middle East. Kafka's hero K. was executed by unnamed assailants within the ominous hegemony of German while his creator drove himself over the brink of life within the secure circle of his family and friends. The inner and outer worlds of Kafka and Brenner traded destinies, but their fiction told the deeper truth: the German atmosphere would harm the Jew; Hebrew would rally round its madmen and bring their stories home.

3

LITERATURE OF THE RUSSIAN REVOLUTION

FROM ISAAC BABEL TO VASILY GROSSMAN

We are the vanguard, but of what?

ISAAC BABEL[1]

The Making of a Russian Jewish Writer

There is nothing in modern Jewish literature quite like the twenty-two-year-old Isaac Babel's appropriation of Russian in his 1916 sketch "Odessa." Writing in the last year of the tsarist empire, Babel was flaunting a Russian identity his country had denied him and attributing advantage to the very Jewishness that most fellow Russians considered his curse:

Odessa is an awful place. Everybody knows how they murder the Russian language there. All the same, I think there's a lot to be said for this great city, which has more charm than any other in the Russian Empire. Just think how easy and straightforward life is in Odessa. Half the population consists of Jews, and Jews are people who are very clear about a few simple things: they marry so they won't be lonely, they make love so their tribe will live forever, they make money so they can buy houses and give their wives astrakhan jackets, they're fond of their children because—well, isn't it a very nice thing to love your children, and aren't you supposed to? Poor Jews in Odessa are very confused by provincial governors and official forms, but it's not easy to get them to abandon positions they took up a very long time ago. You can't get them to do that, but you can learn a lot from them. It's to a large extent because of them that Odessa has such an easygoing, straightforward atmosphere.[2]

Misuse of language being the most serious charge that could be leveled against a writer, Babel opens this little manifesto by throwing the "murder" charge back in the accuser's face: first, he affirms his equal share of the most charming city in the empire, along with his competitive right to move the culture and the language in *his* direction; next he defines Jews as the people of life (as opposed to the gloomier Russians and their writers). Rakish Odessa takes on for him the open competitive style of its Jewish sectors, and he intends to make that the paradigm for Russian literature.

Babel's tongue-in-cheeky conception of Jewish wholesomeness is no less defiant of the modern Jewish intellectual than of his irritant the anti-semite. He professes to admire Jews for their bourgeois virtues and for the stubborn intelligence of their ancient ways. He spurns the politically correct attitude of dismissive contempt for Judaism's moral confidence and slyly affirms its strong tribal loyalties. Many of Babel's Russian Jewish contemporaries—Ilya Ehrenburg, Boris Pasternak, Osip Mandelstam, Viktor Shklovsky—were already the products of assimilating families that may have given their clever children something to be ashamed of when they denied them the self-knowledge that went along with being Jewish. But Babel's father (unlike Kafka's) had insisted that his son study some Talmud, and the Yiddish language spoken at home was the Jewish vernacular of all eastern Europe. Babel's bold prose arose straight out of his Jewish self-confidence.

> If one thinks about it, doesn't it seem that in Russian literature so far there has been no real, joyous, and vivid description of the sun? Turgenev has given us the morning dew and the still of the night. In Dostoyevsky you can feel under your feet the dismal, uneven roadway as Karamazov goes to the tavern, the heavy, mysterious fog of St. Petersburg.[3]

With only half a smile, Babel predicts that "the literary Messiah who has been awaited so long will come from there—from the sunny steppes washed by the sea." A Russian Jew like himself, bearing no moral responsibility for the Karamazovs, the Oblomovs, or the Romanoffs and freed by the consciousness of being modern from the discipline of his own religious community, could extract from each culture what he liked and no more. The overthrow of the tsar in 1917 reinforced this confidence: as once favored targets of tsarist oppression, Jews were ideally able to prove the justice of the revolution that accepted them on equal terms. Babel, who had been primed in childhood by his Jewish family to "know everything" as the only way of surmounting tsarist restrictions, became free under Bolshevism to put that discipline to use.[4]

The extraordinary element in Babel's career as a Russian writer is not his youthful *chutzpa*, which was soon to be tempered by some painful self-doubts, but the reliable voice that he found for himself so early on. When we compare this with the difficulties experienced by Mendele Moykher-Sforim, Sholem Aleichem, and I. L. Peretz, or by the younger M. I. Berdichevsky and Yosef Haim Brenner as they moved between Yiddish and Hebrew in an attempt to create a viable autobiographical narrator, Babel's engaging "I" makes it seem as though Russian were the Jew's ideal language and the Jew the ideal vehicle for Russian. It has been said that Odessa was the place where a variety of factors coalesced—"Jewish and non-Jewish, political and literary, local and more generally Russian."[5] Babel is the voice of that unique symbiosis.

Thus, it is a mistake to assume that Babel's choice of Russian is *prima facie* evidence for his estrangement from his Jewish roots. The learned and insightful Renato Poggioli oversimplifies the relationships between Jews, languages, and identity when he writes that Babel isolated himself from Jewish culture by choosing Russian, "the idiom of the *goyim*," over Yiddish and Hebrew "not merely to escape from the ghetto, but to turn, through Russia, to Europe and to the West."[6] In fact, there was no ghetto in Odessa and no automatic correlation between language and national allegiance in the city of such prominent Zionists and Hebraists as Moses Leib Lilienblum, Ahad Ha'am (Asher Ginsberg), Haim Nahman Bialik, Y. Kh. Ravnitski, Ben Ami (Mordecai Rabinowicz), and Elhanan Leib Levinsky. Sholem Yankev Abramovitch (Mendele Moykher-Sforim), the Odessan architect of Yiddish and Hebrew prose, remained aloof from every ideological impulse. Simon Dubnow, the great Jewish historian, championed—in *Russian*—the counter-idea of Jewish territorialism, idealizing the spiritual power of Jewish communities wherever they had formed. Moreover, Babel's preference for Russian cannot really be interpreted as a rejection of

Yiddish and Hebrew when we consider that he was of the age of Sholem Aleichem's children and Mendele's grandchildren, all of whom were raised in Russian. Babel's muscular Jewishness most resembled that of his fellow Odessan Vladimir Jabotinsky (1880–1940), founder of the Jewish Mule Corps of the British Army during World War I and of the Revisionist wing of the Zionist movement. Jabotinsky might have blamed Babel for failing the Jews in their *political* struggle, but as the author of several Russian novels about assimilating Jews of Odessa and ancient Israel (*The Five, Samson*),[7] Jabotinsky knew that the ethnic allegiance of a text depends less on its language than on the author's spiritual and cultural orientation.[8]

We may understand a little more about Babel's literary self-image as the exemplary insider-outsider if we consider the author with whom he identified—not Gustave Flaubert or Guy de Maupassant or the Russian masters, to whose craft he really did pay careful attention, but Hershele Ostropolier, the semi-legendary Yiddish prankster about whom stories and story-collections circulated throughout Russia. When Lyutov, the autobiographical narrator of *Red Cavalry*, is asked by the Chernobyl rebbe, Motele Bratslavsky, what he does for a living, he says he is setting the stories of Hershele Ostropolier into verse.

> "A great labor," the rebbe whispered, closing his eyelids again. "The jackal moans when it is hungry, every fool is foolish enough to be unhappy, and only the wise man rends the veil of existence with laughter."[9]

The rebbe's enthusiasm for Hershele Ostropolier has been mistaken as a sign of the decadence of his court, its "fabric of lies," and as part of Babel's story's "streak of craziness."[10] But everything in this passage and in Babel suggests quite the opposite. Reb Motele says that while animals and simpletons may be able to express the misery of the human condition, only laughter can get beyond the limits of reality to ultimate freedom. The rebbe ascribes to Hershele Ostropolier a spiritual function as high as his own, and when Lyutov then finds himself seated among the other Hasidim—"the possessed of devils, the liars and the moonstruck"—he includes himself in their inspired brotherhood.

Hershele was part of the Hasidic movement that captivated the Jews of southeastern Poland in the late eighteenth century. The movement was propelled by a new kind of religious personality, one who mediated directly between his followers and the Divine Spirit by using storytelling and magical healing as a vehicle of his populist religion. Hence Hasidism's use of the homier term *rebbe* to distinguish this kind of teacher from the rabbinic authority, the rabbi or *Rav*. Of course, such charismatic authority is vulnerable to accusations of fakery, and Hershele is a comic corrective to the corrective, a countervoice within the revolutionary religious movement, the irrepressible and joyous skeptic who cannot be inhibited from telling the truth.

Babel's only completed Hershele Ostropolier story of the cycle he set out to write adapts a characteristically aggressive tale from the large folk repertoire. Desperate to earn some money for his starving family, Hershele is on his way to the court of Reb Borukhl Tulchiner of Medzhibezh, because "[everyone] knew that Reb Borukhl suffered from black melancholy, and there was no better medicine for him than the words of Hershele."[11] At a roadside inn he finds a golden opportunity for fun and profit when he hears the proprietess sighing in anticipation of *Shabbes Nakhamu*. The term refers to the first Sabbath after the ninth day of the Hebrew month of Av, the midsummer fast day commemorating the destruction of Jerusalem, and it derives from the opening words from Isaiah that are read that week in the synagogue: "*Nakhamu nakhamu ami* [Comfort ye, comfort ye, my people]." In a preposterous subversion of language and faith, Hershele pretends to *be* Shabbes Nakhamu, and as mediator between the imperfect present and the perfected future, he promises to deliver all the bounty that the woman can load onto his wagon to her relatives in the world beyond. When apprehended by her husband, he outwits the poor man by pretending to have been robbed by the rogue who put one over on his wife. I. I. Trunk conceives of Hershele Ostropolier as the Jewish comic response to despair.[12] But Babel appropriated the more ruthless edge of Ostropolier's comedy in order to expose the egotism of the self-proclaimed deliverers and also the credulity of those who agree to be fleeced. Babel believed that he occupied Hershele's position in relation to the redeemers and victims of his own day: his amusement, if truthful, would have to be at their expense.

Babel's own writing also "rends the veil of existence with laughter." There is no funnier scene in Jewish literature than the third act of the Sicilian folk drama in Babel's story "Di Grasso," when the eponymous actor goes flying across the stage of the municipal theater to sink his teeth into the neck of his rival. Or when Zagursky, the violin teacher in "Awakening," tells the family that their prodigy has missed the last three months of classes, as the culprit delays his destiny behind the locked bathroom door. Or when the twenty-year-old seducer in "Guy de Maupassant" leaps up, knocks over the chair, and bumps into the shelf that holds all twenty-nine morocco-leather-bound volumes of the French master. Usually at the narrator's expense and through a violent reversal, the comedy releases some desperately repressed truth, then offers the grace of a luminous ending. In each of these stories, laughter reconciles the fragile individual to his maturer self.

Babel's Russian Jewish prose was almost as secure as Sholem Aleichem's Yiddish. There is no sign in his writing of an "identity conflict,"[13] much less of the kind of language crisis that beset Franz Kafka. But Babel lets us know that the exacting standards he sets for himself respond to the demand that he prove himself as a Jew. The author's confidence that Jewishness would work to his artistic advantage is especially marked in *Red Cavalry*.

Isaac Babel: *Red Cavalry*

It is impossible to read *Red Cavalry*, a compressed epic about the Polish–Russian war of 1920 (the first foreign campaign of the Red Army) without feeling the spiritual charge of that moment in history. At a time when every major European writer seemed to be demonstrating the waste of war, Babel's Jewish narrator, attached as a military correspondent to General Semyon Budyonny's First Cavalry Army, makes his hard peace with the revolution that is entrenching itself on the battlefield. He sees the pillage of old religions—the Catholic churches of Poland, the dashing rites of the Cossacks, and, along with the weary synagogues he remembers from his youth, much of the Jewish population that attends them. Personally, he loathes killing and will not use a gun either to fight the enemy or to fulfill the dying wish of a comrade—or even to save his own life. But he sees in the bloodshed around him the afterbirth of a new society.

Tolstoy, who among European writers of the nineteenth century probably had the widest access to all sectors of his society, was able to stock *War and Peace* with an enormous cast of characters and range of situations drawn from firsthand knowledge. Despite Babel's energetic attempt between 1917 and 1924 to get as much experience as possible in preparation for his life as a writer, many elements in Russian society remained beyond his ken. But he was fortunate enough to have served in the conflict he was describing. Soon after Babel had become a correspondent with YugROSTA, the southern branch of the national wire service, in the spring of 1920, he was assigned to cover Budyonny's Cossack army. The surviving part of the diary he kept during that summer shows just how conscientiously he was sketching for the work to come:

> Korets, describe it, Jews outside a big building, yeshiva bochur in glasses, what are they talking about old men with yellow beards, hunched traders, frail, lonely. . . . Convey Rovno air, badly shaken up, unstable, but life goes on, and there are Polish signboards. Describe the evening. . . . Describe—riding with the divisional commander, a small squadron, the divisional commander's entourage, Bakhturov, the old Budyonny man, a march plays as we move out. . . . Try to convey the spirit of ruined Leszniow, its enfeeblement, the dreary, half-foreign filth.[14]

As Babel interviews Polish prisoners, Cossack comrades, and Jews, his knowledge of Yiddish proves especially useful in discovering the experience of the subject population.

The finished work that emerged from these notes delivers in shrapnel-like dispatches the cramped perspective of the men in battle and the uncomfortable existence of the distrusted Jew. Babel compared himself ambiguously to Tolstoy, who described events minute by minute, by claiming that *he* offered only the "most interesting five minutes I've experienced in twenty-four hours."[15] To follow Babel's action, one must know that Poland launched the war against the Soviet Union to regain territory held by the Russian Empire and took the offensive until Trotsky, commander of the Red Army, sent 700,000 men into battle in the summer of 1920. General Semyon Budyonny's First Cavalry Army, to which Babel (and his narrator, Lyutov) was attached, broke through Polish lines into Galicia and began to march on Warsaw, the Polish capital. But the Poles eventually rallied, sliced through the invading army, and encircled part of it, taking 100,000 Russian prisoners and killing many others. The Jewish civilian population of the towns under dispute had been victims of the Cossacks who fought for the tsars. Then the Polish soldiers killed them for siding with the Russians. Finally, with the Soviet counterattack they fell victim to those same Cossacks, now wearing Red Army uniforms. The thirty-five short stories of *Red Cavalry* cover the summer advance and autumn retreat of Budyonny's Cavalry Army from the disoriented perspective of a Jewish war correspondent, who has to report on the battle while establishing a role for himself among the warring and embattled sides.

The consciousness of his narrator, Kirill Vasilevich Lyutov, is Babel's moral compass in *Red Cavalry*, and his attitude is by no means simple:

> *Nachdiv* 6 has reported that Novograd-Volynsk was taken at dawn today. The staff has moved out of Krapivno, and our transport is strung like a noisy rearguard along the high road, along the unfading high road that goes from Brest to Warsaw and was built on the bones of muzhiks [Russian peasants] by Nicholas I.[16]

The military shorthand (*nachdiv* 6 stands for *nachalnik divizii* 6, commander of the sixth division) of the opening sentence is the stuff of official reportage. Babel stresses that Lyutov is employed as a correspondent of the *Red Trooper*, accompanying the army as political watchdog and voice of the regime. But the follow-up sentence, trailing like a transport along a grammatical high road, betrays the poetic instinct, the acquired learning, and the active conscience of a man who was not raised to be a soldier. That road may be "unfading" because it has been traversed by so many previous Russian armies marching toward and retreating from the Polish capital, because the muzhik bones underfoot testify to the historically irreparable injustice of tsarism, or because the narrator brings a metaphysical perspective to bear on contemporary events.

Ephraim Sicher has identified negative adjectives as one of the hallmarks of Babel's style, his method of rendering ordinary phenomena unique. From *Red Cavalry* he finds such examples as "unprecedented war (Pan Apolek)," "indescribable beehives (The Road to Brody)," and "unforgettable springs (Discourse on the Tachanka)," the negative prefix heightening the horror or beauty of the thing described.[17] Going into battle, the narrator sees the receding landscape in most unbellicose terms: "Fields of purple poppies flower around us, the noonday wind is playing in the yellowing rye, the virginal buckwheat rises on the horizon like the wall of a distant monastery." This moment of grace before the army crosses the river Zbrucz into Poland is set against a theologically defined past. Only he, the narrator, in the imprint of his imagination, sees the fields before him in this unsecular cast. The mood of this lyrical decription is broken as the cavalry fords the river into the war zone and a soldier's expletive drowns the faith as he sinks "and resonantly defames the Mother of God."[18]

The poetic cast of Babel's prose becomes even more obvious if we compare this opening of *Red Cavalry* with the start of Viktor Shklovsky's almost contemporaneous *Revolution and the Front* (1919). The chief theoretician of formalism, Shklovsky concentrates on surfaces and mechanics, and especially on the vehicles—the armored cars and the streetcars and the innovative terminology—that will propel the revolution. His narrator says, "I'll never forget the terrible sense of oppression," then adds, "but most of all I remember the streetcars," deflating the high emotion. Even more demonstratively decremental is his explanation: "[the] reason for this 'war' was that the soldiers crowded the streetcars and refused to pay for the ride."[19] Shklovsky's forced irony may be a protection against the messianic idealism and/or demagogic monomania of the capitalized Revolution, but it fully accepts Marxism's reduction of human experience to its material basis.

Shklovsky admired the "concreteness" of Babel, which consorted so well with his own objectivism, and praised him for being "the only one who maintained his stylistic sangfroid throughout the Revolution." He was much more guarded, however, about what he called Babel's "elevated tone," his "highly colored," "operatic" flourishes.[20] But Babel was not willing to relinquish the reach for transcendence, and his surprising juxtapositions of the concrete and the ineffable are the form that his resistance takes. Lyutov's habitual irony in *Red Cavalry* never extends to the spiritual longings of the characters he encounters. Babel's model of the artist is Pan Apolek, the itinerant painter who is hired by the church to glorify the religion of Christ. By casting the local inhabitants as figures of the sacred story, Apolek subverts both the authority of the established religion and the reductionism of the atheists, exalting the ordinary people and sustaining the idea of holiness within the institutions that once enshrined it. Babel plays the rebel within Bolshevism as Ostropolier does in Hasidism as

Pan Apolek does in Christianity but in reverse, by keeping religious mystery alive.

To return to the opening story, Lyutov's Jewish memory also surfaces in "Crossing the Zbrucz":

> Late at night we arrive in Novograd. In the billet that has been assigned to me I find a pregnant woman and two red-haired Jews with thin necks: a third is already asleep, covered up to the top of his head and pressed against the wall. In the room that has been allotted to me I find ransacked wardrobes, on the floor scraps of women's fur coats, pieces of human excrement and broken shards of the sacred vessels used by the Jews once a year, at Passover.
>
> "Clear up," I say to the woman. "What a dirty life you live, landlords. . . ."[21]

Crossing the river Styx is the Greek topos for passing into death; crossing the Red Sea, after a pell-mell flight from Egypt is the occasion for Passover, the Jewish festival of liberation. The narrator's identification of the shards of Passover crockery betrays his Jewish kinship with the household that serves as his billet. But he seems to be inverting the liberation saga, bringing the wrath of Pharaoh with him into the Jewish fold. Without explaining his mood to the readers or revealing his Jewish identity to his hosts, he is gratuitously harsh to the victims of the desecrated house. When he lies down at night beside the sleeping man by the wall, he has nightmares of *nachdiv 6* in hot pursuit of the brigade commander for having turned the brigade around to flee from battle. Is this his conscience pricking him for betraying his fellow Jews, or does he feel guilty for wanting to betray the Cossacks? His landlady wakes him because he has been shaking his bedmate, her father, in his sleep. With this the story ends:

> She raises thin legs and a round belly from the floor and removes the blanket from the man who has fallen asleep. An old man is lying there, on his back, dead. His gullet has been torn out, his face has been cleft in two, dark blue blood clings in his beard like pieces of lead.
>
> "*Panie*[sir]," the Jewess says, as she shakes up the feather mattress, "the Poles were murdering him, and he begged them: 'Kill me

out in the backyard so that my daughter doesn't see me die.' But they did what suited them. He died in this room, thinking about me. And now tell me," the woman said suddenly, with terrible force, "tell me where else in all the world you would find a father like my father. . . ."22

Critics used "Crossing the Zbrucz" as an example of Babel's manipulation of historical material, his use of epic imagery to represent rebirth, and his attempt to understand the relation between violence and humanity.23 But it is within the continuum of Russian Jewish literature that the daughter's outburst assumes truly "terrible force." The narrator is a Jew-in-hiding, having joined the Cossack army presumably to help liberate his society. Yet whether or not the daughter suspects that he is a Jew, she discounts his help. Describing her father's murder, she mourns not just his loving protection but the loss of the kind of protection he gave her, a male heroism that remained supremely considerate of her feelings even as he was murdered by brutes.

In literature as well as politics, the cowardice of Jewish males had long been a heated topic by the time *Red Cavalry* was written. Already in 1903, after being delegated by the Jewish Historical Commission of Odessa to write up a detailed investigative report of the vicious pogrom in Kishinev, the poet Haim Nahman Bialik had composed instead a prophetic ode, "*Beir bahareyga* [In the City of Slaughter]," a work "more carefully designed to shock Jewish sensibilities than anything heard before."24 The pseudo reportage reached its climax in an exceptionally damning image of Jewish manhood:

> *Note also do not fail to note,*
> *In that dark corner, and behind that cask*
> *Crouched husbands, bridegrooms, brothers, peering from the cracks,*
> *Watching the sacred bodies struggling underneath*
> *The bestial breath,*
> *Stifled in filth, and swallowing their blood!*
> *Watching from the darkness and its mesh*
> *The lecherous rabble portioning for booty*
> *Their kindred and their flesh! [. . .]*
> *How did their menfolk bear it, how did they bear this yoke?*

They crawled forth from their holes, they fled to the house of the Lord,
They offered thanks to Him, the sweet benedictory word.
The Kohanim sallied forth, to the Rabbi's house they flitted:
Tell me, O Rabbi, tell, is my own wife permitted?

Jews who descend from the ancient priesthood, the *kohanim*, continue to be governed by the laws of ritual purity, according to which they may not have relations with a wife who has been defiled. Capping this scene of mass rape, the concern of these priestly descendants for *their* purity is Bialik's emblem of the cowardice to which Judaism had sunk. Bialik's English translator A. M. Klein heightens the accusation by rhyming the way the *kohanim* "flitted" with their scruples about what was "permitted." Bialik knowingly distorted some of the historical facts, ignoring, for example, what he knew about local armed Jewish resistance to the pogrom. But the slander on Jewish manhood had its intended effect; this poem probably did more than any other work of the century to quicken Jewish self-defense and raise Jewish political consciousness.

The Jewish woman of Babel's story defends her father's courage, in literary terms, against both Bialik and the Bolsheviks. Bialik's prophetic oracle and Babel's narrator harden their hearts against this species of martyrdom because they think that Jews must take action to stop the murder of Jews. Bialik, writing in Jewish languages (he also rewrote the poem in Yiddish), ignores the guilt of the pogromists in order to sharpen his condemnation of Jewish passivity. In Babel's "First Love," the narrator's beloved father fails his son's expectations of manhood by getting down on his knees *in the mud* before the Cossack officer. But here the grown-up narrator Lyutov, who wears the uniform of the Revolution, is reproached for being less manly than the Jews he mocks. Babel implicates his autobiographical narrator in the cruelty by placing his burdened conscience at the center of his work. While the *author* of *Red Cavalry* creates a masterpiece of Soviet literature by mining the newly merged postrevolutionary Russian Jewish identity, the *narrator* of *Red Cavalry* stands accused for the disloyalties that such a merger requires.

L IONEL TRILLING WAS the first critic to highlight Babel's dichotomy between Cossack and Jew:

The author, who represented himself in the stories, was a Jew; and a Jew in a Cossack regiment was more than an anomaly, it was a joke, for between Cossack and Jew there existed not merely hatred but a polar opposition. Yet here was a Jew riding as a Cossack and trying to come to terms with a Cossack ethos.[25]

Yet the internal evidence of the stories reveals Babel's far more surprising perception that Cossacks and Jews now shared a common fate. A pervasive parallelism links the decline of the Jews to that of the Cossacks, who are simultaneously harming others. Thus, in the twenty-third story "Afonka Bida," Babel gives us the Cossack counterpart of the bereaved Jewish daughter's cry: with the momentum of victory beginning to turn against the Red Army, "[for] the first time in the whole campaign we could feel at our backs the devilish sharpness of breaches in the rear and of flank attacks—the merciless bites of the weapon which has served us so long and so happily."[26] The prospect of retreat demoralizes the Cossacks (just as pogroms demoralized the Jews). Lyutov's friend Afonka Bida spurs a mock attack against a division of muzhik recruits that has been hastily thrown into battle against the Poles. When the disgusted narrator shouts at him, "What are you playing around for?" the Cossack answers him, "For fun," and then again, jabbing at a boy whom he has pursued into the bushes, "For fun!"

Bida gets his comeuppance when a Polish bullet punctures the neck of his horse. His first extravagant grief over the fallen horse is presented in the most negative terms: "he squeaked like a caught mouse"; "we saw Afonka bowing like a hysterical peasant woman in church." But just as the Jewish daughter's grief acquires sudden dignity, so too does Bida's:

> "He brought that horse from home," said Bitsenko of the moustaches. "Where will he find another horse like that?"
>
> "A horse—it is a friend," replied Orlov.
>
> "A horse—it is a father," sighed Bitsenko. "It saves your life countless times. A fat lot Bida will be able to do without a horse."[27]

Here, in almost identical language, the Jewish woman's grief is transposed into its Cossack equivalent. Two antithetical cultures have both been stripped of their protectors, and each mourns its irreparable loss. The story goes on to describe Afonka's heroic foray against the Poles who have stolen the peasants' horses. "To our admiring ears came echoes of this furious single-handed combat, echoes of the desperate and thievish attack of a solitary wolf upon a leviathan." The repetition of "echoes" in this sentence lyrically anticipates Afonka's heroism, and his return after several weeks with a missing eye and a new horse brings this episode to a redemptive conclusion. But just as the father's reported action in the opening story does not altogether obsure the dreadfulness of Jewish passivity, neither does Bida's reported courage erase his cruelty. The balance of sympathy and condemnation in each case is about the same.

The Jew's attempt to gain acceptance by his Cossack comrades-in-arms is novel, to be sure, but Trilling ignores that Lyutov joins his fate to the Cossacks because he and they are now subject to the same "laws of history." Jews and Cossacks, linked by historical enmity, must now both yield to the Revolution the traditions that kept them distinct. That Lyutov gets to tell the story is the advantage of the literate Jew over the Ukrainian; the physical power and grace and brute justice of the Cossacks is the advantage that they (temporarily) have over him. Lyutov may be "trying to come to terms with a Cossack ethos," but Babel's control of the narrative imposes his Jewish sensibility on the Revolutionary war and forces the Cossacks to ride on *his* terms.

L YUTOV IS NOT JUST a Jew in a revolutionary army. Since the army to which he is assigned is engaged with the enemy on territory thickly populated by Jews, he is alternately a Jew among Cossacks and a Red Army propagandist among Jews. Babel endows Lyutov with his own remarkable ability to move back and forth between the Hasidic Jews and the Cossacks, noting parallels between the two antithetical male cultures. Perhaps the most famous story of the *Red Cavalry* cycle is "My First Goose," in which Lyutov slaughters the landlady's goose to impress the Cossacks with whom he is billeted and is rewarded for his successful rite of passage by their invitation to share their meal of pork. Lyutov concludes the ceremony of brotherhood with these soldiers who sit "straight as priests" by pulling out his copy of *Pravda* and reading aloud a speech of Lenin's. Of course, Lyutov's Jewish conscience punishes him by night for violating it by day: "I had dreams and saw women in my dreams, and only my heart, stained crimson with murder, squeaked and overflowed."[28] The squeak of his heart is the same sound made by the neck of the goose he crushed underfoot.

But this story is lodged between two encounters with religious Jews, who are the moral antagonists of the Revolution. In the episode just before it, set on the eve of the Sabbath, Lyutov meets Gedali, the antique Jewish shopkeeper who questions a Revolution that "creates orphans in the house," and in the episode just after it, the following afternoon, Gedali takes him to the prayerhouse of Reb Motele Bratslavsky, "empty and of stone, like a morgue." Lyutov feels so much at home at the rebbe's Sabbath table that most of what we get to know about him derives from this interlude, namely, that he is from Odessa, that he has studied Bible, and that in his search for merriment he is putting Hershele Ostropolier into verse. Whereupon he is invited to "drink the wine that he will not be served" in the company of "the possessed of devils, the liars and the moonstruck." Hasidism is dedicated to such paradoxical affirmations of the emergence of Aught from Naught; the rebbe's utterances are as far from the straightness of Lenin's prose as his crust of bread is from the Cossacks' feast of pork. But lest we think the story harbors nostalgia for this mystical alternative to the historical imperative, Lyutov catches sight of Ilya, the rebbe's son, publicly smoking in violation of the Sabbath yet still trembling in his parents' house "like an escaped prisoner brought back to prison after a chase." Ilya has not been able to make the final break for freedom, and we will later learn that by the time he does become a soldier, it is too late for a transformation as successful as Lyutov's. Ilya is the casualty Lyutov might have been had he hesitated to join the Revolution.

Though studies of the Jew in modern literature habitually note his marginality, the remarkable thing about Babel's autobiographical protagonist is that he also *belongs* at both the Cossack and the Jewish rites. Lyutov is by no means in the process of metamorphosing from Jew into Cossack, no more than he is about to become a *bal tshuvah* (a religious penitent). He may partake of both the Jewish and the Ukrainian repasts because the Revolution is in the process of crushing the differences between them, and yet he can interpret Lenin to the Cossacks and Hershele Ostropolier to the Jews. In a number of stories, Babel goes one step further; he narrates the stories of Cossacks in their own voice, thus making himself the conduit for their laments, their rages and scorn.

Red Cavalry animates the tension between Cossack and Jew under the system that claims to be liberating them both: two peoples, nurtured in freedom by highly decentralized systems of authority and habits of foraging very far afield—militarily in one case, intellectually in the other—have now to yield their autonomy to a "higher," or at least a newer, power. We read on from one episode to the next to discover what happens to the narrator and what happens in the war, but it is the moral question that dominates the narrative and keeps the reader unsettled from start to finish. For while it is possible for a Jew to learn to ride with the Cossacks in the Bolshevik army and for a Jewish writer to compose the epic of the Russian Revolution, it is impossible to reconcile the values of Jewish civilization with either the Cossack code of honor or the idea of historical necessity. Lyutov fails a crucial test of manly honor when he refuses to shoot the wounded Dolgushov, and he betrays his fellow soldiers by going into war with an unloaded gun. But does Lyutov, then, remain a loyal Jew? What is this book's idea of the good and the right?

"Squadron Commander Trunov" sets out the problem of conflicting moral loyalties in a story of unusually complicated construction that opens as follows:

> At noon we brought the bullet-riddled body of Trunov, our squadron leader, to Sokal. He was killed this morning in a battle with enemy planes. All the hits on Trunov were to his face, his cheeks were peppered with wounds, his tongue torn out. We washed the dead man's face as best we could, in order to make it look less fearsome. We put a Caucasian saddle at the head of the coffin and dug a grave in a ceremonial spot, in the public gardens, in the middle of town, right by the cathedral.[29]

Pavel Trunov's heroism gets its full due in the final paragraph, when we learn that all those hits to his face were sustained in a diversionary action that allowed the rest of his squadron to escape the detection of enemy planes. Meanwhile, as the story opens, his ceremonial funeral is conducted according to the Cossack custom, that is, with a display of trick riding and farewell kisses from his men. Lyutov's poetic voice has never been more at odds with the Cossack ethos. "I stood at the back, I touched with my lips the now serene forehead, surrounded by the saddle, and went off into the town, into Gothic Sokal, which lay in blue dust and invincible Galician dejection."

The body of the story stretches taut against this frame. Sokal, a half-Jewish town of about ten thousand, is home to warring factions of Belz and Husyatin Hasidim. Ignoring the ongoing war between Russians, Ukrainians, and Poles, they stand arguing over the famed Gaon, the Talmudic genius of Vilna who over a century earlier had ignited an internal war within the Jewish ranks by issuing a ban of excommunication against the Hasidim. Having tried to relieve his sorrow for Trunov by jostling for a while among these rival groups, Lyutov takes off after a spectral "Galician Don Quixote" whom he sees among the Hasidim and follows him past the Jewish quarter to a gypsy blacksmith's. There he is recognized by a Cossack soldier and berated for having "maimed" Trunov earlier that day. The story then fills in those earlier events: At dawn, after a pitched battle in which Trunov sustains serious head wounds, ten Polish soldiers are taken prisoner, but they throw off their uniforms before their captors can tell the officers from the men. Trunov is unimpressed by this equalizing tactic. In an attempt to flush out their officers, he stabs one of the prisoners to death and shoots another, though he does not let his men run off with their clothes: "[Our] Soviet Republic is still alive, it's too soon to divide it up." But when Trunov tells Lyutov to cover up his murders by erasing the names of the dead prisoners, it is Lyutov who balks. "It's obvious that Trotsky doesn't write orders for you, Pavel."[30] Speaking for the head of the Red Army, Lyutov will not condone this spontaneous vengeance and warns his Cossack comrade of what true communism demands. Trunov thinks all will be forgiven. "At headquarters they'll see it in terms of the wretched life we lead," he replies. But the two antagonists have no chance to find out which of them is right. At that point the buzzing of the enemy airplanes overhead seems to touch off a buzz in Trunov's head, and he insists that his frightened subaltern join him in his suicidal efforts to down them.

Which of the two does the story favor—Trunov's bold action or Lyutov's insistence on the rules? Judging from the internal parallel in the narrative between Hasidim and Cossacks, it would appear to be a standoff. Certainly, the Revolution leaves no room for Trunov's rough justice or singular heroism, so Sokal, the burial ground of Hasidism, is also the burial ground of the Cossack code. The Polish–Russian conflict was the last great cavalry war: Trunov's stand against the airplanes is as quixotic as the shadowy Galician Jew whom Lyutov follows from the marketplace past the Jewish quarter. Though the Cossacks condemn Lyutov as the Jewish betrayer of Trunov their comrade, the narrator accepts their ostracism as the cost of doing *his* duty by Trotsky, and Trunov's martyrdom may be his way of conceding that he had something to expiate in his behavior as a soldier. Both men are equally conscripts in the war launched by the Russian Communist Party, each doing his duty according to his lights.

But Babel does not let things stand there. He seemed to know that the artistic opportunity of becoming a writer of the Revolution must exact a moral price. Thus, in an autobiographical note written contemporaneously with *Red Cavalry*, Babel said that he had served the CHEKA, the Party's secret police force, a claim that was denied by his wife.[31] I would guess that Babel's desire to implicate himself in the work of the CHEKA was part of his code of honor, his sense that anyone who benefited from the Bolsheviks necessarily had blood on his hands, and that such an artist became especially suspect if he pretended to false innocence. To this end, he wrote two concluding stories for *Red Cavalry*, each burdening Lyutov's conscience in a different way.

The burial of Ilya Bratslavsky at a "forgotten station" in the penultimate story, "The Rebbe's Son," stands in terrible contrast to the funeral of Squadron Commander Trunov nine stories earlier. Trunov lies in state at the center of Sokal, with his head resting on his saddle, the icon of his culture. Lyutov packs Bratslavsky's scattered belongings, the "poems, phylacteries, and foot-bindings" of a Hasidic Red Army recruit, into a trunk. Trunov's men surround him and protect his honor. Looking down at the dying Jew on the train are two Russian typists: "The girls, having placed on the floor the bandy legs of simple cows, coldly observed his sexual parts, the wilted, curly virility of a Semite worn to a shadow."[32] This sentence evoked Viktor Shklovsky's comment, "I'm ashamed to take a close look at Babel."[33] There being no other mourner for the rebbe's son, Lyutov tells Bratslavsky's heroic story in the form of a dirge, a full-throated, pain-soaked lament that must substitute for a marked grave. Lyutov is aware of his Jewish responsibility: "And I—who am barely able to accommodate the storms of my imagination within my ancient body—I received my brother's last breath."[34] Our narrator has come a very long way since his inattentive sleep beside the Jewish corpse in the opening episode; his imagination is now yoked to an "ancient body," the transposition of the adjective from the Jews to himself indicating that his flesh has assumed the weight of his people's history.

Had the story cycle ended there, with Lyutov receiving the last breath of "the last prince," *Red Cavalry* might have seemed an elegy on the expiry of Jewishness—and of all religion—in the birth pangs of revolution, framed by the death of the Jewish father in the opening story and of the Jewish son in the last. But Babel wrote a second ending. After its 1926 publication in book form, *Red Cavalry* was attacked by none other than Semyon Budyonny, commander of the First Army, for its false portrayal of the Zaporozhe Cossacks and of the Russian–Polish war. Maxim Gorky defended Babel, and the argument over the book continued for several years, becoming more dangerous as Stalin kept lowering the level of tolerance for dissident views.[35] It was in that context that Babel added the story "Argamak," named for the horse that completes Lyutov's education. The book that begins with the crossing of the Cossack army into Poland now ends with Lyutov in the saddle:

> Argamak's stride was long, stretched, stubborn. With that devilish stride he carried me out of the ranks, I would become separated from the squadron, and, deprived of my sense of direction, I would wander around in search of my unit for whole days and nights thereafter, end up in the enemy lines, spend the night in a ravine, try to attach myself to other units and be told to go away.[36]

Before being assigned to Lyutov, Argamak had been the special property of the Cossack Tikhomolov, who had trained this steed in his idiosyncratic ways. The Revolutionary Tribunal punishes Tikhomolov for killing two prisoners (the same offense that Trunov committed) by confiscating his horse, and whether carelessly or by design, Squadron Commander Baulin assigns this confiscated animal to Lyutov, earning him the resentment of Tikhomolov and all his buddies. The Jew Lyutov, who has to prove himself worthy of soldiering, is always ready to assume any hardship. Although the horse refuses to be saddled by its new owner and suffers terrible injuries at his hands, Lyutov takes all the risks and absorbs all the pain that finally teaches him how to ride. But he cannot bear the hatred that his sacrifice incurs. "You've given me an enemy," Lyutov complains to his commander when Tikhomolov refuses to make up with him, "but how am I to blame?"

> "I understand you," the commander interrupted, "I understand you completely. . . . Your aim is to live without making enemies. . . . Everything you do is aimed that way—so you won't have enemies."[37]

The Cossack commander defines Lyutov's zeal as a craven need for acceptance. "Give him a triple kiss," mutters one of the bystanders, linking Lyutov to Judas, the betrayer of Jesus. It is in this disquietingly compromising moral atmosphere that the narrator brings the entire work to a close:

> I had to leave. I got a transfer to the sixth squadron. There things went better. Somehow or other, Argamak had taught me to sit in the saddle the Tikhomolov way. My dream was fulfilled. The Cossacks stopped following me and my horse with their eyes.[38]

This achievement might have seemed a triumph were it not framed by serious qualms about Lyutov's integrity. The scene is eerily reminiscent of the conclusion of *Tevye the Dairyman*, with the single Jew surrounded by hostile Ukrainians, except that Lyutov is permitted to remain in their company, thanks to the revolution that has yoked his fate to theirs. Religious Jews like Tevye had always accepted the enmity of their neighbors when it came—however undeserved, however undesired—as the by-product of their service to their own God and their own laws. They were not pacifists nor pacifiers but bore the consequence of having made God the guarantor of their morality and their power.[39] But Lyutov is accused of moral cowardice that masquerades as moral strength. His reluctance to kill, however credible within the sphere of Jewish civilization, becomes suspect in the context of a war that accepts killing as its premise and that does the killing on his behalf. Babel damns Lyutov out of the mouth of his military commander for confusing appeasement with principled action. He invites us to consider whether joining the Revolution and riding with the Cossacks may not have been Lyutov's version of getting down on his knees in the mud.

Babel acknowledged that in proving his own ability "to ride with the Cossacks," that is, to compete with Tolstoy as a master of Russian prose, he had implicated himself artistically in the guilt of the new Soviet regime. The Russia of his epic is winning a war in the process of losing a war, integrating a divided society on the bones of its dying religious traditions. Budyonny condemned Babel for getting it wrong, but Babel condemned himself for having gotten it right. From the perspective of a sentient Jew, the Revolution may have had all the force of historical inevitability, but it could never be granted immunity from moral reckoning. Lyutov controls the conscience as well as the consciousness of the stories, never letting himself off the hook. Playing Hershele Ostropolier to the Bolshevik court, he punctures the mystique of Communist redemption.

The Yiddish Writer Under Communism

At the beginning, Isaac Babel fully expected his artistic self-interest to serve the higher interests of the new regime. But self-interest depends on the nature of the self in question. And this is where the story of Russian Jews under Communism exerts such fascination—at the point that deception colludes with self-deception and the brute state finds its willing conscripts. Because of its theoretical internationalism, Communism offered modern Jews the unique opportunity of quitting Judaism not through defection (conversion to another religion) and not through assimilation (conversion to another nationality) but through national self-transcendence. A boon to lovers of paradox, the multinational character of the Russian state institutionalized the distinction between Jews and other nationalities even as Marxism required that the distinction be erased. There is no parallel in modern Jewish history for quite so contradictory a social contract.

When the Bolsheviks seized control over Russia, Lenin, who had initially considered the Jews a "fictitious nation," was forced to treat them as a national minority, there being no other way of standardizing their presence among the dozens of other peoples that constituted the Soviet Union. Thus, in the decade of political remission between the overthrow of the tsar and Stalin's domination of the Communist Party, a knowledgeable Jew like Babel could talk about everything Jewish as long as it was being left behind. Jewish writers and intellectuals were able to publish, conduct research, and teach in Yiddish as long as they were solidifying the *Communist* future, not the future of the Jews. The only Jews in peril were those who intended to maintain the Jewish way of life or to perpetuate the Jewish people, refusing the bargain of self-repudiation that was being forced on them. The fortunate few among these resisters left or were expelled from the Soviet Union. A dozen Hebrew writers, including Haim Nahman Bialik, Y. Kh. Ravnitski, and Saul Tchernikhovsky, won permission to leave for Palestine in 1921—an exodus that seemed miraculous in retrospect—and the Habima Hebrew theater troupe never returned to Russia from its American tour in 1926. But thousands of others who tried to protect their religion or nationalism were silenced, first by political ostracism, then through internal exile and murder. The Soviet Union in the early 1920s resembled Germany in the mid-1930s—individuals were still able to make their own moral choices, but within a political system that was swiftly becoming totalitarian. By 1925 Babel was already writing to his family in western Europe about the difficulties of working in the odious professional milieu of Moscow ("devoid of art or creative freedom") yet advising them to return, because its conditions were still better "and more interesting" than anywhere else.[40]

M OYSHE KULBAK, two years Babel's junior, was one of several noted Yiddish writers who voluntarily returned to Russia or crossed into the Soviet Union in the late 1920s in order to support the alternative to tsarism, hoping to benefit from a political system that officially designated Yiddish as the language of the Jews. Born in 1896 in Smorgon, near the hub of Jewish culture at Vilna, Kulbak received a more thorough Jewish education than Babel did in Odessa, and he was already immersed in the works of modern Yiddish and Hebrew poets and writers by the time he discovered Russian literature in his teens. Just as the ethnic rivalries of Prague encouraged the rise of a Jewish intelligentsia, so too did the political struggle in Vilna between ethnic Lithuanians and Poles under the domination of Russia impress many young Jews with the logic of developing their own Yiddish culture instead of choosing among the competing local Slavic tongues. Once the tsarist regime relaxed its restrictions on the Yiddish press and the Yiddish theater, the opportunities for a Yiddish renaissance were in place, and a new "secular" culture in Yiddish—and He-brew—gushed from the yeshivas and the houses of prayer.

Like Babel, Kulbak was a new breed of Jew. As his mother's family came from the Jewish farming colony Karka (soil) in the Vilna region, earthiness was for him a native experience that required a whole new Yiddish lexi-con. Kulbak's poetry speaks not of generic trees, but of ash, birch, poplar, fir, and oak; Jews tramp through nettle, brush up against the lichens and moss, trip over stumps, and sleep with peasant girls in hay and grass. Kul-bak's first published poem, *Shterndl*, an anonymous soldier's request that the "little star" become his envoy to his distant home and family, emerged as a folk song out of World War I, sung without attribution throughout the Jewish world. A sojourn in Berlin after the war spiced Kulbak's writing with expressionist bravura. When he returned to Vilna in 1923, he himself became the star that linked the hometown boys and girls of his native re-gion with the distant cities. As instructor of Yiddish in the Vilna Jewish Teachers' Seminary, he was probably the most important local influence on a whole new generation of Yiddish writers. Boys cultivated his forelock and copied his long-breathed poetic line.

In 1928, when Kulbak left Vilna to join his parents in Minsk, he seemed to transport the creative energy of Yiddish literature from Poland to Russia, an impression that was reinforced with the appearance of *Zel-menyaner*, a comic send-up of Soviet collectivization.[41] Shmuel Niger, then the foremost Yiddish critic, claimed that "readers never laughed so hard over a Jewish book since Sholem Aleichem."[42] In Yiddish, Indians are *in-dyaner* and partisans are *partizaner*; hence, *Zelmenyaner* is the name that Kul-bak chose for the offspring of Reb Zelmele (diminutive for Zalman), a little Jew from somewhere "deep in Russia" whose progeny are overtaken by the great Communist experiment. Kulbak's comic novel asks how Reb Zelmele's seed will sprout in the new Soviet soil and how the stubborn and inborn features of the Jewish clan will hold out against the imperatives of history.

The leisurely rhythms of the Zelmenyaners' adjustment to Sovietiza-tion in the opening chapters suggest how freely Kulbak went about his own adjustment in the first years of his resettlement. The patriarch Reb Zelmele dies right off, leaving a carefully calculated inheritance to each of his four sons—Itche the tailor, Zishe the watchmaker, Yude the carpenter-violinist, and Folye the tanner-iconoclast. But Zelmele's widow, Bobbe Bashe, lingers well beyond her time. "Motele, why aren't you going to pray?" she asks a grandson who is wandering around the house, and when he replies, "Grandma, I am a pioneer!" she nods sagely, "Yes, of course, you've prayed already. Where did you pray?"[43] In this benign form, an antique religion may linger almost as long as it likes, commanding some residual piety from its oldest children but wholly deaf to "the something different happening in the world."

The real clash of generations is between the four sets of Zelmenyaner parents and their children, who make up the RebZe courtyard—the contraction for *Reb Zelmele* signifying their adjustment to Sovietized speech. In place of a single Tevye, four uncles of contrasting temperaments try to resist or adjust to change. The hyperbolic Bolsheviks among the children name their son Marat instead of Zalman; they banish the shadows from the courtyard through the introduction of electricity, then connect it to the world through radio. Zelmenyaner stubbornness (standing for Jewish obduracy) is equally distributed between the innovators and their opponents as they confront the demands of Soviet society: intermarriage between Jew and "full-fledged" Russians, the disallowance of religious rituals of birth and death, the pressure of trade unionism on independent craftsmen, the collectivization of private property (including the RebZe courtyard), and the call to participate in Bolshevik ceremony and public life. Since the family is already a species of collective, the comedy plays off the claims of the clan against those of society, pitting biological determinism against Revolutionary powers.

Kulbak's Yiddish epic of Sovietization is perforce more intimate than Babel's. The narrator must be a nephew, since he speaks of aunts and uncles, and judging from his portrait of Tsalke the poet—Tsalke being the diminutive of Bezalel, the biblical artisan charged with building the Tabernacle—he does not take the artist's role all that seriously. Tsalke's habit of hanging himself in the attic at every disappointment is a running gag throughout Book One. He is in love with his cousin Tonke, the only Communist ideologue in the family, who not only rebuffs his advances but informs him that her standard of poetry has been set by "the Zelmenyaner poet Moyshe Kulbak!" She quotes him revolutionary lines that had actually turned Kulbak into something of a radical icon: "*Un bronzene yungen/bafaln/iz demolt/a viln/tsu shtiln/dem tsorn/fun yorn/vos zaynen farlorn* [And bronzed youths/ were then filled/ with a will/ to still/ the rage/of years/ that had been lost]."[44] It is impossible to know just what Kulbak intends by reminding us of his Revolutionary credentials, but since Tonke turns out to be the villain of the plot, her endorsement for the early Kulbak seems less an advertisement than an apology for his youthful zealotry. At the end of Book Two she turns Communist informer against the RebZe court, spewing just the kind of accusation of parasitism that was being used to destroy him.[45]

The Yevsektsia, the Jewish section of the Communist Party with direct control over Jewish affairs, was abolished in 1930, but its thuggish servants of the state remained in a position to impose their decisions on their artistic betters. The intimacy of Yiddish cultural circles worked to their disadvantage, since the smaller unit of power was easier to terrorize. Kulbak depicted this danger in the unrequited love of Tsalke for Tonke: Tsalke's finally successful suicide was Kulbak's concession of defeat in his lopsided love affair with the Revolution, and Tonke's dismissive judgment of her admirer suggests how little the Revolution cared about his demise. Kulbak had miscalculated if he thought that by dealing in humor he could remain politically inconspicuous. In fact, his playfulness may have left him exceptionally vulnerable to charges of subversion. We don't know which denunciation led to his arrest in 1937 or when exactly in which of the labor camps he died. *Zelmenyaner* suggests that his tragic end did not take him completely by surprise.

S OME OF THE YIDDISH WRITERS who returned home to Soviet Russia in the 1920s were ideologically prepared to serve the state. The novelist David Bergelson had placed himself "in harness" to Communism, publishing in 1926 in Germany a magazine of that name. His novel of the same year, *Midas hadin* [The Letter of the Law], threw its support behind the New Economic Plan. The book's hero is Soviet commissar Filipov, charged with enforcing the letter of Soviet law in a Jewish town. Ironically, the liberal who had once objected to Judaism's *midas hadin* was now *attracted* by the punitive absolutism of Bolshevik rule. But other writers rejected this sort of literary compliance and expected to be allowed to exercise artistic freedom, even as they felt censorship tightening. Der Nister (The Hidden One), pen name of Pinhas Kahanovitch, returned to the premodern Jewish world of his native Berdichev in *The Family Mashber* (1939), one of the masterpieces of Soviet fiction. In dark and murky colors that convey his immediate atmosphere, he evokes the crisis (in Hebrew, *mashber*) that threatened Russian Jewry in body and soul. One of the Mashber brothers follows the teachings of Nahman of Bratslav, as does Babel's Motele Bratslavsky, that same Hasidic legacy that counteracts depravity and despair. Yiddish writers, including Peretz Markish, Meir Viner, and even David Bergelson, used historical settings to introduce themes they dared not treat in the present tense.

AMONG SOVIET JEWISH WRITERS none walked the tightrope between obedience and independence as successfully as Ilya Ehrenburg. The most explicitly Jewish of his many novels, *The Stormy Life of Lasik Roitschwantz* (1928), could almost be taken as a lampoon of his own Jewish identity. On one hand, he exploits the perspective of a little Jewish tailor to mock some of the defects of Marxism and Bolshevism: Lasik finds the political intricacy of the Chinese problem "a lot harder than the Book of Zohar" and the attempt to legislate between decadent and revolutionary culture more absurd than the "one hundred absolutely impossible pages" in the Talmud on whether one may eat an egg that is laid on a holiday. On the other hand, Ehrenburg takes his protagonist to Palestine so as to have him say, "I do not feel it to be mine," and to starve him to death at Rachel's Tomb in Hebron, the very place that Tevye cites as the shrine of Jewish homecoming.[46] Ehrenburg exposed Russian antisemitism to ridicule (this book was never published in Russia during his lifetime), but by overcompensating for his suspect Jewish sympathies he supplied a version of the anti-Jewish caricature he wanted to unmask.

The darkest period for Jewish culture under Communism came with the Stalin–Hitler Pact of 1939. Soviet Jewish writers were not permitted to protest Hitler's atrocities—an enforced silence all the more harrowing since Polish refugees who fled to the Soviet zone after the German invasion brought with them uncensored news of what was happening outside Russia. After Hitler attacked the Soviet Union on June 22, 1941, the Germans encouraged local Ukrainians and Lithuanians to join them in killing local Jews, and because the "Soviet people" thus became implicated in the murders, the Jews could not protest those killings. But the war did allow for some Jewish activism when Stalin, prompted by his need for foreign assistance and his exaggerated idea of Jewish influence in the West, tried to win overseas support from the United States and Britain by allowing the formation of the Jewish Anti-Fascist Committee. The Committee became the new central address of Russian Jewry, and swamped with catastrophic reports, it looked for ways to disseminate information about the tragedy.

The Revolt of the Revolutionary Jewish Writer

A mere decade younger than Babel and Kulbak, Vasily Grossman would never have become a Jewish writer had it not been for the Second World War.

> Never, before the war, had Victor thought about the fact that he was a Jew, that his mother was a Jew. Never had his mother spoken to him about it—neither during his childhood, nor during his years as a student. Never while he was at Moscow University had one student, professor or seminar-leader ever mentioned it.[47]

The dawning consciousness that Grossman attributes to physicist Victor Shtrum in his epic novel *Life and Fate* corresponds to what we know about the author's own life.[48] Born 1905 in Der Nister's native Berdichev, a city so preponderantly Jewish it was sometimes mocked as the Jewish capital of Russia, Grossman altogether ignored his Jewishness when he left to study science in Moscow in the 1920s and as he began to write in the 1930s. Whereas Yiddish writers were necessarily dependent on Jewish editors and audiences, the Russian Jew who came of age after the Revolution had no pressing incentive to take an interest in his Jewishness, and every professional reason not to. The repeated "never" in the quoted passage suggests what energy had gone into obscuring Shtrum's origins.

The war forced the Jewish subject into the open. The German massacre of Russian Jews began in Berdichev on September 15, 1941, claiming Grossman's mother among its thirty thousand local victims. Like Victor in the novel, Grossman felt that had it not been for the objections of his non-Jewish wife, he could have brought his mother to live with him in Moscow. Perhaps guilt steeled him to behave with extraordinary physical courage under fire as a war correspondent at Stalingrad and in researching the circumstances of her death. While the war still raged, Grossman joined Ilya Ehrenburg, the Soviet Union's most popular war correspondent, to collect documentary testimony about the destruction of the Jews on Russian soil for *The Black Book,* and he contributed its finest essay on the murder of the Jews of Berdichev.[49] In the aftermath of the war, in the very years that antisemitism was becoming state policy, Grossman began to work on *Life and Fate,* which described the Jewish genocide. He defied the specific objections of the literary commissar Alexander Fadeyev by making his fictional hero, Victor Shtrum, a Jew.

Life and Fate is Tolstoyan in scale, with almost two hundred short chapters touching on the lives of over 150 named characters. Drawing upon his own life and on his journalistic experience, Grossman interconnects the stories of ordinary soldiers and officers (including Soviet commissars and German officers), scientists, and loveworn women in a panoramic overview of the battle over Stalingrad and Russia. But whereas in *War and Peace* Tolstoy represents the victory over Napoleon as a triumph of the Russian spirit and in *Red Cavalry* Babel's narrator speaks for the Revolution, Grossman uses the war and murder of the Jews to uncover the parallel between the Nazi and Soviet regimes. Grossman may have been the first Russian writer to equate Communism with Fascism, compounding the force of his accusation by placing it against the background of Russia's Great Patriotic War.

Grossman's grand inquisitor, Gestapo officer Liss, tortures his Soviet prisoner, the conscientious Bolshevik Mostovskoy, by inviting him to recognize that they are really brothers under the skin:

> [We] learned many things from Stalin. To build Socialism in One Country, one must destroy the peasants' freedom to sow what they like and sell what they like. Stalin [. . .] liquidated millions of peasants. Our Hitler saw that the Jews were the enemy hindering the German national Socialist movement. And he liquidated millions of Jews. But Hitler's no mere student; he's a genius in his own right. And he's not one to be squeamish either. It was the Roehm purge that gave Stalin the idea for the purge of the party in 1937.[50]

Liss predicts that though the good Bolshevik may be momentarily appalled by Nazi treatment of Jews, "[tomorrow] you may make use of our experience yourselves." This prediction is fulfilled in the book's closing sections, when Stalin launches an antisemitic campaign, persuading even the exemplary man of conscience Victor Shtrum to sign a letter of denunciation he knows to be false. The comparison between Hitler and Stalin is clinched by their equally fanatical pursuit of the Jews.

Grossman's book has its artistic shortcomings. As Irving Howe noted, the mimetic approach would fall short when applied to "an event regarding which the phrase 'such as' cannot really be employed."[51] Grossman's sketch of Adolf Eichmann functioning as a Nazi strategist fails as verisimilitude not only because of the very different picture of the villain that emerged when he was later tried and convicted in Israel but because the fictional scene in which he divulges the Final Solution flattens into banal locution what was an infinitely more sinister and complicated process. The horror of the Nazi genocide is inadvertently trivialized when the narrator accompanies prisoners right into the gas chamber to see them become lifeless, "like dolls." But Grossman was trying to expose Stalin's lies, and to record his crimes he used the methods of realism in which he had been schooled.

Grossman injects his passion for liberty into several of his characters. The physicist Shtrum enjoys a scientific breakthrough following a frank political discussion;[52] a heroic Russian commander at Stalingrad realizes that "the only true and lasting meaning of the struggle for life lies in the individual, in his modest peculiarities and in his right to these peculiarities";[53] a woman's attack on the guard on her way to the gas chambers reveals "how clear, fierce and splendid human eyes can be when—even for a fraction of a second—they sense freedom."[54] These bids for freedom, though thwarted, express the relative openness the Soviet Jewish writer experienced when he was able at last to speak out as a Jew.

It was not surprising that Grossman fell subject to the same pressures as his characters. Had Stalin not died in 1953, the author eventually would have shared the fate of the leaders of the Jewish Anti-Fascist Committee, executed on Stalin's orders on August 12, 1952. Instead, Grossman became a victim of the new policy to kill literature while sparing the writer. In 1958 Boris Pasternak was threatened with exile were he to go to Stockholm to accept his Nobel Prize for Literature. Three years later the KGB came to Grossman's apartment to seize all the manuscripts of *Life and Fate*. Grossman was told by the watchdogs of Soviet literature that his work was so dangerous to the state that it would remain forbidden for another 250 years. Thanks to the help of admirers who supplied photocopying equipment, a smuggled microfilm of the epic work reached the West and was published in French translation in 1983, almost two decades after Grossman's death.

It was Shimon Markish, son of the murdered Soviet Yiddish poet Peretz Markish, who first predicted that the life of Grossman would be the stuff of myth. Markish said that by heeding God's charge to Moses—"You shall not lie one to another" (Leviticus 19:11)—Grossman had become the truth-telling Russian Jewish writer in the motherland of doublespeak. Grossman went further than his fellow dissident Aleksandr Solzhenitsyn in exposing not only the corruption of Marxism-Leninism but also the xenophobic "spirit of Russia" that had helped to seal the fate of its Jews.[55] And so we come full circle, from Babel, who thought the Jew could best attest to the Russian Revolution, to Grossman, who thought the Jew could best attest to its demise. Babel invents a uniquely contradictory modernist prose for the moral ambiguity of his situation. Grossman turns clumsy and cumbersome Soviet realism against its inventors to draw clear distinctions between good and evil.

COMMUNISM WAS A VENDETTA of intellectuals who seized control of a state in the name of ideas and used ideas to maintain their control over it. Since it was based on a theoretical misdiagnosis of the human condition, Communism needed writers to maintain the fiction of its progress. Where mendacity maintains those in power, truth is treason. This syllogism was to turn Isaac Babel into a "master of the art of silence" and, implicitly, into an enemy of the state.

The confiscated archives of some 1,500 liquidated Russian writers contain the most macabre literature Russia ever produced. The executioners, needing retroactive legitimacy for their accusations, demanded that their victims invent the crimes that would justify the sentence being imposed on them. It is hard to imagine the "torments of creativity" that Isaac Babel endured in the NKVD investigator's office.[56] In order to satisfy the investigators, not only was Babel forced to admit that he had been involved in a Trotskyist conspiracy and to describe his coconspirators, but he had also to satisfy his torturers' idea of a *genuine* confession. The man who had invented an alter self in so many of his stories now had to implicate himself through the same techniques of narration that he had perfected in his fiction:

> *Red Cavalry* was only an excuse for me to express my appalling mood and had nothing to do with what was happening in the Soviet Union. Hence the emphasis on all the cruelty and absurdities of the Civil War, the artificial introduction of an erotic element and the depiction of only the most outrageous and sensational episodes. Hence the complete failure to describe the role of the party in pulling together the then still insufficiently proletarian-minded Cossacks to form regular forces and constitute the impressive unit of the Red Army that the First Cavalry army became.[57]

Babel had told an audience in 1937, "The only cause I have for satisfaction is that I don't have to take back anything I've written."[58] But he did disavow this confession that was extracted from him though torture. His execution, at 1:30 A.M. on January 27, 1940, would have been carried out irrespective of confession or retraction.

4

BETWEEN THE WARS

The Singer Family of Warsaw

The redemption is at hand and I am at its center.

MELEKH RAVITCH, WARSAW, 1921[1]

He hesitated for a moment and then said, in Polish:
"The Messiah will come soon."
Asa Heshel looked at him in astonishment. "What
do you mean?"
"Death is the Messiah. That's the real truth."

ISAAC BASHEVIS SINGER, *The Family Moskat*,[2]
ABOUT WARSAW 1939

T HE REVOLUTIONARY MOMENT FELL very differently upon the
teenaged Isaac Singer, who was still wearing the traditional caftan
and earlocks in a Polish town south of Lublin:

The few newspapers that arrived in Bilgoraj, late by a few days
or weeks, brought big news. Everything, as it then seemed to me,
was happening at once. In the Ukraine there were pogroms against
the Jews, yet a Jew there became minister. There was peace, England issued the Balfour Declaration, and Poland became a sovereign state. The dates were separated somewhat, but not by much,
and it was all confused in my mind. Every day brought the impossible. Who ever heard of a Jew becoming minister? And when did
it happen that a second Jew, Trotsky, should lead the Russian
Army? And who ever thought that Poland would rise from the
dead? And who could have imagined that a country like England

would take seriously the dreams of a bunch of Zionists and promise Jews a land? In our studyhouse a lame Jew with a fire-red beard and bushy eyebrows, who used to sit all day over Maimonides or reciting the *Zohar*, banged his hand on the table and declared that Trotsky was the messiah. Trotsky's name was Leo, Leo means lion, and lion is that lion of the forest of Ilai, the lion of redemption.[3]

No doubt exaggerating his bewilderment, Singer renders the years 1917–20 as a clash of contrarieties so astonishing that it seemed to augur the messianic age. Events that flow from one another, like the election of Yakov Ze'ev Wolf Latsky-Bertholdi (Wolf Latsky) as Minister of Jewish Affairs in the briefly constituted Ukrainian Central Council, are conflated with pogroms that erupted as part of the Ukrainian–Soviet civil war.[4] Britain's issuance of the Balfour Declaration comes as a bolt out of the blue, rather than as the result of two decades of Zionist effort and persuasion. Whereas Babel's Lyutov reads to the Cossacks "like a deaf man triumphant," watching out for "anything crooked in the Lenin straightness,"[5] Singer gives us a Polish kabbalist who reads history as a text written by God.

Warsaw, the Heart of Polish Jewry

"And who ever thought that Poland would rise from the dead?" Buried in Singer's confused catalogue, this question actually informs all the rest. The reemergence of Poland from World War I as an independent republic had a contradictory effect on its more than three million Jews. In no other country of their prolonged exile, not even in Babylon or Spain, had Jews grown so numerous or sunk such deep communal and cultural roots. Consequently, when Poland regained its national sovereignty in 1919 and then defeated the Russian army in the battle known as "the miracle of Vistula," many expected the country to become a home for "two nations nursed by the same suffering, *Dwa narodny tym samym karmione cierpieniem.*"[6] But Polish soldiers returning from the front attacked the Jews with unprecedented brutality, as if proving their prowess against one enemy they knew they could conquer. Though the new Polish government was obliged by the Treaty of Versailles to grant cultural rights to its minorities, the patriotic spirit turned against the "enemy within." Formally democratic, Poland was actually ruled after 1926 in semiautocratic fashion by its military hero Marshal Józef Pilsudski, and in similarly contradictory fashion, the Jews who were granted formal citizenship faced officially sanctioned discrimination.

The positive model of Polish independence and the negative effects of its discriminatory practices evoked wildly varied Jewish responses. Some Zionists argued for greater autonomy within the Polish Parliament and for cooperation with other minorities in ensuring Polish democracy. The Socialists stipulated that this autonomy rest on the teachings of Karl Marx, and the religious Zionists wanted it based on the teachings of Torah. Revisionists stressed the need for mass emigration and for organized Jewish self-defense. The Jewish Socialist Bund wanted a secular Yiddish-speaking Jewry to unite along class lines with the Polish proletariat. "Folkists" championed a local secular Jewish culture with Yiddish as its official language. A huge proportion of religious Jews intended to continue making political accommodations to Christian Poland while following their own religious discipline. Polonizing Jews tried to launder their distinctiveness, often through the universities and the professions. Jewish Communists wanted to see the Russian Revolution extend its transforming zeal to Poland and the Jews.

But whereas in the United States the democratic process persuaded immigrants that by learning English their children could become full-fledged Americans and in Russia Bolshevism worked to eradicate religion and ethnic loyalties, acculturation in Poland was neither as enticing nor as coercive. With less incentive to replace their mother tongue by Polish, most Jews continued to speak their own language. Almost 80 percent of Poland's Jews declared Yiddish their mother tongue in the census of 1931, and most likely this also applied to most of the 7.8 percent of the population who followed the Zionist directive to declare Hebrew as their mother tongue.[7] With its three hundred thousand Jews (a third of the population), Warsaw became for one heady moment the capital of Yiddish, a cultural free zone—or else a ghetto in the making.

Bewitched by Warsaw, the twenty-seven-year-old poet Melekh Ravitch (pen name of Zekhariah Bergner), former soldier of the Austrian army, quit his steady bank job in Vienna in 1921 to come to live in its penury:

Warsaw. The word possessed me like a dybbuk. I chanted it day and night—a dark and mighty word, simply "Var-she" in Yiddish, but in Polish three black, heavy syllables fraught with destiny and drama and perhaps also with tragedy—"War-sza-wa—"[8]

The tension between his native Yiddish and the heavier portent of Polish, the language he loved second best, was for Ravitch part of the city's attraction. He found Warsaw jammed with refugees who had fled the Bolsheviks, the Germans, and the marauding Polish soldiers. The courtyards with their iron gates that locked at night seemed like fortresses protecting their hundreds upon hundreds of Jewish residents. Warsaw may have lacked the glamour of the Habsburg capital, whose German–Jewish symbiosis had nurtured Schnitzler and von Hofmannsthal, Mahler and Freud, but Ravitch never voiced a moment's regret over moving from the City of Light to the "herring barrel" of Warsaw. Joined by Peretz Markish (from the Ukraine), Uri Zvi Greenberg (also a former Austrian recruit), and the local writer Israel Joshua Singer in a literary "gang" they called "Khaliastre," Ravitch felt he had incomparably improved his cultural standard of living.[9]

Three decades earlier, when I. L. Peretz had come to Warsaw from the smaller Polish city of Zamoscz, he had turned his modest flat into a cultural hub. Many of the institutions that Peretz helped to found survived his death in 1915. A network of modern Jewish schools in Yiddish, Hebrew, and Polish provided not just a combined Jewish and secular education for Jewish children but employment for a large cadre of Jewish writers and intellectuals. These were teachers with a mission, pioneering new textbooks and pedagogical methods to convey their competing visions of the Jewish future. Jewish newspapers and magazines in Yiddish, Hebrew, and Polish sprouted like mushrooms after rain (a potent simile in a land that grew them for export). By the early 1930s, Warsaw boasted eleven Yiddish dailies, in addition to magazines like *Literarishe bleter* [Literary Gazette], the finest weekly ever to appear in Yiddish. Of the 1,500 Yiddish newspapers, periodicals, and miscellanies published in Poland between the two world wars, 681 were published in Warsaw.[10] There was also Yiddish theater and cabaret and a Yiddish film industry, all sustained, needless to say, without government assistance.

The most important of Peretz's legacies, the Association of Jewish

Writers and Journalists, opened its doors at 13 Tlomackie Street in September 1918. As if symbolizing the linked spheres of modern Jewry, the literary headquarters stood next door to Warsaw's largest synagogue, inviting everyone bent on a literary career to argue over modern texts just as their religious counterparts did over the traditional tomes. In its restaurant, bar, and reading room, literary generations collided, visitors from abroad were given a public forum, jobs were advertised, and professional information was traded. According to Isaac Bashevis Singer, this "bourse of Yiddish literature in Poland" was also where young writers conducted most of their romantic liaisons.[11] In line with its growing self-confidence, the *belles lettres* section of Tlomackie 13 appealed to the International PEN Association in London to form an independent Yiddish PEN Club within Poland, arguing that national language is not synonymous with national territory. The accreditation of the Yiddish PEN Club in 1926 was responsible for extending the criterion of membership to include *all* national minorities with independent literatures, paving the way for Hebrew writers to form their own unit of PEN, with its center in Tel Aviv, in 1929.[12]

Without a Jewish government or university to support their national culture, Tlomackie 13 became the dominant cultural institution for Jews living in Warsaw between the world wars. Ravitch, who served as secretary, organized a lecture bureau that sent Yiddish writers out to smaller Jewish communities to give talks on topics like "Expressionism or Impressionism?"; "The Trial of the Jewish Woman"; and "Is Sholem Asch Really the Greatest Yiddish Writer?"[13] Sometimes political clashes erupted during these events, such as at the February 1930 lecture by the anti-Bolshevik Nahum Steinberg on "Jew and Human Being," which was interrupted by young Communists tossing rotten eggs and smashing chairs.[14]

The pervasive youth culture of postwar Poland encouraged enterprising publishers to translate everything modern and novel into Yiddish, from Marx to Marinetti, Charles-Paul de Kock to Georg Brandes. Isaac Bashevis Singer earned a living in his early years by translating Erich Maria Remarque, Knut Hamsun, Gabriele D'Annunzio, and Stefan Zweig; in 1930 he translated Thomas Mann's *The Magic Mountain*.[15] His sister Esther Kreitman translated, also for Warsaw publishers, George Bernard Shaw's *The Intelligent Woman's Guide to Socialism and Capitalism* and Charles Dickens's *A Christmas Carol*.[16]

But simultaneously, and no less vigorously, Jews were also merging into the dominant culture, flaunting their liberation from Jewish concerns. The Polish poet Antoni Slonimski was known to be the baptized grandson of Haim Zelig Slonimski, the Jewish Enlightener who had directed the rabbinical college of Zhitomir from 1862. In addition to Slonimski, the 1918 Polish literary group *Skamander* (named for the river in the *Iliad* where Troy had stood) included the Jewish poet Julian Tuwim, and Jews also formed the majority of its successor group of futurists around *Wiadomości Literackie* [The Literary Monthly]. As part of their attempt to distance themselves from the "Jewish" Jews of Poland, the writers of *Wiadomości Literackie* attacked Jewish separatism more fiercely than they did the Endeks, the political right-wingers who introduced anti-Jewish boycotts and actively promoted antisemitism.[17] But this did not prevent them from being perceived as Jews: in 1931, when the editors were arrested for sedition, the Polish press reported (falsely) that material evidence had been found among these "Jews" of an international Comintern conspiracy, along with huge sums of foreign money.[18]

Thus, Warsaw as a cultural center attracted not only Yiddishists like Ravitch but Jews like Isaac Deutscher, who escaped his rabbinic destiny in favor of Marxism. Deutscher considered Jews the "natural pioneers" of the Communist mission, since who else "was as well qualified to preach the international society of equals as were the Jews free from all Jewish and non-Jewish orthodoxy and nationalism?"[19] Deutscher threw himself into literature and tried to prove himself an internationalist by adopting the language of highly nationalist Poland. Inevitably, the spreading phenomenon of what Deutscher later called "the non-Jewish Jew" compounded the threat to the Jewish Jews: on one hand it raised the expectation that they would cease to be Jews, and on the other hand it fomented the perception among Poles that Jews were inherently Communists.[20]

To describe the fluid Jewish culture of interwar Poland and especially Warsaw, the literary historian Chone Shmeruk spoke not of bilingualism but of a linguistic polysystem, meaning that Polish, Yiddish, and Hebrew, sometimes used interchangeably by the same people, each supported a cultural network with its own institutions. He cites as evidence of multilingualism the 1931 circulation figure of one hundred thousand for the local Polish Jewish press.[21] *Nasz Przegląd* [Our Review], the Polish Jewish daily newspaper that Isaac Deutscher joined as a proofreader (about the time that Bashevis did proofreading for the Yiddish *Literarishe bleter*), was staffed and run by Jews who knew Yiddish much better than Polish, and it was read by a predominantly middle-class Jewish public, much of which still spoke Yiddish or had begun to use Hebrew.[22]

The Remarkable Singer Family

Isaac Bashevis Singer may well have been the most perfectly situated writer in this roiling Polish Jewish literary community. The son of a rabbi, he had absorbed Jewish teachings before he was in a position to question them. The son of a rabbi's daughter, he had spent the hunger years 1917–21 in his mother's native town of Bilgoraj, steeped in the customs and legends of an ancient community that inspired some of his finest work. Owing to his father Pinchos Mendel's refusal to learn Russian and to qualify as an official rabbi at a time when he lived under tsarist jurisdiction, the family subsisted somewhat precariously, first in the small town Leoncin (where Isaac was born in 1904), then in the larger town of Radzymin, and after 1911 in the Warsaw courtyard of 10 Krochmalna Street, where, as neighborhood rabbi, Pinchos Mendel led a prayer quorum and adjudicated every kind of ritual question and personal dispute. The father's ambition to become a published writer of commentaries must be related to some extent to the fact that three of his four children turned their hand to fiction: the eldest, Hinde Esther (1891–1954); the oldest son, Israel Joshua (1893–1944); and Isaac Bashevis (1904–1991), who adopted his mother's name, Bashevis (Batsheva's) to distinguish himself from his highly successful brother. The youngest brother, Moyshe, destined to become a rabbi, was the only one who remained in Poland long enough to fall into German hands.

The Singer family was a study in opposites. Sweet and trusting, Pinchos Mendel was so deeply immersed in kabbalistic mysteries that he prayed he might some day be granted the grace of a miracle. His unworldliness distressed and often angered his wife Batsheva, a quintessential rationalist who energetically defended her faith in God the Creator but remained otherwise skeptical and pragmatic. Hinde felt herself unloved by her rational mother and ignored by her preoccupied father. Israel Joshua was a rebellious youngster who balked at both his family's assumption that he would someday pursue a rabbinic career and the tsarist government's assumption that he ought to serve in what was to be the First World War. By his teens he began bringing radical atheistic ideas into the home, provoking open quarrels with both parents. Although revolutionary fervor claimed him briefly when he moved to Kiev in 1918 and then to Moscow in 1920, by 1921 he was back in Warsaw, inoculating his younger brother Isaac against Communism and all other revolutionary enthusiasms.

Isaac grew up with something like two sets of warring parents—not only the absorbed Batsheva and Pinchos Mendel but also Hinde and Israel Joshua, who had developed a loving rivalry of their own. All four were mavericks with powerful personalities, but while the older pair reined in their passions through Jewish self-discipline, the younger vented theirs in writing. By the time Isaac came of age, his older brother had already emerged as a bright star of the literary avant-garde: in 1924, Israel Joshua became one of the founding editors of the *Literarishe bleter*, and at that same time, he was discovered and hired by Abraham Cahan as European correspondent for the New York *Forverts*. He helped to get Isaac his first job in literature, as proofreader on the Warsaw weekly, and in 1935, after his own emigration to America, he secured for his brother an entry visa to the United States.

The conflict between tradition and enlightenment had already been raging in Poland for a century when it erupted as a domestic clash within this one extraordinary household. The dynamics of the family determined the Manichaean nature of the struggle. One of Bashevis's biographers traces the children's rebellion to Israel Joshua's realization that "father and mother would have been a suitable couple were mother the father and father the mother."[23] But the moral integrity of their parents' way of life equally spoiled the children for any competing enthusiasm. Though the religiously raised Singers became writers of modern fiction and led a more or less secular way of life, they found the proposed alternatives to orthodoxy much more repellent than the spiritual intensity of their parents' home. In their psychological and moral scheme, there was no going back, and no going forward.

The three Singer siblings were exceptionally fortunate in being able to leave their native soil for English-speaking lands. Of several hundred Yiddish writers in Warsaw when the Germans invaded in 1939, some 150 are thought to have escaped to the Soviet zone, most of them to perish when it, too, was overrun. And of the estimated 190 Yiddish writers who were walled up inside the Warsaw ghetto, only four remained alive.

The Singers had grown up in a household so religiously intense and so morally challenging that they could never trust their flight from it. Almost simultaneously, between 1932 and 1935, they evinced their conflict in the best books they were ever to write: a historical novel about the rise and fall of the Jews in Poland, the fictional autobiography of a modern woman who tries to escape the centripetal force of her formative past, and a pseudo chronicle about messianic deception. If they escaped the physical fate of Polish Jewry, they joined it on the page. One hardly knows which is the greater marvel, the differences in artistic strategy among the three novels, as though each had deliberately diverged from the others, or the way each reaches a version of the same emotional and philosophic end.

Israel Joshua Singer: The Brothers Ashkenazi

Israel Joshua (or I. J., as he signed himself) was the first of the siblings to become a professional writer, after what may be the briefest flirtation with literary modernism on record. After having gotten his literary start in Kiev, just after the Bolshevik Revolution, in the magazine *Eygns* [Our Possession], he was conscripted by the poets Markish, Greenberg, and Ravitch to participate in their journal, *Khaliastre*, but as the least enthusiastic member of this circle, he was the first to repudiate its ostentatious radicalism. Alone among his siblings, and rare among his colleagues, he entered upon a stable, happy marriage and raised two beloved sons. Artistically, too, he turned conservative, censuring the sensationalist trends in journalism and expressionist trends in art. In one of his earliest works, dedicated to those for whom "earth is not easy [*vemen erd iz nisht gring*]," a corpse rises from behind the fence—the designated burial place for Jewish suicides and renegades—and leads the community of Jewish cripples forth into the world preaching the erasure of boundaries, which were so precious to expressionism.[24] It was just this sort of experimental form and seditious faith that I. J. Singer repudiated as a mature writer of fiction. In one of his stories, a Jewish "townie" who has seduced a Jewish country girl is compelled by her village community not just to honor but to celebrate his wedding and his paternity. Like the Jewish villagers, the author forces out into the open the couple's erotic secret, destroying the potential for sentimental romance in favor of responsible consequences. In another story, an assimilated Warsaw antiques dealer subjects his pets and his acquaintances to a sadistic and tyrannical regime, until he finally goads his frenzied tomcat into ripping out his eye. Here the suppressed violence implicit in assimilation erupts and takes its vengeance on the self-rejecting Jew.[25]

In the spring of 1928, Singer briefly forswore the writing of fiction, declaring that under prevailing conditions Yiddish could no longer nurture the creative imagination, that "it was impossible to write Yiddish now."[26] Whether this impulsive act was prompted by disappointment in his own first novel, *Shtol un Eisen* [Steel and Iron, 1927], or by a related crisis of faith in his language or in literature, Singer injected this despair into his subsequent work. A remarkably intense novel, *Yoshe Kalb* [Yoshe Calf, 1932] shows the irreparable damage that Hasidism does to a sensitive young man who feels he must extinguish his personality to expiate for the sin of having yielded to an illicit passion. The separation of the novel into two parts corresponds to the hero's fatal inability to live either within the bonds of his religious community or as a voluntary pariah, a penitent outsider.

In 1933, the same fateful year that Hitler came to power, Singer's younger son died of a sudden illness, and the family set out for America. All his private grief and fears for the world he left behind coalesced in the novel that he began serializing in the *Forverts* in December 1934, nine months after arriving in America.[27] Despite his earlier pessimism about the prospects of Jewish literature, *The Brothers Ashkenazi* is a book of enormous ambition, the kind of panoramic study that no Yiddish writer had attempted before World War I. Lacking the indigenous literary traditions and the necessary vocabulary for a work of epic scope and accustomed to seeing themselves as part of a powerless minority incapable of initiating political change, the best Yiddish writers had hitherto concentrated on the "little man" of the small Jewish market town rather than on the larger (predominantly Gentile) arena. Only after they themselves had set out for America did Yiddish writers begin to construct large-scale historical and panoramic novels that placed the Jewish story within its European setting. For example, Joseph Opatoshu's *In Polish Woods* interweaves the saga of the troubled Hasidic dynasty of Kotsk with Poland's failed 1863 uprising against Russian domination, and Sholem Asch in *Three Cities* follows the rise of the revolutionary movement from St. Petersburg, through Warsaw, and finally, in 1917, to Moscow. But while Opatoshu and Asch used the novel to confirm the integration of Jews into European history, I. J. Singer demonstrates its failure. Through a twist of creative logic, he expressed his regained confidence in Yiddish literature by repudiating his trust in Poland and Europe.

A book about rivalries, *The Brothers Ashkenazi* itself appears to be an act of literary rivalry with earlier representations of the Jew in Polish literature. At the end of the nineteenth century, Wladyslaw Reymont, the first Polish winner of the Nobel Prize for Literature, had published a sprawling novel, *The Promised Land*, that deplored the industrial growth of Lodz, "the Manchester of Poland."[28] The involuntary villains of Reymont's book are the Jews, who in trying to turn Poland into their "promised land" corrupt the country for its (Christian) Polish citizens. When Reymont's hero, Charles Boroviecki, leaves his father's estate to become a chemist in the Lodz textile industry, he is depraved by the city's greed and lust. Germans and Jews have unleashed in Lodz a competitive frenzy that swallows up good Poles against their will: "You have the delusion of doing business with civilized people of central Europe. But Lodz is a forest, a jungle—in which, if you have good strong claws, you may fearlessly go ahead and do away with your neighbours; else they will fall upon you, suck you dry, and then toss your carcass away."[29] Reymont the writer is a little like his hero in the way he battens on the frontier spirit of Lodz's textile industry while not really trusting the mix of ethnic groups that fuels the city's growth. Meanwhile, the prophet of false progress is a Jew who loves Lodz to distraction, ignoring its terrible, never-ceasing, doomed struggle, "a struggle that carried off more worn-out victims every year than the most frightful epidemic would have done."[30] The fact that this particular spokesman for capitalism is as poor as some of its other victims only reinforces the treachery of his belief in capitalist expansion.

As though parrying some of Reymont's charges, Singer tells the story of Lodz industry from its inception, when Germans and Jews were *invited* to develop the weaving industry that rural Poland never could have started on its own. Poles hardly figure at all in the Yiddish novel, except as the beneficiaries of other peoples' profit. The Jewish novelist does not share Reymont's nostalgia for the hardier morals of an agricultural society, nor does he show nostalgia for any equivalent golden age of Jewish tradition. The doomed struggle of Singer's novel is not with capitalism or modern industry, though these certainly figure in its images of corruption, but with the Jews' vain effort to survive on an increasingly predatory continent.

Each of the three books that constitute *The Brothers Ashkenazi* opens with an "invasion" of immigrants to Lodz, the city that lies southwest of Warsaw and became second to it in Jewish population. The arrival of German weavers before the mid–nineteenth century sparks the rivalry with local Jews. Competition between the two minorities is good for the textile industry, but the Germans exploit their Christian advantage by asking the tsarist ruler for sanctions against the Jewish weavers. The Germans bring their own brand of antisemitism along with their looms. "When a Jew occasionally stumbled into German Wilki [the German settlement], flaxen-haired youths pelted him with rocks and set their dogs on him with the ancient cry 'Hep, hep Jude.'"[31] The Hep Hep Riots, as they were known, had begun in Bavaria in 1819 to intimidate the Jews and discourage the government from granting them full citizenship.[32] The importation of this slogan into Poland signaled the beginnings of a more virulent antisemitism. Defying strict Marxist analysis, Singer associates the rise of capitalism and antisemitism not only with the concentration of resources in the hands of the owners of industry but with German *drang noch osten*, the national appetite for more land in the east.

A very different kind of invasion opens Book Two. The assassination in Russia of Tsar Alexander II in 1881, followed by pogroms and anti-Jewish decrees in that country, floods the traditional community of Lodz with thousands of Jewish refugees from the Russian heartland, the so-called Litvaks (Lithuanians) with their "non-Jewish ways." Some of these Russian Jews are the conduit of socialist ideology: they try to replace the interethnic rivalries of Lodz by organized class warfare. Their cry "Long live the brotherhood of workers!" splits the Lodz community horizontally, the masses against the bosses.[33] The several agitators in the novel enjoy a temporary triumph when the Revolution overthrows the monarchy, and the novel moves briefly into Russian territory to savor the moment. As the only group without political protection, Jews are keen to develop competing models of political power, but these calculations backfire: the new forces turn against them upon coming to power.

Book Three opens with a grimmer reprise of Book One. The Germans emigrated originally "because in Germany there were many people and not enough bread. In Poland there was bread but no goods."[34] The Germans invade Poland in Book Three "because in Germany there were many people but not enough land. In neighboring Russia, there was plenty of land, fields, cattle, wood, minerals. So the German rulers took men from their fields, factories, workshops, and schools; set local women in their place; and sent the men into the neighbor's land to burn, pillage, and conquer. They began with Poland, which was across the border."[35] The impulse that once spurred a peaceful immigration has become the excuse for armed aggression. In no other respect does Singer deviate so sharply from the accepted historical record as in his depiction of the German invaders of World War I. As it happened, the relatively benign experience of the Jews under this earlier German occupation was one of the reasons they so badly misjudged German intentions in World War II. But the Germans of Singer's novel are already proto-Nazis in the ruthlessness of their conquest and in their sadistic antisemitism; the atmosphere of the 1930s permeates his descriptions of the 1910s.

Competition is the book's main conductor of energy, including among the Jews. No sooner do a few dozen tailors gain permission to settle in Lodz than they get into a dispute with Jews in the smaller neighboring town. Quarrels over religious jurisdiction predate economic rivalries with the German weavers, and once steam-generated factories employing hundreds of workers replace the home industry of the weavers, Jewish Social ists find it easier to threaten Jewish owners with strikes than the Christian capitalists who seem beyond their reach. Jewish family life is equally contentious. Abraham Hersh Ashkenazi, whose family name casts the story as a metaphor for Polish Jewry, is the responsible head of the Lodz Jewish community as well as a prosperous businessman. The birth of his twin boys (in the mid-1860s) ought to have been the occasion for great joy. But just before Passover, a holiday he is accustomed to celebrating in Hasidic fashion in the male court around his beloved Rebbe of Warka, Ashkenazi refuses his wife's entreaties to stay home for the impending birth. In revenge, instead of naming the eldest boy Simcha Bunem for the Przysucha Rebbe as her husband instructed, she splits the honors with her rabbinic grandfather Jacob Meir and divides the two names in half. Their names "ring false" to the enraged husband, thenceforth poisoning his relations with both Simcha Meir and Jacob Bunem. Overlooked in critical literature about this novel is the importance that Singer ascribes to women's dissatisfaction in the disposition of Jewish affairs. In the four Jewish homes to which this book introduces us, two rich and two poor, all the wives are fatally estranged from their husbands, and the novel supports their frustrated protest against the authority that undervalues them.

Fraternal rivalry between the Ashkenazi brothers represents the elemental characterological dimension of human conflict. Simcha Meir is the jealous runt who tries to compensate for his early deprivation and biological disadvantages through the accumulation of power. As a young husband he contrives to take control of his father-in-law's textile mill, and he discards the vestiges of "Jewish solidarity" that the older man felt for his workers. Transmogrified into "Max," he replaces his father as manager of the city's first steam-generated factory, developing new products, opening new markets, and contriving to buy out the owners. The handsome and charming Jacob Bunem is his brother's opposite. Born with the natural appeal of a front-office man, he attains through rich marriages the positions for which his brother has to fight. Max schemes to marry his brother's childhood sweetheart, Dinele, and succeeds in doing so, much against her will. Years later, their daughter Gertrud falls in love with her uncle, and Jacob Bunem, now Yakub, takes his niece for his third wife.

Intergenerational conflict is compounded by conflicts within the generations. Where Sholem Aleichem conceived a negotiated transition between fathers and daughters, Singer depicts a fatal breach between fathers and sons. To secure the faith of his brilliant son Simcha Meir, Hersh Ashkenazi takes his rebbe's advice and, forgoing a prestigious *yeshiva*, sends him to the local scholar, Reb Nuske, who is as uncompromising for God as others are for gain: "Within his long, bony, skull there was no room for anything but the Torah, the thousands of commentaries and annotations he had committed to memory and in which he immersed himself. He knew that there was only right or wrong, no in between, for to be partly wrong was to be totally wrong."[36] Reb Nuske's zealotry alienates even his own family, much as Hersh Ashkenzi did by going to the Hasidic court when his wife was about to give birth. In the harsh *cheder,* Simche Meir becomes the rival of Reb Nuske's son Nissan, and once Nissan rebels against his father to become a Marxist revolutionary, the two boys compete on the stage of history. Whereas the material and spiritual values of their parents complemented one another in a Jewish society of merchants and scholars, Max and Nissan become fanatical rivals, embracing the extremes of greed and egalitarianism.

THE YOUNG JEWS OF Singer's saga burst forth onto the stage of history with talents honed by their highly disciplined civilization. It is as through Max, Yakub, and Nissan are competing over who has the most to offer their society—industry, charm, or moral improvement. Max Ashke-nazi, the book's principal source of energy, excites grudging respect for his adaptive brilliance. In one classic sequence (based on a passage in Rey-mont), he spots a woman on the street wearing a dress of vivid red, and within the space of two pages he negotiates to buy the garment from its startled owner, goes to Germany to find a chemist who can copy the for-mula, and dazzles the market with his product. With similar dash, he re-bounds from the blows of the Germans and the Russians. Even after his incarceration under the Bolsheviks, he returns to Lodz to rebuild his busi-ness for the third time, and is hailed "the King of Lodz." Max is the effec-tual version of Menakhem-Mendl, but Singer lacks Sholem Aleichem's faith in the value of resiliency. After the German occupation, the Polish nationalists reconfiscate Max's property and drive him to ruin, along with their economy. Max dies on the final page, reaching vainly for the ser-vants' bell.

Yakub fares no better. The kindlier of the twins, he maintains his Jew-ish demeanor as long as his father is alive. He slaps Max across the face when he contrives to oust their father as factory manager. Much later in the novel, Yakub travels to Russia to rescue Max from prison, and "moving so confidently that the guards didn't even challenge him," he negotiates their safe conduct to Poland through a landscape of utter chaos.[37] But at the last station before Lodz, they come up against the Poles, who have only one way of celebrating their newfound sovereignty. A Polish officer orders the two brothers to dance for his amusement. Max obeys him (as he would not obey his father). Jacob slaps the officer just as he once slapped Max—and is shot to death.

> "Why did you do it?" Max screamed, struggling to raise him from the ground. . . . A trickle of warm blood ran down Yakub's face and into his dyed beard.
>
> Jesus looked down from the wooden walls of the station where he hung nailed to the cross.[38]

Singer does not reward Yakub for playing the romantic hero. The blood in the dandified beard exposes the aging Jew's pathetic camouflage. The spotlight on Jesus is an even more ironic touch. Just when Singer was be-ginning this novel, Józef Pilsudski, Poland's strong man, had awarded a medal to Sholem Asch that seemed to acknowledge him as evangelist of Judaeo–Christian and Judaeo–Polish reunion. Asch thought he recognized in Polish and Jewish nationalisms a common yearning for redemption, and he particularly enjoyed portraying Jesus as the exemplary Jewish martyr; in an early story of his that had gained notoriety, Jesus descends from the cross to join his brother Jews in their martyrdom.[39] Thumbing his nose at Asch's sentimentality, Singer leaves Jesus fixed woodenly on the wall.

No one in Singer's book is spared. Nissan is in Moscow when the Revolution overthrows the tsar, and he can hardly contain his joy as he attends the first Council of Soviets. "How long had he waited for the first meeting of the freely elected deputies of a liberated Russia! How long had he struggled to achieve it, how much confinement and torture had he endured!"[40] But he is kicked out by the Bolsheviks with curses and guns. Felix Feldblum is a minor character who tries to prove himself a Polish patriot, first by joining the Polish Socialist Party and later in Polish uniform during the war. After the Poles set fire to the Jewish section of Lodz in the most brutal pogrom in the city's history, Feldblum's blue uniform appears at the mass funeral in the black sea of Jewish mourners. No matter how much creative energy the Jews manifest, political thugs will appropriate whatever they build for themselves and pervert whatever they try to accomplish for others.

DESPITE ITS IMPORTANT animation of Jewish life in Poland, *The Brothers Ashkenazi* suffers from structural and stylistic defects. Singer drives the book the way Max whips up his ambition, often ignoring refinements while tearing toward his narrative goal. He invests so much energy in this story of Jewish accomplishment that one is amazed at the remorselessness with which he snips all the tendrils of plot. Singer offers historical evidence for his gloom: the political forces of Europe are trapping the Jews— the Germans from the West, the Russians through Bolshevism, the Poles with their xenophobic nationalism—and Reymont's misconception of Jews has become the regnant ideology, guaranteeing the collapse of Poland along with its Jews. But it is finally Singer himself who heightens this sense of tragedy through the narrative device of alternatives that cancel each other out. His pessimism about posttraditional society determines his historical vision, not the other way around. There is no hint in the novel of the mass emigration to America or of the Zionist impulse that figured in actual history. The crowd returning from Max's funeral knows that "everything we built here we built on sand," because the *novel* opens with the vista of sand on which the Jews determine to build their city. By concentrating Jewish history into the story of Lodz, and by sealing its borders in a literary sense, the novel lets the weight of that last phrase fall on the "everything" that Jews accomplished before the Germans and Poles and Russians crushed their efforts.

Esther Kreitman: The Devils' Dance

Although she was the first of her siblings to begin writing, Hinde Esther (Singer) Kreitman felt thwarted in her career by a lack of encouragement. In a stark autobiographical story, written from the perspective of the fetus inside the womb, she describes "thrashing, heaving, often punching her mother in the side" in an effort to get out into the world.[41] All in vain. She had not only to wait out the full nine months but also to then experience the humiliation of being fobbed off to a wet nurse as an unwanted girl. Kreitman's fictional autobiography describes a similarly useless rebellion in adolescence, ending with an arranged marriage and (as she experienced it) physical banishment from the family. Its heroine is urged by her mother to throw away all her writings lest the officials accuse her of revolutionary sedition.

Hinde Esther was, in fact, married off to the son of a diamond dealer, and her removal from Warsaw in 1912, first to Antwerp, then to London, was both the start of and a severe setback to her literary prospects. Though she only began to publish fiction after her marriage (as signified by the use of her married name), in quitting the city she also left the most vibrant center of Yiddish publishing. Had she remained in Warsaw, she might have joined Kadya Molodovsky, Reyzl Zhikhlinski, Rokhl Korn, and Rokhl Auerbach—the small but significant cadre of women that began publishing locally after the First World War—in literary comradery. Though female poets and writers were still a rarity in Yiddish and Hebrew, women were among the leading liberal voices in Polish literature—hence, greatly beloved by Jewish readers—and their work confirmed the woman's particular ability to sympathize with children and the disadvantaged. Molodovsky, who knew the Jewish sources and spent many years teaching in Jewish schools, turned poetry into a conduit through which the biblical matriarchs could express their fellow feeling for every kind of sorrow:

> For poor brides who were servant girls,
> Mother Sarah draws forth from dim barrels
> Pitchers of sparkling wine. . . .
> For high-born brides now poor,
> Who blush to bring patched underclothes
> Before their mothers-in-law,
> Mother Rachel leads camels
> Laden with white linen.[42]

Rokhl Korn wrote as a daughter of the Polish countryside:

> I'm soaked through with you, like earth with spring rain,
> And my fairest day hangs
> On the pulse of your quietest word,
> Like a bee near the branch of a flowering linden.[43]

The women of this generation, including both poets quoted here, were as socially and politically engaged as the men, but in taking women's experience as the special province of their writing, they often favored the solitary, isolating emotions, choosing poetry over prose, and the domestic and erotic veins of language. In the same way that immigrants penetrated the economies of their adopted countries by supplying what it lacked, women writers discovered in literature a dearth of what they could best provide. The Jewish emphasis on study and learning that had done so much to develop male intellect had curtailed competing forms of emotional experience, so confessional writing of Jewish men consisted of complaints of stifled hunger for physical release. The women, conversely, exulted in their sex. One wonders what kind of writer Kreitman might have become had she spent the formative 1920s in Warsaw, as did her brothers, instead of in London, where the Yiddish writers formed only a tiny enclave within Anglo Jewish literature.

It took Esther much longer than her brothers to develop as a writer, but she was the first of the three to exploit the autobiographical form of fiction, for which Isaac would eventually become renowned. Her maiden novel, *Der sheydim tants* [the Devils' (or Ghosts') Dance], published in Warsaw in 1936, mirrors the facts of her life. Its powerful narrative consciousness prompted the English translator, Kreitman's son Maurice Carr, to rename the novel *Deborah*, after its heroine.

> Ever since childhood she had longed to receive an education, to cease being the nonentity of the family. She would learn things, gain understanding, and then not only would papa be a great Talmudist, not only would her mother possess a boundless store of knowledge, not only would Michael be a brilliant student, but she, Deborah—the girl who, as her father had once said, was to be a mere nobody when she grew up—would be a person of real consequence. She would make her own life.[44]

In order to become a person of real consequence, Deborah would have to know what "making her own life" means, and this turns out to be the central conundrum of the book. When a student of her father's *yeshiva* gives her Russian books to read, she becomes the first member of her family to cross the cultural divide into non-Jewish literature. But there is no social context for her intellectual craving, as there is for her brother, neither in the towns where she spends her childhood, nor in Warsaw, where she comes as an adolescent. Whereas Michael rebels outright, she is not able to reject the family whose acceptance she seeks. Her dependence on the approval of others means that "her own life" is never hers to define—except through writing.

In the family relationships that dominate the novel, the sibling rivalry between Michael and Deborah runs parallel to the rivalry between the two parents. The good rabbi's problems derive not so much from the poverty to which his unworldliness condemns the family as from the disdain of his skeptical wife. In one marvelous scene, the bedridden mother, Raizela, oversees the negotiations her husband is conducting in the other room with the young man who is about to replace him as local rabbi. The older rabbi wants his wife by his side to clinch the deal:

> This annoyed her. Preparing a little speech for Reb Avram Ber when he had to face the village council, well, that was one thing, but haggling with a merchant on his behalf was another—no, she

would not lower herself to that. She scribbled down a few words and sent them in [. . . .] Reb Avram perused the scrap of paper. A smile settled in his beard.

"Well, gentlemen," he said, "I shall now accept six hundred rubles, and here's good luck!"[45]

Deborah develops a version of her mother's strategy, using dissatisfaction and illness as a means of emotional intimidation, both in her parents' home and when she marries. The husband she allows her parents to choose for her (as did her mother before her) is a much coarser version of her father but no less dependent on her mood swings and approval. The novel itself may be considered a form of "scribbling down a few words" from another room with the certainty that they will determine the course of the action.

Among the siblings, Kreitman was the only one who continued to harbor sentimental notions about the socialist movement. Deborah's brief involvement with the "movement" is summed up by the verdict that she is "an idealist without a definite ideal."[46] In Kreitman's second novel, *Diamonds* [*Briliantn*],[47] set in London and Antwerp and based on observations and experiences garnered through her in-laws' involvement in the diamond trade, the most upstanding character is the socialist Leybush, who acts as conscience for the novel as a whole. Yet Leybush is just another ineffectual idealist. His wife is seduced and has a child by his wealthier friend; he is last seen on the eve of World War I arguing the case for pacifism on a soapbox in Hyde Park, drowned out by the patriots, missionaries, and feminists all around him. Socialism seems to have aroused in Kreitman a longing for goodness like her father's and a skepticism like her mother's: she credits its good intention while damning its impotence.

The heroine Deborah accommodates her family by accepting an arranged marriage. As her parents accompany her to a kosher hotel in Berlin, where she will meet and marry her intended, the bride-to-be enjoys her only carefree moments in that brief period between being a daughter and becoming a wife. The next day, she is confronted by the hotel keeper's daughter, who witnessed her wedding the previous night.

"Please don't think me inquisitive, Madam, but . . . er . . . could you tell me, what is the name of that dance you all entered into after supper last night?"

"It was . . . a devil's dance!"

"Beg your pardon? I didn't quite catch that."

"Even if I were to tell you, you wouldn't know. The dance is quite peculiar to Polish Jewry."

"Yes, but do tell me what it's called. I'm so interested, for it's the strangest dance I've ever seen. So beautiful, though; so fantastic!"

"It's a ritual dance," Deborah said, on the verge of tears.[48]

This "fantastic" dance, which lends the Yiddish book its title, pits Deborah against the Western girl she might have been. The wedding has condemned her to pandemonium, the domain of ghosts and devils, and to the condescension of this vivacious girl, only two years older than herself. Yet being an anthropological specimen has some advantage: Deborah finds herself an object of curiosity. By analogy, the background Kreitman so resents is worth its weight in gold if she is willing to market herself as an exotic specimen. Indeed, the English feminist press that reissued the novel in 1983 advertised it as "the woman's voice that has never been heard before—from the depths of the ghetto, the ghetto of Jewish women."[49]

Yiddish readers would have recognized in Kreitman's wedding scene an allusion to the famous drama by Sh. Ansky (Shlomo Zanvl Rapoport), *The Dybbuk*, where the bride Leah is drawn into the beggars' dance just before she is "possessed" by the soul of her dead beloved. In Ansky's play, Leah's father had tried to marry her off for money, ignoring her attraction to the *yeshiva* student Khonen. Khonen's rebellious soul rises from the dead and penetrates Leah in the form of a *dybbuk*, the soul of a person pursued by demons that finds a temporary resting place in the body of a living person. Ansky animates Jewish folklore to undermine scientific rationalism: spiritual-moral yearning triumphs over material necessity as the two lovers consummate their union through death. Esther Kreitman debunks this spiritual triumphalism, just as her brother Israel Joshua debunked Sholem Asch's optimistic view of history. The devil's dance in her novel is not a symbolic gateway to any kind of transcendence but a joyless tradition that has lost its purpose. The heroine's capitulation to her family's expectations seals both her material *and* her spiritual fate. The legacy of the Jewish past can only charm those who don't have to live by it.

And yet just before the book ends, Deborah is possessed by a dream of returning from Antwerp to her parental home in Warsaw and by a fear of the madness that accompanies that dream. She experiences imaginatively what it would be like to return through Germany to Warsaw, only to find her parents' apartment "all empty, quite empty." "It was outrageous! Her parents had not even deemed it necessary to inform her of their change of address, and now, after such a long and weary journey, she found herself stranded. The disappointment was too great for her to bear."[50] The nightmare merges with reality when her husband wakes her with the news that World War I has just erupted, closing off any prospect of returning to Poland.

Kreitman sets out alternatives for the heroine that cancel one another out. Like Israel Joshua, Kreitman admires her uncompromising parents almost as much as she is exasperated by them, creating an emotional impasse between her desire for autonomy and her need to be as they are. The home she quits is no longer hers to recover, yet its power over her grows stronger the farther she moves away from it. In I. J. Singer's fiction, the political forces combining against the Jews overpower everything they do on their own behalf. In Kreitman's work, history merely shuts the trap that personality has already sprung.

Isaac Bashevis Singer: Satan in Goray

In 1935 the Yiddish PEN Club in Poland determined to stimulate good writing by publishing annually the most promising first book by a local writer. To launch the series, a committee selected Isaac Bashevis's novel *Satan in Goray*, which had appeared serially between January and September 1933 in *Globus*, the literary monthly he coedited with his friend Aaron Zeitlin. However, just prior to his book's publication, Bashevis received something even more precious than this recognition from his peers—a certificate of entry to the United States from his brother Israel Joshua. He left Poland for New York in April and did not see a copy of his book until after he had reached the safer side of the globe. For the rest of his life he would continue to write fiction and memoirs about the Jewish world he had known in Poland, but of all his novels only this one was conceived within the society that had formed him.

Isaac Bashevis had begun publishing in Yiddish in 1924, after a brief attempt to become a writer in Hebrew (possibly to avoid competition with his older brother), and according to Melekh Ravitch, he became the first professional Yiddish writer to earn his living solely by the pen. Early on,

Bashevis developed multiple literary personalities, contributing pseudony-
mously to the yellow press while defending the advantages of realism in
the literary magazines. In private life, he advertised his promiscuity, fathered a child with a woman he never married, and later married a woman
with whom he had no children. But to maintain the separation between
pulp fiction and serious prose he published *Satan in Goray* in a literary magazine he had founded, not in one of the local tabloids. With hindsight, it
seems appropriate that the PEN Club, "the highest representative of Yiddish literature in the world," should have opened its series with the maiden
novel of the writer destined to become its most famous member.

Satan in Goray opens at the start of the Jewish year 5426, or 1666 C.E.,
eighteen years after the Cossack massacres. In that awful time—the greatest Jewish slaughter since the destruction of the Second Temple—Cossack
armies under the leadership of the hetman Bogdan Chmelnicki rose up
against Polish overlords and, fearing no resistance from unarmed Jewish
villagers and townsmen, attacked Jews with exceptional brutality.
Whereas Isaac Babel plays up the irony of national perspectives as Lyutov
observes the memorial to this Ukrainian liberator, Isaac Bashevis situates
his novel in a Jewish town, "isolated from the world," whose survivors are
still painting over the blood-and-marrow-splattered walls. What assaults
the town in the *aftermath* of the massacres are rumors that the Messiah has
come in the east. Heralds of Sabbatai Zevi, the self-proclaimed Messiah,
infect Goray with reports of impending redemption. The snowballing new
faith crushes its reasoned opposition. By the time the town discovers that
the "redeemer" has converted to Islam, the Jews have brought a greater
devastation on themselves than the one they suffered under Chmelnicki.

Belief in redemption, one of the principles of Jewish faith, runs like
charged electrical current through Jewish history—charged because, unlike Christians and Muslims, Jews do not acknowledge that the prophet of
redemption has yet appeared. When modern Jews determined to trans-
form history on their own, they often argued their positions in the language of messianism, either to claim or to deny that they were actualizing
the redemptive dream. The apocalyptic nature of the First World War in
tandem with the Russian Revolution suffused modern Jewish literature
with images of would-be redeemers. Writers looked for political precedents in Jewish history, such as the aftermath of the Spanish Inquisition,
when David Reubeni (1500–35) showed up at the papal court proclaiming

that he had come to restore the Jews to their ancestral kingdom, and inspired the Marrano Solomon Molcho (1500–32) to declare himself Reubeni's fellow liberator. Or when, according to legend, the great kabbalist rabbi Judah Loew Ben Bezalel (known by his Hebrew acronym Maharal, c.1525–1609) created a *golem* out of clay in order to protect the Jews of Prague from an impending pogrom. Or when the darkest of all false messiahs, Jacob Frank, led a large following of Polish Jews into Catholicism. Sholem Asch, Moyshe Leib Halpern, Moyshe Kulbak, Aaron Leyeles, H. Leivick, Aaron Zeitlin, Haim Hazaz, and Uri Zvi Greenberg were among the many Yiddish and Hebrew writers who returned to these historical characters to interpret the events of their own time. In Leivick's 1919 poetic drama *The Golem*, the Maharal succeeds in training his creature to subvert the Christian blood libel, but then he cannot staunch his creature's appetite for blood; supernatural powers arise to warn the well-intentioned rabbi against "forcing the end" of history. Uri Zvi Greenberg's work called upon the Jews to rebel against the culture of expectancy and to quit "the Kingdom of the Cross" lest only ten Jews remain to confirm that "there *was* once such a nation on Christendom's woeful soil."[51]

Excepting only the Bar Kokhba revolt against Rome in 135 C.E., sixty-five years after the destruction of the Second Temple, Sabbatai Zevi inspired the largest and most influential messianic movement in Jewish history. Gershom Scholem, the great scholar of Jewish mysticism and Bashevis Singer's near contemporary, wrote a magisterial historical study of this enigmatic figure, whose idea of reaching into the depths of sin to achieve cosmic redemption took such hold of the Jewish imagination that even upon his conversion to Islam in 1666—the year of the prophesied return to Jerusalem—some of his followers continued to believe in his divine mission.[52] Scholem charts the whole sweep of the movement that "shook the House of Israel to its very foundation." Bashevis Singer, as if looking through the opposite side of the lens, imagines the experience of Sabbatianism in a small town in Poland while the messianic outcome was still in doubt.

When the surviving Jews of Singer's novel straggle back to Goray after the massacres of 1648–55, they seem fortunate to have their rabbi back at his post with all his former authority and half his family intact. The distinguished descendant of generations of Goray rabbis, Benish Ashkenazi—sharing the emblematic patronymic of the *Brothers Ashkenazi*—wants to reimpose the full discipline of Halakhah, the Jewish Law. This means, for example, maintaining the separation of the sexes, to guarantee chaste behavior, and obeying strictly the laws of *kashrut* (dietary laws) and ritual slaughter. Before the catastrophe, when Jewishness was in high repute, Benish had held his community to an absolute standard. "Often Rabbi Benish discovered too late that he had ruled an animal kosher when it was not. Half of the housewives of the town then had to smash their earthen vessels, scald the iron ones, and pour the soup and meat into the swill heap."[53] (The earthen vessels had to be smashed because clay may absorb the properties of the food that is cooked in it, whereas iron need only be scalded to render it kosher.) But after the massacres, Benish is unable to reimpose discipline even on his own household, much less on his town. He is no longer confident that he understands God's will. The religious discipline that once sustained Goray cannot be forced back on a congregation of mourners who see no purpose to their tragedy. Messengers to Goray touch off an epidemic of hope that the old rabbi is too weak to stop. By the end of Part One, Rabbi Benish has been routed, and with his departure from Goray the Sabbatians gain full control.

The forces opposed to Rabbi Benish are uncoordinated but cumulatively effective. The lame and irascible Mordecai Joseph hates the rabbi for his superior knowledge. Itche Mates the packman, his temperamental opposite, is an ascetic so stripped of bodily desire that he cannot consummate his marriage to Rechele, his local bride. (It is rumored that he has several others.) For Rabbi Benish's younger son Levi and Levi's wife Nechele, a childless couple, Sabbatianism is license to indulge in erotic excess. They provide the salon, the alternative synagogue, for the Sabbatian school. Individually weak, these misfits become a potent force when they are united in messianic faith. Once Rabbi Benish quits the struggle, there is no one to oppose Gedaliya the slaughterer, who arrives in Goray in the name of Sabbatai Zevi to prepare the Jews for the imminent redemption.

Rechele Babad is the book's central character. Born several weeks before the massacres, placed when her mother dies in the care of a widowed uncle, a ritual slaughterer, and raised from the age of five by his aged mother-in-law, she is terrorized into submission by tales of punishing demons. When the crone dies one Yom Kippur, Rechele, left alone with the corpse, experiences a paralyzing shock that leaves her partially crippled. She can no more resume a "normal" life than her father Reb Eleazar Babad can regain his former wealth and position in their native town. In Rechele the author creates a character who has never developed any moral balance. Overwhelmed in childhood by terror and punishment, she never learns how to distinguish right from wrong. Later, when she is approached by suitors, she is unable to protect herself from the "dead eyes" of one or the lechery of another.

The psychologist and literary scholar Janet Hadda has drawn a convincing parallel between some of Rechele's symptoms and those of Hinde Esther, suggesting that the author may have unconsciously provided a psychological basis for his sister's peculiarities in this study of an emotionally disturbed young woman.[54] This child with an inflamed imagination also resembles descriptions that Bashevis Singer wrote of himself as a fearful child. But in the novel Rechele is the emblem of the historical trauma, the "image of the lost generation" that grew up between the pogroms and the failed messianism of 1666.[55] She is the only character whose life is covered from beginning to end. Less a heroine than the foil of events, she is born just when catastrophe befalls the Jews, and she dies as a result of the even greater catastrophe they bring upon themselves. Her damaged childhood leaves her susceptible to all kinds of influences, including the mass hysteria that overtakes Goray when she is in her teens. Thus, when this child survivor begins to transmogrify the terrors she experienced into prophecies of the coming redemption, she cannot be blamed for the "voices" issuing from her. Perhaps the author means us to realize that he is also not to blame for having emerged as the voice, or interpreter, of the demonic forces of his time.

Gedaliya's religion of joy seems the perfect antidote to Benish's strict regimen. He counsels leniency in precisely the areas where Benish was most firm. As a ritual slaughterer, he allows Jews to eat meat again, and his relaxation of dietary, sexual, and ritual taboos invites his flock to enjoy what was formerly proscribed:

> He demonstrated by means of cabala that all the laws in the Torah and the Shulchan Aruch referred to the commandment to be fruitful and multiply; and that, when the end of days was come, not only would Rabbi Gershom's ban on polygamy become null and void, but all the strict "Thou shalt nots," as well. Every pious

woman would then be as fair as Abigail, and there would be no monthly flow of blood at all; for impure blood comes from the Evil One. Men would be permitted to know strange women. Such encounters might even be considered a religious duty; for each time a man and a woman unite they form a mystical combination and promote a union between the Holy One, blessed be He, and the Divine Presence.[56]

Bashevis Singer reveals how evil penetrates Goray in the language of sanctity, how license can be packaged as moral advantage. The language of inversion is the seduction whence evil flows. Gedaliya justifies his cohabitation with the married Rechele as part of his duty to turn sin into sanctity, foul into fair.

Rechele's damaged soul is fertile ground for irrational expectations. When Reb Gedaliya seats her at his right hand during the public Passover *seder*, she is ignited by a feeling of exceptional potency and begins to relay his visions of the "true messiah" Sabbatai Zevi. Her spontaneous prophecy grants the Jews of Goray an authentic miracle, and for once, the local balance of power appears to shift: "The gentiles who had crowded about the prayer house stepped back, terrified at the sight; they kneeled and bowed, and God's name was sanctified abroad."[57] As the summer wears on and a terrible drought parches the fields, the two communities react in opposite ways: the peasants turn wrathful in their hunger, but the Jews have ceased worrying about tomorrow. Neglecting their normal preparations for the winter, the Jews dream of the golden jackets and marzipan candy that will soon be theirs for eternity.

At first the reader is invited to maintain a skeptical distance from this miracle: having been supplied with information about Rechele's childhood, including that she had studied the Bible with her uncle and remembered parts of it by heart, we may read her inspiration as a case study of hysteria. But Bashevis Singer is after more than psychological realism. At the point that demonic forces take possession of Rechele, he joins her reality to that of the text:

> Rechele had been impregnated by Satan. She confessed this herself to her husband: Samael had come to her at night and had violated her. A destroyer demon grew in her womb.[58]

The narrative turns wholly credulous. When Reb Gedaliya sees things getting out of hand and tries to talk Rechele out of her tortured imaginings, the imps blow out the candles and threaten him, too. Satan revisits Rechele nightly and torments her beyond madness. Whatever else may be imagined or rationalized, evil is real, and the ravishing of Rechele is Satan's special treat. The consequences for Goray are almost equally cruel, as the humiliated community faces starvation and exposure to a winter without provisions. Redemption can be promised for only so long before the day of reckoning finally comes. There is nothing so abject as a civilization that destroys itself.

Satan in Goray was Bashevis Singer's laboratory, the proving ground of his subject, style, and theme. The modern author exploits Rechele much as Gedaliya does, "taking advantage" of her susceptibility to describe deviant and abusive sexual behavior. Possession by a dybbuk was a familiar trope in Yiddish folklore. Under the protection of a twice-told tale, the author introduces pornographic details that would otherwise have exceeded the boundaries of contemporary taste. In later years, some critics accused Bashevis of exploiting aberrancy to gain fame among an American readership. Explicit and violent sex offended large segments of the Yiddish readership, including both traditional Jews, who retained strict notions of modesty, and radicals, who subordinated passion to politics. Once the Jewish communities he was describing were exterminated by the Nazis, Bashevis was charged with violating the memory of the martyrs. But as we see from his earliest novel, Bashevis Singer had devised this pornographic vocabulary for evil a decade before the Jews of Europe were destroyed. This was the only raw material he possessed, and he had to either "import" the horror of his times into that circumscribed community or not voice it at all. The rape of Rechele was his first, and arguably his most effective, use of this technique, using sexual perversion as shorthand for all the other kinds. Horror does not stalk Rechele as an invasion of an otherwise orderly rational life; her demons are on the inside, like the devil's seed that grows in her womb.

Bashevis Singer's cramped literary perspective derived from a deeply conservative estimate of his artistic opportunities. He felt that in order to be authentic—and the inauthentic writer was of no interest to him—Yiddish fiction had to stay within the actual sphere of the spoken language, of the "religious school, study house, shop and . . . the streets of Jewish Warsaw."[59] The Yiddish writer could not write effectively about "peasants, hunters, fishermen, coal miners, sportsmen, railroad workers, mechanics, policemen, military personnnel"; even attempts to describe intellectuals and quasi intellectuals were doomed to failure, since these creatures were shedding the cultural traditions and language within which they were being described. Bashevis admitted that without having spent the war years in the Jewish town of Bilgoraj, which was still mired in the old traditions and folklore, he would not have gained the resources for a historical novel like *Satan in Goray.*[60]

This meant that the only tools the modern Yiddish writer had at his disposal were the concepts and vocabulary of a Judaism in which he no longer believed. Bashevis forswore his brother's broader canvas, confining all the action to the space in which Yiddish was actually spoken.[61] Yiddish was the obvious outgrowth of a religious civilization, since nothing less than religiously mandated social separation could have generated an autonomous Jewish language in the middle of Europe. The modern Yiddish writer might now want to put the religious content of the language to secular use, but his task was charged with contradiction: "it was godly without a god, worldly without a world." Bashevis concentrated into his first major novel this conception of Yiddish as a severely *limiting* vehicle that would disappoint the writers who tried to exceed its grasp. The Yiddish writer was in the same position as the Jews of Goray: he, too, would come to ruin if he tried to escape his boundaries.

THE STRONGEST driving force in *Satan in Goray* is the narration itself.

In the year 1648, the wicked Ukrainian hetman, Bogdan Chmelnicki, and his followers besieged the city of Zamosc but could not take it, because it was strongly fortified; the rebelling *haidamak* peasants moved on to spread havoc in Tomaszow, Bilgoraj, Krasnik, Turbin, Frampol—and in Goray, too, the town that lay in the midst of the hills at the end of the world. They slaughtered on every hand, flayed men alive, murdered small children, violated women and afterward ripped open their bellies and sewed cats inside. Many fled to Lublin, many underwent baptism or were sold into slavery.[. . .] For weeks after the razing of Goray, corpses lay neglected in every street, with no one to bury them. Savage dogs tugged at dismembered limbs, and vultures and crows fed on human flesh. The handful who survived left the town and wandered away. It seemed as though Goray had been erased forever.[62]

The narrator propels the prose as relentlessly as the Cossacks perpetrate their slaughter. This descriptive rush, which became one of the hallmarks of Bashevis Singer's writing, is not limited to scenes of violence: whether he is describing the penetration of the messianic news into Goray, the betrothal of Rechele and Itche Mates, the storm that menaces Rabbi Benish in his final attempt to control his flock, or any number of moments on the way to the anticipated redemption, the author communicates his urgency through declarative sentences that produce momentum without reflection, giving the impression of energy that is not subject to human control.

Rhetoric is the other key to *Satan in Goray*. Rabbinic civilization is embodied in the "letter from Lublin" that comes to warn Rabbi Benish against the messianic herald Itche Mates. Studded with formalities, slowed by circumlocutions, and inflated by hyperbole, the Hebrew epistle from the great rabbi in Lublin takes far too long to get to its warning about the messengers of the false messiah and offers its recipient too little ammunition to stop them. Its information is proven correct, but nothing can be done about it. Only after the hysteria has spent its force and most of the Sabbatians have acknowledged their error is the language of religious discipline able to reimpose its moral certainties. This occurs in the final two chapters of the novel, where the narrative takes the form of a tight exemplum that clearly distinguishes good from bad. Here we are told how Rechele died, Gedaliya was punished, and Mordecai Joseph repented of having spearheaded the Sabbatian heresy. With a sudden switch in style, accompanied by a change to the typeface and layout of the religious chapbooks, the author seems to be reimposing order on the universe. Yet if the moral order is as plain as its concluding summary, why were the forces of evil so persuasive in their time? Why couldn't the characters in the novel control history as firmly as the narrator does after the fact? Far from returning us to moral certainties, this recapitulation of the narrative suggests that evil in history is unstoppable, whether it comes in the form of Cossack murderers or messianic promise. What is more, distinctions between good and evil can only be made with hindsight, since in the heat of a struggle every contestant justifies his cause. Readers of the concluding chapters cannot readily credit the sanctification of Mordecai Joseph or the demonization of Reb Gedaliya, since these posthumous judgments distort the impression we formed while reading the novel. If anything, the author invites us to see how relatively puny and emotionally unsatisfying are the resources of rabbinism—and its rhetorical strategies—in the face of the strongest human passions. The book's final homiletic warning against "forcing the end of history" cannot dislodge the memory of Rabbi Benish, at the end of Part One, being swept out of town in defeat.

This novel of "epic simplicity" turns out to be divided against itself,[63] the libertarian and judgmental sides each exposing the insufficiency of the other without any possibility of compromise. Bashevis Singer's later novels were often to follow the same pattern: the protagonist breaks free of traditional observance and gives in to his appetites until he reaches the point of nausea and repentance. Yasha Mazur, the "magician of Lublin," experiments ever more recklessly as a lover and performer until he becomes a species of criminal, then walls himself up against temptation in a cell of his own making. Aaron Greidinger, the hero of *Shosha*, goes from woman to woman until in self-disgust and moral yearning he marries the retarded playmate of his childhood. The survivor-narrator of *The Penitent* indulges in wild excess in America, then walls himself up in Meah Shearim, the ultra-Orthodox enclave within Jerusalem. The epigraph from the English edition of *The Family Moskat* at the start of this chapter warns that all of modernizing Jewish Poland has been spiraling forward to its end. *Satan in Goray* was the primal version of this story, providing ambiguous closure with a religious text after it has fully indulged the riot of sin.

Bashevis knew where he stood in this conflict between remorseless idealism and religious restraint:

My brother freed himself from revolutionary phraseology, but he continued to believe, or rather to hope, that the human species would come to its senses. He still believed in so-called progress. Little by little, humankind would learn from its mistakes. My brother needed this faith in moral progress, although the facts refuted him left and right. In a sense, I had taken over the role of our parents: in our conversations I mercilessly destroyed his humanistic illusions. Now I regret it, because with what could I replace them? At least my parents preached religion. I had nothing but the power to destroy.[64]

A comparison between their novels confirms that Israel Joshua's lingering faith in humanism is always subject to fresh disillusionment, a loss he plays out with each character in turn. Hinde Esther remained openly sentimental about the socialism she knew could not effect the transformation it promised. But Bashevis never believed with the humanists or socialists that rational beings could progressively improve their species. He did not trust any version of ameliorative history and saw no middle ground between disciplining religion and wantonness. Moral life was either/or—either Rabbi Benish or Reb Gedaliya. He insisted, as his parents had done, on the ontological reality of good and evil, but he could not reconstruct the religious discipline that alone could uphold these distinctions. He did not think that what was morally necessary was possible.

IT IS BY NOW commonplace to recognize that every historical novel is also a commentary on its own time. This seemingly antiquated story about the followers of Sabbatai Zevi throbs with the hysteria that Marxism generated in the ruins of eastern Europe following World War I, a hope that continued to dominate Jewish intellectual circles in the 1930s. It is not strictly a political fable, like George Orwell's *Animal Farm* or *1984*, which invited readers to enjoy the parallels between Big Brother and Joseph Stalin. Rather, Bashevis Singer's "story of long ago" re-creates the circumstances of political hysteria without direct contemporary allusion. A pure tapestry of ethnographic and historical threads, the novel recalls the 1930s only for those who already know something about the political climate of those years, or who recognize correspondences with other epidemics of hope. But for such readers, this "splendid anachronism" looms as one of the finest political novels in the Western canon.[65] Evil is never so powerful as when it claims to be redemptive, the promise of redemption is never so persuasive as when it follows great suffering, and no suffering will compare with the consequences of "forcing the end" of history.

5

A FAREWELL TO POLAND

Jacob Glatstein and S. Y. Agnon

Zol ikh nor nisht blaybn der lebediker eyner.
Farze mikh nisht mit mayne dineh beyner.
Let me not remain the only one.
Do not pass over me with my thin bones.

JACOB GLATSTEIN, JUNE 1938[1]

READERS MIGHT EXPECT this book about the modern Jewish canon to speed up a little at this point. After all, the 1930s are called the period "between the wars," as though they had been lived in anticipation of Hitler's invasion of Poland on September 1, 1939. If literary history were to follow the pattern of political history, all eyes would be looking forward, to the events that would change the Jewish people forever. But our book lingers on this period of creative consolidation, when Jewish literature reached the climax of a developmental curve that had begun in the latter part of the nineteenth century, battening on the rise of Jewish population that had grown to an unprecedented seventeen and a half million. Some of the finest and boldest literary experimentation occurs in the 1930s in Europe, Palestine, and America.

This chapter is devoted to two works in which the protagonists return from their new societies to rejoin the unsafe present of Europe in the 1930s. When I write "unsafe," I am mindful of Michael Andre Bernstein's salutary concern for what is called foreshadowing, the tendency of certain historians and writers to see historical events, and most especially the Holocaust, as preordained, resulting in "judgmental callousness and historical distortions" that appear to hold victims responsible for not having avoided their doom. Foreshadowing values the present, "not for itself, but as the harbinger of an already determined future."[2] I share Bernstein's discomfort with the deterministic cast of this rhetorical strategy and the political uses to which it can be put. But in promoting the cause of free will on the part of the subjects and interpreters of history, Bernstein ignores the obvious counterpart to his discussion of foreshadowing, which is the inability of some writers and historians to acknowledge the bleak truth about their own times because they, too, value the present—but as the harbinger of an already determined and *improved* future. Their excessive optimism about man's potential—the rosy edge of the palette whose other side is black—is also incompatible with free will, and with Judaism, because it denies the reality of the present danger. The two authors discussed in this chapter cannot be accused of foreshadowing because they could not have known what lay ahead. Their evocation of an unsafe Europe seems prophetic in retrospect because they did not erase the shadows from the world as it was.

The Divergence of Yiddish and Hebrew

At the end of the 1930s, with no apparent knowledge of one another's work in progress, the foremost modernists in their respective languages— the Yiddish poet Jacob Glatstein in New York and the Hebrew writer S. Y. Agnon in Jerusalem—wrote autobiographical novels about visits they took to their native cities in Poland midway on life's journey. It was highly unfashionable at that time for a modern Jewish writer to identify with his people and to draw attention to their political isolation. In those years when Hitler was coming to power in Germany and capitalist economies appeared to have collapsed, liberal and leftist elites, especially among the Jews, were convinced that the Soviet Union was the only bulwark against the fascist threat. In the United States, ambitious Jewish writers were beginning to enter mainstream English culture. Supported by the twin pillars of modernism and Marxism, they expected to transcend bourgeois society, the parochial concerns of their immigrant parents, and the national crises of their fellow Jews. Intellectuals in Palestine, at the Hebrew University as well as on the kibbutzim, debated the nature of the ideal society of Eretz Israel that would erase the humiliation of the centuries in exile through new secular institutions and a new secular culture. Glatstein and Agnon, however, turned conservative against the liberal and radical tide. Their almost simultaneous departure in the same counterclockwise literary direction is the more unusual because of the way they rejoined their artistic fate to the Jews of Poland, then later cast themselves as witness-survivors.

Prolonged sojourn in a European retreat was the literary premise of *The Magic Mountain*, a novel of enormous influence on our two authors. Thomas Mann had turned one of his own visits to the Swiss clinic where his wife was in treatment into the fictional basis of Hans Castorp's stop at the tuberculosis sanatorium. The hero's temporary withdrawal from a life in flux to a relatively static sanctuary allowed Mann to arrange his book as a meditative medley of themes in place of the usual linear plot. It let him probe the mystery of time in a historical sense by presenting the inner significance of an epoch and by depicting his young hero in an extended here and now where the entire contemporary world of ideas coalesces.[3] Agnon and Glatstein did something very similar: they placed their heroes back where time began for them, collapsing the tenses into a sustained hermetic present, and returned them to the center of Europe, where the historical tensions of centuries were coming to a head.

As if between a third-person fictional protagonist like Hans Castorp and personal travel notes, such as Alfred Doblin used in his *Journey to Poland* (1925) or Walter Benjamin in his 1926–27 *Moscow Diary*, Agnon and Glatstein placed their autobiographical narrators at the center of modernist works of fiction, splitting the focus and the narrative tension between the creative, mobile narrator, the implied author of the book, and the community he has come to review.[4] They invited identification of the narrator with the author by attributing to their narrators their own lives and works, confessional revelations, and discussions of their literary craft, while maintaining fiction's prerogative of critical distance. Through disjunctive methods of narration they drew attention not only to the modernist's anxieties over the existence of coherent personality but also to his ambition to encompass everything in a single work. Each drew on psychoanalytic methods: Glatstein's narrator locates the source of his adult crisis in the traumas of earliest childhood, Agnon's explores the nexus between personal and collective myth.

But writing in different languages, the Yiddish and Hebrew authors experienced their literary opportunities in opposite ways. Once twinned in the premodern period, the destinies of Yiddish and Hebrew had diverged so sharply by the end of the First World War that competing ideological parties had actually formed along linguistic lines. Yiddish was the adaptive diaspora language, easily turned into an argument for "diasporism," for the perpetuation of Jewish autonomy through a national culture wherever Jews lived in sufficient numbers. Hebrew was the centripetal language, the only tongue that united the Jews through time and space, hence the only potential unifying language of a sovereign Jewish nation; it carried the aura of remembered majesty. Writers in these languages might be equally concerned about Jewish destiny, yet they followed the logic of their languages to opposite ideas of salvation. As Yiddish declined and Hebrew miraculously began to take root in Palestine, one of the most wrenching problems of modern Jewish existence became the erosion of the language in which European Jews had fashioned their nationhood for almost a millennium, a language that was everywhere being exchanged for "that abstraction known as the future."[5] Although Glatstein and Agnon were among the least ideological writers of their day, their artistic intuition was guided by the potential of their languages, one of which was waning and the other gaining strength.

It cannot be accidental that, of the two writers, Glatstein lost the race with history, although Agnon began his work much later. The creative instinct that prompted Glatstein to organize a major work of fiction around a voyage back to his native city made it impossible for him to complete the project as planned. He published only two volumes of the projected trilogy—*Ven yash iz geforn* [Yash's Outbound Voyage], 1938, translated as *Homeward Bound,* and *Ven yash iz gekumen* [Yash's Homecoming], 1940, translated as *Homecoming at Twilight,*—eventually abandoning the third volume when the mass murder of European Jews began.[6] The literary scholar Dan Miron writes that Glatstein told him in private conversation shortly before his death that the flow of the trilogy had been "choked off" by the war.[7] With the passage of years, that incompletion became an organic part of the work.

Jacob Glatstein: The Yash Novels

Glatstein had left Lublin in 1914 and arrived in New York at age seventeen. After trying his hand unsuccessfully at jobs in the sweatshops, he registered at New York University Law School. While there, his classmate Nahum Borukh Minkoff drew him away from law and into a new movement of Yiddish poetry for which he was then laying the theoretical groundwork.[8] In 1919, Glatstein coauthored with Minkoff and the poet Aaron Leyeles the manifesto of Introspectivism, which contained as many points as Woodrow Wilson's peace plan of the same year and exuded the same progressive zeal. Positing an intensely subjective model of Yiddish free verse and placing no limits on the intellectual range of their interests, the Inzikhists proposed to distill through the prism of self—*in zikh*— everything from politics to personal memory in a poetry that was alert to the world in all its contrariety, "unclear or confused as it may be."

> We insist that the poet should give us the authentic image that he sees in himself and give it in such a form as only he and no one else can see it. If such a poem then becomes grist for the mill of Freudian theory . . . we do not mind. Art is ultimately redemptive, even if it is an illusory redemption or a redemption through illusion . . . Only a truly individual poem can be a means of self-redemption.[9]

Inzikh falls well within Benjamin Harshav's observation that every modern movement of change, either personal or institutional, is borne by negative and positive impulses alike.[10] As one manifest proof of their independence, the poets of *Inzikh* rejected the Jewish practice of maintaining the orthography of Hebrew root words in Yiddish and spelled them phonetically instead so that the eye could rejoice in what the ear perceived. In the Soviet Union, the Yiddish literary establishment was neutering Yiddish orthography for blunt political ends, to deprive the Hebraic component of any pride of place; ideologues of the Revolution leveled Hebrew as the first step toward eliminating the language that represented the religious and learned components of Yiddish. Though Glatstein and his fellow *Inzikhists* dissociated themselves from the campaign against Hebrew, they insisted that the time had come for the son to "set up his own tent," and so they decided to "naturalize the sacral component of Hebrew" (the phrase is Leyeles's) to free up the sound patterns and rhymes and to gain equal status for all Yiddish words.[11] Their rebellion was cast as an American declaration of independence, much as E. E. Cummings tried to democratize English by deemphasizing its capital letters. They exploited the suppleness of their vernacular by incorporating vocabulary and sounds from other languages, paralleling the modernists, like Ezra Pound and James Joyce, who had reimagined English as the universal tongue. In concert with this aesthetic of freedom, Glatstein published the first of these two novels (but only the first) in the de-Hebraized spelling the group had adopted.[12]

In becoming a Yiddish poet rather than a lawyer, Glatstein had cast in his economic lot with the immigrant community, and since poetry could not earn him a living, he had to turn, as most Yiddish writers did, to the Yiddish press. In 1926 he took a job on the news desk of the *Morgn Zhurnal* (Jewish Morning Journal), a Yiddish daily with a traditionalist Zionist orientation that prided itself on the high level of its writing and the reliability of its coverage. Glatstein was a clever man, an intellectual as well as a poet: "Why should I say, he *may have been* our smartest writer?" one critic blurted. "He *was* our smartest writer."[13] The daily bombardment of news could not help but challenge some of his aesthetic priorities. While modernism and the rhetoric of class conflict insisted that national boundaries were obsolete, political antisemitism everywhere was targeting the Jews. The same opportunities that allowed the Yiddish poet in America to cultivate his cosmopolitanism and selfhood also encouraged his fellow Jews to switch over to English—so that they might read English rather than Yiddish verse. Glatstein's poetry quickened with such contradictions, and under assumed names he also registered his conflicts in short stories and political commentary.

But he had never undertaken a large-scale literary project until his mother's illness summoned him home to Lublin and provided him with the scaffolding for a major narrative. In practical terms, the mother's fatal illness allowed for his first "furlough" in twenty years, mandating an extended trip abroad that he would otherwise never have taken. The Polish epigraph to his book, from Marya Konopnicka's poem "And When the King Went to War," casts the poet's journey in an ominous light: the gurgling springs and murmuring wheat and corn sympathize with the fallen soldier who dies far from his homeland so that the king may return victorious to his throne.[14] The "Yash" of Glatstein's titles seems to derive from another work of Konopnicka's, a popular Polish tale about the adventures of a little boy named Janek who goes far away from his mother's house before returning home again.[15] The name Yash, which appears nowhere else but in the title, is a version of Janek, which, along with Jas or Jasio, is a variant of Jan. Glatstein had entitled his first book of poems *Yankev Glat-*

shteyn, projecting the confidence of an integrated Yiddish author. But for this autobiographical fiction of the voyage home, *Yash's Outbound Journey,* he chose a Polish name, perhaps the one he had been assigned in adolescence before coming to America. He associated Konopnicka's poems with his childhood in Poland and Polish may have been the first language in which he had imagined himself a poet. Yash seems to be the displaced Polish Jew who will die unmourned on foreign soil.

Glatstein began writing this book with obvious chagrin about his prospects as a Yiddish author. The first installment, which appeared in October 1934, opens with a disparaging reference to the Yugoslavian American writer Louis Adamic, whose book *The Native's Return: An American Immigrant Visits Yugoslavia and Discovers His Old Country* had just become an American bestseller. Since the two contemporaries had arrived in America at almost the same time, Glatstein took note of how far he had fallen behind.

> Louis Adamic, a Yugoslav, arrived in America as a young man of sixteen and spent nineteen years in the land of blessed opportunity. He plowed with his nose, plowed through the entire country, until he made his way right up the ladder of fame.
>
> Last year he traveled home. Kindly Uncle Guggenheim paid his expenses and he came back to his parents as the "boy who made good."[16]

Supported by grants, hailed as a literary success, Adamic had enjoyed a royal reception both in his birthplace and in America. Not so the Yiddish writer! No rooster had crowed, no dog had barked when Yash arrived home after twenty years. The Yiddish writer was no one's native son: independent Poland was not the same country Glatstein had left. Moreover, who wanted to hear about Jewish Europe? "How can I serve up exoticism for a Jewish audience that already knows the shtetl too tiresomely well?" At the same time, Glatstein does not hide his contempt for Adamic's middlebrow pap. The Yugoslav may have won himself a huge audience by writing in English, but Glatstein knew the satisfaction of having mastered his native Yiddish, achieving a level of artistry he could never have matched in an adopted tongue. By the time Glatstein published *Yash* in book form three years later, he had deleted the whole comparison with Adamic and began his novel at the point of boarding the ship.

Before the *Olympic* even leaves the harbor, Yash is confirmed as its ideal passenger-observer. Once at sea, he exults at being able to meet so many strangers on equal terms. He converses about faith and literature with fellow Americans of various backgrounds, and because he also knows Russian, he spends hours chatting with a group of homebound Soviet citizens about politics and Revolution. One of the passengers later compliments him on his "golden ears." But, contrary to the expectations that he and the travel genre arouse in us by throwing strangers together, Yash has none of those intense, transforming interactions that threaten to change the direction of a life. Isaac Bashevis Singer complained that Jules Verne wouldn't have spent ten lines on so unadventurous and unromantic a trip.[17] The missing dramatic action of this novel takes place *in zikh,* within the narrator, between the middle deck where Yash moves by day and the cabin to which he retires by night.

Three short passages from the first section of the book illustrate how Yash's layers of consciousness constitute the main "action" of the novel. The first night out to sea in his narrow bunk, Yash is reminded of the "teacher Fishl Dovid who is going home for the holidays in a rowboat." This is the first Jewish reference in the book, and it appears without commentary, just as it emerges unbidden in Yash's mind. Fishl Dovid is the hero of Sholem Aleichem's "Home for Passover," a teacher from the *shtetl* Khatchevate who must earn his living in the distant city of Balta but who really lives for his twice-yearly visits back home with his family. The *melamed*'s journey is threatened, as happens so often in Sholem Aleichem, by a succession of obstacles that evoke the nightmare of Jewish life, ending with a trip across a thawing river in a narrow boat rowed by a sadistic Gentile ferryman. Yash's literary allusion connects the terrified Fishl Dovid, stretched out on the bottom of his potential coffin, with the dapper American poet who is being ferried across the water. Jewish apprehension overtakes the narrator at the boundary between wakefulness and sleep, anticipating the conclusion of this book that leaves us wondering whether Yash did, indeed, reach his mother before her death. Yash's identification with Sholem Aleichem's teacher is his first reminder that his birthplace is also the birthplace of Yiddish and Yiddish literature, hence his professional as well as physical home. The anxieties of Fishl Dovid, who left and returned to the same Jewish home, have been vastly compounded for Yash by the greater distance he has traveled, the permanence of his settlement abroad, and the militancy of the antisemitism that now sweeps the world.

Meanwhile, the daytime Yash is conducting his homeward journey through real historical time. In the early hours of June 30, 1934, Hitler executed his former comrades among the storm troopers, and that slaughter, reported by the ship's bulletin on the third day out at sea, introduces a political anxiety that suffuses the book. Until that point, Yash enjoys conversations with Christian and Jew alike, pleased to shuck off, at least temporarily, his concerns for the Jewish people. But now the equanimity of his Gentile shipmates oppresses him:

> I realized that Hitler means something different to them and to me. Hitler is to them (with rage or without) the German dictator, and to me he means 600,000 German-Jewish brothers—my 17 million brothers and our hysterical fear of fascism; [. . .] Hitler is a paw forcibly writing chapters of Jewish history and so I have to pay bloody attention to him.[18]

The jolt of news sends him looking for his fellow Jews, who are either reluctant to be discovered or eager to talk. Of course, neither Yash nor any of the other Jews he meets has any notion of how to respond to Hitler's threat. The tension between politics and poetry that is central to this book has no practical issue.

Glatstein called this tension between self and society "the yearning of the poet and the journalist for one another." In an essay written concurrently with this novel, he argued that there was no necessary conflict between these opposing genres, that "modern journalism satisfies the elemental hunger for publicisitic expression and leaves to the true poet the difficult task of developing plain, momentary phenomena into new contemporary mystery."[19] Journalism registers the threat that poetry may surmount. Missing in between is the social fabric of realism, of a resident society, the stuff of which novels are usually made. In effect, the indeterminate shipboard community is the best Yash can hope for, since there is no other community he can call his own. In uncovering his absent society, Glatstein's experimental Yash novel demonstrates why the American Yiddish writer finds it so hard to write a novel.

Memory is the third and murkiest level of action. The poet composes within his tradition of texts, the journalist is alive to people and events, and buried in the grown man are the formative impressions that only very occasionally bob to the surface. Thus, when Yash seeks his fellow Jews because he needs political reassurance, the sight of a pious Jew in bedroom slippers triggers a remembered sensation of his parents' Sabbath, a pure memory he could not have summoned up at will:

> The Jew exuded the atmosphere of Sabbath rest that hung like a secret in our home, when parents closed the door and went to lie down for a while after the *tcholnt* [baked stew]; a calm that was broken only when father removed the iron bars and unbolted the store. The smell of iron-rust, the frozen scrape of cold keys, and the first customer of the long week were the signals that God Abraham had turned on all the lights and Holy Sabbath had departed and the careworn week had returned.[20]

The Jew in slippers connects Yash's formative years at home with the present journey to see his mother, whose ears "are yellow as wax" according to his aunt's letter.[21] Only now, with this flash of memory, does he really begin to feel the magnetic pull of the still-living past. The mystery of Sabbath remains associated with the marvelous but impenetrable mystery of his parents' union, the erotic-sacred origins of his being that remain beyond his ken. There is something protective in this child's remembrance of the difference between sacred and profane, as though he recognized behind the door to life the promise of death. Glatstein is not inclined, nor does he have the artistic luxury, to enter a Proustian reverie. The poet works with fragments, not extensive narrative sequence.

The kaleidoscopic interaction among these strata of reflection, actuality, and memory shifts as the narrator approaches his destination. The closer Yash gets to home, moving by train from France through fascist Germany, the more the "flutter of talk" yields to "the sad tonality of home." By the time he enters Poland, Yash has to apologize to his train companion for his silence. He approaches Warsaw as though it were Zion:

> See, I have never been false to you. My tongue may be cleaving to my gums, but I have never forgotten you, my Jewish Poland,

with all your terrors and sorrowful festivities. Do not forget my right hand, as I have not forgotten thee.[22]

The logic of his inward and outbound journeys brings him home to the land that is the crucible of his Jewishness. He has dedicated his right hand, his writing hand, to the Yiddish language that is cradled in Poland, so he must pray for continued inspiration from the sourceland of his devotion. Jewish Poland is to the Yiddish poet as Jerusalem is to the psalmist: Yash will reiterate a version of this pledge and prayer when he is about to take leave of Poland at the end of the second volume. Meanwhile, his journey ends where his life began, in Lublin.

BUT HERE IS SOMETHING STRANGE. Despite the organization of this planned trilogy around the return home of a native son, Glatstein's emphasis falls on the caesura, on the empty space between the anticipation and the aftermath of homecoming. His home itself is missing. Yash's reunion with his father and other relatives is not described. Only a preview encounter with his mother's sister on the way to Lublin and an account of his unpleasant negotiations with the burial society constitute the story of Yash's time at home. Instead of the social substantiveness of a reunion with members of his family, and perhaps with his fellow Yiddish writers, we next meet the narrator resting up from "several weeks in Poland" at a Jewish resort hotel that specializes in arteriosclerosis, a condition that betokens both the calcification of the arteries and a hardening of the brain. *When Yash Arrived* is the claustrophobic, insular sequel of its cosmopolitan predecessor. Unlike Thomas Mann's sanatorium for the treatment of tuberculosis, Buchhendler's Jewish hotel, situated on the margins of European society, holds out no expectation of cure, only such relief as the host can provide through his board and the guests can gain through the huddle of association. As the book opens, a charismatic storyteller is holding a group of random guests spellbound, like some latter-day Hasidim around their rebbe, but his stories and melodies reinvigorate the tatters of this community of faith only somewhat and temporarily. This ailing Steinman, who has an only unmarried daughter, soon locates in Yash his potential spiritual heir. The narrator, however, is destined to disappoint his hopes.

Ever the curious listener, Yash records encounters with remarkable person-alities, but he can no more become their cultural spokesman than he could save his mother.

Glatstein casts his fictional self as Joseph from the land of plenty, ap-proached by his starving brothers, "the community of the poor [. . .] their hands extended, addressing themselves not to me personally, but to me as the messenger holding out the promise of the mythical bread."[23] But unlike the biblical provider, the Yiddish poet controls no granary and can only become the conduit for Jewish suffering through the medium of this book. Yash's Benjamin is a sixteen-year-old Hasidic prodigy, a manic dreamer who wants to inspire a protean new Jewish literature that is like a "creative encyclopedia" containing everything in itself—poetry, prose, philosophy, drama, psychology, astronomy, epigrams, even the false mes-siahs who should not be penalized for having dreamed.[24] Lacking only the power to keep itself alive, Jewish Poland is rich in storytellers, wild ge-niuses, and an incredible past.

While the first Yash novel steers its course through international waters, the second is set in the context of history. Steinman, the guests of the ho-tel, and visitors whom Yash knew in his childhood—all reminisce about the past, and he, too, is prompted to recall sequences of his youth. This motif of historical self-knowledge gains prominence at the end of Yash's stay, when he accompanies the novel's only wealthy character, a retired lawyer named Neifeld, on an impulsive excursion to the town of Kazimierz. Neifeld enjoys the ambiguities of history embedded in this place where, ac-cording to legend, King Casimir the Great (1310–70) fell in love with a Jewish Esther and installed her in his palace. How delicious that the coun-try's most popular tourist attraction should be the palace a Polish king built for his Jewish concubine! But the narrator finds that the ambiguity of the Polish–Jewish love affair is losing its charms to the blight of antisemitism. Neifeld admits that he has become a tourist in his own country and that this trip to Kazimierz is probably his last. Yash sees the wretched Jewish life at the foot of the palace hill, where Jewish artisans paint images of a dreamy past that belie the misery in which they raise their families. He sees the grotesque reality behind the exotic veneer: the warts on the restaurant owner's nose were not "the practical kind that sprout in later life so that one's eyeglasses may be held up by something. This woman's warts were on either side of a thick nose and gave it the look of some curious growth."[25]

Yash returns from his excursion to learn that Steinman lies dying, and this expiry of the soul of Polish Jewry on the eve of his own departure from Poland strikes so elegiac a note that the book seems to be folding up the Jewish tent. Steinman, who opened the book with a Yiddish *de profundis* ("Even from the *blote*, from the muck, do I sing to you, O Lord"), can barely get his "Hasidim" to hum the melody that he has taught them. During his sojourn at Buchhendler's, the poet has undergone a process of integration that has restored his broken connections with his youth and formative culture, but his deepened attachment only sharpens his foreboding:

> I remembered a Spanish book I had once read. The author, Ramon del Vale Inclan, divided the book into four "movements" corresponding to the four seasons. In the first part, the hero, a knight, is full with spring; in summer he is consumed with success like a Casanova; in fall his decline sets in; and in winter we find him lying with one hand shot off, waiting for the end.[26]

Yash fears he may be that knight, facing the winter of European civilization. "All of us—myself and everything I remembered, and everything I forgot—would soon find ourselves in winter with a hand shot off. That would be the hand which, I had vowed, I would let wither if I forgot thee, and thee, and everything that had ever been reflected in my eyes and in my brain."[27] The soldier of Konopnicka's poem who dies abroad is joined to this second image of the wounded warrior, this Yiddish poet-combatant in the ubiquitous war against the Jews. Memory, the Jew's primary weapon in exile, is concentrated in the psalmist's vow never to forget Jerusalem, and Yash had pledged to Jewish Poland this armed hand in its struggle for survival. But the last things Yash sees as he drifts into sleep at the dawn of his departure are the half-opened suitcases near his bed, "the sharpest and most solid objects in the room." These American grips will carry him off to safety, separating him forever from the Jews of Poland.

Glatstein sensed that he could not complete the task he had begun. When Yash sets out on his journey to Poland, he is as free as any man has ever been, the secular Jew free from observance, the American free from persecution, the citizen free to travel the world—and, in this book, even the writer freed from daily routine. Yash's freedoms are precisely the properties of Yiddish in America, liberated, just as the Introspectivists insisted, from religious discipline, collective responsibility, and artistic conventions—but therefore also divested of power, community, and God. The Yiddish poet in America has neither shored up the influence that once allowed Joseph to help his brethren in Egypt nor invested the kind of trust in Divine Authority that would justify a prophecy of hope. Glatstein did not forget Poland. During and after the Hitler years, he wrote some of his most powerful poems of rage and quietude, poems of revolt and vengeance, an entire Holocaust psalter. The lyric from which the epigraph to this chapter is taken, dated June 1938, compresses into one evocative scene of "homecoming" the anxiety of the second Yash novel. In the perfect stillness of evening, mournful wagons return to town with no one there to meet them. As a few sickly Jews climb down from the wagons:

> . . . a clever word falters
> In every brooding head.
> God, on your scale of good and bad,
> Set a dish of warm porridge,
> Toss some oats, at least, for the skinny mules.
> The deadness of the town grows dark.
> A cruel silence afflicts the Jewish beards.
> And each sees in the other's eyes
> A prayer of fear:
> When death comes,
> Let me not remain the only one,
> Do not pass over me with my thin bones.[28]

For this observer-participant, fear of separation has displaced the fear of death. He is not anxious about confronting but about *escaping* the common fate. Glatstein himself returned to America to write the Yash books, but he failed to complete the story of the Yiddish writer.

Shmuel Yosef Agnon: *A Guest for the Night*

Throughout the foregoing discussion anyone familiar with Agnon's *A Guest for the Night* would have noted points of contrast between his work and Glatstein's.[29] Yash sets out for Poland as the consummate cosmopolitan; Agnon plunges his traveler directly into Jewish space and time:

On the eve of the Day of Atonement, in the afternoon, I changed from the express to the local train that runs to my home town. The Jews who had traveled with me got out and went their way, while Gentile townsfolk, men and women, made their way in. The wheels rolled sluggishly between hills and mountains, valleys and gorges; at every station the train stopped and lingered, let out people and baggage, and started up again. After two hours, signs of Szibucz sprouted from both sides of the road. I put my hand to my heart. My hand throbbed against my heart, just as my heart throbbed under my hand.[30]

In the most charged hours of the Jewish calendar, the unnamed protagonist approaches his city of origin, where he plans to spend the ensuing year. The eve of Yom Kippur is for him not merely a date but the core of moral time. The pace of movement slows, *rallentando*, as the heartbeat picks up. The city he approaches in Gentile Europe bears the Hebraized name Szibucz, from the root sh-b-sh, "to make crooked or to spoil," being the moralized version of Agnon's native city Buczacz.[31] The uneasiness that overtakes Yash in his cabin at sea is here at the forefront of waking consciousness. As Yash rushes across the globe to rendezvous with his mother's still-beating heart, the Szibucz guest slows down for an appointment with himself. The missing ground of Glatstein's home is Agnon's exclusive location. The two Jewish narrators are not perched on the same axis: while the Yiddish writer balances on the horizontal tightrope between Gentile history and the Jewish experience of it, the Hebrew traveler stands on a vertical axis, between a weakened Almighty and a demoralized people. Already in the second sentence he accepts the distinction between Jews and Gentiles in the same uninflected way that he notes the gender separation between men and women. Agnon's narrator never experiences the freedom from Jewishness that liberates and then dooms his Yiddish counterpart. His freedom and anxieties are of another kind.

To say that this "man," as Agnon refers to him, enters Jewish moral time and space is of course not to suggest that he is returning to the *shtetl* or to the contained world of Tevye and his horse at the dawn of modernity. Such a faithful Jew and his horse do appear in Agnon's cast, but the horse (Henoch) and his master (Hanoch) freeze to death in the winter of this novel and pass into the realm of myth. Mutation, not familiarity, greets the narrator from the moment he reenters his hometown. The town's skeptics tell him there may not be any suitable lodging for a Jew like him—one who keeps his head covered. His guide, Daniel Bach, has lost a leg and his faith and gets along as well as he can with man-made substitutes for both. That the narrator himself is not quite able to maintain the traditional life of yesteryear is signaled by his arrival at the inn too late to eat the pre-fast meal. Nevertheless, he is the most confident Jew in sight. Agnon's narrator is arriving from Jerusalem, and though he reports that his house there had been destroyed by Arab marauders, he projects the state of mind of someone who has a metaphysical as well as physical home.

Yom Kippur is the Day of Judgment. Agnon's fully cognizant Jewish narrator approaches the place and the moment of his reckoning as an informed participant, indeed, as the controlling author of his process, his *prozess*. He fashions his own key to the house of his fiction, he conducts his own prosecution and defense, he spins his own parables, and he provides his own commentary. The Yom Kippur liturgy is saturated with appeals to the King of Kings who occupies the Seat of Judgment. Despite his arrival at the eleventh hour, the dubious welcome he is accorded, and his unsettled status as a visitor in his altered home, the narrator *intercedes for* the God whose will he does not know:

> Does the king refrain from putting the crown on his head because it is heavy? On the contrary, he puts it on his head and delights in it. The king's reward for the crown being on his head is that everyone exalts and honors him and bows down before him. What good does this do the king? That I do not know. Why? Because I am not a king. But if I am not a king, I am a king's son and I ought to know. But this man has forgotten, he and all Israel his people, that they are sons of kings. The books tell us that this forgetfulness is worse than all other evils—that a king's son should forget he is a king's son.[32]

In *The Trial*'s parable of the priest, the ignorant man from the country waits a lifetime to be admitted to the Law, leaving his freedom untested. Agnon's narrator, using the familiar rhetoric of Jewish Midrash, stands like the gatekeeper between the man from the country and the Law, negotiating the traffic between them. The Jews as a people represent God's authority, and should they abdicate their privilege—forgetting that they are the sons of a king—they reduce the moral potential of the universe. Agnon's self-accusation falls differently from Kafka's because he bears responsibility for his readership in a way that Kafka doesn't. K.'s anxiety is circumscribed by his isolation. Agnon's anxiety extends from himself to the Jews of Europe, to those beyond Europe to the world they inhabit, all the way to the Ruler of the Universe, who is in danger of being isolated from modern man. Far from diminishing anxiety, as some moderns assume that Jewish allegiance necessarily does, the cognizant Jew recalls the anxiety of the Hebrew prophets, who throb with the anticipation of a national catastrophe that they have the means only to foresee, not to prevent. Agnon has the temerity to be anxious on God's behalf.

A S COMPARED WITH the radical impersonality of Kafka's prose, Agnon's narrator experiences each and every moment according to an implicit standard. Yet in the following passage, the narrator's emphasis on close and patient scrutiny, the twice as long it takes him to do the ordinary, is complicated by the fact that he is inspecting only ruins and garbage, not a well-fashioned urn or a sacred place:

> It takes an ordinary man a half hour to walk to the center of town; carrying baggage, it takes a quarter of an hour more. I took an hour and a half: every house, every ruin, every heap of rubbish caught my eye and held me.[33]

The debased objects of his attention contradict our concept of value. Those who emphasize Agnon's modernism point to his "use of paradox, the fusion of antonomies, the breaking down of logically marked categories, the revelation of chaos in the belief systems of apparently naive legends whose heroes appear to be models of mental and spiritual integrity, and the subtle reversal of readings that he himself has constructed."[34] Situating Agnon among the modernists, however, should not negate his insistence on moral judgment that requires deliberate discrimination between good and evil. Agnon's narrator is morally overdetermined. When a friend invites him to stop off for a glass of ale, he gives two reasons for accepting: first, to please his friend and, second, to assuage his conscience, saying nothing about quenching his thirst. A hundred pages earlier he had tipped the postman but then told him not to squander the money on brandy, thereby inadvertently reducing the innkeeper's trade. He wants to repair that damage by going in for a drink, because a man cannot excuse having wronged one individual by the good he has shown another. This level of reckoning, however tongue in cheek, cannot leave a man with a clear conscience, because anyone with such a powerful awareness of his multiple motives will find the human flaw even in the most altruistic acts. Moral prose does not imply moral certainty. The complications in Agnon come from having full access to the Law but little trust in the man who tries to obey it.

Agnon's narrator is not a tourist. Like a Western hero, neither resident nor stranger, he comes to town attempting to relieve its residents from the evil threatening them. He remembers a better time, "when there was peace in the world, and joy, when a man had his victuals in plenty and his belly carried his legs."[35] But not being a gunslinger, the European Jew cannot shoot up the town to restore the forces of good. Politically handicapped and unarmed, he is limited to incremental cultural and economic improvements, such as reopening the house of study, dispensing charity, boosting the economy by buying and ordering local goods, and paying his upkeep at the local inn. All this time the surrounding "Indians"—the Gentiles— are sharpening their knives, and his money is running out. Recognizing from his own predicament that in order to cease being a guest one must have a house of one's own, he does what he can to inspire passion for the Land of Israel, knowing that most of the town will never reach it.

THE PHRASE "a guest for the night" has at least three referents. Its plainest allusion is to the narrator himself, a tantalizing blend of autobiography and invention. Born Shmuel Yosef Czaczkes in 1888 and raised in a traditional family that appreciated his precocity from an early age, Agnon assumed his literary name shortly after he arrived in Eretz Israel in 1907 as part of the Second Aliyah, when he published his first local story "Agunot." *Agunah*, the legal term for a deserted married woman who is neither divorced nor widowed, signifies a condition of tragic suspension that cannot be unilaterally dissolved. The adoption of this Hebrew name suggests that the writer will always remain within the bounds of tradition but without full security, like that afforded a wedded spouse. The ambivalence signified by the choice of name seemed to express itself four years later when Agnon left the Land of Israel in 1913 to sojourn in Germany. There he secured his reputation as a Hebrew writer, married, and acquired a life-long patron, the publisher Zalman Schocken. During his stay in Germany he visited his native Buczacz twice, once to see his ailing father and again to observe the week of mourning for him. In 1924, after a fire destroyed his home in Hamburg along with all his books and manuscripts, he settled with his family permanently in Jerusalem. Upon this second coming to Israel, Agnon adopted a religious way of life and built himself a house that figured prominently in his writings. His only extended trip abroad from that time on, triggered by the destruction of his house in the Arab pogroms of 1929, was a stay in Leipzig between March to September 1930, with a weeklong visit in August to the city of his birth, which became the kernel of this book.

Hence, the literal "guest for the night" is the one whose arrival in Szibucz opens the book at the beginning of the Jewish year 5689 (autumn 1929) and whose return to Eretz Israel concludes the book one year and eighty chapters later.[36] By slowing his narrative pace, just as he does in the description of the narrator's arrival, Agnon turned his weeklong visit to Buczacz (August 13–20, 1930) into his fullest autobiographical work, replete with information about his ancestry, his early life and works, childhood friends, and so forth. Yet the reliability of the novel as autobiography is called into question by the artistic manipulation of events. Like Glatstein, Agnon interprets himself as a character of fiction—the traditional modernist, transient native, artistic bourgeois, and sovereign subject of the Jewish God.

The designation "guest for the night" also emerges straight out of contemporary Polish–Jewish political discourse, describing the ambiguity of Jewish settlement on European soil. The Poles, eager for Jewish support of their reconstituted nation yet uncomfortable with the sizable Jewish community in a modern Polish republic, tried to emphasize the generous welcome they had once accorded the Jews even as they expressed their present resentment. The Zionist movement brought out the contradiction of Polish politics: while Polish nationalists agitated against the Jews and even instigated pogroms as a way of driving them out, they simultaneously accused the Zionists who promoted emigration of having treated Poland as a "guest-house for the night."

Since the destruction of the Second Temple in 70 C.E., Jews had founded their sacred communities wherever they settled, and the narrator's magnetic attraction to Szibucz dramatizes this spiritual affinity to his Jewish birthplace. Far from producing a nomadic tribe of wanderers, the Jewish concept of exile had encouraged the proliferation of autonomous communities (*kehilloth*) that substituted the Beit Midrash, the house of study, for the Beit Hamikdash, the Holy Temple. Doubled loyalty was the Jewish problem, because the Temple in Jerusalem had proven no more or less permanent than many a Jewish sanctuary in Asia and Europe and the Jew developed metaphysical as well as physical attachments to whichever place housed his study and prayer. When Agnon's narrator is persuaded to address local congregants one Sabbath, he elects to speak on the virtues of "the house of Israel" without specifying whether his text points to the newly reclaimed Szibucz house of study or to the newly reclaimed Land of Israel.

The political crisis of interwar Jewry is rendered in this novel more vividly than in any other I know. Agnon's contemporary Simon Halkin called it the new Midrash Rabbah on the Book of Lamentations for the way it communicated the "physical and spiritual sensation" of the destructive process that culminated in the Shoah.[37] Its individual testimonies of horror constitute a black book of 1914–29: Friede, the family nurse, recalls the rape and murder of her two daughters by a soldier who tricked them into his trust. Mrs. Zommer recounts how a farmer, pretending sympathy for her plight, sold her a sack of potatoes that turned out to be clods of clay. The narrator's childhood friend Schutzling learns that all three of his daughters were mowed down by soldiers when two of them came to prison to pick up their sister upon her release. These acts of sadism supplement a good deal of other incidents of random and explosive violence.

The narrator walks a political tightrope between urging immigration to Israel and cautioning against messianic expectations. Several times during the course of the novel, he is accused of having "misled" his fellow Jews on the question of Eretz Israel, either because he promised his listeners too much or because he encouraged them too little. Yerukham (Hofshi) Freeman, who had been inspired to move to Palestine by the example of the narrator's *aliyah*, his ascent to the holy land, and by his maiden poems that rhymed *Jerusalem* with *heaven* (*yerusholayim, shomayim*), tells how betrayed he felt to discover that the narrator had gone back *down* from the holy land to Germany. That the poem Freeman quotes is Agnon's own aims the accusation through the narrator at the author. Contrarily, the narrator's childhood friend Dr. Jacob Milch bears him a grudge for having dissuaded him from emigration, advising him to "stay where you are and do not try to settle in the Land." Against this accusation the narrator replies that he who wants to come to the Land would not be put off by advice to the contrary.

Agnon's narrator passionately defends the Jewish settlement in Palestine against the barbs of its Orthodox critics and its disillusioned idealists. He imports the fragrance of Palestine to Szibucz through a crateful of oranges and forwards to Israel—on the grounds that there it will be more needed—a manuscript that is said to have powers of easing the travails of women in childbirth. All the same, the narrator reminds us that just before this trip to Szibucz his home had been destroyed by Arabs. Yes, it is far better to leave for Eretz Israel than to go on living in hate-driven Europe, but the narrator cannot guarantee the Jews a greater degree of safety there. Daniel Bach is still alive in Europe, despite his wooden leg, while his brother who had emigrated to Palestine was murdered by Arabs in his settlement at Ramat Rachel. The return to Eretz Israel never before brought Jews political security, and the realization that there may be danger inside as well as outside the land dare not slow the momentum that is driving the Jewish people back to Zion.

Without question, the condition of being a "guest for the night" points to the need for a Jewish homeland. At the book's conclusion, the narrator postpones his departure from Szibucz until the circumcision of the Freemans' son, whereupon he retraces his steps in leaving the city with almost ritual exactness.[38] The return to the Land of Israel with his family is described as a blessed return to a permanent home.

Now let us see what happened to that man who will live in Jerusalem and what he did in the Land; or rather—since he is settled in the Land and is only a tiny grain of its soil—who will deal with a single grain when the whole Land is before him?

The story of the guest is ended; his doings in Szibucz are done.[39]

This ending is precisely what Glatstein the American Yiddish writer could not provide—the formulaic inclusion of the individual within a people, the people within a land, in a language resonant with precedent and promise. During his first return to Europe in 1916, Agnon had composed a version of the legends "our fathers told us, how the exiles of Israel came to the land of Polin (Poland)." In quasi-biblical rhetoric, he rehearsed the story of how during their passage through the Polish forests the Jews discovered a tractate of the Talmud incised on every tree, prompting those who seek the origin of names to say, "This is why it is called Polin. For thus spoke Israel when they came to the land, 'Here rest for the night [*Po lin*].' And this means that we shall rest here until we are all gathered into the Land of Israel."[40] Now the man who had supplied the earlier legend was providing its sequel, for the time of removal to the Land of Israel had urgently arrived. The same person who is privileged (*shezakhah*) to live in Jerusalem becomes, in the destiny of the people and from the divine perspective, no more than a grain of earth. Yet compared with the drifting impermanence that claims the Jews of Lodz at the end of *The Brothers Ashkenazi*, the final resting place of this narrator, who may be a grain, is arable national soil.

The term "guest for the night" (*oreakh nata lalun*) also refers to a force beyond the narrator or the dislocated Jewish people's return to Zion. It was the prophet Jeremiah who used this expression to refer not to himself or the Jews but to Almighty God. Prophesying the drought that is about to descend on Jerusalem, Jeremiah reminds God that His reputation suffers whenever His people is punished:

> *Though our iniquities testify against us,*
> *Act, O Lord, for the sake of Your name;*
> *Though our rebellions are many*
> *And we have sinned against You.*
> *O Hope of Israel,*
> *Its deliverer in time of trouble,*
> *Why are You like a stranger in the land*
> Like a traveler who stops only for the night? [*oreakh nata lalun*][41]

Jeremiah resorts to the Jews' strongest defense against their avenging Lord, namely, the warning that if they are to be judged by the strictness of His wrath, He will also be judged by their punishing fate. Agnon takes this logic a step further, knowing that the Jewish God may be abandoned by Jews out of indifference. Displacement and exile have become so routine that there may be nothing left to warn against. After the catastrophes of his own lifetime, Agnon's narrator has no more outrage to expel against the people who inhabit the cities of slaughter, or against their Guardian. What is more, he fears that God may be eclipsed not only by the ruin of His people but also by Jews who insist they are redeeming Israel on their own. He is not afraid of God but afraid *for* God. Nothing is as contingent in the modern world as its Eternal Judge.

Thus, everything depends on that man in the middle, the narrator who forms an organic link between the Jews and the King of Kings, using the traditional language of their interaction to remind each of their interdependency. On the morning of Yom Kippur, the narrator notices that the Torah scrolls had been stripped of their sacred ornaments by soldiers who had seized them during the war to pay for their guns and ammunition:

> The Trees of Life, the staves on which the Scroll is rolled, protruded sadly, their faded color wringing one's heart. See how humble is the King who is the King of Kings, the Holy One, blessed be He, who said, 'Mine is the silver and mine is the gold,' but has not left Himself even an ounce of silver to adorn His Torah.[42]

Here, yet again, is the quotation from Haggai that was used by Tevye, this time with pathos directed toward the denuded Master of the Universe, who shares the humiliating fate of all Szibucz. The government's confiscation of synagogue property is noted by the narrator even as he observes that God "has not left Himself" the slightest adornment of his Law, as though there were no conflict between the political fact and the theological metaphor, as though one were expected to sustain two such contradictory views of life. This ontological irony readmits God into the modern text on the only basis possible, as an enfeebled authority who lives on human sufferance. Jeremiah anticipated this divergence between religious claims and political realities in his image of *oreakh nata lalun*, but whereas the biblical prophet remained in thrall to God's power, Agnon's narrator awakens compassion for the King who has been stripped of the divine right of kings.

GNON'S VERY COMPLEX BOOK is organized, appropriately enough, around the symbol of a key—"that which opens up, discloses, or explains that which is unknown, mysterious, or obscure."[43] Like the title phrase, the key symbol figures substantially in the plot and virtually demands an exegetical process to interpret its many layers of reference. Thus, one recent psychoanalytic reading of the novel suggests that while the key functions on the manifest level in accordance with the Hebrew word *mafteakh*, from the root word "to open," the preponderance of Agnon's references to locked doors recalls the negative function of keys as represented by the German-Yiddish term *shlisl*, from the verb "to shut, close or lock."[44] According to this reading, while the narrator's attempt to hold the key to doors is obviously a redemptive effort to reopen the houses of study and the gates to Israel, his wish to repenetrate the security of his childhood is also a latent wish to regress into the womb, and an expression of the death wish and of an innate pessimism that runs parallel to the restorative endeavor.[45]

The Narrative Potential of Hebrew and Yiddish

Although it is true, as Robert Alter writes, that fiction offers "no solutions to the problems of existence, only the imaginative and linguistic means for thinking about the problems, for seeing them with a depth of vision," what Alter subsumes under the word *only* becomes in Agnon a powerful solution.[46] The Jewish way of life is also, when all is said and done, less an answer than a means for living with questions, and Agnon's narrator persuades us by example, precisely through the texture of his book, what advantages accrue to the person who experiences his life within its framework. The narrator often feels guilty because the money in his pocket and his home in Palestine give him an unfair advantage over the Jews of Szibucz, but his true advantage in the book is his proprietory right to the great chain of tradition and of its resonant literature. He explains that he is *not* a prophet: "a prophet knows nothing by himself and is only the agent of the Almighty, neither adding to nor taking away from the Almighty's message, and since the day the vision was blocked, prophecy has been taken away."[47] Yet why else disclaim prophecy but to remind us of its potential?

Here is how Agnon goes about trying to find lodging for the Divine Guest: There is no one in the novel whom the narrator dislikes as consis-

tently as Erela Bach. His aversion for this young woman is the more remarkable because, as he himself admits, it is independent of her achievements. She is not only the daughter of the Bach family, otherwise the most
sympathetic family in the novel, but a teacher of Hebrew and a practical
Zionist, both admirable from the novel's point of view. Why, then, does
the narrator so strongly dislike Erela? "First, because of the way she articu-
lates her speech, for she slices up her words as if with a sword, and second,
because of the spectacles in front of her eyes."[48] The way she slices up Hebrew may refer to her ostentatious use of the Sephardic pronunciation that
was taking hold among the young pioneers who wanted to distance themselves from the Ashkenazic Hebrew of their religious parents; the spectacles are the handicap she turns into a weapon, unlike her father's ironic
acceptance of his missing leg. But elsewhere the narrator explains his dislike more plainly: "[Erela] boasts that she has no concern with anything
that cannot be explained by reason alone."[49] As the purest rationalist in the
book, she is the narrator's greatest enemy, for the Hebrew she teaches is
deprived of its living resonance and her rational scrutiny pretends to heal
the wound that it actually inflicts. She has stripped the Bible of its exegetical splendor, as the conquerors did the Torah scrolls in the synagogue.
She has turned it into mere archaeology and literature.

Agnon's cast of Jews includes plenty of other problematic characters
and opponents of Zionism. As the book nears its end, a number of characters voice despair. Schutzling says that we know what the generations to
come will look like: one-third will be like Daniel Bach (who has a wooden
leg), one-third like the train conductor Rubberovitch (who has an artificial
arm), and one-third like Ignatz (who has a hole in the middle of his face
where his nose used to be). A sweet-tempered scholar confesses:

> Sometimes . . . I come to the conclusion that it is not worth a
> man's while to live, for even if he does good and never sins, surely
> his very existence only brings about more evil and leads to sin, be-
> cause his fellows have not reached this standard, and therefore
> they are compelled—both because they are evil themselves and
> because he is good—to do him evil.[50]

This may be a commentary on Agnon's own kind of Jewishness, which
stirs more hatred by so strenuously trying to be good. But none of this

negativity arouses as much antipathy as Erela. The narrator reiterates his dislike for her without self-doubt or apology, as if to demonstrate that this is the only way the materialist worldview is to be resisted: viscerally, unequivocally, and on principle. Either the spirit will live free and breathe or it will be pinioned by spectacles and sliced up by reason's sword. Besides finding a home for himself and the Jews, the narrator seeks one for God, and in that endeavor no one is as harmful as the ideological materialist who has taken up the sacred language only to pervert the soul of Israel's schoolchildren.

In Agnon's prose, which is the antithesis of Erela Bach's, there is no such thing as a strictly denotive sentence, and while different levels of meaning may be distinguished, the text resists the separation of what is organically blended. The effect of totality that James Joyce achieves through stream of consciousness and a syncretic English (by describing Ireland in the fused language of European humanism) Agnon accomplishes through the interpenetration of symbolic, midrashic, homiletic, and realistic layers of narrative in the simultaneity of Hebrew. Agnon appears to be doing this naturally, because the Hebrew exegetical tradition has already read so many meanings into every word of the classical vocabulary. The style pits its congruence of spheres against the wreckage of postwar reality, so we experience the disintegration of a world in an integral, comprehensive language. Those who have a share in Agnon's tradition have said that he applies to modern fiction the rabbinic concept *hafokh ba v'hafokh ba*, the idea of delving into the mysteries of the Torah by turning over and over again its every jot and tittle because *everything* is to be found in it.[51] The result of so much compression is not necessarily comforting. The reader who follows Agnon to the heights and into the depths must consider God's agony of exile along with those of the Jews and the narrator.

A GNON AND GLATSTEIN had seized their freedom early on, each quitting his home while still in his teens, exchanging the place of his birth for the country of his choice, and assuming the kind of artistic authority in youth that most writers achieve only after half a lifetime. Each had insisted on the autonomy of the self, with a sense of separation from the community of fate to which he remained bound through language.

Their creative independence was so authentic that they had no fear of seeming reactionary when they enmeshed themselves again with Jewish Europe, returning to seek artistic nourishment from the place where they began. Each author, through his autobiographical narrator, attests to the grim condition of his people according to the logic of his language: Yash the Yiddish narrator discovers that the unparalleled freedom he attained in America has left him no secure future as a writer and no powers as a Jew. Agnon's Hebrew narrator is humbled by the realization that in a dying world his language has been reborn but is shorn of the holy grandeur that gave it glory.

6

SHOAH, KHURBN, HOLOCAUST

TESTIMONIES IN NATIVE AND ADOPTED TONGUES

We are casting out this letter on our way to Ponar, so that
good people should deliver it into Jewish hands . . . so that for
the 112 of us, at least one [of our betrayers] should be killed in
revenge. This is the duty of every Jew to our nation. With
tears in our eyes we plead—avenge us! avenge us! Therefore I
write in Polish, because were someone to find a letter in Yiddish, he would burn it, but in Polish some good and decent
person will read it and deliver it to the Jewish resistance."

LETTER FOUND ON THE WAY TO PONAR (10 KILOMETERS
FROM VILNA), DATED 26 JUNE 1944[1]

IF WE ACCEPT the increasingly popular notion that "Holocaust literature has grown into a genre of its own," Adolf Hitler would be the first
ruler in history to have inspired a new literary genre.[2] Hitler did not,
like Elizabeth I or James Stuart, merely lend his name to works commissioned or created during his reign. His imagination, fueled by the power
he acquired, created a social system so exceptional that those who were
subjected to it felt they had to bear witness to what they had seen and experienced. Hence the diaries, chronicles, reportage, and scrawled messages by the victims of Nazism, most of whom did not survive the war.
Hence the postwar depositions submitted by survivors of the ghettos and
death camps. And hence the thousands of volumes of memoirs and autobiographical fictions by individuals who might otherwise never have undertaken to write a book. What Alexander Donat called "the Holocaust
Kingdom" elicited an outpouring of testimony, which has gathered mo-

mentum for fifty years and will probably continue to generate an interpretive literature for many decades more.[3] This was not what Hitler had in mind when he promised a thousand-year Reich, but no other regime (let us pray, no other regime) will ever be remembered so intensely.

This body of writing bears a strange relation to its source. Unlike the bulk of historical research on World War II, which concentrates on Hitler and on those whom Daniel Goldhagen calls his "willing executioners," memoiristic literature emerged mostly from the side of the victims. This literature responding to Hitler's initiative is not about him; the writers have no access to those who masterminded the killings and can rarely provide a description of their executioners. They have as little imaginative empathy for the Nazis as the Nazis had for them. The literature shifts attention from the instigators to the victims, from those who determined events to those who endured their consequences. The result is as lopsided as the war itself. Rokhl Auerbach, one of the chief memoirists of the Warsaw ghetto, argued that the unique fate of the Jews made them uniquely responsible for the prosecution: "We, numerically the smallest of the nations that was conquered by Hitler, gave relatively the largest—and in absolute figures also one of the largest—number of sacrifices of the war."[4] Auerbach credits Nazi psychology for the way it atomized, disoriented, separated, and divided every group and family, crippling reflexes of protest and coaxing people to their deaths. Hunger, thirst, crowding, surprise, and terror were the aggressive weapons of the massive Jew-hunt, while the Lie encouraged hope that the Jews could save themselves if only they tried.[5] Dedicating her life to documenting the prosecution, Auerbach argued (vainly) that Jews should not accept monetary reparations from the Germans, lest this be construed as a form of expiation. Yet Auerbach's firsthand testimony, like most of the thousands of testimonies gathered by Yad Vashem, the Israeli documentation center she helped to found, contained much more information about how Jews reacted to imprisonment and deportation than about Nazi conduct, much more analysis of the Jewish than the Nazi mind. By the time Auerbach got to Treblinka, where most of Warsaw Jewry had been gassed and incinerated, she found only bones and ashes.[6]

The literature of the Holocaust inverts the hierarchy of values that Hitler imposed. Hitler drew strength from depriving other people of theirs, demanding obedience from his own subjects and reducing to ciphers those categories of human beings he determined to eliminate from

his Reich. Yet the most impressive feature of Holocaust literature is its reliance on the first-person singular. In wartime diaries and postwar memoirs, the ego claims its due, even against its author's wishes. "I had planned
a contemplative, essayistic study," writes Jean Améry (pseudonym of Hans
Meyer) in *At the Mind's Limits,* but "what resulted was a personal confession
refracted through meditation." Améry overcomes his distaste for personal
revelation to document the torture he endured at the hands of the
Gestapo, and having come face-to-face with his torturer, he insists on
identifying his Gestapo officer by name: "P-R-A-U-S-T." He credits his experience at Auschwitz with having murdered abstraction about the human
condition, taking special exception to Hannah Arendt's argument in *Eichmann in Jerusalem* about the "banality of evil" in totalitarian society. Améry,
who had seen the torturer at work on his body, records "how the plain, ordinary faces finally became Gestapo faces after all, and how evil overlays
and exceeds banality."[7] His German torturers saved him from ever again
thinking about the world in German philosophic categories.

The Nazi genocide rendered its most vulnerable targets extraordinary
against their will. Beyond anything previously imagined about the capacities of children, the powers of observation and human sympathies are as-
tounding in the memoirs of victims like twelve-year-old Dawid
Rubinowicz of the village Bieliny, near Kielce, Poland; thirteen-year-old
Eva Heyman of Budapest, Hungary; and Anne Frank, the most famous diarist of our century, only fifteen years old when she expired at Bergen-
Belsen.[8] Here is fourteen-year-old Yitskhok Rudashevski of Vilna,
Lithuania, responding to the Nazi decree that Jews must wear identifying
badges:

> I felt a hump, as though I had two frogs on me. I was ashamed to
> appear in them on the street not because it would be noticed that I
> am a Jew but because I was ashamed of what [they were] doing to
> us. I was ashamed of our helplessness. We will be festooned with
> badges from head to foot and we cannot help each other in any
> way. It hurt me that I saw absolutely no way out. Now we pay no
> attention to the badges. The badge is attached to our coats but has
> not touched our consciousness. We now possess so much con-
> sciousness that we can say we are not ashamed of our badges! Let
> those be ashamed who have hung them on us. Let them serve as a

searing brand to every conscious German who attempts to think about the future of his people.[9]

Captivity had heightened rather than crushed the child's moral confidence. Elsewhere he says, "We are like animals surrounded by the hunter." But no animal ever left such a record of its attempt to evade the hunter; no cohort of children ever demonstrated such literary skills.

Hitler's Final Solution ironically enlarged the Jews' prominence in history. Like many a demagogue, he had chosen for his target the people with the world's most inflated image and weakest political base. He could execute his plan of genocide for the very reasons that antisemitism had grown in Europe; because the Jews were politically unprotected. Yet Jewish civilization had also developed its "weaponry." David Weiss Halivni, survivor of Auschwitz and Nazi labor camps, recalls pleading with a German guard to give him the wrapping of his sandwich, which he recognized as a *bletl*, a page from the *Code of Jewish Law*. He then used this page as a "rallying point" for his fellow inmates.[10] The survivor Rafael Scharf noted that Hitler had been unlucky in this one respect—that he had targeted a population renowned for its literacy. Stalin's Gulag also inspired a vast literature of survivors, but since his victims were his own subjects, most of that writing resonates within Russian bounds. Hitler assembled the landless Jews from all over Europe, but those who managed to survive his reign then spread accounts of his evil throughout the world.

Even Hitler's Gentile victims granted Jews priority as sufferers under Nazism. When the Spanish Christian expatriate Jorge Semprun wrote his fictional autobiography about his incarceration in Buchenwald, *The Long Journey*, he described his "best friend in the maquis" as a Jew, although, as he later clarified, his colleague had actually been a Burgundian.[11] He linked his narrator to Jews out of a sense that the Holocaust "belonged" to them over all the other victims Nazism had claimed. Tadeusz Borowski, knowing that he had arrived at Auschwitz after the Germans had stopped gassing Aryans, casts the Polish narrator of his stories as the Jews' guilty beneficiary: "Between two throw-ins in a soccer game, right behind my back, three thousand people had been put to death."[12] Already in 1938, the German writer Ernst Wiechert had singled out the torture of Jews in his memoir of Buchenwald (which he kept buried in his garden until after the war): "Jews did not count for men nor even for animals; they were merely

vermin to be squashed to death."[13] But Wiechert goes unmentioned by
those who write about Holocaust literature, having been eclipsed by Jewish survivors who testified for themselves.

Furthermore, by singling out the Jews as the prime target of his aggression, Hitler increased their mythic potency. No matter how effectively the
German people will alter the course of their national politics in the years
ahead (and no matter how wholeheartedly most Jews—in contrast to
Rachel Auerbach—want to clear "the German people" of collective responsibility), Germany cannot erase its crime against the Jews, because
even its self-transformation will be understood as a reaction to its earlier
deeds. In this sense, Romain Gary's black comedy *The Dance of Genghis Cohn*
is prophetic: although former executioner Schatz has been denazified and
is trying to put the past behind him, he is haunted by the dybbuk of the
Jewish nightclub comedian Genghis Cohn, who showed him his naked
backside before he was shot and who now taunts him from beyond the
grave.[14]

Most of all, the literature of Hitler's victims confounds the uniformity
he tried to impose on them. Mocking both the rabbinic definition of the
Jew and the multifarious ways that European Jews had chosen to classify
themselves, Hitler decreed through the Nuremberg Laws that a full-
blooded Jew was anyone with three or more Jewish grandparents or anyone with two Jewish grandparents who practiced Judaism. He enjoyed
humiliating the Jews by imposing his definition on a notoriously individu-
alistic and culturally diversified people. But though Hitler was able to
grind millions of Jews to a common death, survivors went home to their
native languages or adopted new ones in order to describe their experience of the death camp, and just as the prisoners in the camps had naturally grouped themselves according to their language, their narratives bore
the cultural stamp of the language in which they were recorded. Holocaust writing obeys the internal laws of culture, not the imposed laws of
Hitler. The Dutch youngster Moshe Flinker kept his diary in Hebrew, and
drawing inspiration from biblical and Zionist sources, he sounds more like
the middle-aged Hebrew educator Chaim Kaplan in the Warsaw ghetto
than his contemporary and Dutch-speaking compatriot, Anne Frank. No
matter how abominable the experiences they describe, writers reimpose
their cultural imprint on the record, recreating a virtual taxonomy of European Jewishness within the literature that derives from its destruction.

Critical and theoretical literature on this subject is similarly culture bound. Had Theodor Adorno been writing in Yiddish or Hebrew, we would never have had his formulation "To write poetry after Auschwitz is barbaric."[15] Adorno's maxim derives from his own epistemology, from disillusionment with his own brand of cultural criticism, or perhaps from the taint of his German language or from the rhetoric of the Frankfurt School.[16] Adorno's dictum recalls the radical saying of his colleague Walter Benjamin: "There is no document of civilization which is not at the same time a document of barbarism." Benjamin was speaking as a historical materialist, making the argument that cultural treasures represent the spoils of the victor, that they owe their existence "not only to the efforts of the great minds and talents who have created them, but also to the anonymous toil of their contemporaries."[17] Adorno's essay, echoing Benjamin's apprehension about democratic society and the culture that is produced under market conditions, throbs with dismay over the "sinister, integrated society of today," "the open-air prison which the world is becoming," and the way that traditional culture—"neutralized and ready-made"—has become worthless. It is in this context, and not in any consideration of Jewish martyrdom or Jewish writing, that Adorno uses Auschwitz as the ultimate metaphor. Meanwhile, poets in Jewish languages found that poetry alone resisted the degradation, and at least one of them, Abraham Sutzkever, attributed his very life to that proposition.[18] David Roskies, a scholar of Yiddish and Hebrew sources, demonstrates how the literature of Hitler's victims stands "against the apocalypse," assimilating even this unique catastrophe into an unbroken literary tradition that begins with the destruction of Solomon's Temple in 586 B.C.E.[19]

By and large, literary scholarship has echoed Adorno in homogenizing the Holocaust, posing such questions as whether the horror of the Lager and the extermination process can be rendered in language, within prevailing linguistic and literary forms.[20] An ever more generalized inquiry into the capacity of language, in the abstract, to represent the Nazi genocide ignores the influence of actual languages in determining how the question continues to be answered. Such an approach tends unconsciously to replicate the reductionism of Nazism by assuming that the writers became what they were subjected to. It responds to Nazism's singling out of the Jews by refusing to deal with their Jewishness at all, reinforcing the negation of the Jewish people through the refinement of abstraction rather than physical extinction. I would like to advance a different view and argue that the nature of literature during and after the war depends in large part on the language and context within which it was written, as well as on the author's relation to his language, whether Jewish or non-Jewish and whether native or acquired after the war, and that where problems of language reflect conflicts of identity, they predate the war and were not caused by Hitler alone. And if we are to accept as a category the literature of the Holocaust, we should be equally prepared to recognize its function of reversing Hitler's plan of annihilation and overturning his definition of the Jews. Jewish resistance to Hitler was mounted primarily through literature, Jewish writing of the war is primarily a literature of resistance, and Jewish writing forms the bulk of Holocaust literature. This part of the Jewish canon is the hardest to contain, since everything that claims authenticity as testimony asks to be included.

I am in complete sympathy with the philosopher Berel Lang's suspicion of the term *Holocaust,* because "its theological or at least mediating overtones . . . are confined to the viewpoint of the victims, and they fail to suggest the specific role of genocide as it figured in the deeds of the Third Reich."[21] Lang shows how Holocaust terminology transposes the destruction of the Jews from the political realm in which it occurred into the religious realm. I use the term reluctantly, to analyze what others since the 1960s have called by that name.[22] But the problem goes even deeper than Lang suggests, ignoring not only the political war against the Jews but the substantiveness of the Jewish people whom Hitler tried to eliminate. The term *Holocaust* seems to craft a new secular version of the crucifixion, a version in which the Jews are cast as the sacrificial figure in a denationalized saga of evil and innocence. As against the syncretic concept of the Holocaust—a religious burnt offering that is wholly consumed—the terms *Shoah* (meaning "destruction" and used in this context in Hebrew in Eretz Israel as early as 1938)[23] and *khurbn* (the generic Yiddish term for national catastrophe)[24] yield diachronic conceptions of what the historian Lucy Dawidowicz called the war against the Jews and what Lang calls the Nazi genocide against the Jews. Both *Shoah* and *khurbn* derive from the Bible, with different weights of memory attached. All language is national, in the sense that it is generated and spoken by a group of people; all "literature of the Holocaust" is shaped by a particular culture, however complicated it may be by the author's crisis of identity.

The Yiddish and Hebrew Diarists

Yiddish was the European language most directly affected by Nazi rule. Although linguistic assimilation had become the norm by the 1930s among Jews in western Europe, the Soviet Union, and the United States, it was slowed in Poland by some of the external and internal forces of exclusion and renaissance alluded to in the previous chapters. Thus, Yiddish was the main language of the ghettos, and of the majority of Jews targeted for annihilation, though most Jews also knew at least one coterritorial language. When a lending library was established in the Vilna ghetto, it was announced after the one hundred thousandth book had been borrowed that 17.6 percent of this total were in Yiddish, 2 percent in Hebrew, 70.4 percent in Polish, and the rest in Russian and other languages.[25] That hundreds of Jews managed to pass for Poles on the Aryan side of the ghetto wall despite a veritable army of bounty hunters trying to detect them proves the high degree of acculturation indicated by the above statistics. At the same time, the widespread translation of literary works *into* Yiddish and Hebrew during the interwar period demonstrates not merely the avidity of the Jews for foreign cultures but their faith in the development of their own. In the Vilna ghetto, Yitskhok Rudashevski and his school chums drew their models of resistance from *Der giber in keytn* [The Hero in Chains], a shortened translation of Victor Hugo's *Les Miserables*.

Vilna—"the mecca of Jewish nationalism in the interwar period"[26] or, as Jews typically referred to it, "the Jerusalem of Lithuania"—is an apt example of Jewish cultural autonomy during the period of World War II. Here, a generation of Western-trained scholars had founded their own quasi university in 1925, the YIVO Institute of Jewish Research, and here the Jewish Teachers' Seminary trained pedagogues for its network of secular Jewish schools. Modern and traditional Jews benefited from common Jewish medical, social, and philanthropic institutions and studied side by side in the famed Strashun Library. Writers, poets, artists, actors, and journalists maintained a competitive press and theater. When the Germans occupied Warsaw in September 1939, thousands of Jewish refugees fled to Russian-occupied Vilna, further swelling the ranks of the local intellectual community and reinforcing the hope that communal discipline could be maintained within hostile surroundings. In trying to comprehend and respond to the shift of power around them, the Jews of Vilna drew upon a long history of cultural resistance to physical might.

The Germans began mass executions immediately after they took Vilna on June 24, 1941, and forced the remaining Jews into adjoining ghettos at the beginning of September. Mark Dworzecki, a physician and wartime diarist, reports that during the first hours of confinement, everyone had the same thought: "We have to write memoirs; each of us has to record what he sees, so that future generations should know it."[27] This idea had already taken hold of Herman Kruk at the outbreak of the war two years earlier, when he fled his home in Warsaw in order to reach the Russian zone. Now, trapped in Vilna by the German invasion of Russia, he felt he lacked the energy to run any further:

> If I am to remain here and become a victim of Fascism, I will take up my pen and write the chronicle of a city. Clearly, Vilna may also be seized. The Germans will begin to Fascisize the city Jews will enter the ghetto—and I will record it all. My chronicle has to see, has to hear, and has to become the mirror and conscience of the great catastrophe.[28]

To describe his literary intentions, he uses not Dworzecki's term *memoir* but the Hebrew-Yiddish term *pinkes,* a community register in which a local registrar recorded such legal, social, and historical events as the community felt it necessary to preserve for posterity.

An amalgam of Jewish public servant, scribe, and socialist functionary, Kruk has been likened to the "hard-working, decent party officials that one may have found in the German SPD or the British Labor Party in the 1920's."[29] Separated from his wife, who had stayed behind in Warsaw, he threw his energies into projects, like a ghetto lending library, that brought him into daily contact with hundreds of people of all ages and types. When the Nazi ideologue Alfred Rosenberg set up an agency in the YIVO to collect Jewish documentary and historical material for transfer to Germany, he put Kruk in charge of the project. This work involved him with German officials, leaders of the Jewish community council, and members of the Jewish resistance, who by the spring of 1942 had begun using the YIVO—which stood outside the ghetto—as a base for their underground activities. As what the Germans called a "useful worker," Kruk was initially protected from the periodic roundups and from hard physical labor. He was able to dictate most of his text to his secretary, Rachel Mendelsund-Kowarski, who typed it in triplicate for hiding in different locations. His diary maintains professional discipline, alluding only rarely to personal affairs ("Today marks three years since I decided to leave my home, my wife, all my dear ones in Warsaw").[30] Kruk mentions having been ill only as it interfered with a public duty.

Writing, recording, and testifying were the first spontaneous acts of resistance by Jews of the eastern ghettos against the Nazis. This form of resistance was determined "not only by the experiences of the past, considered in the light of existing knowledge, but also by the dominant values of Jewish tradition and culture."[31] The most famous of ghetto chroniclers, Emanuel Ringelblum of Warsaw, a professional historian who had already written parts of the history of the Jews of Warsaw before the outbreak of the war, organized a team of researchers in the winter of 1940 to assemble a definitive ghetto archive; cloaked as a weekly gathering for the enjoyment of the Sabbath, *Oyneg Shabbes* insisted on comprehensiveness and "objectivity" from its informants and reporters—an odd priority for a people under siege, unless they intended history to reverse Hitler's temporary rule over them.[32]

Although Kruk was not, like Ringelblum, a trained historian, in his *pinkes* he sets himself the same goals. But he finds it hard to record "with trembling hands" the testimony of the first eyewitnesses to mass murder, those who clawed their way out of the mass graves at nearby Ponar and reached the ghetto hospital. "How can one write about this? How can one gather one's thoughts? If the heavens are heavens, they should pour down lava, drowning every living thing once and for all."[33] Later, he returns to the hospital to interview two additional witnesses, who "confirmed everything that has been recounted here in such reporterly fashion [*azoy khronikmesik*]," and the next day he is back at his post, reporting German confiscation decrees and the mixed record of Jewish compliance.

Since German intentions can be grasped only after the fact, Kruk knows he lacks the context to form proper judgments. "Every German order elicits a hunt for meaning, intention, the need to outdo them in cleverness."[34] Already in July 1941, during the first weeks of occupation, Kruk records an incident under the heading "They wanted good, and the result was evil, a story about 150 men." To prevent the Ipatingi, special units of Lithuanian collaborationists, from conducting random manhunts of Jews in the streets, the Jewish Council (the Judenrat) suggests that it itself would provide the recruits on an orderly basis. But when the Lithuanians, acting for the Germans, accept the offer, the Judenrat realizes its error. "How can you send people away when there is no guarantee of what will become of them?"[35] This was the first of many such dilemmas to which Kruk gradually realizes there can be no "good" solution, because the moral problem is actually cognitive and the German scheme remained utterly independent of any and all Jewish actions.

In a decision made famous by Joshua Sobol's play *Ghetto*, Kruk, as a member of the Jewish Socialist Bund, opposes ghetto theater as unseemly diversion from political actuality. The Bund printed placards scolding, "You don't make theater in a graveyard."[36] Yet when the boycotted concerts prevail and the halls are filled, Kruk comes to see that popular theater may sustain public morale.

As an avowed secularist, Kruk emphasizes the social behavior of the Jews. Zelig Kalmanovitch, also a member of the Rosenberg workforce in the Vilna ghetto and the head of the ghetto's Jewish Museum, concentrates on the Jewish spirit, which has to sustain the will to live. Whether Kalmanovitch chose to keep his diary in Hebrew because he needed to express himself in traditional language or felt he wrote under the aegis of eternity because he was writing in Hebrew, his writing is suffused with a national-religious feeling quite unlike the style of Yiddish fellow diarists like Kruk and Emanuel Ringelblum in Warsaw. The use of Hebrew as a vernacular by European Jews before the creation of Israel signified a heightened commitment to Zionism, the resumption of a national life that began with the Bible and carries its resonance into modern-day Eretz Israel. While the demarcation between wartime writings in the two languages is not absolute, the choice of language clearly reflected and influenced narrative style and tone.

Hebrew was by no means a natural choice for Kalmanovitch, who had been a Jewish Diaspora–nationalist in his youth and had supported the "territorialist" idea of autonomous Jewish communities wherever Jews settle in sufficient numbers, with Yiddish as their common language. Sometimes mistaken for resignation, Kalmanovitch's religiously tinged rhetoric—he believed that Jews should follow the accommodationist policy of the Judenrat, under its leader Jacob Gens, to save as many lives as possible—was actually far more militant than that of Kruk, who supported the ghetto fighters. The Hebrew diarist finds his model of resistance in the Jewish child of a Polonized family whose first exposure to the Bible has come in a ghetto school. Upon hearing the story of Jacob and Esau, this child suddenly called out: "Teacher, we are the descendants of Jacob and they [i.e., those who wrong us] are the descendants of Esau. Is that right? Very well, then. I want to be of the descendants of Jacob and not of the descendants of Esau."[37] Kalmanovitch wants to make this the ghetto's standard. Anyone not *choosing* to remain with Jacob would no longer be considered a Jew. Kalmanovitch is so keen to avoid the Nazi's coercive definition of the Jew—that reactive identity that Jean-Paul Sartre defined as the Jew's existential condition—that he defies rabbinic criteria to make Jewishness under Nazism entirely voluntary.

Yiddish, the European vernacular, was tied to the fate of the Jews of Europe, but writers in Hebrew could feel that they transcended the continent. The sixteen-year-old Moshe Flinker, trying to survive with his family in Belgium in 1942-43, realizes that his diary has become less an account of everyday events than "a reflection of my spiritual life," and particularly of the struggle to understand how God's covenant with the Jewish people is reflected in the Nazi Jew-hunt. The more isolating his concealment, the more strength he finds in individual Hebrew words like *emunah* (faith) and in the phrases of prayers ("Behold our poverty," "Heal us and we shall be healed").[38] Flinker's trust in redemption outlived its author. When his diary surfaced in Israel after the war, it was read and published by the legendary polymath and Zionist activist Dov Sadan and the Hebrew writer S. Y. Agnon, who found it to be source of personal inspiration.[39] Unfortunately, translators of ghetto material from Jewish into non-Jewish languages are apt to eliminate or grossly simplify the intertextual references and quotations, assuming that their national and religious allusions will not strike a chord with the English reader.[40]

The Jewish ghetto diaries are quite at odds with Paul Fussell's discussion of writing in wartime, based on his analysis of a Dutch boy's diary of the Second World War. Fussell first unmasks the diary as a literary fabrication (designed to persuade America to enter the war), then draws general conclusions about the "benignity" of wartime writing that promotes the innocence of one's own side. All this sounds logical and true. Fussell describes the sentimentality, "emotional primitivism," and "moral simplification" of writers during and even after the war, writers whose analytical faculties were softened by the assurance that they fought on the side of the angels.[41] Yet the Jewish diarists give the lie to this model. They are highly critical of their fellow Jews, often more so than of the Germans, whose actions lie beyond their ken. To guard against any possibility of "benignity" in gathering evidence from hundreds of informants, Emanuel Ringelblum told everyone to write "as if the war were already over," fearing neither the Germans nor the Jewish Council: only thus would *Oyneg Shabbes* material serve the future tribunal, "which, after the war, will bring to justice offenders among the Jews, the Poles, and even the Germans."[42]

What accounts for this difference? Fussell's writers are trying to assist their military command by putting literature at its service. They intend for their armies to win the war; hence, their writing subordinates itself to the military goal. The ghetto diarists, by contrast, represent a noncombatant polity that cannot fight back in kind; they can only try to secure their posthumous judgment through an alternative standard of victory and defeat. For whose sake would they write propaganda, if they have no allies to hear their appeal? The last words attributed to the historian Simon Dubnow as he was being deported in Riga were *"shraybt un farshraybt* [keep the record]." Chaim Kaplan's last recorded words were, "If my life ends—what will become of my diary?"[43] Kruk continued his diary after he was taken to the Estonian labor camp Klooga, where he was killed just one day before its liberation by the Red Army.[44] Like soldiers who die for their country, these Jews obeyed the imperative to document over the imperative to live.

*L*ITERARY RESISTANCE became the chief weapon of even the ghetto fighters and partisans. As soon as Vilna was liberated by the Russians, they rushed back to the city to retrieve this buried "Jewish ammunition" and then to provide more of it on their own. Mark Dworzecki, Shmerke Kaczerginski, and the poet Abraham Sutzkever wrote memoirs at once, incorporating the depositions of other Vilna survivors, whom they interviewed in the ruins of the city.[45] The first collective Yiddish postwar anthology about the destruction of Jewish Vilna, compiled by survivors repatriated from the Soviet Union, lists several dozen subjects to be documented while memory is still fresh: the nature and methods of German

terror before and during the ghetto period; the role of the local population; the Jewish ghetto police; family life in the ghetto; cultural life in the
ghetto; religious life in the ghetto; problems of prostitution in the ghetto;
traitors, informers, and spies; political parties and organizations; and
places of hiding.[46] The list goes on. And the forest of diaries and memoirs
was soon expanded by hundreds of collective memorial volumes written
by survivors to commemorate their destroyed Jewish communities.

After the war, Yiddish generated virtually a "*khurbn* literature." Elias
Schulman wrote, "It is no exaggeration to say that every Yiddish poet and
prose writer, whether he was in the camps or not, wrote about some
aspect of the catastrophe."[47] In becoming a literature of *khurbn*, Yiddish
became more overtly Jewish. Once the instrument of Jewish cosmopolitanism, Yiddish literature more or less abandoned the "world" to mourn
the particular civilization that had given it birth. Yiddish traded places
with Hebrew, becoming the language of the past, of sacral and historical
memory.

By contrast, Jewish writers outside the confines of Yiddish were not immersed by the *khurbn* to the same degree. Hebrew was energetically becoming the workday language of a Jewish country. Survivors of the Vilna
resistance movement like Ruzka Korchak and Abba Kovner, of the Polish
and Hebrew spheres of Polish Zionism, settled in Israel to build a living
community, and also thereafter began to write and gather the historical
record, she in Polish, he in Hebrew. But Hebrew literature in Israel, preoccupied with nation building, was slower in coming to grips with the Holocaust than Yiddish, which was largely consumed in its flames. The paths of
Yiddish and Hebrew widened as never before.

Writers in Search of Language

On the day he entered the ghetto, Zelig Kalmanovitch was heard to say,
"*Abi tvishn yidn* [as long as I am among Jews]."[48] Kalmanovitch had become
so disillusioned with the rest of Europe that he felt prepared to accept incarceration for the gain of Jewish society—and this despite a lifetime of
disagreeing with most of his fellow Jews. In the ghetto Kalmanovitch
wrote a long study of I. L. Peretz, who in a similar spasm of disgust, with
Polish antisemitism on the eve of World War I, had rededicated himself to
communal self-help. Jewish writers and intellectuals like Peretz and

Kalmanovitch had sought an accommodation with European culture essentially on their own terms, within their own Jewish languages. Europe's decline into barbarism strengthened rather than undermined their moral and cultural confidence.

How very opposite was the experience of writers whose Jewishness was forced on them by Hitler, or of those who had been raised by their parents not to betray a Yiddish accent or a Jewish gesture! Reluctant Jews, uninstructed Jews, they were first saddled with an unwelcome identity, then targeted for extinction as what they least wanted to be. Whatever the hopes that had led them or their parents or even grandparents to adopt the non-Jewish language, the process that targeted them as Jews had to complicate their identity, especially when they were being hunted by speakers of their language. Most complex was the case of those who had to change their language during or after the war and to write about their experience in a language other than the one that had shaped it.

Jerzy Kosinski: The Painted Bird

Jerzy Kosinski's eponymous image in *The Painted Bird* (1965) is the most dramatic representation of the artificially segregated Jew under Nazism. An unnamed six-year-old boy from an unnamed city in eastern Europe is separated from his family in the first weeks of World War II and tries to survive for its duration among peasants in the countryside. There he witnesses and experiences ghastly horrors not as a member of some group that is being herded toward extermination but as one who is solitary and uninformed. The swarthy complexion that marks him as a "Gypsy-Jew" invites a heightened level of mistreatment from the fair-haired locals. The boy loses his speech when he is immersed by the peasants in a pit of manure—this being his punishment for having accidentally dropped the missal during the Corpus Christi Mass. Nevertheless, he retains his instinctual will to live. After the war he is reunited, reluctanctly, with his parents, and in the final paragraph of the book he begins to talk again.

The image of the painted bird is glossed early in the novel, when the boy finds temporary shelter with Lekh the bird dealer, an outsider like himself who has devised a ritual reenactment of the cruelty he sees. Lekh selects the strongest of his birds, paints its wings, head, and breast in vivid colors, then sends it flying toward a flock of its own species.

For an instant the birds were confounded. The painted bird circled from one end of the flock to the other, vainly trying to convince its kin that it was one of them. But, dazzled by its brilliant colors, they flew around it unconvinced. The painted bird would be forced farther and farther away as it zealously tried to enter the ranks of the flock. We saw soon afterwards how one bird after another would peel off in a fierce attack. Shortly the many-hued shape lost its place in the sky and dropped to the ground. When we finally found the painted bird it was usually dead.[49]

Lekh's sport is an attempt at exorcism: he is the lover of a woman called Stupid Ludmila, who lost her wits after she was gang-raped by a rejected suitor and a herd of drunken peasants. Rather than punish those responsible for her condition, the villagers excoriate the woman for her changed behavior, and one day, overpowering Lekh, they bludgeon her to death. Lekh recognizes both the parallel between human and animal instincts and this difference: human beings enjoy their privilege of toying sadistically with their own species. Kosinski reenacts this same ritual when he releases the boy, his own painted bird, into the brute world of this novel.

Kosinski's book has been widely praised for its universalism, for capturing the horror of "the Nazi mentality" stripped of its national uniform or historical base. Sidra DeKoven Ezrahi calls it the "most relentless example of the imaginative representation of the Holocaust," because of the way it universalizes the demonic values of Nazi civilization.[50] Critical argument has turned on whether its violence is gratuitous (gratuitous not simply because the boy is treated brutally but because of the book's uninflected descriptions of brutality). The level of deviance is so high it has led readers to wonder "whether The Painted Bird is a terrifying and obscene book or a book about the terrors and obscenities of the Nazi period." Alvin Rosenfeld, author of this distinction, suggests the latter and calls the book the most extreme literary representation we have of terror at the point that it evolves into myth.[51]

Universalism is indeed the key to the special horrors of this novel. To make the point that the boy is deracinated, Kosinski leaves him uncircumcised, trading in a feature of historical probability to gain the advantage of myth. (Had the boy been circumcised, the game would have been up for him the first time the peasants caught sight of his little "tassel.") Moreover, the boy remembers nothing of his childhood that would place him among any one people as opposed to any other. There are no nurturing parents. All that the boy recalls of his moral training are the animal tales his nurse used to read him from a picture book. Since he had always been taken to church on Sundays, but without instruction in his faith, the child never does know who or what he is. "Was it possible that God's wrath was reserved only for people with black hair and eyes, who were called Gypsies?"[52] He cannot conceive that there might actually *be* Gypsies (much less Jews), people with a different moral code. When the dark-skinned Kalmuks descend on the village in a rampage of brutality, the boy is convinced that he must belong to them, and weeks later, when a soldier of the liberating Red Army instructs him in Stalin's greatness, he finds a temporary affinity with the Georgians, who are "swarthy, black-haired, with dark burning eyes," just like him.

Thanks to the biography by James Park Sloan, we know that Kosinski's father was able to save the family during the war by passing for a Gentile (and being allowed to pass for a Gentile) in a small Polish town.[53] From Kosinski's brilliant fiction, we learn that the child must have been as frightened by his father's ability to dissimulate as he was by the thought that the extended charade might not succeed. In a sense, Kosinski's later move to America and his dazzling self-transformation into an English author—not to mention his lifetime habit of assuming different disguises and roles—reenacts his father's ordeal of survival at the cost of being himself.

His parents, not Hitler, deprived Jerzy Kosinski of an identity, and though that absence of identity might have saved his life, it left his salvaged life hollow. Kosinski writes out of a cultural void that would be terrifying under any conditions, and is all the more so during a genocide against a people supposedly "his." The "trope of muteness" in this novel is not generated by the war alone, and not by the Holocaust primarily, but by the author's cultural autism.[54]

Piotr Rawicz: Blood from the Sky

In contrast to Kosinski, the Ukrainian-born Piotr Rawicz, of multicultural Lviv (the Russian Lvov, Polish Lwow, and German Lemberg), recounts the adventure of a circumcised Jew who must trick his pursuers into ignoring the evidence on his flesh. Whereas Kosinski's primitive style undercuts the possibility of civilization (he said he was helped in this by the thinness of his acquired English), Rawicz, who was fluent in many languages, was so highly self-conscious about the interplay of acquired and native cultures that he had lost the ability to write other than ironically. We meet up with the autobiographical narrator of *Blood from the Sky* (1961) in a Parisian cafe, where he is pretending to describe his hero Boris as the customer at the adjoining table. Writing in adopted French, he warns that he will speak in metaphors, because he doesn't really trust his audience or himself:

> I'm scared of your cops, of your summonses, of your justice, of just plain you. So I'm not telling you straight out what the title [of Book One, "The Tool and the Art of Comparison"] refers to. You'll get no strong language out of me. Later on, you will see for yourselves. When a man's papers aren't in order, when ambiguity— strained and creaking ambiguity—is the one remaining bridge which occasionally allows him to steal, in the evenings, into the encampment of the human, it is better for him not to expose himself to the censor's thunderbolts. You won't be cheated, though. As time goes by, you will see what tool I mean.[55]

These broad hints about self-exposure, strong language, and the telltale tool imply that the Nazis' determination to uncover the Jew through the penis will be parried by the narrator's attempt to recover his life through his pen. The cultural Houdini will deny the apparently irrefutable evidence of the circumcised penis. Rawicz transfers the atmosphere of danger from the German manhunt to the French cultural front, assuming as an author-in-hiding the same defensive posture that he had once adopted as a hunted Jew.

Boris's mentor before the war had been Leo L., "the greatest orator [he had] ever come across," a modern Jewish nationalist (much like Jacob Glatstein's Steinman) who takes over from religious authority the task of inspiring his fellow Jews. When Jews are driven into the ghetto, Leo L. declares himself glad to have turned down a professorship at Harvard: "I wouldn't want to be without us. Absence, in itself, would have been a crime, an unforgiveable crime."[56] He entertains Boris with Heinrich Heine's *The Rabbi of Bacharach*, a work that transmutes Jewish tragedy into German high culture. Later, in the final stages of starvation, Leo L. turns mystical, kabbalistic, recasting the Jews as players in a "Performance of

Nothingness," that is, a performance of no earthly importance because it is being played out in the mind of God. Once the death deportations begin, however, Leo urges Boris and his girlfriend Naomi to save themselves:

> "Of you who are leaving, a few may survive. I am by no means certain. But should you happen to do so, remember everything, remember carefully. Your life will be no life. You are going to become strangers to yourselves and to everyone else. The only thing that matters, that WILL matter, is the integrity of the witnesses. Be witnesses, and God keep you."[57]

The Jewish spokesman stays with his people but charges his student with the same obligation the diarists assumed in the ghettos.

Boris becomes a picaro on the loose, perpetually reinventing himself to escape slaughter. Early on, disguised as a Gentile, he witnesses a German raid on a makeshift school during the "great sweep" of the ghetto. Boris recognizes Yaakov, a child he had once met in the park beside the statue of a great philosopher. Yaakov had been surprised to learn that the statue was of a man who was "someone who thinks about thought." Why did such activity merit honor? "How could anyone who didn't do it, BE?" Now, this cheeky little philosopher sticks out his tongue at his German pursuer, "a red tongue, so long and so wide, an endless purple-pile-carpeted corridor, a tongue that was only too real, appallingly real, in this setting which wasn't real at all." Boris then sees the offending instrument sliced out by the German officer, followed by the "lovely eyes" of a Jewish girl. His consciousness roils behind the Gentile mask he wears:

> The belly of the Universe, the belly of Existence was gaping open, and its filthy intestines were invading the room. The dimensions and categories of consciousness, time, space, grief, vacancy, and all astronomies were indulging in a masquerade or tussle, in a wedding or ride, and the stuff of dreams was sprawled on the Throne of God, who lay in a swoon on the concrete, surrounded by His own vomit.[58]

Not painted birds at all but bold little Jews, these children are murdered in a rout of God's Universe. The prose tumbles toward madness so that it should not have to admit how soberly it testifies. Boris holds his tongue yet again when a cultivated young German invites him into the officer's mess, and he sees from its window pigs gnawing at five human heads he had thought were cabbages. He follows Leo's instructions to survive as a witness, and also fulfills the other part of his prophecy by becoming a stranger to others and himself.

Rawicz's narrative presents Boris alternately in the first and third persons, analogous to the game of hide-and-seek the protagonist plays with Poles, Ukrainians, Germans, and fellow-Jews-in-hiding—a game that reaches its climax when he falls into Gestapo hands. With false identity papers of a certain Yuri Goletz, Boris sees "how childish these precautions seem when set beside the deadly obviousness of the tool, now laid bare again." Nevertheless, for months he refuses to tell the Germans what they insist on knowing. Neither his torturers nor his cellmates can get him to admit he is a Jew, until one day he discovers a strategy better than mere denial. When his torturer says, "We've seen more than our share of 'Poles' like you," Boris blurts out:

> "Yes, Lieutenant, you are quite right. I am not a Pole. I am a Ukrainian. I know you are going to kill me. You cannot possibly release me now. You have worked me over too thoroughly. None too proud of the idea of my parading myself with a face like this, are you? I've no illusions on that score. . . . All the same, I'm not a Pole. Nor a Jew. And if I am to die now, I want to die as I was born: a Ukrainian."[59]

There follows an interview with the Ukrainian intellectual, which is quoted in this book's Introduction, in which Boris proves his Ukrainian identity beyond the shadow of a doubt. Under the German's nose, he even taunts his Ukrainian interrogator in their common language for collaborating with the enemy. Later, when his contrite cellmates beg his forgiveness, Boris absolves them in the name of "our Lord." In this flip side of Kosinski's fable, the overdetermined Jew outwits all the antisemites at once—the Poles, the Ukrainians, and the Germans.

But who is it that survives? "[The] man with the tool steeped in shoddy misfortunes and the head brimming over with comparisons" emerges as a mere composite of European disguises. The gaunt refugee sitting in the

Paris cafe at the end of the novel tells us he doesn't wear a hat, doesn't even own a hat: he is no longer even a symbolic Jew. When it comes to in-gratiating himself, though, he is prepared to remove the nonexistent hat in order to beg a spare coin or cigarette. France is where the Jew completes the process of his "naturalization." It is in this light that we read Boris's postscript, his final act of self-repudiation:

> This book is not a historical record.
> If the notion of chance (like most other notions) did not strike the author as absurd, he would gladly say that any reference to a particular period, territory, or race is purely co-incidental.
> The events that he describes could crop up in any place, at any time, in the mind of any man, planet, mineral.[60]

Some readers have taken this disclaimer at face value, to mean that Rawicz is confirming that events did not occur, "at least not as recorded here," and that fiction cannot be a reliable means of representing the Holocaust.[61] Yet the narrator is obviously playing a self-protective game of inversion with his readers. If Boris could remain an undetected witness to the slaughter of children, discuss literature in the presence of men buried alive, and con-vince the Gestapo that he was not a Pole but a Ukrainian, he can also sat-isfy the French intelligentsia's philosophical fancy by recasting the destruction of the Jews as the story of a metaphor. To make sure we grasp his bitterness, the Jew lays on this relativistic metaphorizing with a trowel. The veracity of the Holocaust is not what is questioned but rather the pre-tentious culture that Boris/Juri or the customer-narrator discover in France.

This novel indicts the act of bearing witness as a corrupt exchange be-tween a Jew who has ceased to be one and his depraved audience. Early in the novel, when the narrator describes the murder of Boris's mentor Leo L., he adds in a footnote that when Leo was murdered, the Jews lost their bid for posthumous justice: "For he alone would have been capable of speaking for us."[62] The French will accord the survivor a place in their cafe only if he has given up being a Jew. Some twenty years after Rawicz wrote this, Alain Finkielkraut described with refreshing candor how a young French Jew, unschooled in his own culture, could play at being persecuted by forging "a tragic spectacle from the tragedy of [his] people." Shielded from antisemitism by the precedent of the Holocaust, he wraps himself in the identity of the victim "with all but certain assurance that [he] would never be one."[63] But while Finkielkraut examines the shamefulness of being an imaginary Jew, the literary scholar Elaine Marks sees no irony at all in having discovered Jewishness through "an obsession with death and absence to which the Jewish story became attached." Without apparent regret or apology for her negative definition, she conceives of the Jew as a "metaphoric Marrano," and thus fleshes out the culture of emptiness and phoniness that Rawicz foretells.[64]

Elie Wiesel: Night

Paris was also the place where Elie Wiesel transformed himself—with phenomenal repercussions—from a writer of Yiddish and Hebrew into a French novelist. Refused a permit to Palestine by the British after his liberation from Buchenwald on April 11, 1945, Wiesel came to France with a cohort of young refugees, studied French and Jewish subjects under more or less private tutelage, and began a gritty career as correspondent for a Hebrew daily in Israel.[65] The almost random circumstance that brought him to France rather than to nascent Israel after the war determined not only the language but the direction of his life as a writer. In 1956 he published the Yiddish memoir . . . *un di velt hot geshvign* [And the World Was Silent], then transposed it into French as *La Nuit* (translated into English as *Night*).[66] As with the work of Isaac Bashevis, the translation rather than the original became the basis of all successive translations, not only because so many more translators know French and English than know Yiddish but because the transposition into a Gentile language had already accommodated a Gentile readership.

It was as the 117th volume in an Argentinian Yiddish series called Polish Jewry, devoted almost entirely to memoirs of prewar Europe and the war years, that . . . *un di velt hot geshvign* first appeared. Although its subject, the author's deportation to Auschwitz along with the other Jews of Hungarian Sighet, aligns it solidly with other books in the series, this memoir is exceptionally solitary. Most Yiddish memoirists try to fix the identity of as many murdered relatives and friends as possible, and for some of them that act of recalling the dead seems the very purpose of writing. Wiesel— the youngest author in the series—crafts a highly selective and isolating literary narrative. Although he resists the description of his work as fiction, readers have had no trouble distinguishing "the book's principal tropes—*night* and *father-son*"—its recurrent imagery, and coherent plot.[67] Having never studied literature before the war, Wiesel drew his literary models from the French existentialists and writers of the "Catholic renaissance" he read after the war, for whom individuality and individual conscience constituted the essence of art.

The scene at the dramatic center of his book illustrates how tightly the narrator controls the action. Three prisoners charged with sabotage, two adults and a boy, are hanged in the presence of the inmates. "Long live freedom!" cry the two adults as they mount the scaffold. The child is silent. "Where is God?" asks "someone" from behind the narrator. I translate the end of the chapter from the Yiddish:

> Both adults were already dead. The noose had choked them at once. Instantly they expired. Their extended tongues were red as fire.
>
> Only the slight Jewish child with the lost dreamy eyes was still alive. His body weighed too little. Was too light. The noose didn't "catch."
>
> The slow death of the little *meshoresl* [assistant] took thirty-five minutes. And we saw him wobbling, swaying, on the rope, with his bluish-red tongue extended, with a prayer on his grey-white lips, a prayer to God, to the Angel of Death, to take pity on him, to take his soul, liberating it from its death-throes, from the torments of the grave. When we saw him like that, the hanged child, many of us didn't want to, couldn't keep from crying.
>
> —Where is God?—the same man asked again, behind me. Something in me wanted to answer him:
>
> —Where is God?—Here he is, hanging on the gallows. . . .
>
> That evening the soup had no taste.
>
> We hid it away for the next day.[68]

Given that the witness of this hanging could not have known what the boy was thinking or whispering, the author is not so much describing as virtually creating this scene. The overheard anonymous man behind him and the "something in me" situate it within God's domain. The suspended child who is praying (in Yiddish he also has "angelic eyes"; in French he is described as an angel) evokes the suffering servant, an allusion made ex-

213

plicit by the diminutive *meshoresl* (little servant) for a *Kapo's* assistant, a eu-phemism that does not derive from the Lager but that conveys the boy's symbolic role in the execution.[69] The second interchange between "some-one" and the silent self then interprets the hanging as the "Death of God." Although we are told that the boy (probably not much younger than the sixteen-year-old witness) was hanged for the same act of sabotage as his two elders, Wiesel imaginatively recasts him as God's abandoned child.

Assisting in the translation from Yiddish into French, Wiesel improved the book artistically and also neutered it culturally. The quoted passage, for example, was compressed to about half its length; the projected prayer was dropped and this "objective" description added:

> For more than half an hour he stayed there, struggling between life and death, dying in slow agony under our eyes. And we had to look him full in the face. He was still alive when I passed in front of him. His tongue was still red, his eyes were not yet glazed.[70]

The closure of this passage was also rendered more credible. The French text reads, "Ce soir-la, la soupe avait un gout de cadavre [That night the soup tasted of corpses]."[71] By all accounts, no one at Auschwitz could have left his soup for the next day.

Translation obviously cost the author his intimacy with the Yiddish reader. In the Yiddish version, the author, like the ghetto diarists, hectors his fellow Jews about their false illusions. "We believed in God, trusted in Man, and lived with the illusion that each of us harbors a holy spark of the heavenly fire, that each of us bears in himself, in his eyes and his soul, the image of God. That was the source—if not the cause—of all our mis-eries."[72] The first-person plural pronoun and collective self-blame are ex-cised from the French. Missing, too, are the historical ironies, as when scraps of bread tossed into the prisoners' wagon remind the narrator of God's gift of manna in the desert: "Too bad that the Torah doesn't tell us how the Jews reacted to the first manna. Whether [. . .] the same dread-ful scenes were played out there as among us."[73] The change in title shifts the emphasis away from the "silence of the world"—meaning the uncon-cern of the non-Jewish world for the fate of the Jews—to the divine si-lence, meaning something like Nietzsche's death of God. The Yiddish author smarts with pain at the world's indifference:

Now, ten years after Buchenwald, I see that the world is forgetting. Germany is a sovereign state. The German army has risen
from the dead. Ilse Koch, the bestial sadist of Buchenwald, is happily raising her children. War criminals promenade through the
streets of Hamburg and Munich. The past is being erased. Forgotten.[74]

That no such disappointment in the Gentiles is voiced in translation
demonstrates how the conventions of national discourse override the exi-
gencies of the subject.

In her investigation of the Yiddish and French versions of *Night*, Naomi
Seidman suggests that the influence of François Mauriac, whom Wiesel
befriended, was responsible for turning "the survivor's political rage into
his existentialist doubt."[75] Mauriac's generous endorsement of *La Nuit*, in
which he connects Wiesel with that other Jew, "the Crucified, whose
Cross has conquered the world," became the prism through which the unknown Jewish writer attained renown. Mauriac wrote:

For [Wiesel], Nietzsche's cry expressed an almost physical reality: God is dead, the God of love, of gentleness, of comfort, the
God of Abraham, of Isaac, of Jacob, has vanished forevermore, beneath the gaze of this child, the smoke of a human holocaust ex-
acted by Race, the most voracious of idols. And how many pious
Jews have experienced this death![76]

Seidman assumes that because Mauriac gave the book a Christian interpretation—in a manner that many Jews have found offensive—Wiesel re-
ciprocally "negotiated" his memory of the Holocaust, presenting the Jew
"as the Christian is prepared to accept him, the emblem of suffering silence rather than living rage."[77] This idea of causality seems at once too
broad and too narrow. In truth, there is not much *rage* at all in the original
Yiddish, either against the Germans for their barbarism or the Jews for
their passivity, and there is more disappointment than anger with "the
world." Wiesel muted his emotion even further in translation, obeying
what Irving Howe called the aesthetic impulse to "lower the temperature"
when transposing Yiddish into a Gentile language. Moreover, Wiesel's Orthodox education had not included studies in modern Jewish literature, so

his formative models for writing about his own experience came mostly from the books he read after the war. The thinness of his artistic inheritance is also the source of his power, as his story emerges in stark and simple terms. With the instinct of a writer rather than a memoirist, he does not describe his reconciliation with his surviving sisters after the war and concludes instead with a confrontation of himself in the mirror. It was as though he had written the gospel of a survivor. How could Mauriac fail to see it, through Christian eyes, as the story of Lazarus risen from the dead?

Aharon Appelfeld: Badenheim 1939

Aharon Appelfeld experienced the war as Kosinski only invented it. His mother and grandmother were killed in the summer of 1941, and he was separated from his father soon afterward. Born near the polyglot city of Czernowitz, Rumania, with German as his mother tongue and Ukrainian learned from the household maids, he was probably well served—at least for the duration of the war—by the assimilated atmosphere in which he had been raised, because it allowed him to go unnoticed, as if a non-Jewish child, under changing occupations. In 1944, at the age of twelve, he attached himself to the Russian army as a kitchen helper, and at the war's end he made his way with eight other boys first to Yugoslavia, then to Italy. He reached Palestine in 1946, only to be interned by the British, but he started learning Hebrew in a school that was set up within the camp. It was in his acquired language that Appelfeld began to write, first poetry, then prose, eventually becoming one of Israel's most appreciated authors.[78]

Appelfeld's fiction is a landscape of deprivation. The author uses the absence of childhood memories, want of a native culture, the experience of prolonged homelessness, and belated acquisition of a literary language to evoke the cruel waste of the European legacy, an emptiness that can never be filled. His work is classified as Holocaust literature because it is situated in relation to the war and its dangers, yet his writings are actually more engaged with the world into which he was born than with the forces that determined its extinction. Like Kafka, the writer whom he acknowledges as his artistic savior, Appelfeld felt the coolness toward Jewishness in his own home before he encountered it in society, and it is this initial discovery that remained the more decisive. When the spiritual meanness of those trying to escape their Jewishness meets up with the forces of destruction, it has no resistance to offer, and if such Jews do manage to elude the enemy, they are left in the wilderness of post-war Europe without any cultural allegiance.

Language, the problem of the author, is the central problem for Appelfeld's characters. The narrator of an early story loses his voice the moment the cover is lifted off the bunker in which he has been hiding. Another, recuperating in the hospital, wants someone more intact than himself to record the refugees' stories "with the kind of detachment that makes observation possible."[79] One of Appelfeld's most sympathetic protagonists is an ambitious Jewish family's retarded daughter, Tzili, whose slowness of speech and mind becomes her moral as well as physical salvation. The first of his novels to be set during the war itself, *Tzili* seems to convey the author's sense of himself as a semi-mute, an educationally handicapped child who is better off because his parents had not had the time to turn him into the European sophisticate they would have wanted him to become.

Tzili's cultural shortfall is also an advantage when she is on her way to Eretz Israel at the end of the novel. Between those who trumpet "rebirth in Palestine" and those who want to shut down the Zionist rhetoric—"We've had enough words. No more words"—Tzili carries herself and her unborn child with quiet dignity.[80] Just so, the author contributed more to Israeli literature by revealing his privation than he could have done through Zionist zealotry. Critics have noted how the characteristic lacunae of Appelfeld's narrative style seem to credit what is missing more than what is there. Into the purposeful, dynamic, and highly vocal context of Israel, the Jewish state affirming its independence, Appelfeld admitted orphancy— loss for which there can be no compensation.

Appelfeld's best and best-known novel, *Badenheim 1939*, is a parable about modern Jewish culture. The book that introduced English readers to Appelfeld, it chronicles the last season of an Austrian summer resort frequented by Jews at various stages of assimilation. The book's English title signals its prevailing mood of predestination (the original, with subtler foreshadowing, is called *Badenheim: Resort Town*). As spring returns to Badenheim, bringing with it the vacationers who sustain the town's economy, the routine of townspeople and visitors is interrupted by ominous changes. The pharmacist's wife Trude, the novel's Cassandra, has been having hallucinatory visions about her daughter, who has married a Gentile, and about her native Poland, which seems to be summoning her home. Her husband gradually recognizes the logic of her premonitions when the "Sanitation Department" extends its jurisdiction into many areas of once unassailable privacy, requiring all Jews, permanent residents as well as visitors, to register for purposes unknown. In abbreviated chapters that distance us from the characters, as if from people in a dream, the novel forces the Jews in Badenheim to realize that they will be subject to the Nazi definition of them. The compressed quality of the prose endows every gesture and word with symbolic resonance.

A resort is a protected environment, a retreat from everyday concerns. In *Badenheim 1939*, Jewish life in central Europe is cast by Appelfeld as a misguided vacation from reality. For many years, the impresario Dr. Pappenheim has been organizing a cultural festival in which Jews were the main purveyors of and customers for German literature, music, and art. By the summer in question, their zeal has reached a maniacal pitch: the twins who recite Rilke are almost ethereal, "like people who had visited hell and were no longer afraid of it."[81] Professor Fussholdt spends all his time correcting the proofs of his latest book, which attacks Jewish scribblers who fall short of German literary perfection. Through the various guests, performers, and inhabitants of the town, the novel presents a composite study of German-speaking Jews, who seem to accept the ineluctable denouement of their drama. The final image, of Jews sucked into the trains "as easily as grains of wheat poured into a funnel," leaves a pregnant sadness but no sharper emotion—no outrage, no disquieting hatred of the murderers, no panic about the human condition. It suggests that the "return to Poland" was implicit in the initial attempts of Westernizing Jews to transcend their identity and that the best of them *accepted* the ironic reversal that restored them to their origins.

Though one can see why Appelfeld's story of fatal entrapment has been compared to Kafka's, Appelfeld stands in a different relation to his subject. Kafka's view of incomprehensible authority arose from within himself and was then projected outward. Appelfeld internalizes the real terror that was imposed from without, but it is as though the Hebrew prose in which the book is being written were separated from a fictionalized experience that was undergone in German. Appelfeld's Hebrew creates an atmosphere of remoteness even when he later writes about people whose language is Hebrew. The language of remoteness also insulates him from the past, as though the Hebrew narrative were the closed scar over the wound.

Quite unlike Kosinski and Rawicz, who remained men without a culture, and even unlike Wiesel, who wrote outward for a foreign audience, Appelfeld was clearly affected by the centripetal force of his acquired national language. As Appelfeld begins to write about Israeli immigrants, his Jewish characters form a community against their will, and his novels hint at the presence of a resurgent family and nation. The Immortal Bartfuss in the novel that bears his name is a thuggish survivor-immigrant imprisoned in paranoid self-isolation who begins to recognize in himself the desire for companionship and community that he had foresworn. The author followed a similar literary path in his acquired Jewish language.

Each of these four Jewish survivors of East-Central Europe—Kosinski, Rawicz, Wiesel, and Appelfeld—had to reinvent himself culturally after the war because he could not return to his native land or language. My colleague Susan Suleiman, who contends that all Holocaust memoirs are essentially "homeless," makes a useful distinction between postwar memoirs that were written "at home" in the native language and works that were "in translation from the start, with no original," that is, written not only far from home but in an adopted tongue.[82] Nor are the anxieties that attend these two types of dislocation limited to survivors of the war; they have become a staple of modern literature, as more and more refugees, exiles, and ordinary immigrants become writers overseas or in adopted languages. But to the distinction between native and adopted language must be added the more crucial distinction between Jewish and non-Jewish language, since Jews writing in Jewish languages may have been geographically displaced after the war but often seemed no more homeless than they had been before. Jews who had always lived within the metaphysical category of exile were no more or less in exile after the great destruction, and for some such writers the state of Israel created a sense of home that helped to offset the trauma of homelessness. As for the Jewish writers who continued in, or went home to, their native languages after the war was over, their confidence was at the mercy of the local climate.

Writers in Possession of Language

Anne Frank: Diary

Not by chance did the *Diary* of Anne Frank become the world's most beloved representation of the Holocaust. When the American Jewish writer and war correspondent Meyer Levin discovered the *Diary* in its French translation in 1952, he realized it was the ideal vehicle through which the Nazi genocide could be brought home to Americans.[83] His enthusiasm helped the *Diary* became the most famous book by a Jewish author after the Bible, selling over 25 million copies in fifty-nine languages by 1996. Anne Frank had charm, humor, honesty, literary talent, and good powers of observation. Her adolescent awakening, a favorite theme of modern literature, occurred during history's most dramatic manhunt. But the book's cultural context was equally decisive in putting readers at their ease. The removal of the family from Hitler's reach for the duration of the book prevents the horror of the Holocaust from invading the work, while the Westernmost Jewishness of the Frank household, which is hardly distinguishable from liberal Christianity, invites Gentiles to identify with the Jewish experience. The book became so popular that the Dutch government turned this Jewish child into a national icon, confirming the book's legitimacy and further extending its author's fame.[84]

The *Diary* radiates moral and cultural security. Anne had moved with her family from Frankfurt to Amsterdam when she was four years old, young enough to adopt Dutch as a mother tongue, and she regarded her new city, which was famed as an asylum since the Spanish and Portuguese Inquisitions, as a refuge from Nazism, the new Inquisition. In 1941 Anne was transferred to a Jewish school, something her cosmopolitan father would never have encouraged were it not required by the new racial laws that had been implemeted after Germany's conquest of Holland. In the Jewish school she not only was spared the indignity of exclusion by Gentiles but was surrounded by Jewish children, some of them from religiously devout or Zionist homes. She was instructed by Jewish teachers in the history of her own people; thus, by the time the family was forced into hiding, she was well armed to face the assault against her as a Jew. Confident of her acquired Dutch tongue, convinced of her personal innocence and of the rights of the Jews, Anne conceives of herself as the heroine of an adventure story in which a persecuted prey must remain undetected by the wicked bounty hunters in its "secret annexe." Because the families in the annexe are being sustained at great risk to themselves by wonderfully decent Dutch Christians, she knows all the Jews on the inside are not hated by all the Gentiles on the outside. Kitty, the addressee of her diary, is that undefined sympathetic friend for whom K. vainly reached but who Anne Frank always assumed was there.

The *Diary* invites us to experience the abnormality of the Final Solution from within a serene soul. "Miep often says she envies us for possessing such tranquility here," Anne records in November 1943, seventeen months after the family has gone into hiding, wondering, though, whether for those who have experienced the fears of entrapment "the world will ever be normal . . . again:"

> I see the eight of us with our "Secret Annexe" as if we were a little piece of blue heaven, surrounded by heavy black rain clouds. The round, clearly defined spot where we stand is still safe, but the clouds gather more closely about us and the circle which separates us from the approaching danger closes more and more tightly. Now we are so surrounded by danger and darkness that we bump against each other, as we search desperately for a means of escape. We all look down below, where people are fighting each other, we look above, where it is quiet and beautiful, and meanwhile we are cut off by the great dark wall; it tries to crush us, but cannot do so yet. I only cry and implore: "Oh, if only the black circle could recede and open the way for us!"[85]

In Anne's cosmology, the moral center stands firm, even as the inhabitants begin to fear their isolation and danger.

Not until April 11, 1944, after the burglary that almost exposed the Franks' hiding place (and may very well have led to the betrayal), does Anne express for the first time the humiliation of her situation:

> We have been pointedly reminded that we are in hiding, that we are Jews in chains, chained to one spot, without any rights, with a thousand duties.[. . .] Who has made us Jews different from all other people? Who has allowed us to suffer up till now? It is God

that has made us as we are, but it will be God, too, who will raise us up again. If we bear all this suffering, and if there are still Jews left when it is over, then Jews, instead of being doomed, will be held up as an example. Who knows, it might even be our religion from which the world and all peoples learn good, and for that reason and that reason only do we have to suffer now. We can never become just Netherlanders or just English or any nation for that matter, we will always remain Jews, we must remain Jews, but we want to, too.[86]

Her dialectic swings restlessly between affirmation in God as the guarantor of Jewish dignity to the need for approval from the world and all its peoples. Though her Jewish self-affirmation is as proud as Yitskhok Rudashevski's, Anne thinks of Jewishness in relation to Gentiles, and she concludes this diary entry resolving to lay down her life—"like a soldier on the battlefield"—for her beloved Holland. She is so firmly a Dutch Jew that any expression of loyalty to one part of her forged identity elicits corresponding pride in the other. Only as the diary nears its sudden end does she begin worrying about Dutch antisemitism and collaborationism, but she is arrested before she can record its consequence.

Anne Frank testifies to the Jewish–Gentile symbiosis in Europe during the very years of its annihilation. This led some of her Jewish countrymen to fear that her optimism might eclipse the brutal record. In order to document the "final, unwritten chapters" between her arrest on August 4, 1944, and her expiry at Bergen-Belsen at the beginning of March 1945, the Dutch Jewish filmmaker Willy Lindwer interviewed Anne's surviving classmates and acquaintances for his documentary and book, both entitled *The Last Seven Months of Anne Frank*. The testimony of these women, who shared the incarceration of Anne, her mother, and her sister Margot in Auschwitz and Bergen-Belsen, admits the murderous reality that the writer of the *Diary* still hoped to be spared. One of these surviving friends wrote in the registration book of Anne Frank House, the popular museum that recalls her years in hiding: "Anne Frank didn't want this."[87] But the Dutch government may well go on protecting Anne's aura of optimism, since the image of her in hiding, assisted by righteous Gentiles, presents the country in much better light than does the Westerbork detention camp, guarded by Dutch police, from which all the inhabitants of the secret annex were deported, along with one hundred thousand other Dutch Jews, to Sobibor and Auschwitz.[88]

Ironically, the affirmative power of the *Diary* made it equally threatening to extremes of the political Right and Left. Neo-fascists called its authenticity into question as part of their effort to deny the historicity of the Nazi genocide. Holocaust deniers feel they have to discredit the work through which most people in the world first learn about the destruction of European Jewry.[89] The attack from the other side of the political spectrum was no less pernicious. Selected at least in part for their leftist credentials, the American dramatists Albert Hackett and Frances Goodrich, who adapted the *Diary of Anne Frank* for stage and screen, accentuated its faith in humanity at the expense of its Jewish anxieties. Garson Kanin, who directed the *Diary* in its definitive stage version, found Anne too disturbingly Jewish:

> Anne says "We're not the only Jews that've had to suffer. Right down through the ages, there have been Jews and they've had to suffer." This strikes me as an embarrassing piece of special pleading. Right down through the ages, people have suffered because of being English, French, German, Italian, Ethiopian, Mohammedan, Negro, and so on. I don't know how this can be indicated, but it seems to me of utmost importance. The fact that in this play the symbols of persecution and oppression are Jews is incidental, and Anne, in stating the argument so, reduces her magnificent stature.[90]

Kanin insisted on deracination as a condition of performance. He refused to admit Anne's resolve as a Jew, turning her thought inside out to make her say, "We're not the only people that've had to suffer. Sometimes one race . . . sometimes another." Those opposed to Jewish self-determination, as Kanin was, did not want Anne's Jewishness to reinforce Jewish national consciousness. Meyer Levin was driven half mad by the attempt to neuter Anne's text, and subsequent histories of the public quarrel between him and Lillian Hellman, whom he held chiefly responsible for this attempt, have taken up the argument.[91] But it has to be said that the humanistic Judaism of Anne Frank's Reform home is the basis of her broad appeal. The leftists were only exaggerating, not inventing, the universalism implicit in her idea of the Jewish mission.

Primo Levi: If This Is a Man

Primo Levi, called "the great memoirist of the Holocaust" and, despite his grim subject, "one of the outstandingly beautiful and moving writers of our time,"[92] had the advantage over Anne Frank in being able to complete his own account of the war years, and to keep returning to it until his death, or suicide, in 1987. He became for the intellectual reader what Anne Frank was for the masses, the preferred guide to Hitler's Europe, and for some of the same reasons. H. Stuart Hughes distinguished Levi from among his more assimilated Italian coreligionists as a "real Jew" because he had celebrated his bar mitzvah and accepted his Jewish heritage.[93] But Levi admits that until Mussolini's passage of the racial laws in 1939, he had always considered his origin "as an almost negligible but curious fact, a small amusing anomaly, like having a crooked nose or freckles."[94] Levi is the cultural antithesis of Kosinski, who had to invent himself as a writer from scratch; of the East European Piotr Rawicz and his chameleon protagonist Boris, who are trying to satisfy Paris; and of the Orthodox-educated Hungarian Elie Wiesel, who wrote in Hebrew and Yiddish before settling on French. Levi was a culturally integrated European, a native and lifelong Italian Jew who was educated in the language and literature that he then made his own.

His memoir *If This Is a Man* (originally published in English as *Survival in Auschwitz*) opens with a comment on this firm identity: "I was twenty-four, with little wisdom, no experience and a decided tendency—encouraged by the life of segregation forced on me for the previous four years by racial laws—to live in an unrealistic world of my own, a world inhabited by civilized Cartesian phantoms, by sincere male and bloodless female friendships."[95] Many of those friendships were with non-Jews who lived, as Levi did, beyond caring for such distinctions. Considerably older than Anne Frank when the war broke out, already a working chemist and with several published stories to his credit, he was far more at home in his native language and culture, being able to trace his Italian lineage back for generations, whereas she had come to Holland from Germany as a child and felt demonstratively grateful to her adoptive homeland.

It has been suggested that Levi's memoir of Auschwitz is an inversion of the *bildungsroman*, since the narrator has to *unlearn* rather than to learn all the stages of civilization.[96] Levi confirms that during his stay at Auschwitz he evolved from a Cartesian into a Lagerian, a creature of the concentration camp. Yet there is not the slightest indication that Levi really exchanged one set of values for another or came to doubt the humanist credo with which he had entered the camp. Whereas Elie Wiesel opened his Yiddish memoir with a statement of his lost faith, Levi was able to write at the end of his life, "I . . . entered the lager as a nonbeliever, and as a nonbeliever I was liberated and have lived to this day," stressing the continuity rather than the discontinuity with his prewar beliefs.[97]

Though Primo Levi says he suffered the common inmates' nightmare that no one back home would want to listen to his story, the manner in which he addresses his readers hints of no such anxiety:

> All took leave from life in the manner which most suited them. Some praying, some deliberately drunk, others lustfully intoxicated for the last time. But the mothers stayed up to prepare the food for the journey with tender care, and washed their children and packed the luggage; and at dawn the barbed wire was full of children's washing hung out in the wind to dry. Nor did they forget the diapers, the toys, the cushions and the hundred other small things which mothers remember and which children always need. Would you not do the same? If you and your child were going to be killed tomorrow, would you not give him to eat today?[98]

Levi's scene is finely and musically calibrated, with the mendicants, drinkers, and fornicators off in their shadowy corners and the children's washing etched on the barbed wire fence. The narrator involves us in the plight of these mothers, who commit what are meaningless acts only from Nazi perspective, not ours. The humanist, eschewing both supernaturalism and naturalism, does not believe we serve any higher purpose or that man is reducible to the sum of his animal parts. Thus, he speaks with true moral assurance, in the language he shares with his readers, a language that, despite Italian fascism, is not implicated in the horrors he must describe.

Levi's art of mediation reaches its high point in a somewhat longer description of his work team at Buna on a rare "good day" at the coming of spring:

We look around like blind people who have recovered their sight, and we look at each other. We have never seen each other in sunlight: someone smiles. If it was not for the hunger!

For human nature is such that grief and pain—even simultaneously suffered—do not add up as a whole in our consciousness, but hide, the lesser behind the greater, according to a definite law of perspective. It is providential and is our means of surviving in the camp. And this is the reason why so often in free life one hears it said that man is never content. In fact it is not a question of a human incapacity for a state of absolute happiness, but of an ever-insufficient knowledge of the complex nature of the state of unhappiness; so that the single name of the major cause is given to all its causes, which are composite and set out in an order of urgency. And if the most immediate cause of stress comes to an end, you are grievously amazed to see that another one lies behind; and in reality a whole series of others.

So that as soon as the cold, which throughout the winter had seemed our only enemy, had ceased, we became aware of our hunger; and repeating the same error, we now say: "If it was not for the hunger!"[99]

Here the humanist with his embracing sympathies returns to the age-old question of happiness. Extrapolating from his own experience, as scientists from Archimedes to Freud have done, he arrives at a new law of emotional perspective whereby the greater source of displeasure obscures the lesser. As opposed to those who dwell on the aberrant features of the Nazi experiment in evil, he wants to communicate what the Lager has to teach not only about deviancy but about normalcy. The same Renaissance ideal that once prompted humanists to formulate the codes of the courtier inspires Levi to figure out the codes of the Lager so that he can share his acquired knowledge with the rest of Europe. Only a cultural poise acquired long before the war allows for this possibility.

Just once in the memoir does his narrative sympathy fail him. Following a "selection," the narrator sees old Kuhn praying on his bunk, and upon the assumption that "Kuhn is thanking God because he has not been chosen," he explodes in fury:

Kuhn is out of his senses. Does he not see Beppo the Greek in the bunk next to him, Beppo who is twenty years old and is going to the gas chamber the day after tomorrow and knows it and lies there looking fixedly at the light without saying anything and without even thinking any more? Can Kuhn fail to realize that next time it will be his turn? Does Kuhn not understand that what has happened today is an abomination, which no propitiatory prayer, no pardon, no expiation by the guilty, which nothing at all in the power of man can ever clean again?

If I was God, I would spit at Kuhn's prayer.[100]

Each rhetorical question invites condemnation of the religious impulse. The passage "provides rejection of any religious perspective and something unusual, [Levi's] angry moral judgment."[101] Primo Levi assumes that Kuhn's prayer is selfish in the same way that Wiesel speaks for the angel on the gallows, attributing his own meaning to an utterance the content of which he could not have known. Levi's unique show of anger, not with one of the Germans or *Kapos* or even with the most bestial of the prisoners but with a believing Jew, alerts us to a problem in his humanism that excludes believers from his range of sympathy and attributes to the observant Jew an idea of chosenness as callow as his own.

This problem of humanism is acknowledged in the last of Levi's memoirs, *The Drowned and the Saved,* when the author recalls the moment of entering Auschwitz, waiting to file past the "commission" that would spare him or send him to the gas chambers:

For one instant I felt the need to ask for help and asylum; then, despite my anguish, equanimity prevailed; one does not change the rules of the game at the end of the match, not when you are losing. A prayer under these conditions would have been not only absurd (what rights could I claim? and from whom?) but blasphemous, obscene, laden with the greatest impiety of which a nonbeliever is capable. I rejected the temptation: I knew that otherwise, were I to survive, I would have to be ashamed of it.[102]

Having once joined the cult of self-reliance, Levi feels it would be dishonorable to admit his limitations. But his concept of sport and team loyalty is inadequate to the test to which he is being put. Although prayer may indeed be used as a desperate plea bargain with the Almighty, the Hebrew Psalms are sufficient evidence of many other possibilities. Who knows? Perhaps the young man who entered Auschwitz yielded to temptation when he *resisted* his impulse to pray? Culturally induced by his upbringing, Levi's humanism serves him well as a chronicler, but also fails him at the crucial point of spiritual need, when man cannot fathom what he is forced to endure.

By contrast, the happiest moment in Levi's account of Auschwitz—an exalted moment, really—comes when he is carrying a huge pot of soup with a fellow prisoner, Jean, an Alsacian Jew. For some "unknown" reason, a canto from Dante's Divine Comedy comes to mind, the passage where Ulysses, as sought out by Dante and Virgil in purgatory, recalls how he exhorted his followers to sail beyond anything that they had ever known before:

> *Think of your breed, for brutish ignorance*
> *Your mettle was not made, you were made men,*
> *To follow after knowledge and excellence.*[103]

The prisoner struggles to remember lines he had learned by heart as a schoolboy so that he might inspire his partner—who knows no Italian—with a reminder of man's noble potential. When his memory falters, he says he would have given "today's soup" to find the connecting lines, a sentiment so improbable that the author confirms its truth decades later. Levi has been called "the Dante of our time," testifying to the reciprocal influence he enjoys with the Italian literary tradition. Professor Lino Pertile of Harvard University is probably not alone in opening his course on Dante with this above-quoted passage from Primo Levi. Yet Dante's inspiration was divine, after all, and the Jew obviously read him selectively for this particular secular illumination.

Levi took his artistic responsibilities to the Jewish people very seriously. Decades after the war, deviating from his practice of writing only about what he knew firsthand, he researched the history of a band of Jewish partisans in order to dramatize a Holocaust "counternarrative" of resistance. The resulting novel, *If Not Now, When?*, is touching evidence of a great artist's determination to write a work out of a sense of duty, even if it

meant going against the grain of his talent and beyond the range of his experience.[104] But Levi's Jewish fellow-feeling did not extend to the religious
tradition. His poetic revision of the Shema, the holiest prayer in Judaism—"Hear O Israel, the Lord Our God, the Lord is One"—replaces
God by victims of the death camp as the supreme object of veneration; it
is they who are to be engraved on our hearts, as it says in the original
prayer, "When you are in your house, when you walk on your way/When
you go to bed, when you rise [*Stando in casa andando per via,/Coricandovi alzan-
dovi*]."[105] The title of his memoir, *Se questo è un uomo* [If This Is a Man], which
is drawn from this poem, follows Christianity in placing suffering man
(though without divine parentage) at the pinnacle of its eschatology, as an
end in himself.

Henryk Grynberg: The Jewish War; The Victory

Henryk Grynberg, born in Poland in 1936 and a resident of his native land
until 1967, serves as our final and most complicated example of the Jew
who writes about the war in his native non-Jewish language. Grynberg's
parents lived on such intimate terms with the local townspeople in their
region of Minsk Mazowiecki that his father assumed he could trust some
of them with his money while the family tried to hide from the Germans.
But most of the family was discovered and killed, and the father was axed
to death one night when he returned to pick up his deposit. The mother
was able to save only the elder of her two sons through a series of adventures that the author eventually turned into literature. Since mother and
son remained in Poland after the war and after the imposition of the Communist regime, Polish was Grynberg's altogether natural language once he
became a writer and a journalist, and it remained his language after he
sought asylum from antisemitism in the United States. Polish had saved
him but betrayed him. He had to reveal himself in the language of his
concealment.

Grynberg's career as a writer was necessarily affected by the status of
the Jews in Poland, which became even more ambiguous after the war
than it had been before. Poles did not change their stereotypic view of
Jews as a result of their annihilation, especially if they had taken over Jewish property and were afraid that claimants to it might some day reap-
pear.[106] Hatred of Jews that had been fanned under the Germans could no
longer express itself freely once the Soviet Union imposed Communist

rule, but the prominence of Jews in party leadership made it possible to hold them responsible for Communism's dictatorship. Grynberg was not merely confined like the German Jewish writers to the language of his antagonists but blamed as a Jew by his fellow Poles for the Communist regime that throttled *their* national independence. The ironies multiplied when the Communist regime he was accused of abetting began fomenting anti-Jewish propaganda following Israel's victory over the Soviet-supported Arab armies in the Six-Day War in 1967. This was the final assault that drove Grynberg and many thousands of other Jews from their homeland.

Once in the United States as a Polish émigré, Grynberg began reconstructing the story of his family in a series of autobiographical fictions. He called his first book *The Jewish War,* conveying the intention of his literary counteroffensive.[107] At the basic level, this was the war his parents had waged for their lives and the lives of their children, against the Poles as well as the Germans, since without the help of the Poles the Germans could never have identified them as Jews. His father is immensely resourceful, amassing the ransom he knew he needed to protect Jewish life:

> And he was proved right . . . he was right to have amassed money so laboriously. He bought with it the bread he was holding under his coat. One can always count on money. Money proves that one is human, he thought. And if you get killed for it, you are not killed like an animal, but like a human being, for money.[108]

Grynberg might have trained his irony on his father for a strategy that failed, but instead he praises him for having thought like a man. There is no foreshadowing here. Like a military historian, the author explains his father's strategies and then, after his murder, tells how his mother masterminded their survival. Mother and child take increasing risks, finally boarding with local Christian families in a remote village. His mother serves as the local schoolteacher, offering instruction in catechism and going regularly to confession. So genuinely does the child adopt his role that he is stricken with conscience when he must take Communion without telling the priest that he has not been baptized, and his mother can only persuade him to commit this "mortal sin" because the alternative would cause her death. At a much more impressionable age than Rawicz's Boris, he is forced to make his subterfuge *natural* by turning into what he pretends to be.

The tactics Grynberg adopts as an author are precisely those his mother taught him for outwitting the Poles, and later the Russians. Don't hang your head. Don't knock softly, like a Jew, but rap short and sharp to demonstrate that you expect to be let in. March out in front, never show fear. Manifest the freedom that you are being denied, and never seem to be concealing anything lest you are recognized as the prey that you are. Looking back, the author wonders how such a posture could have been maintained:

> My stance had become upright. I stopped walking with my toes turned in. Mama told me to look people straight in the eye. I did. I was a child and I did not find it difficult. But what if I had been older? Like Mama, for instance? Could I have done it? Probably not. Just as the others couldn't. They did not look people in the eye and they perished. It was said that they had "Jewish eyes."[109]

Grynberg adopts the unsentimental style of the survivor to recount his story, but he includes himself among those who would not have passed the test. The naive point of view of the child who would have perished is contrasted with the determination of the mother whose plucky realism pulled them through. But Grynberg is quite unlike Rawicz and his hero Boris in the conclusions that he draws from his strategy of survival. The literary equivalent of what Grynberg was taught as a child is now to face the world with unblinking *Jewish* eyes, since only thus can Jews claim to have survived. The Jew has now to affirm the identity he was once forced to conceal in order to emerge victorious from the Jewish war.

Grynberg's war imagery assumes this new meaning in the postwar period. At first the child reaches certain obvious conclusions as a result of his adventures. When his mother wants to return to see whether any of her family is still alive, he does not want to go back home. "Why?" his mother asks. "Why don't you want to go back to Dobre?" His answer is straightforward: "Because I don't want to be a Jew anymore."[110] With the Russian liberation of Poland, the Jews may technically emerge from hiding, except that now everyone knows that they are expendable. "Once the way has been shown, any fool can do it the second time."[111] The Bolsheviks who "liberate" Poland expect the child to learn their catchwords and catechism while the Poles revile him for mouthing Russian propaganda and expect him to recite their patriotic verse. The boy and his mother have risen one notch by becoming pawns instead of just targets; whereas the Germans invited the Poles to help them kill the Jews, the Russians use the Jews to impose their power on the Poles. But the danger is now doubled, for the Jews are morally suspect as well as politically vulnerable.

In the second volume of the memoir, entitled *The Victory*, the boy is reconciled to being a Jew to the point of becoming the chronicler of Jewish experience. The child's point of view gives way to eye-level sympathy for the desperate adults who are trying to "take up a new life." Two families fight for possession of a girl who had been left in a convent, each claiming her as their own. Jewish men marry the women who saved them and become part of the same Christian communities that helped eliminate their original families. Grynberg tells the story of himself, his mother, and his new stepfather Uszer in a way that encompasses the history of postwar Jewry in Poland:

> There were tears wherever Jews assembled. [. . .] But at no other time did things ever reach the extremes they did one Sunday morning when [. . .] they showed the prewar Jewish film, *The Town of Belz*. It's hard to say how many Jews were in Lodz at that time. Seven hundred and seventy had survived in the ghetto. Maybe a few hundred more had returned from the concentration camps. A few hundred had arrived with the Polish-Russian army. There were also some two thousand survivors from other cities and towns, people like us. And all of them wanted to get into the hall, which could not hold more than five hundred people. They broke the doors, all the mirrors, railings, and windows. The tickets, bought at black market prices, meant nothing now since nobody could check them. The throng pressed from every side and through every possible entrance. My mother never even made it into the lobby. Uszer pushed me in front of him. The lobby was so packed I couldn't breathe. I started shouting, "Let me out, I'm suffocating!" Women started shouting, too. But nothing could be done, there was no way to get out. People tried to remove the women who had fainted by passing them over their heads. Uszer managed to lift me

up and seat me on his shoulders and walked me inside. Three or four people seemed to be on every chair. All the space around the walls and between the rows was filled. There was little air, as if there were an invisible throng hovering above us. The lights went out and, for a moment, complete silence reigned. But when the well-known song came on—"Oh Belz, my beloved Belz, my little shtetele where all of my family . . . "—terrible cries burst from everyone. Not weeping, not wailing, but a great collective groan and cry of pain. As if a mass execution had taken place. You couldn't hear the words of the song or the melody. You couldn't even see the screen because everyone had risen and was standing on tiptoe to see. But at the same time, people covered their eyes and faces with their hands. This went on until the film was over.[112]

This passage illustrates the difficulty of invoking the words *Art* and *Holocaust* in tandem. The destruction of the Jews was so extensive and final that nothing *but* words and music could recover its actuality. For those who had lost their world, the quality of the document was less important than the fact of its existence and the images it held. A prewar film made to serve the market for nostalgia, a song that had become the very byword for sentimentality—these acquire the emotional force of an earthquake once their subject lies buried under rubble. But when the author describes the event many years after it occurred, he has to compose *his* scene with care. He relegates to analogy what was real for the people in the theatre—the invisible throng hovering above them, the mass execution that had taken place. He provides demographic information about the remnants of Polish Jewry to explain the extremity of the behavior we are witnessing. Readers who have been following the story of one boy and his mother have to be swept up into the hysteria of mourning and made to experience for one long claustrophobic moment Jewish grief that is too great to be borne. Grynberg is thoroughly at home in his language, in the Polish city, in recounting his life. He is at home, too, in opening up his "theater" to the Poles.

Grynberg concludes these two books with a rueful observation: "The war was over, but who had won?" He appreciates how important it is for teachers and parents to insist that good always wins out over evil, as could be surmised from Hitler's defeat. He has sought justice by trying to discover his father's murderer. Yet he finds no resolution to the war in Poland, a country that feels abused not only for its suffering under the Germans but by the very Jews it displaced, whose spoils it appropriated. His own war never really ends "but only hides beneath the surface of life and continues its course there . . . In a certain way real war may be better—during a war you can wait for peace. And truly believe in it."[113] Fussell's propagandists conscripted literature to political ends because they were fighting a winnable war. The war for Jewish life that Grynberg prosecutes in literature has only won the freedom to record its losses.

The Fate of Yiddish

Hitler's war against the Jews was simultaneously a war against Yiddish, which was the creation of European Jewry and the main repository of its modern culture. The dangerous potential that Kafka recognized in the unequal relation between German and Yiddish was fully realized in the ghettos of eastern Europe by the Jews who kept diaries and records to transcend the finality of being murdered. Prior to the war, Yiddish had nurtured one of the most determinedly secular literatures of the West. Along with much of the rest of Europe, its writers were swept up by newfound confidence in the powers of human beings to resolve their own problems on earth without the supervision of divine authority. The war that destroyed the base of their language cut away the foundation of these secular hopes; more than that, it seemed to leave open no appeal to history.

Many Yiddish writers and poets turned away from the all-too-present world to the absent God and composed a new liturgy. On May 22, 1943, the poet Abraham Sutzkever wrote a song in the Vilna ghetto that reaches up from his cellar hiding place to a white hand as pure as a shroud: "Beneath the whiteness of your stars, / Stretch out to me your white hand; / All my words are turned to tears—/ They long to rest within your hand."[114] Kadya Molodowsky prays after the war, "Merciful God / choose another people/ Elect another."[115] Aaron Zeitlin admits that being a Jew "means, even if you wish to, you cannot escape His snares, / you cannot cease to pray—even after all the prayers, / even after all the 'evens.'"[116] Jacob Glatstein casts the displaced Jewish God as the dependent of a vanishing tribe: "Without Jews, no Jewish God. / If, God forbid, we should quit this world,

Your poor tent's light / would out."[117] Chaim Grade commands himself, "Pull on rotting shoes from the deathcamp Maidanek / And go to heaven to find their cremated feet." Z. Segalovitch asks, "Oh God, for whom are you God?"[118] In his remarkable poem dated London 1941, Itsik Manger brings Eve back at sunset to the apple tree, which is not the Tree of Life but the Tree of Death;[119] he recasts that primal moment as portent of the *khurbn*. When the Yiddish poets lost their people, the Jewish God became their ideal reader by default.

Chaim Grade dramatized the dilemma of the postwar Yiddish writer in his most famous story, "My Quarrel with Hersh Rasseyner."[120] Set briefly in Bialystok (1937) and Vilna (1939) and then at length in Paris (summer 1948), the story traces the ongoing quarrel between two former *yeshiva* classmates: Hersh Rasseyner, who remains within the tradition, and Chaim Vilner (Grade's *yeshiva* name), who becomes a secular Yiddish writer. When the two survivors rediscover one another, both are incredulous. Vilner cannot believe that after the *khurbn* anyone can still believe in God. Rasseyner cannot believe that after the *khurbn* anyone can still believe in man. The catastrophe that destroyed their families and their way of life was powerless to interrupt, much less bring to an end, the debate that they had entered into when Vilner left Jewish observance. This story is not only anti-Hitler, it is resolutely anti-Holocaust, in the sense of reestablishing the continuity that had been shattered by the events of 1939–45. Like the Hasidic paradox "There is nothing as whole as a broken heart," Grade uses the inherent contentiousness of Jewish culture and of his own divided self as proof that the "modern Jew" has survived the war intact.

The German Jew-hunt did not destroy or even redefine its target. The difference between Jewish Jews, attenuated Jews, conflicted Jews, reluctant Jews, and non-Jewish Jews emerges every bit as sharply from wartime and postwar writing as it did earlier in Europe. As a general rule, writers in Yiddish and Hebrew experienced the *khurbn* or *Shoah* as a national catastrophe. The act of writing about the destruction of the Jews in the Jewish languages reinforces a sense of collective responsibility even when—or especially when—it complains of Jewish behavior and protests against the God of Israel. Only in "postmodern" Israel, once its writers began to absorb Western influence to the degree that Jewish writers had once done in Europe, did Hebrew start playing around with the *Shoah*, even to the point of suggesting that German and Jewish nationalism are similar.[121]

The experience of the East-Central European Jewish writer whose native tongue was not Jewish or who emigrated linguistically from a Jewish to a Gentile tongue was quite different. Paul Celan nailed his poetry to the paradox of his native German tongue, the language he was doomed to share with his parents' executioners. The suicides of Celan, Jerzy Kosinski, Piotr Rawicz, Jean Améry, and Primo Levi divulge the toll of writing about the destruction in Gentile tongues. Did their loneliness overtake them? Did they experience a common despair?

Grynberg's question ("The war was over, but who had won?") fuels the continuing conflict over what constitutes the literature of the Holocaust. The war over history perpetuates the war within history. Jewish literature absorbs the catastrophe but cannot contain it. The Jews may have been left to die, but now their death is appropriated by the world in many different branches of "Holocaust literature" and "Holocaust studies." There is powerful pressure from Christian and liberal culture, all the stronger for being unconscious, to interpret the slaughter through its own universal symbolism rather than as a political process aimed at a particular people. The term *Holocaust* itself works hard to spiritualize the war against the Jews. The dominance of Gentile over Jewish languages, in literary scholarship as well as in literature, the preponderance of Jewish writers who work in Gentile languages, and the growing distance from the events—all suggest that although Jews will continue to be recognized as Hitler's primary victims, they will have as much trouble keeping *their* experience of the war in contention as they had keeping themselves alive in Europe.

7

THE ZIONIST FATE
IN ENGLISH HANDS

FROM GEORGE ELIOT TO A. M. KLEIN

> This earth means something different to us than Croatia to the
> Croats or America to the Americans. They are married to their
> countries; we are searching for a lost bride.
>
> ARTHUR KOESTLER, *Thieves in the Night* (1946)[1]

UNTIL THIS POINT, we have been looking at a modern literature
that arose in tandem with ideologies and political movements
hostile to the existence of a Jewish people. This hostility is reflected in each and every work we discussed so far, culminating in Holocaust testimonies. In turning now to the rise of Zionism as reflected
through the prism of English literature, our interest is not with how badly
the Jews have fared at the hands of English authors from Chaucer to Graham Greene—the usual theme of such investigations—but rather how *well*
Jews manage in the world's most hospitable culture.

Perhaps the most important insight of political Zionism was its recognition of the paradox of emancipation. At the end of the nineteenth century, the Viennese journalist and playwright Theodor Herzl, then
stationed in Paris, realized as he witnessed the Dreyfus affair that the more
Jews blended with their Christian neighbors, the more they provoked
anxieties. The Parisians who a century earlier had proclaimed "liberté,
egalité, fraternité" were now out in force yelling "Death to the Jews!" A
Jewish army officer was being publicly vilified not because he wore Jewish
earlocks and spoke Yiddish but because he had so successfully transformed
himself into a Frenchman that he was suspected of undermining the
Frenchness of the state. Herzl, who had once considered leading Jews en

masse to the baptismal font, founded the Zionist movement in 1897 with the goal of creating a modern Jewish state that would lessen the risk facing the Jewish people by removing them from Europe.

But Zionism was not merely a negative reaction to Europe, it was also the product of enlightenment and emancipation, drawing special inspiration from the spirit of liberalism that emanated from Britain and the United States. If Benjamin Disraeli, an obvious Jew despite his father's decision to have him baptized, could head a modern state as prime minister of England, why could there not be a state of self-emancipated Jews with a leader of their own? If pilgrims fleeing religious persecution could establish their independence in brand-new colonies, why shouldn't Jews—who had introduced the idea of religious freedom to the world in the Book of Exodus—now emancipate themselves from the Egypt of Europe? England was hardly free of anti-Jewish sentiment, providing such stereotypical portrayals as Shylock and Fagin, but England and America were also the beacon of political tolerance for Jews fleeing persecution and seeking national renaissance. Could English literature also allow for the autonomy of a modern Jewish people? Could Jewish writers convey in English their religious distinctiveness and the competitive potential of their civilization? Would English allow for the kind of cultural security we found in Sholem Aleichem and S. Y. Agnon? Since Zionism was both the fruit of British liberalism and the declaration of Jewish independence, what happens to the self-affirming Jew in English literature?

Similar questions have been addressed in recent investigations of British and American influence on countries and cultures that have come under their sway. I do not share the rancor that is often implicit in the use of the term *colonialism*. The record of relations between the Jews and the English-speaking world is mixed. The declaration of Lord Arthur Balfour in 1917 that "His Majesty's Government view with favour the establishment in Palestine of a national home for the Jewish people" was probably the single most potent support for Zionism to come from outside the Jewish community. Yet the British blockade of Palestine in response to Arab pressure in the 1930s was probably its cruelest setback. Had it not been for England and America, Hitler would have consolidated the Third Reich. Yet had the Allies acknowledged Hitler's war against the Jews, there would not have been six million Jewish dead. These same contradictions come into play in English literature, which often betrays Christian assumptions toward the Jews even as it extends them its most generous hospitality.

Before seeing how Jewish literature deals with this subject, it is useful to discuss two prominent representations of the Jew in modern literature that demonstrate how Jews can, and cannot, survive the dilemma of English generosity. What is obviously at stake in both these works is not the fate of the Jew alone but the fate of an unassimilable minority in a Christian culture.

The Classic of Zionism: George Eliot's *Daniel Deronda*

George Eliot was at the peak of her powers and recognized as the finest novelist in England when she began to research *Daniel Deronda* (1876). Among its probable sources, biographers single out her friendship with the Talmudic scholar Rabbi Emanuel Deutsch (1829–73), who had visited Palestine in 1869 and provided her with the "inspirational model of a man committed to race, faith, tradition" and the ideal of a Jewish national homeland.[2] In Eliot's previous two works, the Italian historical novel *Romola* and the dramatic poem *The Spanish Gypsy*, she tried to rouse the imagination of her fellow English men and women "to a vision of human claims in those races of their fellow men who most differ from them in customs and beliefs."[3] In choosing a Jewish subject, she certainly accomplished that goal. We are introduced to Deronda as a young man of uncertain background; as the adopted son of a wealthy British peer, he has to find a profession, a wife, and what would today be called an identity. As Deronda gropes to discover who he is and what he should make of himself, the novel poses the question of what Christians and Jews were to make of themselves once formal discrimination was outlawed and British citizenship extended equal rights to all.

The book opens as Daniel Deronda watches an unknown woman flushed with triumph at a roulette table:

> Was she beautiful or not beautiful? and what was the secret of
> form or expression which gave the dynamic quality to her glance?
> Was the good or the evil genius dominant in those beams? Proba-

bly the evil; else why was the effect that of unrest rather than of undisturbed charm? Why was the wish to look again felt as coercion and not as a longing in which the whole being consents?[4]

Deronda's attraction to the woman touches a moral nerve in ways that a Hebrew or Yiddish writer would almost certainly have rendered in the terminology of the *yeytser tov* and the *yeytser hore*, the vying impulses of good and evil that struggle in the soul of man for ascendancy. As the plot develops, Deronda experiences many of the conflicts and anxieties that were later associated with the "alienated Jew"—with one difference: he intends to resolve the conflicts so that his "whole being" may consent to his behavior. Although we are not yet privy here to the source of Deronda's scruples, from the outset he will not yield to the beautiful unless it is also good.

The woman at the gambling table, Gwendolen Harleth, is the novel's marvelous heroine, and were this a generic romance, the spark that is struck between her and Deronda in this opening scene would, after several hundred pages of adventure, result in their felicitous union or in their tragic separation through death. In *Middlemarch*, George Eliot had satisfied this element of romance by consummating the union between Dorothea Brooke and Will Ladislaw after mistakes and anguish on both their parts. This does not happen here. Instead of being resolved through eventual union, Deronda's initial doubts deepen into the realization that he must renounce miscegenation (from the Latin *miscere*, "to mix," and *genus*, "race") in order to fulfill his own destiny.

Hence, the novel is written in the form of an anti-romance: even as the mutual attraction between hero and heroine raises expectations of love—a secular version of Christianity's universal love—Deronda is caught up by a competing subplot that leads him to the Jews. Acting on impulse and intuition, he rescues Mirah Lapidus, a Jewish girl, from suicide; no less intuitively, he discovers Mordecai, a prophet of Jewish nationalism, hidden away in London's immigrant district and learns from him about the grandeur and self-sacrifice of the Jewish historical mission. Deronda reestablishes the link between this parted brother and sister in the course of seeking his own family and faith. His evolving attraction to Judaism culminates in the determination to restore the Jews to independent political existence, and as the corollary of his self-discovery, he persuades Gwendolen Harleth that she, too, would do better to live within conservative limits.

In their advanced liberal society the hero and heroine of this anti-romance, a Jew and a woman, could both aspire to positions other than those determined by their birth. Though Gwendolen learns that her family has suddenly been impoverished by a collapse of the stock market, she is able to arrange a striking marriage with the wealthy Henleigh Grandcourt. Likewise, lingering prejudice against the Jews no longer prevents them from marrying well. Protesting that the Jewess Mirah Lapidus will never find a mate among her own tribe, Hans Meyrick, Deronda's artist friend, says, "She will see no Jew who is tolerable. Every male of that race is insupportable—'insupportably advancing'—his nose."[5] Yet as Meyrick himself wishes to marry Mirah, it is his love rather than his prejudice that constitutes the real threat to her Jewishness, and the same is true of his doting family, who wish Mirah would give up her attachment to her people so that they could adopt her more completely. When the musician Herr Klesmer (whose name is Yiddish for musician), "being a felicitous combination of the German, the Sclave, and the Semite," marries the only daughter of the aristocratic Arrowpoints, both the parents and their social circle are quickly reconciled to the match and continue to regard the groom as their highest arbiter of musical taste.[6] George Eliot's Jews are not confronted with hostility but with a liberalism so confident of its tolerance that it cannot understand why anyone should resist its embrace.

Eliot sensed the ominous potential in all this apparent freedom. The "spoiled child" Gwendolen falls prey to an aristocrat who is bored with everything but the game of power. There is nothing in Eliot's earlier fiction to prepare us for the sadism of Henleigh Grandcourt, who uses his inherited title and wealth to intimidate his social inferiors the way Blackshirts would soon sport their boots and pistols.[7] Nor does the menace of egoism spare the Jews. By the time we meet up with the baptized Princess Leonora Halm-Eberstein, her career as the famed actress Alcharisi is far behind her, and she has summoned her son Daniel to meet her to settle a debt of conscience before she dies. Her Orthodox father had forced her to marry her cousin, but as soon as her father died, she abandoned Judaism to pursue a career on the stage. When her husband then died, she gave her unwanted son to one of her admirers, Sir Hugo Mallinger, to be raised as an Englishman. Still bristling with resentment at what Judaism demanded of her, she tells Daniel:

"[Your grandfather] never comprehended me, or, if he did, he only thought of fettering me into obedience. I was to be what he called 'the Jewish woman' under pain of his curse. I was to feel every thing I did not feel, and believe every thing I did not believe. I was to feel awe for the bit of parchment in the *mezuza* over the door; to dread lest a bit of butter should touch a bit of meat; to think it beautiful that men should bind the *tephillin* on them, and women not,—to adore the wisdom of such laws, however silly they might seem to me. [. . .] Ah!"—here her tone changed to one of a more bitter incisiveness—"you are glad to have been born a Jew. You say so. That is because you have not been brought up as a Jew. That separateness seems sweet to you because I have saved you from it."[8]

With emancipation, many Jews like Leonora sought not the freedom to live as Jews but rather freedom from the burdens of their Jewish birth, and though the book's thematic sympathies are not with the princess, Eliot invests her with the dramatic and intellectual powers to express this position better than it has ever been done in fiction. The novel agrees with this reluctant Jew and mother that where choice has become possible, "separateness" is best appreciated by those who freely choose it.

It is left for Daniel, the forsaken child, to find his way back to his people without the help of native language, inherited traditions, or such vestigial memories as are said to form the basis of national identity and—unlike the biblical Moses to whom he is often compared—*against* the wishes of the parent who guarantees his biological membership in the Jewish people.[9] Thus, when Daniel takes his leave of Gwendolen in the penultimate chapter, the parting scene with his mother is played out in reverse. He explains his intention of restoring a political existence to his people, "making them a nation again, giving them a national centre, such as the English have, though they too are scattered over the face of the globe."[10] The terms of this parting relate as much to England as to Zion. Like himself, Gwendolen may learn that a free human being may voluntarily assume the obligations and the limitations of having been born one thing and not another. As romance strains to eliminate boundaries, the anti-romance conserves the distinctiveness of self and others.

In one sense, *Daniel Deronda* is, of course, a thoroughly liberal book. It championed the Jews the way *Uncle Tom's Cabin* opposed the black slave trade, by engaging the imaginative sympathies of readers on the side of its vulnerable minority. George Eliot and Harriet Beecher Stowe corresponded about using literature to fight the prejudices of their respective societies, but their books diverge thematically precisely as their subjects do. Abolitionism demands liberty for individual men and women whereas Jewish survival requires precisely the opposite—recognition of a *collective* identity. In order to erase the classification of human beings through skin color, Harriet Beecher Stowe paints the black family "as white as she can make them" and demonstrates to her readers that Uncle Tom is almost certainly a better Christian than they.[11] The embodiment of the book's conscience, Augustine St. Clare (a descendant of persecuted Huguenots), declares that no man can consistently profess Christianity "without throwing the whole weight of his being against this monstrous system of injustice that lies at the foundation of our society; and, if need be, sacrificing himself in the battle."[12] The universal message of Christianity is well served by the abolitionist theme and Stowe's sentimental novel.

George Eliot faced a tougher literary task. Imaginative identification, which helps to collapse the barrier between the reader and an alien character, cannot explain why Jews are unassimilable. The author had to demonstrate that while Jews, like Christians, may be individually lovable or alienating, good or bad, they also have a separate culture, history, and national destiny. That the positive value of such national identity had been theoretically advanced by thinkers like Johann Gottfried Herder did not make it any easier to substantiate in fiction. Just as Daniel spends long hours with Mordecai learning Hebrew and Jewish history and studying Jewish texts, so too does the novel educate the reader, through conversations and arguments in the claims of a people whose "religion and law and moral life mingled as the stream of blood in the heart"—but mingled in a manner quite alien to the Christian heart.[13] In order to establish Daniel's eventual goal of "separateness with communication," Eliot had to include in her narrative an independent context of ideas to represent the Jewish tradition on something like its own intellectual merits. The chapter in which Daniel Deronda witnesses a debate over the Jewish question at the club Hand and Banner figured for many Jewish readers as the epitome—

and for many Gentile critics as the nadir—of the book, perhaps not only because of its nationalist argument but because of its presentation of the different status of argument itself in the two cultures.

Daniel Deronda illustrates the problem the English novel would continue to face in its treatment of the Jews, which resembled their condition in real life. The Jews as a people could only be absorbed, aesthetically and politically, to the degree that they yielded their particular identity, meaning that the novel would either take aesthetic risks to represent their difference or else marry them to Gentiles and divest them of their difference. Critical reception mirrored these alternatives. News of the novel gave it near-mythic status among East European Jews even before most of them had a chance to read it.[14] It was accorded an "unquestionable" place of honor among English writers who understood Zionism in all its depth and breadth.[15] Contrarily, leading English critics like Henry James and F. R. Leavis, echoing the sentiments of the Mallingers and Meyricks in the novel, who were distressed that Jews did not surrender their distinctiveness, pointed to the "inferior" aesthetic quality of the Jewish section, Leavis going so far as to propose rescuing Gwendolen Harleth's half of the book from the rest.[16] George Eliot, however, in an attempt to win freedom for her Jews and her women, grants her characters absolute moral freedom, the intelligence to doubt and to question, and the nerve to gamble and explore. *Daniel Deronda* is the imaginative equivalent of the Balfour Declaration, a book that expanded British sympathies in appreciation of difference, suggesting that the Empire should learn to live within bounds.

The Classic of Modernism: James Joyce's *Ulysses*

James Joyce is much admired for having created in *Ulysses* (1922) an interpretation of the Jew that is opposite to *Daniel Deronda's*. In the epic novel that defined English modernism, he follows Leopold Bloom through the city of Dublin on the most memorable single day in all of literature: 16 June 1904. The son of a Jewish father, Bloom feels himself a "reluctant exile" in his native Dublin. "A secret voice unceasingly urges his return to the warm light and blue shadow of the East."[17] When during a morning stop at Dlugacz the butcher's Bloom buys himself kidneys for breakfast, he picks up a Zionist flyer and catches sight of some advertisements for the purchase of land in Palestine. In the molten style that seduced a generation into modernism, Bloom's thought flows from consideration of the animal flesh he is purchasing to the flesh of the young girl buying sausages just ahead of him to the newspaper's offer of land:

> He walked back along Dorset street, reading gravely. Agendath [Agudath?] Netaim: planter's company. To purchase sandy tracts from Turkish government and plant with eucalyptus trees. Excel-lent for shade, fuel and construction. Orangegroves and immense melonfields north of Jaffa. You pay eight marks and they plant a dunam of land for you with olives, oranges, almonds or citrons. Olives cheaper: oranges need artificial irrigation. Every year you get a sending of the crop. Your name entered for life as owner in the book of the union. Can pay ten down and the balance in yearly instalments. Bleibtreustrasse 34, Berlin, W. 15.

The name of the street in Berlin is Bleibtreu (stay true), which underscores the Zionist project that is lodged there. But though Poldy Bloom plays around with the idea of Zion, he does not take the prospect seriously:

> No, not like that. A barren land, bare waste. Volcanic lake, the dead sea: no fish, weedless, sunk deep in the earth. No wind would lift those waves, grey metal, poisonous foggy waters. Brimstone they called it raining down: the cities of the plain: Sodom, Gomor-rah, Edom. All dead names. A dead sea in a dead land, grey and old. Old now. It bore the oldest, the first race. A bent hag crossed from Cassidy's clutching a naggin bottle by the neck. The oldest people. Wandered far away over all the earth, captivity to captiv-ity, multiplying, dying, being born everywhere. It lay there now. Now it could bear no more. Dead: an old woman's: the grey sunken cunt of the world.[18]

Images of the Jew as the accursed wanderer overtake the prospect of re-claiming the Land of Israel, and instead of the dead cunt of the world, Bloom eventually finds his way back to the living flesh and the warm bed of his voluptuous wife Marion (Molly) in Dublin, where they both reside. He throws the Zionist pamphlet into the fire. The national question is de-bated at Barney Kiernan's Tavern in Dublin, just as it was at Mordecai

Lapidus's London club Hand and Banner, but all that Leopold Bloom and his creator are at pains to prove under the xenophobic attack of Irish bar-mates is that the Jew is no traitor to his country. Both in this scene and later in Nighttown with his spiritual son Stephen Dedalus, Bloom defends the Jews against antisemitic aspersions and proves himself "as good an Irishman" as any.[19]

Indeed, Joyce seemed to be paying the cosmopolitan Jew the ultimate compliment by making so much of Bloom. He absorbed the Jew into Eng-lish literature on the same terms that he thought the Jew ought to be ab-sorbed into Ireland, as an unexceptional citizen trailing exotic origins. He exploded the myth of Irish tolerance and exposed local bigots in ways de-signed to make Bloom more endearing to the reader.[20] What a welcome departure this magnification was from the unsympathetic Jewish portraits by T. S. Eliot, Wyndham Lewis, Ezra Pound, Ernest Hemingway! Many Jews felt special affection for the writer who had granted them pride of place in the modernist canon. Harold Fisch was thrilled to see the Jew functioning "as a symbol of the universal condition," as "a persona of Everyman."[21] Not until the end of the century did some Jewish disciples of Joyce perceive that he may have cuckolded the Jew politically as well as maritally as the cost of starring him in the modernist epic.

Everyone was meant to know that James Joyce's *Ulysses* is patterned on the Homeric model: to prepare for the critical reception of the book, Joyce guided novelist and critic Valery Larbaud in its symbolic correspon-dences. Within a decade of the book's appearance, Stuart Gilbert had pro-duced an exegetical guide that related the domestic triangle of Bloom, his wayward wife Molly, and the student Stephen Dedalus to the myth of the warrior-wanderer Ulysses, who makes his way home to his wife Penelope and his son Telemachus. But in a remarkable (and hitherto unremarked) departure from the *Odyssey*, Joyce's Jewish hero does not return to Ithaca—to his wife and spiritual son, yes, but to his "land of origin," no. Bloomsday happens to be set just three weeks before the death of Theodor Herzl, when the Zionist movement was already fully active. Had this novel truly followed the story of Odysseus/Ulysses, the Jewish hero would have prepared for return to the Jewish homeland. At the very least, Bloom would have bought an orange grove near Jaffa instead of tossing the Zion-ist handbill into the grate. Yet Joyce's modern Jew remains in Ireland, as-similated into the Christian mainstream. For all the author's famed opposition to Irish nationalism, the Jew of Joyce's Christian imagination is homogenized into his Irish Christian society and considers himself lucky to make that his home. No doubt Joyce was responding to the expressed wish of the Jews he knew personally, like Italo Svevo, by favoring their assimilation, and to have promoted a Zionist motif would have left him open to charges that he discouraged integration. But the ambiguity of the political situation did not dictate the artistic choice. In this single respect, Joyce's generous modernism is no more respectful of Jewish distinctiveness than is the mean-spirited modernism of Eliot and Pound.

At least one spiritual son of Joyce later felt he had been betrayed by the master into denying his Jewish birthright. Midpoint in the fictional autobiography that he wrote at the end of his life, Henry Roth describes the moment when Ira—his fictional representation—"kicked over the apple cart" and, at a celebration of Bloomsday at which he was to have been the guest of honor, struck a blow against the writer who had led him astray·

> Oh, there were a hundred indictments he could hurl at Joyce; and reading Stuart Gilbert's salaaming adulation, ground-kissing obeisances, incited a hundred more. On every page: commencing with the scarce nominal Jew that the great Guru foisted on the reader, a Jew without memory, without wry anxiety, exilic insecurity, not merely oblivious of his heritage, but virtually devoid! Of the Kishinev pogrom the year before, nothing, of Dreyfus, nothing, nothing to say to Dlugacz, or whatever his name was, the Hungarian butcher, no sally about the pork kidney: was it kosher? No inference, no connection between a newspaper offering plots in Palestine and the possibility of a Jewish community in Dublin. No recall of Friday candles, no recall of *matzahs*. Jeez, what a Jew, even one converted while still a juvenile—no *cheder*, no *davening*, no Yom Kippur, no Purim or *hamantashen*, no *brukhe*, no Hebrew, no Yiddish, or naught but a negligible trace. And despite the lack, daring to depict the Jew's "stream of consciousness," the inner flow of a Jew's psyche, an Irish quasi-Marrano of the year 1904. What unspeakable gall that took, gall and insufferable egotism! Gall and ignorance![22]

Although Roth acknowledges that this "excessive" protest against Joyce's "vanities" (the words are his) attests to the master's ongoing influence, he is convinced that it was Joyce's prose—more than Marxism, more than anti-semitism—that lured him into the "stupendous gravitational field" of modernism and erased whatever had made him and could have maintained him as a Jew. Interesting also is Henry Roth's perception that along with its erasure of the Jewish Jew as a separate intelligent being, Joycean modernism fails to allow for intellectual partnership with a mature woman.

Three Zionist Writers:
Ludwig Lewisohn, Maurice Samuel, Arthur Koestler

The contrast between Eliot and Joyce exemplifies the predicament of the Jew in Anglo American culture: while English invites everyone into the common tent, that image itself stigmatizes those who inhabit the tents of Jacob. What did it take, then, for a Jewish writer in English, professionally dependent on the English publishing industry, to define a Jewish destiny that diverged from the Anglo American model of acculturation? What kind of fiction would emerge from such an impulse, and what sort of writers could sustain it? The following three very different English writers, all of whom were European-born and felt compelled to tell the Jewish national story, will help one to understand the answers to these literary questions.[23]

IN THE 1920S, German-born Ludwig Lewisohn became a Zionist with the gratitude of a patient in remission. Born in Berlin in 1882 and brought as a child to Charleston, South Carolina, Lewisohn was exactly the sort of Jewish intellectual who would later flourish in City College in the 1930s, except that he was coming of age a full generation earlier in the American South. Lewisohn was dismayed to discover that despite stellar credentials, as a Jew he was unable to attain a university position in the East; the teaching job he did find eventually in the Midwest nearly drove him to distraction. Turning handicap to advantage by writing and by becoming a critic, translator, and interpreter of German literature, he was the first American writer to introduce the ideas of psychoanalysis into fiction. He joined other such dazzling public intellectuals as H. L. Mencken and

George Jean Nathan in exposing the puritanism and parochialism of America's elites and in trying to cultivate their appreciation for higher intelligence and better art. Lewisohn, however, was less a mocker than a passionate believer in the "nobility and universal significance of creative expression." "More strikingly than any other in a generation of critics who wished to write like artists," he carried over into his novels the tensions of his life.[24]

Lewisohn drew a set of negative conclusions about intermarriage from a disastrous first marriage to a much older Christian woman, and from his experience with nativist antisemitism in America he drew further inferences about the limits of integration. What he came to feel through personal trial and error, and under Freudian influence, was that the Jew who begins to hate his Jewishness under the pressure of antisemitism reinforces that hostility in an escalating cycle.[25] He conveys this conclusion tendentiously, if not altogether persuasively, in his most influential novel, *The Island Within* (1928).

This novel traces the Levy family from its origins in Vilna, Lithuania, through three generations of westward migration to New York. As the immigrant parents prosper in America, their children come to equate success with assimilation. Their son Arthur attends Columbia University, becomes a psychiatrist, marries the daughter of a Protestant minister in a civil ceremony, and seems oblivious, but for the pain that it causes his parents, to the issue of identity. While Jewish self-hatred almost destroys the life of his sister and drives one of his most talented acquaintances to suicide, Arthur feels no tension until his marriage begins to disintegrate. Only then does he realize that in becoming less of a Jew, he had become less of everything. "[Just] as the artist must express himself through some medium—words, sounds, paint, marble—even so in the larger sense human expression is effected through the medium of some national culture."[26] The impoverished Jew lacks the cultural substance to be an adequate husband and father. The thesis of the novel is summarized in one brief exchange between estranged husband and wife, with the Gentile wife rather than the Jewish husband pronouncing it definitively:

> "It's kind of an argument, isn't it, against mixed marriages?" Her eyes were sad.
> "I'm afraid it is," he anwered. "One among many others."[27]

The Island Within became a best-seller, going through sixteen printings in the first five months. It was also extremely popular with the American Jewish leadership, touted as "the finest study of Judaeo–Christian relations that has appeared up to this time" and as "the tale of a Jew manfully, tragically, withal triumphantly, facing his innermost problem—that of belonging to himself instead of being possessed by the world, which will have him only to break him."[28]

The title of the novel evokes the familiar passage from John Donne's *Devotions*: "No man is an island," which Ernest Hemingway appropriated in *For Whom the Bell Tolls* as the motto of the rare American who went to fight in foreign wars. But Lewisohn portrays the Jew who is washed away from the bedrock of his people because he is *too eager* to join himself to others. His American novel rejects the integrationist ideal by asking readers to share the perspective of the threatened Jew.

Yet this focus creates an odd set of problems. For one thing, the narrator is obsessed with visible traits of Jewishness. When Arthur visits his sister in Boston, he notices that she drew forward her little girl, "a dark beautiful, glowing, very Jewish-looking child with clear wise eyes."[29] When John, the son of Arthur and Elizabeth, returns to the city, the little boy appears sturdier and more vivid. "His nose was almost as straight as Elizabeth's. But he was, in coloring and expression, a Jewish child."[30] This concern for Jewish appearance creates some uneasiness in a novel that presumably deals with the ability of a man to determine his identity. If Arthur and his narrator are so self-conscious about racial signs of Jewishness in children, wouldn't marriage to a fellow Jew simply exacerbate this neurotic condition?

Similarly, as if to admit Arthur's discomfort, the book renders his father's immigrant speech with its heavy accent. Although the father seems a sound parent, moderate in his beliefs and a decent embodiment of receding Jewish authority, how seriously can one take a man who has this to say about antisemitism?

Now, as I heard Doctor Katzmann say et a meeting de odder day, it vould be all right if dey vere bet people. But some det hate us most are fine ent honest people in every odder vay. Ent it vould be all right if ve vere bet people ent deserved to be hated. But ve are a goot people, honest ent hart-vorking ent kint end charitable ent an educated people. Nobody is bet—neider dey nor ve . . .[31]

Lewisohn may have wanted to show how hard it is to appreciate someone who speaks "a distorted tongue." He uses dialect selectively (and imprecisely) to create the discomfort from which Arthur and his sister hope to free themselves. But no English reader could easily credit the dignity of positions that seem to caricature the language.

The association of Jewishness with psychoanalysis is particularly disturbing. Arthur's evolving interest in Freudian theory is a practical element in the plot, justifying his introspection and granting him the authority to psychoanalyze others. But the more Arthur connects Jewish self-denial with mental breakdown and Jewish self-acceptance with professional analysis, the more being Jewish becomes an essentially *problematic* condition, an illness in search of a cure. The same is also true of being a woman. Thus, whereas George Eliot introduced the Jewish brother and sister, Mordecai and Mirah, as the positive mind and soul of the Jews that draw Deronda back to his heritage, Lewisohn can only work the negative side of his topic, raising the specter of insanity, failure, and death for those who deny their heritage.

The Island Within was the first English novel to engage the linked problems of acculturation and antisemitism, confronting the Jew's readiness to remain a Jew. The aesthetic liabilities Lewisohn incurred in presenting this case arose in part from the task that he had set himself, which was to demonstrate from the inside the defective nature of the integrationist solution to the Jewish question. But fiction has a different standard of authenticity. For this to have become more than a thesis novel, we would have had to care about Arthur and about Jewishness before we cared whether he remained a Jew. And even as a thesis, the mere stand against assimilation does not necessarily translate into Jewish confidence.

WHEREAS LEWISOHN EXPOSED the psychological harm of assimilation, Maurice Samuel assailed Christian society on moral grounds. Samuel defined relations with English culture as a conflict between "the gentleman and the Jew." The gentleman "is the noblest ideal of man in a society which immorally accepts competition and rivalry as the basis and meaning of life."[32] Its bywords are the stiff upper lip, the chivalric code, the level playing field—the codes of manhood that accept the necessity of conflict and try to dignify it by rules.

Contrasting the cult of the sporting Englishman who seeks honor in cricket and war with the moral passion of the Hebrew prophets whose only fight is for justice and charity, Samuel removes morality from the realm of the prudential and ascribes it to the realm of the prophetic, an emphasis that sets him equally against the Marxists—those "mechanical moralists" who argue that if you "make social conditions perfect . . . bad behavior will disappear."[33] Samuel did not defend the Jews against their attackers but took prophetic Judaism and Zionism as the standard against which other civilizations and ideological movements ought to be judged. Cynthia Ozick has noted that in Samuel's writing "the Jewish view is never yielded up through simple declaration or exposition; it is wrested out of the engagement with, and finally a disengagement from, an alternative world view."[34]

Samuel was a masterful interpreter of Jewish peoplehood in his memoirs and several books about Yiddish culture. He wrote five books on Zionism and Israel between 1929 and 1968 and an equal number about antisemitism and the Arab war against the Jews. Only in his fiction did Samuel shy away from direct involvement with the Jewish national project. Samuel's novel *The Outsider* was published in 1929, the same year as his account of the Arab pogroms, *What Happened in Palestine*. In the novel, a demobilized American at the end of the First World War wants to escape the bourgeois attachments that await him back in his puritan New England home by remaining in Paris. He picks up a girl with the understanding that they will make no demands on one another beyond biweekly trysts in a cafe and in his room. But he has trouble maintaining his sense of liberation and neutrality until "the suspicion [occurs] to him that he was finding little of what he thought to find."[35] His Jewish buddy, also an American expatriate, becomes addicted to heroin and then sells it to support his habit, and his own callous behavior proves fatal to the girl.

It is not difficult to see how the moral education of this "ugly American" corresponds to Samuel's decision to assume responsibility for the Jews, but neither here nor in any of his later novels does the author incorporate the contemporary Jewish drama into his fiction. Ronald Sanders remarked on this bifurcation in his work: "Why did he persist in this odd reticence about putting a Jewish content into fiction? Was it because fiction had become something of a vacation area for him, in which he could occasionally escape from the dense atmosphere of Jewish concerns . . . ?"[36] Samuel may have ascribed this thought to the protagonist of *The Outsider*, who says, "I confess I like writing without obligation."[37] Fiction may have been his respite from polemics, or perhaps his adversarial construct of gentleman and Jew prevented him from writing Jewish novels in the language of gentlemen. Whatever the reason, it is significant that the leading Zionist of his day, who was also a talented novelist, could not integrate the passion of his life into English fiction.

ARTHUR KOESTLER CONSIDERED Zionism not the consummation of Judaism but its political alternative. Born in Budapest to nonpracticing Jewish parents, exposed in childhood to World War I and the Hungarian Revolution, raised with no Jewish instruction either at home or at school, and, indeed, lacking firm moral guidance from either of his parents, Koestler might well have joined many other European youths who tried to erase all traces of their origins. But he joined a Jewish dueling fraternity in Vienna when he came to study at the University in 1922, and he attributed his understanding of the Jewish question to the instruction that he was given as a potential member:

> [The] Jews had been persecuted during some twenty centuries and [. . .] there was no reason to expect they would not be persecuted in the twenty-first. To argue with anti-semites was all the more hopeless as the Jews were in fact a sick race. They were a nation without a country, which was like being a man without a shadow. [. . .] If Jews wanted to be like other people, they must have a country like other people.[38]

This reflexive Jewishness, adapted from the Zionist program of Vladimir Ze'ev Jabotinsky, seemed to young Koestler so perfectly obvious that he marveled he had not arrived at these conclusions on his own. Yet defining acceptance by the Gentiles as the measure of health engendered an intrinsically troubling relation to the Jews and Judaism, since it required the

Jewish people to reconfigure itself just for the sake of becoming like others—and perhaps like others capable of hating the Jews.

Koestler's *Thieves in the Night* (1945), "a novel about the settlement of a commune in Palestine and the growth of Jewish terrorism as an inevitable response to British policy,"[39] was meant to change that policy through the force of persuasion. The hero Joseph is not a Jew at all according to Jewish law. The son of a Russian Jewish musician who died when he was eleven and a Gentile mother whose family never approved of her marriage, Joseph traces his conversion to Zionism to an affair with an older woman, someone he had been chastely in love with for two years who casts him away in horror when she discovers "the sign of the Covenant on his body" the first time they make love.[40] Though many readers objected to the improbability of this premise, Koestler may have been echoing his own life experience with a mother who had always encouraged him to transcend the shameful flaw of having been born a Jew. Joseph reacts to his rejection by trying to learn something about the Jews, and he then goes off to Palestine to help build the Jewish homeland. While Joseph overcomes his intellectual doubts in physical struggle for Israel, he (consistent with his character and the political thrust of Koestler's book) can never make his home with a Jewish woman or learn to enjoy Jewish society. The woman he does fall in love with, Dina, is a refugee from Nazism who has been so damaged by six months of abuse by the Gestapo that she cannot allow herself to be touched by any man. She is raped and murdered by the son of the Arab *mukhtar,* increasing the book's sense of moral urgency: Like the attack on the biblical Dina, whose brothers avenged it, the attack on her modern counterpart will have to be answered by her brothers in Eretz Israel.

Thieves in the Night is not a subtle book (as Koestler had already proven in his anti-Soviet novel *Darkness at Noon* that he could brilliantly wage political warfare in fiction). Here he demonstrates how the Arab society of Palestine and the Arab bias of the British foreign office in 1937–39 virtually compelled Jews to resort to violence in order to secure a place for the Jewish victims of persecution, how the British forcibly restricted Jewish immigration into a country to which they had far less right than the refugees they were excluding, and how the Jews desperately tried to erect Jewish settlements and to absorb the damaged refugees while fighting off the Arabs. When Joseph joins the Jewish underground, he agrees to broadcast secretly to Britain, because he is convinced that if the British knew what evil they were perpetrating, they would repudiate their policy forthwith. Koestler thus incorporates an appeal to the English conscience in the information that he "broadcasts" through this book.

Koestler was far too complicated a writer (and far too ambivalent a Jew) to reduce fiction to thesis. Joseph is accused of having "that intellectual squint" that makes him see both sides of the coin at the same time, a luxury he believes that twentieth-century Jews can no longer afford.[41] Yet Joseph's value to the novel is precisely this "Jewish" habit of requiring moral and rational justification for elemental self-defense. Koestler's critics and even some of those who admired the book objected that when Joseph prevails over his scruples to support limited acts of terror, the author seems to be justifying the subordination of means to ends that he had opposed in *Darkness at Noon.* This was to overlook Koestler's emphasis on political context, which made him write a novel instead of a tract. The Jewish underground argues that Jews are targeted for murder because of their *disinclination* to wield power. Koestler's two political novels could thus be read in tandem as a demonstration that moral argument can never be absolute. The embattled Jewish community of Palestine was the antithesis of Stalin's Russia; it was therefore required to take the opposite position in order to arrive at the same goal of justice.

The book's more serious internal flaw is that its advancement of Zionism comes at the expense of the Jews it was intended to help. Joseph writes in his diary, "I became a socialist because I hated the poor; and I became a Hebrew because I hated the Yid," sentiments his biographer David Cesarani says was not unique among Jewish intellectuals and therefore no automatic proof of Jewish "self-hatred."[42] Perhaps not, but this compound of negations seriously inhibits the book's emotional impact. Joseph's attraction to Dina, the only character whose isolation exceeds his, contrasts with his visceral distaste for Ellen, the kibbutz member he marries and whose child he fathers. Without any corresponding affection for his fellow Jews, Koestler in this novel grants Zionism the right to fight its enemies as a means of solving the Jewish question.

Lewisohn, Samuel, and Koestler were among the very few Jewish writers in English to concern themselves with the Jewish fate in the middle of the century, and the limits of their accomplishment in fiction testify to the aesthetic problems they faced.[43] The desperation of the Jews made it harder to treat individual Jewish men and women with the nuance that George Eliot has used in a much quieter time to draw Daniel Deronda. Engaged Jewish writers could hardly face an English public without the bitter awareness that it was probably indifferent to the threat facing their people. Koestler records his antipathy to the Jews while championing their cause. Pushed to the defensive and isolated from their peers, Jews who tried to write chapters in the epic of Zionism attested mostly to the loneliness of their struggle.

The Zionist Best-Seller: Leon Uris's *Exodus*

All this seemed to change with the birth of Israel in 1948 and its successful wars of self-defense. The unexpected grit shown by the tiny Jewish community of Palestine resulted in the securing of a Jewish homeland that changed the image of the Jew, at least temporarily. Whereas the great majority of Anglo American Jewish writers and artists had shied away from Zionism during the 1920s and 1930s, and may have gravitated to socialism and communism because of their promising internationalism, Jewish self-determination became *salonfähig*, fit for elite liberal taste, and even culturally popular once it appeared to have accomplished its goal.

The best-selling *Exodus*, published by Leon Uris in 1958 and never since out of print, signaled this transformation of the Jewish image. A best-seller must by definition satisfy the cultural expectations of a mass audience, and that English readers thrilled to the story of the rebirth of Israel meant that Israel had become a popular cause. Blurbs for the book—"towering novel of the twentieth century's most dramatic geopolitical event" and "the story of an American nurse and an Israeli freedom fighter caught up in a glorious, hearbreaking, triumphant era"—advertised the rise of Israel as the book's chief attraction.

The book is set, like *Thieves in the Night*, during those final years of the British mandate in Palestine, when the Jewish settlement is trying to bring home its refugees from Europe under mounting Arab attack. An American nurse, widowed during World War II, goes grudgingly to Palestine and quickly gets involved in the efforts of the embattled Jewish *yishuv* to win its independence. Ari Ben Canaan, a crack agent of the official underground and also a species of widower—his childhood sweetheart was brutally murdered by Arab marauders—is charged with various dangerous missions that spotlight his resourcefulness, courage, and flawless judgment. There is also a large supporting cast of Jews, Arabs, and Englishmen, each representing another political position or historical type.

From a literary point of view, Uris's formulaic novel was never in serious contention for the status of a Jewish national epic. Even by potboiler standards, the writing was dreadful:

> [Katherine Freemont] was one of those great American traditions like Mom's apple pie, hot dogs, and the Brooklyn Dodgers. For Kitty Freemont was the proverbial "girl next door." She was the cliché of pigtails, freckles, tomboys, and braces on the teeth; and true to the cliché the braces came off one day, the lipstick went on and the sweater popped out and the ugly duckling had turned into a graceful swan.[44]

The whole book is filled with such self-advertised clichés. The Jewish victims of Europe pop into heroic Israelis as subtly as the contents of Kitty's sweater; we are as far removed here from the experiential density of George Eliot as commoner ever was from king. Crude historical summaries function in place of characterization to create an illusion of narrative depth: Zionism in Russia is the heroic team of Ari Ben Canaan's father and uncle; the conflict between Labor Zionism and Revisionism is represented by the same brothers, now estranged. German Jewish assimilation cum Danish resistance to Hitler is the refugee Karen Hansen; Polish Jewry and the Warsaw Ghetto Uprising, the refugee Dov Landau. And so on. Yet so great was the cultural impoverishment of the American Jewish reading public that it learned its national history from the pages of this book. Circulated surreptitiously in translation in the Soviet Union, it is credited with having rekindled the embers of Jewish identity for many Russian Jews.

To be taken seriously, then, on account of its enormous impact, *Exodus* is constructed, like *Daniel Deronda*, around the attraction of a Gentile woman for a Jewish man, except that this romance is written from the Gentile's perspective and ends with the Jew begging the Gentile to stay with him forever. Since the all-American Kitty Freemont admits that she "always felt uncomfortable around Jewish people," her evolution into an admirer, a lover, and about-to-be wife is meant to bring the American reader along the same path from suspicion to acceptance of the Jews, through sympathy to love. Yet Kitty admits that Jews attract her for their un-Jewish qualities: "This Ben Canaan doesn't act like any Jew I've ever met."[45] She wants to adopt the German-Danish Jewish refugee child Karen Hansen, whose appearance is so un-Jewish she has been able to pass as a Christian throughout the war. Uris combines sympathy for the survivors of Nazi Germany and admiration for Israeli military prowess as the twin pillars of Israel's popularity, which is probably as good a sociological insight as we will ever have into the nature of Israel's appeal to the American liberal imagination. Since Kitty has to be won over for the romance to succeed, only those non-Jewish qualities succeed in attracting her.

Miscegenation is not just acceptable to Uris, it is the only kind of union that he allows. Each of the other two subordinate Jewish romances ends with the death of one of the partners: Dov loses Karen, and Ari's sister Jordana loses David Ben Ami. Thus, there are no Jewish marriages in this book about Israel, no more than there are in Hollywood films or television. And the final union between Kitty and Ari, though only hinted at and never consummated, is conceived as an act of emotional capitulation. "Don't leave me!" Ari cries after a lifetime of self-sufficiency, sparking one of the sloppiest, most curious passages in the book:

> Ah, how she had wanted to hear those words! Yes, she thought, I will stay, this night and for a few tomorrows, for you need me now, Ari. [. . .] You need me now but tomorrow [. . .] you will be all the strong Ari Ben Canaans who inure themselves to tragedy. And then . . . you will no longer need me.[46]

What will she do, Kitty is thinking, now that she has caught her Jewish man? How badly she had wanted his capitulation, his confession of need, but does she really want to settle down with a Jew in a *Jewish country?* Uris's concept of American sensibility comes to the rescue of the de-Judaized Israelis with the expectation that they will not become a liability. It wants just enough tragedy to warrant compassion but not enough to cause any real concern.

The point here is not to fault the formulaic best-seller for pushing the right buttons nor to show ingratitude for popular culture when it occasionally comes down on the side of the Jews. Powerful currents within Zionism itelf sought to create just the kind of un-Jewish farmer-warrior-hero that Uris inadvertently caricatures in the figure of Ari Ben Canaan. But Uris's defense of the Jews is based solely on the approval of Gentiles, and on an approval that imagines that the Jews really *are* Gentiles and that Israel is a smaller America. Yet the Jews, a minority, are in many ways the antithesis of the English, a political speck in a hugely Arab Middle East, a quirky tribe with its own customs and legacies. To its eternal credit, the biblical story of *Exodus* never minimized how tortuous the return of the Jews to Zion was likely to be. In literary terms, Uris's best-seller wins Israel the popularity of a dance around the golden calf, a seemingly innocent diversion until you consider how much tougher it makes facing up to reality.

A Realized Zionist Novel: A. M. Klein's *The Second Scroll*

Abraham Moses Klein was born in 1909 in Montreal, a city more European than American whose local myth of "two founding nations" encouraged permanent competition, between the English Protestants and French Catholics, rather than the integrative American ideal of a single people with a single language. As the first prominent minority to settle in Quebec, Jews were declared to be Protestant in an educational structure divided along religious-linguistic-ethnic lines; thus, they grew up formally identified with the English yet clearly not of them. Klein's situation as an English poet in a French-speaking city had much in common with Kafka's position as a German writer among a local majority of Czechs, and he felt similarly uneasy about joining the more powerful English culture at the expense of its politically weaker French rival. Klein spoke Yiddish in his traditional home, learned Bible and Talmud at *cheder*, attended local English high schools and McGill University, and then studied law at the French Univérsité de Montréal; he was thereby thoroughly prepared to take advantage of the cultural ferment in the three communities. In his famous collection, *The Rocking Chair*, the Jewish poet functions as cultural mediator between French and English Canadians.

As a schoolboy, Klein had developed a fascination with hapaxlegomena: "Isolated words. Lonesome words. They occur but once in the whole Torah, and are related to no other word."[47] He enjoyed both the singularity of the word and the cultural mediation involved in acquiring it. His adoration of language led him to its English master, James Joyce. As well as paying Joyce the compliment of imitation, Klein spent many years working on an interpretive commentary on *Ulysses* that applied the technique of Talmudic exegesis to the modernist text. He did not, however, follow his idol by going into literary exile. Klein remained not only physically rooted in Montreal but edited a Jewish journal and became increasingly involved in rescue efforts as the situation of Jews worsened through the 1930s and '40s. One of his earliest editors said that were he a Zionist, he would hang Klein's georgics in his study and read them every day.[48] Ludwig Lewisohn called him "the first contributor of authentic Jewish poetry to the English language."[49] Canadian criticism began to take notice of the Jews because it had to accommodate A. M. Klein.

Klein's only published novel was an exuberant response to the creation of Israel. *The Second Scroll* (1951) tells the story of an intertwined quest. Shortly after the establishment of Israel, a Canadian Jewish poet is commissioned by his publisher to put together a translated anthology of Hebrew verse, and he sets out for Israel to gather his material. Since early childhood, the narrator has heard stories about his mother's brother Melech Davidson, and a letter from this long-lost uncle who has survived the war prompts him to look for his relative on the way to the holy land. The search for a reconstituted national culture thus runs parallel to the search for Melech Davidson (the King, son of David), a figure whose messianic name betokens his symbolic role in the book. Melech had started out as a Talmudic genius in a traditional Jewish community in Russia. When his faith was crushed during the Ukrainian pogroms, he pinned his hopes on Communism, which had triumphed in the Revolution. This allegiance was shattered in turn by the Nazi–Soviet pact of 1939, and then Russia was betrayed when Hitler attacked it. Though Melech escaped from a Jewish mass grave, he cannot recover his confidence as a believing Jew. By the time his nephew begins to look for him, he has considered and rejected conversion to Christianity and has led a minor uprising of Jews in protest against their conditions in Arab Casablanca. The narrator thinks he is about to catch up with Davidson when he arrives in Israel, but he learns that his uncle was killed at the very moment that the modern nation was born. The messianic quest cannot be consummated in the flesh, not even in a reconstituted Jewish state, but "Melech Davidson" has played an inspiring role in restoring the Jews to a national existence.

Superimposing the story of modern Zionism on the biblical story of

Exodus (as James Joyce had set Dublin against the *Odyssey*), Klein connects each of the five chapters thematically to its counterpart in the Torah and adds a "gloss" for each at the back of the novel to evoke the Jewish exegetical tradition. The task of the modern Jew was to escape not only the German lime pits but the ideologies that enslaved him before and after Nazism came to power, beginning with Communism. When he becomes Comrade Krul, Davidson yokes Talmudic discipline to Communist praxis, just as Nissan had done in *The Brothers Ashkenazi*: "Krul's quotations from European writing had the thoroughness, and in a sense the quality, of a concordance, and his argumentation was like nothing so much as like the subtilized airy transcendent *pilpul* of Talmud-commentary commentators."[50] Comrade Krul then speaks for a significant sector of modern Jewry when he becomes disillusioned and repents: "My ideology had been a saying of grace before poison."[51]

Klein's boldest polemic is with Christianity. In the third and central chapter, "Leviticus," the section of the Bible that contains the core of the Law, Klein casts the dominant religion of Europe as the beckoning "Torah" that has tried so hard to convert the Jew. He reminds us of the example of Israel Zoller (1881–1956), chief rabbi of Rome, who converted to Christianity in 1944 as a gesture of gratitude to Pope Pius XII. Likewise contemplating conversion after the war, Uncle Melech is sent by Monsignor Piersanti, his would-be baptizer (Saint Peter), to see the tableaux of Michelangelo in the Sistine Chapel. The monsignor is certain that there his prospective convert will be overawed by the visible splendor of Christianity. In his reportage of the actual voyage he took to Europe and Israel, Klein writes in his notebook that upon seeing Michelangelo's statue of Moses in Rome he was momentarily "saddened at the existence of the Second Commandment which had deprived us of the potentiality of similar achievement." He then comforts himself with the thought that Jews had produced the original Moses.[52] Melech Davidson stares up at the masterpiece of Christian art as the Jews once looked up at Mount Sinai, but instead of Christian glory Melech sees "the manner in which Christian history had interpreted Christian art." "Since Adam is created in the image of God, the killing of man is deicide! Since Eve is a reproductive creature, the murder of the mortal is a murder of the immortal!"[53] Michelangelo's premise that humanity is divine confirms just how heinous was the crime of Christendom against the Jews. Thus, viewing the humanizing masterpiece of the Christian Renaissance, the Sistine Chapel, as an indictment of Christianity's collapse into barbarism, Melech is released once again from ideological captivity, and he determines to quit Europe for Eretz Israel.

But Melech extends his trek through the desert of exile to where the Jews still lie subject under Arab rule. The book's descent into the *mellah*, the Jewish quarter, of Casablanca in the fourth chapter, "Numbers," is its most sensuous part:

> We entered, we slid into the mellah; literally: for the narrow lane which gaped through the gateway at the clean world was thick with offal and slime and the oozing of manifold sun-stirred putrescences; metaphorically: for in a moment we knew that the twentieth century (with all its modern conveniences) had forsaken us, and we were descending into the sixteenth, the fifteenth, twelfth, eleventh centuries. The streets, narrow and mounting, mazed, descending and serpentine, formicated with life. Everywhere poverty wore its hundred costumes, tatters of red and tatters of yellow, rags shredded and rags pieced, a raiment of patches, makeshifts, and holes through which the naked skin showed, a kind of human badge. Brightness, however, fell only from rags; if a garment was whole, it was black, the somber ghetto gaberdine.[54]

Jewish poverty shines like a reproach through Klein's voluptuous description of Casablanca. But compared to Melech's response to Christianity, his formal reproach to Muslim civilization is relatively mild. The gloss on this chapter takes the courtly form of a three-part drama in which the Jew appeals to the cadi, the Muslim judge, for equal treatment on three counts: the Jew is a brother and his kinship should be recognized; the homely Land of Israel was the promised bride of the Jew and belongs to him by right; and Muslims should realize that Judaism, Christianity, and Islam illumine the same God. The sweet reasonableness of Klein's playlet reminds us that in 1951 one could still hope that Islam would eschew the excesses of Jew-hatred that had corrupted Christianity and respond to the Jewish appeal of a common Semitic heritage. Yet Melech does not indulge his messianic expectations of brotherhood at the expense of the exodus. He spearheads a revolt of the *mellah* Jews against their oppressors that eventually results in their departure for Palestine.

Klein's most persuasive proof that the Jews have passed from slavery into freedom is the texture of his prose. Maurice Samuel rejoiced that the novel delivers a harmonious new American Jewish language, "our first intimation of what might be called Judaeo-English"; Klein intended, Samuel said, "to recapture the lyric bliss which the Return inspired in the Prophets."[55] As against those English writers who tried to imitate Jewish immigrant rhythms or dialect or irony, Klein created a celebratory prose that would be commensurate with the miracle he was recording. The narrator describes himself as a little *cheder* boy struggling with the Hebrew vowel signs—"those beneath the letters, like prompters prompting, and those beside the letters, like nudgers nudging, and those on top, like whisperers whispering"—conveying the charm of learning the mysterious ancient language.[56] The incredible diversity within the Jewish people emerges from the official records the narrator consults in his search for Melech Davidson, each name "somehow . . . like his alias" because the alphabetical list *is* actually made up of "synonyms" for the messianic name, from Lazarus Achron (the last, but one who rises from the dead) to Jochanan Zefany (John the hopeful), each deriving from a different branch of the Jewish family tree. Klein is imposing on his reader no less than James Joyce does when, translating from the Yiddish idiom, he says that the ignorant looked on the Torah "as knowingly as did the rooster on the page of the prayer of *Bnai Adam*" or when he describes the trumpets sounding out of the stone of the Arch of Titus "not as aforetime the sound of jubilee, but the broken murmur, the *shvarim*, the tragic triad of wandering and suffering and exile." Gentile or uncultivated Jewish readers might not hear in the term *shvarim* the reverberation of the shofar's broken notes, but they would feel the gravitational pull and mystery of the Jewish past.

The novel promotes language as the essence of culture. Asked by his English publisher to undertake, "for my spiritual advantage and his profit," a volume of translations of the poems and songs of the new Hebrew society, the narrator-poet thinks the task eminently suitable: he has only to seek out his best counterparts in Hebrew and to choose their finest works. Yet in the final chapter, "Deuteronomy," the narrator realizes that he has been on the wrong track:

> They were not members of literary societies, the men who were
> giving new life to the antique speech, but merchants, tradesmen,

day laborers. In their daily activity, and without pose or flourish, they showed it to be alive again, the shaping Hebrew imagination. An insurance company, I observed as I lingered in Tel Aviv's commercial centre, called itself *Sneh*—after Moses' burning bush, which had burned and burned but had not been consumed. Inspired metaphor, born not of honored laureate, but of some actuary, a man of prose! [. . .] A dry-cleaner called his firm *Keshet*, the rainbow, symbol of cessation of floods! An ice cream organization, Kortov, punned its way to custom fissioning *kortov*, a drop, to *kor-tov*, cold and good! [. . .] Nameless authorship flourished in the streets.[57]

The narrator has no trouble locating the Hebrew poets of Israel, but Jewish creativity is far better captured by the Hebrew language itself. The vision of Ezekiel 37 assumes linguistic form. "It was as if I was spectator to the healing of torn flesh, or *heard* a broken bone come together, set, and grow again." We therefore have this novel instead of the anthology, a tribute to the people who revived the language.

Because of Klein's obvious debt to James Joyce, *The Second Scroll* was mistakenly considered an act of homage. But Klein had turned the cultural tables on Joyce by Judaizing English, channeling all its resources into the Jewish master narrative. Reversing the current of Anglicization, Klein wanted the universal language to exalt the Jew, who most assuredly *did* return from his European exile to his homeland—and against greater obstacles than were ever faced by Ulysses. In this tale of two languages, English modernism pays homage to Hebrew not through translation but through Klein's wit.

The author's passion comes through in the passage that describes the formal founding of the Jewish state:

> When as a young boy, the consolations and prophecies of Isaiah before me, I dreamed in the dingy Hebrew school the apocalyptic dream of a renewed Zion, always I imagined it as coming to pass thus: First I heard the roar and thunder of the battle of God and Magog; then, as silence fell, I saw through my mind's eye a great black aftermath cloud filling the heavens across the whole length of the humped horizon. The cloud then began to scatter, to be diminished, to subside, until revealed there shone the glory of a bur-

nished dome—Hierosolyma the golden! Then lower it descended and lower, a mere breeze dispersed it, and clear was the horizon and before me there extended an undulating sunlit landscape.

My childhood vision, no doubt the result of a questionable amalgam between Hollywood and Holy Writ, was indeed fulfilled; but not in all its details and particularities. The cataclysmic war was there, the smoke, the thud and brunt of battle; but no golden dome. What was to be seen instead on the fifth day of Iyar was a forgathered company of men hitherto obscure, as anonymous as the *Bnai Brak*, who too had spent a night expatiating upon the miracles of exodus, met in surroundings not palatial, in a city which forty years earlier had had neither being nor name, to announce to the world on behalf of a people for whom they were as yet *noms de plume*, hardly *noms de guerre*, that henceforward in the domain of their forefathers they, nullifying all hiatus, intended to be, beneath the sovereignty of the All-Sovereign, sovereign.[58]

Jewish experience is conveyed through its own cultural vocabulary—the prophecies of Isaiah; the battle of Gog and Magog; the scholars of Bnai Brak, whose nightlong study is recalled each year in the text of the Passover Haggadah; the dating of the declaration of Israel's independence according to the Jewish calendar, Iyar not May. Klein does not domesticate the prose by calling the holy city *yerusholayim* but reaches for *Hierosolyma*—the Latin no less—forcing English up to its highest registers to suit the occasion. The wit connects the "penning-names" of the declaration's signatories, many of whom had Hebraized their names upon coming to Palestine, and the *guerre*, the war these signatories are going to have to wage upon declaring the sovereign state. The narrator pokes fun at the Cecil B. DeMille nature of his boyhood imagination, but he creates for the occasion a high prose of his own. The long sentence beginning "What was to be seen instead" builds, through a series of postponed objects, predicate, and adjectival and adverbial clauses, an experience of anticipation that subordinates historical precedents and analogies and even divine intervention to the nominal adjective "sovereign," standing alone.

Instead of accommodating the Jewish subject to the requirements of English, Klein creates an alienating English to convey the Jewish experience. In the language of the majority he exercises the right to appear alien to others rather than becoming alien to himself. Klein's work was akin to a hapaxlegomenon in that no one was ever likely to repeat this experiment in jubilation. Yet the Jews' need to tell their story in English far exceeds the bounds of this particular work and the mode of this exalted theme. George Eliot was correct in her perception that the prospects for Jewish survival in liberal democracies is closely linked to the problem of whether Jew and Gentile can resist the motif of romance. The way in which the Jewish national story is told in the world's most powerful language remains of no small importance to both.

8

THE IMMIGRANT PHASE

AMERICAN JEWISH FICTION FROM 1900 TO 1950

He had been fixed in infantilism as deep as a bronze boundary
marker was fixed in the ground, deep as a utility pole.

HENRY ROTH, *From Bondage*[1]

The Child as Hero

Motl Peysi the cantor's son might have been speaking for American Jewish
literature when he exclaimed, "*Mir iz gut, ikh bin a yosem* [I am lucky, I'm an
orphan]!"[2] As the frisky seven-year-old son of an ailing cantor in a Russian
shtetl, Motl is freed from parental discipline by the death of his father.
Sholem Aleichem had been writing about this boy all his life. He is the
hero of his first successful story—a boy who craves a penknife but has to
give up the dream of owning one in deference to his sickly father. He is
the child who desperately wants to play the fiddle in one story and to
dress up with the Purim players in another, ever prevented from following
his creative impulses because his father wants him to grow up a proper
Jew. Sholem Aleichem's comedy is stretched taut, as in *Tevye the Dairyman*,
between the playfulness, aggression, and eroticism of the child and the
civilizing responsibilities of the Jewish adult. But finally, and not coincidentally, during his first sojourn in New York in 1907 Sholem Aleichem
created Motl, whose father *dies* in the opening chapter. The furniture is
sold off to pay the doctor's bills. The mother's tears become her trademark.
The older brother has to take up the burden of caring for the family. But
Motl is finally freed from guilt. As the family sets out for America, "a new
world for Jewish children,"[3] Motl becomes their miniature Moses, the
chronicler of their voyage to liberation.

The real Mary Antin was not much older than the fictional Motl when she described her migration from Polotzk to Boston.[4] When Mary was ten years old, her father went off to America to earn the family its passage, and by the time she and her mother and siblings rejoined him three years later, she had emerged as "a new being, something that had not been before"—a young writer of impressive self-possession. The process of immigration not only emancipated her from parental supervision but inverted the family hierarchy. "Did I not become the parent and they the children, in those relations of teacher and learner?"[5] Mary's confidence in her own mind was so complete that she soon cast off Divine Authority, provoking a "toy riot" in the school yard when she declared to her classmates that she did not believe in God.[6]

Motl and Mary led the way to the promised land. Almost exact contemporaries, they faced similar conditions. Motl, however, was conceived as the child of Yiddish imagination, still carrying his father's name. When he met up with their former neighbors—Kletsl (now Sam), Velvel (who had turned into Willy), and Philip (né Faytl)—he treated English as palimpsest and delighted in divining what had lain beneath. Mary Antin did not superimpose but instead substituted one culture for another. Progress was for her a straight line from antisemitic Russia to free America, benighted religion to rational self-reliance, cloistered Yiddish to universal English. "I shall never have a better opportunity to make public declaration of my love for the English language," she writes at the point of describing how she learned to pronounce the dreadful English *th*:

> I am glad, most of all that the Americans began by being Englishmen, for thus did I come to inherit this beautiful language in which I think. It seems to me that in any other language happiness is not so sweet, logic is not so clear. I am not sure that I could believe in my neighbors as I do if I thought about them in un-English terms. I could almost say that my conviction of immortality is bound up with the English of its promise. And as I am attached to my prejudices, I must love the English language![7]

Not for nothing did Mary Antin become the poster child of American public school education. She accepted that the organic connection between language and culture required more of the Jewish immigrant than mere mastery of another tongue. By so patiently instructing her in the new language, her teachers intended to make her indistinguishable from her fellow Americans so that she might thenceforth suffer no handicap in competition with them and enjoy every benefit in association with them. The hospitality of America flowed from the English language—the same liberal emanation of British Christianity George Eliot warned against— that was now forging a nation out of immigrants like herself. An avowed atheist, Antin found the promise of eternity in the prospect of fame as an English writer.

As she celebrated English, Mary might have shouted, "I am lucky. I've been adopted!" Yet the unintentional irony in her writing almost matched the deliberate irony of Sholem Aleichem's: the only works for which she was to win "immortality" were the evocations of her Jewish past. She remained interesting to others, and to herself, not as the integrated American citizen she became but as the Yiddish-speaking child she had once been.

The child was the natural hero of immigrant fiction. Antin is surely right that children are the prow of their immigrant families. Their adventure of discovery is an ideal vehicle for the experience of a new society in a new land.[8] But the perspectives of child and adolescent continued to dominate American Jewish writing long after the immigrants had settled in, as though its practitioners could not accept that they had evolved into adults. American Jewish literature was not merely centered on the family, as its critics have often observed, but on perpetual children, the sons and daughters who could not or did not want to evolve into Jewish parents. American Jewish writers had trouble imagining themselves as people in charge, and they tried to make a literary and artistic virtue of the independence that adolescence demands. Writing in English, for a broad American audience, they particularly did not imagine themselves taking charge of Jewish destiny.

Abraham Cahan: *The Rise and Fall of David Levinsky*

A classic of the American immigrant novel genre, Abraham Cahan's *The Rise of David Levinsky* (1917), was the first to define the immigrant Jew's filial dilemma. As a boy in Antomir, Russia, David is encouraged by his widowed mother to redeem their life of poverty by becoming a great

Talmudic scholar. When she is killed by a Christian mob during Easter, trying to find the hooligans who had attacked her son, he is both freed from responsibility and saddled with an impossible moral debt. He forms an inchoate plan to become a learned man in America, but ambition leads him instead to become a wealthy clothing manufacturer. David pays for this perceived disloyalty to his mother by never finding mature happiness with another woman. The whole book is cast as a rehearsal of failure by a man who exemplifies socioeconomic success. Unlike the low-key New England hero of *The Rise of Silas Lapham*, the novel by Cahan's friend and literary champion William Dean Howells, Levinsky cannot behave honorably as an American businessman because he feels he has traduced his mother's values by *becoming* an American businessman.

Cahan brokered the marriage between the Jews and America with a sense of superiority to both sides of the match. He was not exactly humbled by his encounter with literary America. Howells may have smoothed his way into English literature, but it was Cahan who initiated Howells and his fellow journalists on the *Commercial Examiner* into the Russian classics, taught them about continental socialism, and introduced them to the life of Jews on the Lower East Side.[9] Simultaneously, as founding editor of the New York *Forverts* [Forward], he became the public educator of the Jewish immigrant community, and by the time he created Levinsky, he was running the largest circulation Jewish newspaper in the world. Cahan's skills as a cultural arbiter are in evidence, for example, when David on first catching sight of America is compared to its earliest settlers, who "fell on their knees and a hymn of thanksgiving burst from their souls. The scene, which is one of the most thrilling in history, repeats itself in the heart of every immigrant as he comes in sight of the American shores. I am at a loss to convey the peculiar state of mind that the experience created in me."[10] Cahan tactfully reminds his English readers that the ethos of the Pilgrim fathers was courtesy of the Hebrew Scriptures and that Jews feel no less gratitude for religious freedom than those who founded the country. However, this promising accommodation to America exacts its price from the Jew who is making the accommodation. Cahan works so hard to make Levinsky palatable to the English reader that in the process he sacrifices whatever the hero would have needed to sustain himself as a Jew.

What tantalizes the reader in *The Rise of David Levinsky* is the gap between the protagonist's accomplishments and his dissatisfaction. Since there is no one but himself to keep him from exercising the right to happiness, and no one but the author to keep him from enjoying the fruits of his labor, why cannot Levinsky take any pleasure in his newfound home? His character is certainly not beyond redemption. Yet for all his material success, Levinsky never marries and never fathers a child. One source of his deficiency is the narrative method I have been describing; by interpreting Levinsky outward, Cahan guaranteed the collapse of his Jewish soul, progressively ridding him of private associations of language and memory, the habits of dipping into the Talmud, reading the Yiddish press, attending synagogue, worrying about his fellow Jews in Europe and Palestine. Cahan builds up the English reader's trust in Levinsky at the expense of his inwardness, the "untranslatable" parts of his being. Had Levinsky created a Jewish family or intellectual life for himself in America, the author would have been required to explain the need for some continuing Jewish separatism in America, what Herman Wouk would much later describe as the conflict between Inside and Outside.[11] Cahan faced the choice between alienating the English reader or alienating the Jew from his tradition, and he resolved the problem, as did the vast majority of Jewish writers in English, by tracing the progress of his hero in terms that are favorable to the audience. What had blocked the hero's emotional development was not Levinsky's wish to succeed as an American manufacturer but Cahan's wish to succeed as an American novelist.

When Isaac Rosenfeld "rediscovered" Cahan's book in 1952, he offered a very different view of Levinsky's failure-in-success: "Levinsky's character was formed by hunger. The experiences of his life—poverty, squalor, orphanage, years of religious study and sexual restraint, the self-sacrificing love of his mother and her violent death—all these experiences contain, as their common element, a core of permanent dissatisfaction."[12] Applying a psychoanalytical model of child development, Rosenfeld argues that Levinsky's experience of deprivation so deeply formed his personality that he had to reproduce the experience of deprivation throughout his adult life. This hunger expresses itself as a yearning for fulfillment, but since it is the organic habit of his life, he must preserve it at all cost:

> For hunger, in this broader, rather metaphysical sense of the
> term that I have been using, is not only the state of tension out of
> which the desires for relief and betterment spring; precisely be-

cause the desires are formed under its sign, they become assimilated to it, and convert it into the prime source of all value, so that
the man, in his pursuit of whatever he considers pleasurable and
good, seeks to return to his yearning as much as he does to escape
it.[13]

In a bold leap from the particular to the general, Rosenfeld interprets
Levinsky's personal dissatisfaction as an instance of the Diaspora Jew's
"yearning after yearning" that is embodied in the Psalmist's vow "If I forget
thee, O Jerusalem, let my right hand wither." The Diaspora Jew's yearning
has gone on for so long that it has become the substance of his being, the
archetypal form of his relation to the world. According to this theory, the
Jew preserves his longing for Jerusalem as its own object: he wants less to
satisfy his desire than to keep the sense of incompletion alive.

Rosenfeld then links this Jewish habit of yearning to something similar
in the American spirit. Although they may be hot in pursuit of material
gain, Americans suspect that true happiness in personal fulfillment cannot
be secured by money alone. The teaching "Money isn't everything" undermines the false security of wealth and reaffirms the appetite, the hunger,
for a deeper satisfaction; a structural congruity in character and culture between Jews and Americans derives from this equivocal rush to success that
leaves Levinsky a lifelong bachelor and self-declared failure. Whereas Cahan had tried to recast the Jewish experience in terms familiar to his American readership, Rosenfeld finds an essential affinity in the psychology of
Jew and American that predisposes each to understand the other. Cahan
had been looking for a resolution such as George Eliot ascribes to
Deronda: "a longing in which the whole being consents." The strange
consequence of Rosenfeld's essay is to reverse Cahan's judgment on his
hero, for while Cahan deplores Levinsky's inability to become a husband
and father, Rosenfeld interprets his "yearning" as protection against rank
materialism and seems to uphold adolescence, incompletion—the condition of yearning—as an attractive moral state.

Immigrant writers of the early twentieth century were still addressing
the artistic problem of how to bring Jewish experience to the American
reader. Anzia Yezierska, a much more combative writer than Mary Antin,
could never get beyond the story of how she left her immigrant home.
Whereas Antin "made herself over" into a genteel writer[14] and Cahan ac-

commodated the English reader by treating Yiddish as a foreign language, Yezierska brought the immigrant streets to life by imitating their cacophony and fractured English. "My voice was like dynamite," boasts the ten-year-old herring salesman of *Bread Givers*. "Louder than all the pushcart peddlers, louder than all the hollering noises of bargaining and selling."[15] Yezierska's resistance to genteel authority and to the humiliations of poverty bursts through the prose and hauls readers down to her level of cultural subsistence. But once her autobiographical heroines move out of their neighborhoods and into their new tailored suits, the author loses the Yiddish pungency that was her trademark. How meekly our heroine yields to her principal, Mr. Seelig, when in front of the public school class she has been hired to teach he tries to correct her telltale immigrant pronunciation of "the birds sing-gg" by putting his cool fingers on her throat and showing her how to soften the consonant! "'Now say it again,' he commanded. And I turned pupil myself and pronounced the word correctly."[16] This image of a throttled writer resurfaced in the title story of Yezierska's posthumous collection, *The Open Cage*, when the heroine releases the bird that had flown into her apartment, then returns into "[her] own cage."[17] As the internal evidence of her writing gives notice, Yezierska and her heroines no longer had a story worth telling once they took their cues from the perfectly assimilated German Jew Seelig, whose name connotes bliss.

The Romance of Poverty and Assimilation

Writers of the American Left soon developed a special ideological fondness for immigrant childhoods that were lived in poverty. Dissatisfied with democracy's tolerance for human imperfection and persuaded by the Marxist critique of capitalism, many admired the Russian Revolution and hoped that socialism could be imported, either through radical upheaval or through democratic persuasion, into America as well. They expected Marxism, not business, to forge an alliance between the Jews and native Americans. Just as "proletarian" origins became a valuable commodity in Russian literature following Maxim Gorky's forceful autobiography, a Jewish immigrant past could be used as the touchstone of reliably lower-class origins.

Already a Communist mercenary by the time he wrote his fictional memoir *Jews Without Money* (1930), Michael Gold justified his sentiment for his Jewish immigrant family *because* they were without money, and hence implicitly aligned with the proletariat against the bourgeoisie. Among the charms of his book is the portrait of the "buttinsky" mother who tries to reform the prostitutes as well as her family; among its tendentious inventions is the killing off of a sister under the wheels of a truck. The book's appearance at the beginning of the depression created a natural audience for its anticapitalist message and aroused sympathy for those plunged into want. But the vicious implications of Gold's nostalgia can be found in his introduction to the second edition, written two years after Hitler came to power in Germany. He presents the following defense against the Nazis' taunt that Jews are all international bankers:

> I have told in my book a tale of Jewish poverty in one ghetto, that of New York. The same story can be told of a hundred other ghettoes scattered over all the world. For centuries the Jew has lived in this universal ghetto. Yiddish literature is saturated with the ghetto melancholy and poverty.
>
> And Jewish bankers and fascists are everywhere. Hitler has received their support, both with money and ideas.[. . .] Jewish bankers are fascists; Jewish workers are radicals; the historic class division is true among the Jews as with any other race.[18]

Whereas Yiddish writers like Sholem Aleichem had resolved not to let poverty or the insult of the ghetto deny the resiliency of Jewish life, the ideological Left transposed this system of values to credit Jews with resiliency only as long as they remained poor in the ghetto.[19]

Indulgent of the Jewish poor, the second generation of writers on the Left were unsparing to those who made it in America. Their negative prototype was Sammy Glick, the Jewish hustler of Budd Schulberg's novel *What Makes Sammy Run?* (1941), who gets himself promoted from copy boy to radio columnist and then advances through a broken field-run of thefts, lies, and seductions to "success" as head of a Hollywood studio. Though the book answers its title question in part by filling in details of Sammy's deprived childhood, it punishes the greedy little Jew for climbing to the top: Sammy feels the younger dogs nipping at his heels at the moment of his triumph and discovers on his wedding night that he has married a woman even more calculating than he. Whereas I. J. Singer pronounced the doom of the hustling Max Ashkenazi as part of a total political rout, Sammy is punished for being the wrong kind of Jew.

Budd Schulberg was the son of a studio executive in Hollywood, but the novel reveals him rather than Sammy as the Jew who is really on the make. To play up to his *goyish* audience, Schulberg takes for his narrator Al Mannheim, a New England Jew with genteel credentials: his father, "the town's only rabbi, had led a life of community service and true Christ-like gentility that had won him Middletown's approval and genuine respect."[20] Mannheim, ever the tattle-teller, enjoys relating how Sammy tricked him into spending a night with hookers, ascribing to the "bad Jew" the morals of a pervert while congratulating himself for his sensitivity and tact. "Maybe I'm a Puritan, but there has to be somewhere you draw the line and this was always it for me. . . . I wasn't exactly surprised to find that Sammy approached the most elemental emotion in life with all the sensitivity of a slaughterhouse worker slitting a steer's throat."[21] Sammy is portrayed as a hack and a "red-baiter," while Mannheim the *honest* writer—supports the Communist-backed Screen Writers' Guild and boasts of his political sensitivity. The concluding words of Al Mannheim reveal Schulberg's state of mind:

> Now Sammy's career meteored through my mind in all its destructive brilliance, his blitzkrieg against his fellow men. My mind skipped from conquest to conquest, like the scrapbook on his exploits I had been keeping ever since that memorable birthday party at the Algonquin [when Sammy had waylaid and conquered a famous Broadway playwright]. It was a terrifying and wonderful document, the record of where Sammy ran, and if you looked behind the picture and between the lines you might even discover what made him run. And some day I would like to see it published, as a blueprint of a way of life that was paying dividends in America in the first half of the twentieth century.[22]

The diction betrays what was going on as the book was being written— the *blitzkrieg* that had struck Europe *in all its destructive brilliance,* launched by the Nazi predator who *skipped from conquest to conquest* compiling a *terrifying and wonderful* record of annihilating the Jews. Schulberg displaced the evil being done to the Jew as a way of insulating himself from both Hitler's war and the need to defend against it, animating the stereotypical object of antisemitism in order to repudiate the Jew it caricatures. The novel's implicit ideal of assimilation is realized by the marriage of both Jewish men to non-Jewish women, Mannheim to a fellow Leftist, Sammy to a fellow predator. If Abraham Cahan deplored Americanization as an unwitting betrayal of Jewish values and the Jewish past, Schulberg apologized for the stereotype that antisemitism had created.

Isaac Rosenfeld noted that it was in the Jewish tradition and in the American grain to attack the "gospel of success." But when such novels as *What Makes Sammy Run?* and its Canadian parallel, Mordecai Richler's *The Apprenticeship of Duddy Kravitz* (1959), criticize Jewish success from the Gentile rather than the Jewish perspective, they turn ambition into a particularly Jewish form of corruption.[23] Richler's Duddy Kravitz is flanked by a gentle English Canadian boy who becomes his victim and a pure-hearted French Canadian girl who wants to save his soul. The ethnic labels define the Jew as the brilliant manipulator who takes advantage of Canada's two founding peoples. In Tillie Olson's leftist short story *Tell Me a Riddle*, a dying grandmother tries to recapture the freedom of her Revolutionary adolescence by disengaging from the Jewish bourgeois family she has inadvertently spawned. The grandmother is appalled by her daughter's primitive Sabbath candle-lighting but is later charmed by the Pan del Muerto, the shortbread cookie baked by immigrants from Mexico in the image of their little girl who has just died. These works are less schematic than is their antipathy for Jewish society and Judaism, but on no account did these North American Jewish writers seem able to imagine the value of perpetuating Jewish life. Thus, the ideology of the Left helped turn assimilation into a virtue by implying that Judaism had given way to purer social ideals.

The Classic of Disinheritance: Henry Roth's *Call It Sleep*

Henry Roth's *Call It Sleep*, an acknowledged classic of American literature (1934), is a shattering epic of immigrant adjustment to the land of opportunity. By the time Roth began writing the book, the story was already commonplace.[24] The ominous prologue, in which Father, after a separation of two years, comes to Ellis Island to pick up his wife and the child he has never seen, compresses into a few pages the by then standard experience of arrival in the new land, relying on the reader's familiarity with the setting in order to imply that something new is being done with the theme. We are told that "there was something quite untypical" about the scene we are witnessing, and its oddity awakens our curiosity. How is this family different from others? Or, how will this story of immigrants differ from those we have already heard? The story is different because the boy arriving with his mother from Europe is entering a much more dangerous zone than America: he is beginning a new life in his hitherto unconstituted family under suspicion by a father who doubts that he is really his son. When his father tosses the child's old-fashioned hat into the ocean, he strips the book of any lingering notion of divine grace. The fate of the hat warns the child that he will have to muster more than the usual capacities of mind and spirit if he is to survive.

Henry Roth's book presents childhood as the archetypal immigration. Every child hopes to arrive in a friendly land. Happy families may all be alike in at least one respect, that the fortunate pairing of the parents is retroactively confirmed by their beloved children, but children born into angry marriages remind parents of a regrettable bargain. Having never *earned* dislike, they cannot fairly anticipate how or why they provoke punishment, yet they have to figure out the connections between cause and effect if they hope to avoid abuse. Child and immigrant must both learn a new language. The burden is on each to adjust to a world already complete without him. In one important respect, however, the two conditions differ, for the child, unlike the immigrant, can never select the home in which he must learn to live.

As we are joined to his consciousness in the opening chapter, David Schearl is already aware that "this world had been created without thought of him." Too small to reach the faucet, he cannot drink without the help of his mother—"tall as a tower." "Have little fear," she says. Indeed, were it only a matter of growing taller, David might look forward to mastering his environment in the natural course of time. The physical world is not his only challenge, however. His mother expects something from her son in return for the water she gives him: a kiss with lips as cool as the water that wet them. This kiss alone has the power to erase, albeit momentarily, her "reserved and almost mournful air," but it is part of the ritual she has forged that she will not ask for it directly, expecting her son, like a storybook hero, to intuit it on his own. David must find the propitiating formula to slake her thirst, then solve the much more tangled riddle of his family.

David's mother is his only teacher and protector in this early stage of his life. Unlike neighbors who holler at their children, Genya Schearl cares tenderly for David and speaks to him so poetically that we don't have to look far beyond her conversation for the source of his own powers of expression. In a stunning, significant reversal of the technique of most immigrant novels, Roth renders Yiddish as the poetic "home" language of the text and English as the distorted language of the streets. Yet Genya's warmth has a darker, smothering side: held under suspicion by her husband, she often exploits David's presence to save herself, and she compounds his anxiety by designating him as the mainstay of her love, a role he cannot refuse without risking the loss of her protection. "Waltuh, Waltuh, Wiulflowuh," chant the little girls of the vulgar street chorus in Roth's characteristic counterpoint of inside and outside the home. The young ladies pronounce themselves ready to die for this object of their passion, and although it is long before he really knows anything about his mother's past, so attuned is David to her yearning for love "somewhere else" that upon hearing this evocation of the far-off land of wildflowers he is himself overcome with her longing for it.

The oedipal paradigm seems to fit relations between this mother and son so closely that many a reader thinks he has discovered in it the key to the boy's neurosis. But Genya's heart was driven wild in another land, in another language, and by another lover, not the boy's father. Betrayed by her Christian lover and humiliated by her own father, she became a pariah and married her first eligible suitor—Albert Schearl. Since the only home Genya can subsequently provide for her infant son is in exile, he must become the more alien the closer she binds him to herself. She is not the typical immigrant mother, nor the embodiment of Jewish old-country virtues, but an outcast who had already overthrown the tradition and forfeited the trust of her community before leaving for America. Schearl is likewise marked by the unprosecuted charge that he was implicated in the death of his father. Thus, banished by their families, David's parents live like fugitives within the great immigrant community, a self-imprisoning family that is divided against itself by suspicion and guilt.

Albert's frustrated rage is the counterpart of Genya's longing for love. The day we join him, David is going somewhere alone with his father for the first time. Albert needs no persuasion by God to sacrifice the son whom he holds responsible for his failure. He sends David to collect his unpaid wages, and there the boy learns that his "crazy" father had been fired for wanting to kill a man in rage. Forbidden to talk about this errand, David also conceals from his father what he has discovered about him. The boy thenceforth imagines Albert with a poised hammer, about to strike, and knows that he cannot expect a staying miracle should he ever become the target of his father's fury. First by his mother, then by his father, David is given responsibilities beyond his capacities to discharge, and without being able to appeal to the other parent for help.

Henry Roth differs from James Joyce, to whose narrative technique he is consciously indebted, in this perception of inheritance. Joyce opens *Portrait of the Artist as a Young Man* with the child's discovery of language from a face that is welcomingly intimate:

> Once upon a time and a very good time it was there was a moocow coming down along the road and this moocow that was down along the road had met a nicens little boy named baby tuckoo. . . .
>
> His father told him that story: his father looked at him through a glass: he had a hairy face.[25]

The unpunctuated, uninflected opening of the artist's story, heard from the firm perch of a father's lap, invites the child to experience himself as a part of the natural world. He is surrounded by people who know just what they want to make of him. By the time he is fully grown, Joyce's young artist will want to shake himself free from excessive instruction of tenacious authorities in order to go forth as the repository of a multilayered national culture "to forge in the smithy of his soul the uncreated conscience of his race." In sharpest contrast, Roth's denuded young artist has to work his solitary way out of the cellar of fear and ignorance. The meadow happens to figure prominently in the memory of both David's parents, but as a sinister place. Nor does anyone else in the new world apart from his parents offer David instruction. Public school is notably inconsequential in the boy's development, as though Roth were telling us that it had nothing to teach him about what he most needed to know.

David is introduced to sex by his disabled neighbor in a cupboard where traps are set for mice and rats. He encounters death when another child is carried off in a black box. His mother inadvertently alerts the boy to further dangers when she uses his presence to ward off the unwelcome advances of the father's friend Luter and to keep this knowledge from her husband. The strange tension between his parents teaches David mistrust. "(Don't believe. Don't believe. Don't believe. Never!)"[26] The street reinforces this lesson that "Id ain' no Sendy Klaws, didja know?"[27] It is thus, by learning not to expect salvation, that David steels himself to the real and imagined terrors that beset him. He succeeds not so much in overcoming his fear as in defying it, "as though he had slammed the door within him and locked it."[28] In the parlance of the time, Roth's child immigrant was on his way to becoming an existential hero.

THE ARRIVAL FROM EUROPE of Aunt Bertha into the Schearl household forces the family conflict out into the open. Like the sweat that pours from her, Bertha brings information to the surface. It may seem strange that this coarse woman should be the one to introduce David to the Metropolitan Museum of Art, dragging him around its exhibits in a parody of art appreciation, yet without her candor David could never have penetrated the secret of his parents' marriage—and could never have mastered the art of representation. Her vulgar speech breaks the family's contract of silence, and in the way that literary realism determines to get to the bottom of things, she insists on knowing and speaking the truth.

Few detective novels unravel their mystery as suspensefully as this second section of *Call It Sleep*. Yoked to the perspective of the child who has to elude his mother's watchfulness while following her story in a language he does not know, the reader experiences David's urgency as the matter of life or death that it is for him. David tries to learn his mother's secret from the Polish conversation between his mother and his aunt by catching her occasional lapses into Yiddish. His dawning comprehension is rendered through the drama of language.[29] In this moving, artistically exalting sequence, the child's curiosity is satisfied at great expense. For to solve a mystery is to learn the truth, namely, that his father's suspicions about David's paternity are only biologically, not psychologically, unfounded. Genya, whom we encounter as David's mother and Albert's wife, had already spent her romantic passion on a church organist, a man whom, given the chance, she would have followed into marriage and into the

Church. The clue to his mother's emotional life is the picture she hangs in their home of a field of cornflowers, the landscape of her thwarted love. As for Albert, having failed to rescue his father when he was attacked by a bull and hence suspected by the family of having abetted his father's death, he is rendered impotent by his certainty that Genya would not have married him unless she had been desperate to protect her bastard. David will eventually clear up the misunderstanding between husband and wife, but in the process he will shatter the myth of the family—and of the Jewish family as font of nurturing values and love. David's later attraction to his Catholic friend Leo, and his hope to be saved by the magic of Leo's cross, reenacts his mother's buried love.

Along with the family secrets, coarse Aunt Bertha forces the conflict over language out into the open. Thus, although the Yiddish of the home is Roth's language of eloquence, it functions in the book as an isolating rather than a socializing tongue. At no point, not even in the Yiddish the-atre that Albert attends in his disappointing friendship with Luter, does this book introduce the possibility of a sustaining Yiddish institution or cultural cohesion. The richness of Genya's Yiddish does not connect her to fellow Jews or to a Jewish way of life but separates her from surround-ings that seem uglier by contrast. Bertha punctures this privacy, forcing English into the home, as when she recounts her visit to the dentist she hopes to entrap in marriage:

> "In Veljish," she continued, "they say that 'kockin' will clear the brow of pain. But here in America—didn't he call it that? 'Kockin'?—will clear the mouth of pain.
>
> His father's newspaper rustled warningly.
>
> "Cocaine?" said her sister hastily.
>
> "Oh, is that how you say it?"
>
> 'Kockin,' as David had learned long ago, was a Yiddish word meaning to sit on the toilet.[30]

Bertha is goading her brother-in-law with the same *shtick* that borscht belt comedians used to provoke their immigrant audiences into laughter. They force their listeners to sacrifice false dignity and get down into the trough of the real. Bertha is David's first teacher in the verbal play his author re-discovered in Joyce. Born in linguistic exile, Roth would have to tell his story not in Yiddish, the language of his people, nor in Polish, the language of his homeland, but in a mongrel English that draws attention to its impurities. In this respect, he may have felt even more authentic than Joyce, because he had earned the right to English through such a traumatic effort and because the displaced Jew of his novel was the real thing.

IN ITS THIRD SECTION, "The Coal," the novel crushes the notion that a religious tradition can help to compensate the immigrant child for the loss of family cohesion. Roth does not depict American schooling—described with such gratitude by Antin and Yezierska—but the afternoon *cheder* of Yidel Pankower, the custodian of David's ancestral myths. The project is doomed from the start. His father enrolls him in *cheder* to make him "at least something of a Jew." Genya weighs in with memories of her *cheder* teacher's onion breath. Reb Pankower's debased authority is confirmed by his attempt to shore it up with switches. When, against all odds, the child begins to perceive through the Hebrew Bible the "increasing nearness of God" and believes that he may be able to find in the recalcitrant text the truly protective Power he seeks, his attempt to gain that knowledge, by clambering through the window into the schoolroom, is thwarted by the teacher who suspects that he must be trying to steal from him. In other circumstances, Yidel Pankower might have found the ideal student in David Schearl, and the sensitive boy a spiritual father in this lonely old man. Instead, the teacher's isolation from his pupils provokes one crisis with David after another and finally triggers the bloody climax of the struggle between the actual father and son.

David's imagination is fired by one of the most famous chapters of Isaiah. Its image of the angels calling "Holy, holy, holy is the Lord of Hosts" has made its way into the Jewish liturgy, with Jews rising to their toes in emulation of the sacred chorus. But David is too preoccupied with his own crisis to respond to the glory of the language or the scene. He is fascinated by the coal that the seraphim pluck from the altar to touch the prophet's lips and purify him from sin. He needs to harness the prophet's power to protect himself from his father. Without trivializing the mythic resonance of Roth's description, we recognize in David's quest for magical powers what his Jewish contemporaries were looking for when they created the comic book characters Superman and Batman—the power to restore a stolen sense of justice. When David is ridiculed by his *cheder* teacher for thinking that he may have located Isaiah's light between the crack of the streetcar tracks, he gives up on Isaiah, but not on the search for redemptive power.

On the eve of the Sabbath, an old woman pays David to light the stove for her in a scene that seems to have little purpose other than to demonstrate the hypocritical circumvention of Jewish law. David's first exposure to Jew-baiting occurs on the eve of the festival of freedom. "It was Monday morning of the first Passover night. One was lucky in being a Jew today. There was no school."[31] Enjoying none of the ironic "luck" of Sholem Aleichem's Motl Peysi, David is humiliated by the janitor when he tries to perform the ritual burning of the crumbs of leavened bread, the *khometz*, in front of his house, and he later denies being Jewish when threatened by a Gentile gang. All that the battered David asks as he approaches his door on Passover eve is that his mother will give him only clean underwear, not an interrogation, so that his ordeal on the street will not precipitate a tougher confrontation at home.

Roth demystifies the Jewish holiday, the Jewish family, and the immigrant experience, dismantling tradition as part of his liberation from the nightmare of history. He was, of course, telling the story of a generation that assumed it was becoming more culturally advanced as it left Jewishness behind, but unlike them, he intuited that his achievement would destroy the creative sources of individual talent. How could you simultaneously forfeit your formative culture and go forth to forge the uncreated conscience of your race?

I N CONTRAST TO GENERATIONS of Jews who grew into adults by assimilating the cumulative wisdom of their elders, David Schearl peels off false hope and false mythologies. By the fourth and final section of the novel, he feels "secure at home and in the street—that was all the activity he asked."[32] Because the story is so closely confined to the boy's fears, we are in danger of forgetting how bravely he overcomes them. There is something unassailably strong in the child's character. The book rests as much on David's courage as it does on the quality of the prose and the epic scope of the narrative.[33]

As David makes his way outward from the cocoon of family, his autonomy grows with every loss and punishment he suffers. Both Genya and Albert were beaten by their fathers in the old country, but neither triumphs over the ordeal as does David. His father's raised hand, looming over the boy since the opening chapter, comes down on him in earnest when he is conscripted into assisting his father on his milk deliveries, and fails to stop two men from stealing a couple of bottles from the wagon. David experiences his father's punishment most intensely as he imagines it coming, then again when his father catches up with the thieves and uncoils his practiced whip against them, and finally when the brass-buckled ends of the reins bite twice into his shoulder. "He never winced. He hardly even felt them, so frozen with terror he was."[34] But this terror does not prevent David from accepting his punishment yet again. In a frenzied scene in which all of David's accusers seem to converge—the child is charged with having abetted forbidden sex and Leo's rosary beads fall to the floor incriminating him as traitor to the Jews—David offers himself to his father without waiting to be sacrificed. He hands his father the whip he had broken in the earlier fit of rage, saying, "It was me, papa—" inviting his father to punish him for the sin of his being.[35]

Roth's fiction differed from earlier American Jewish writing in the burden of punishment that it took upon itself. Sinfulness in the book is often directly associated with sex—the "dirty" play of the children in the cupboard, Leo's insistence that David become his sexual procurer, the boys' spying on Genya from the rooftop as she bathes. But the sense of "original sin" as forbidden sexuality envelops the entire experience of the novel. It recalls a story by the American Yiddish writer Lamed Shapiro in which a Jewish family of father, mother, and son immigrates to New York after a pogrom. Told from the perspective of the uncomprehending child, the story reveals through the father's growing rage that the mother is bearing a pogromist's child, hence America will never be able to erase the consequences of Europe's violence.[36] Similarly, Roth seems never to have enjoyed the liberal assumption that man is born rational and innocent or the corresponding notion that America extends to all its children an equal right to happiness. He thinks he must prove himself to America, not America to himself.

When David invites his father to beat him without waiting to be called, he strips the ogre of his menace and begins to reveal the wretched man beneath. David forces his parents to recognize the compromise each had made in marrying the other; he deconstructs the mythic past so that all may live in the humbled present. But to say it thus is like portraying Niagara with a garden hose. As David plans his expiation (by sticking a milk dipper between the streetcar rails to ignite Isaiah's healing flame), the sound within him becomes a roar:

—If it lights, so what? What'll I do? He'll ask me. What'll I do? What? What? Papa, nothing. I wanted . . . I wanted. What? The— The—on the floor. Beads. Fell out—pocket. What for you—? Ow! Papa, I don't know what? Why? He'll look. He'll say. Ball. Ball I wanted Ball? He'll say—ball? Yes. Ball. In my head. Ow! I can't tell. Must! In my head seen. Was. In the corner. By milk-stink baby-carriages. White. Wasn't scared. What? What? What? Yes. Wasn't scared. How I seen one once, when—When? Sword in the fire. Tenth street. Ask the rabbi. Sword. In the crack light and he laughed. When I read that he—Fire. Light. When I read. Always scared till then—and they made me. Goyim by river. And They— So had. So lost. Wanted back, Papa! Papa! Wanted back. And he said yes. Leo. Like inside-outside guts burning. And he said would. Come out of box. Said God on—Wait, Papa! Papa! Don't hit. Don't Ow![37]

This frantic confession evokes all the dangers that beset the boy, all the objects through which he had sought redemptive light. Even as he harnesses the stream-of-consciousness technique, Roth lashes out against it; he seems to be shouting "Ow!" against Mollie Bloom's "Yes," anticipating his later, more sustained criticism of James Joyce, who would replace his father as the authority to be overcome.

David finds shelter from his family in the street. An American chorus of voices surrounds the boy as he puts himself to the final test. Unlike many admirers of this sequence, I feel the author straining here to enlarge his work, as though he were trying to do justice to the extraordinary achievement of the young protagonist. Or, possibly, Roth needed to remove himself from David's consciousness, to escape the intensity of the narrative before bringing it to conclusion. Whatever its creative genesis, the passage establishes David as a "ward" of the city, its uncommonly plucky new offspring. Amid the sailors and the prostitutes, the toilers and the boozers conducting their business and their arguments, he thrusts his milky weapon between the rails: *"Power! Power like a paw, titanic power, ripped through the earth and slammed against his body and shackled him where he stood."*[38] He has dared to seize the electrical power of the city that is mythic and real, that momentarily hobbles him and forever sets him free. When the policeman carries him into his home, he hears the shaken voice of his father answering his questions and knows he has triumphed. The reader knows it too: *"'Yes. Yes,'* he was saying. *'My sawn. Mine. Yes. Awld eight. Eight en'—en' vun mawnt'. He vas bawn in—'"*[39] As Albert humbles himself to acknowledge that he has sired this child, he is revealed in all his immigrant pathos, doomed to ungrammatical stammer while his son goes on to expose him in "English literature." Childhood may be an especially vulnerable species of immigration, but by harnessing the power of the local language, the child can triumph over his immigrant parent.

David knew the world was created without thought of him, and so did Henry Roth. He did not have the choice of Jewish writers before him: Hebrew remained a dumb mystery; Yiddish was the wall its native child had to scale in order to escape the family. Roth lacked the nurturing tradition for the individual talent, and in T. S. Eliot's *Waste Land,* which he discovered when he was in his early twenties, Roth recognized his own fallen condition. Eliot and Joyce had contrasted the nobler past with the ugly present. Roth saw that he could write a similar epic about the wasteland of his own deracination. But the effort proved so draining that the author needed the sleep of half a lifetime to restore him to purposeful energy. To what purpose had he undertaken the ordeal? Child and author had taught themselves to live without most of the things that others live for. When an earlier generation of East European Jewish writers had asked, "For whom do I toil?" the largely rhetorical question implied that the true artist thrived on service to a people, and withered in its absence. Roth's novel unwittingly showed how little the artist would be worth to himself once he stood free and clear of his people. Jew without Jewishness, American without the inspiring heritage of America, Roth had entered the emptied world that Jean-Paul Sartre conceived in his philosophy, and it is not surprising that he expressed his existential selfhood the same way Sartre did, by becoming a Communist. At that point in his life, Roth might as well have called it sleep. His masterful novel illumined like no other how the impulse of self-empowerment could result in the need for self-enslavement.

* * *

Henry Roth's artistic resurrection—as remarkable as his debut—began with the *American Scholar's* 1956 symposium on the question "What do you think is the most neglected book of the past twenty-five years?" *Call It Sleep* was the only novel to be cited more than once, by Leslie Fiedler and Alfred Kazin, and was subsequently recalled to public attention with a drumbeat of acclaim that revived the dormant author.[40] Soon he was writing and publishing again. Always mining his own experience, which was the only subject he had ever trusted, he allowed his Italian translator Mario Materassi to help him arrange a complete retrospective of his writing, "to exhibit the continuity within the desolating discontinuity that had taken place over all those barren years."[41] The two men designed a "connective tissue" of commentary, quotation, and reminiscence that let the mature Henry Roth pass judgment on his earlier writing. *Shifting Landscape* takes up the same theme of expiation that permeates *Call It Sleep*. Since the past could never be rewritten, only atoned for, Roth reprinted opinions he had held as a Marxist and an opponent of Israel, such as his 1937 defense of Joseph Stalin and the Moscow Trials, written four years after he had joined the Communist Party, and his 1963 pronouncement: "I feel that to the great boon Jews have already conferred upon humanity, Jews in America might add this last and greatest one: of orienting themselves toward ceasing to be Jews."[42] Lillian Hellman would make a career of falsifying her Communist past and win the plaudits of "fellow travelers" for perfecting the art of lying. Arthur Miller would spend a lifetime attacking McCarthyism as a safe way of obscuring Communist crimes. Henry Roth thanked God that he had once "put it down there" on paper, so that he would have all the evidence for his self-prosecution. He attributed his transformation to the fear for Israel's safety that had overtaken him during the 1967 Six-Day War.

> Only one force of a social and political nature had stirred him in the last decade, had ruptured the tight shell surrounding his self-absorption. . . . That force was *Israel!* Only Israel had sundered his well-nigh impervious preoccupations with his psyche, burst open the pod of his self-engrossment, and had set his predilections flying—as if his partisanship were an accelerator.[43]

Anxiety about Israel's welfare had breached his habitual introspection—
the way the Red Sea had parted to let the Israelites pass. The waters returned "(alas, without engulfing the foe)," but Roth felt that he had
emerged on firmer moral ground.

For his epic memoir *Mercy of a Rude Stream*, Roth invented a dialectical,
confessional style very close to the commentary of his *Shifting Landscape*.
Set off by different typefaces, the present-day aging "author" in front of
his computer, "Ecclesias," interrupts and passes judgment on the saga of Ira
Stigman, the fictional version of his adolescent self. Like an analysand on
his own couch, or a prosecutor in his own dock, the mature Jew prods
himself to recall all the details of his incest with his sister and the betrayal
he believes that he practiced in his art. He admits that he had escaped his
parents by adopting surrogates—for his motherly muse, Eda Lou Walton,
the professor of literature at New York University, and in the paternal role,
none other than the father of modernism, James Joyce—and at this point
he acknowledges the self-betrayal in that love affair with English modernism:

> *Ulysses* demonstrated to him not only that it was possible to
> commute the dross of the mundane and the sordid into literary
> treasure, but *how* it was done. [. . .] No more awesome master of
> every phase of syntax, no more authoritative mentor—nay,
> taskmaster!—of subtlest effects, subtlest distinctions of word or
> phrase, had Ira in his desultory way ever encountered than Joyce.
> Wryly, Ira remembered the old saying about the Chicago packing
> houses: that they used every part of the pig except the squeal.
> Joyce elucidated ways to use even the squeal: lingo as well as lan-
> guage, the double entendre, the pun, the homely squib, the
> spoonerism, the palindrome, pig Latin and pig Sanscrit.[44]

Roth examines among his many debts to Joyce those marvelous but corrupting influences he thinks turned him porcine—*treyf*. It was Joyce who
showed him how language could free him from the "depraved exile," from
the "immutable bondage" of his Jewish family.[45] He does not blame Joyce
for his own sly sinfulness but for something hollow in Joyce's plenitude,
for whatever was lacking in Joyce's generosity that comes through in the
un-Jewishness of his Jew Leopold Bloom. This is the false part of Joyce's

influence, the part from which Roth felt he had to liberate himself before he could return to telling his story in a brand-new "Jewish" contrapuntal style. If *Call It Sleep* is the classic of disinheritance, *Mercy of a Rude Stream* is the messier, wordier, classic of repossession, but repossession of a culture from which he has grown apart. After a lifetime of disaffection, Roth has no Jewish subjects to draw upon other than his youth before he became a modernist and the Israel he loves but does not know. His Jewish passion resembles Isaac Rosenfeld's idea of Jewish yearning, for by the time he is aroused to the task, he is too isolated from his fellow Jews to do more than *long* to protect the people he has rejoined.

Passing from Home and Making a New Life: Isaac Rosenfeld and Bernard Malamud

If asked at what point American Jewish letters gave notice of its independence from Anglo American modernism, I would cite the day Isaac Rosenfeld, with the help of Saul Bellow, composed a Yiddish parody of "The Love Song of J. Alfred Prufrock." T. S. Eliot was the giant who could not be ignored. The giant had charged the Jews with corrupting his culture. What better way to credit him as a poet and discredit him as an antisemite than by Yiddishizing the poet who so feared the Yid? "Let us go then, you and I" became "*Nu-zhe, kum-zhe, ikh un du*," the repeated participle *zhe* turning Prufrock's civil invitation into a nagging prod. The evening spread out against the sky "Like a patient etherized upon a table" was likened instead to "*a leymener goylem af Tisha b'Av*," a clay golem on the midsummer Jewish fast day commemorating the two destructions of the Jerusalem Temple, the golem being the creature of Jewish folklore who, when animated by magical formula, defends the Jews against their Christian attackers. The women in the room who "come and go/Talking of Michelangelo" discuss something more likely in their Jewish context: *In tsimer vu di vayber zenen/Ret men fun Marx un Lenin.* (In the room where there are women/The talk is about Marx and Lenin.) Most notably, "I grow old . . . I grow old . . . /I shall wear the bottoms of my trousers rolled" became *Ikh ver alt . . . ikh ver alt . . . es vert mir in pupik kalt*"; that is, the old Jew at the seashore was more likely to feel his *pupik*, his belly button, growing cold than to roll up his trousers. Rosenfeld and Bellow never published "Der shir hashirim fun Mendl Pumshtok," probably unwilling to advertise their mockery of a critic whose literary standards they hoped to satisfy or surpass. But like the pebble that brought down Goliath, the Yiddish spoof gave notice that the immigrants were confident they could take over the hallowed tradition.[46]

Rosenfeld's intelligence irradiated his generation of writers and intellectuals without ever finding its artistic form. He seems aware of the deficiency in his only published novel, *Passage from Home* (1946). After trying to find greater spontaneity and freedom than he enjoys at home in a surrogate bohemian family that he hobbles together, the book's adolescent hero, Bernard Miller, is reconciled to his rigid father and stepmother but without achieving the breakthrough to joy and love. This emotional failure conveys the disappointment of a novel that is much more intelligent than it is artistically persuasive and that is most memorable for Bernard's (hence Rosenfeld's) reflections. Rosenfeld's tropes became so familiar that it is hard to remember how fresh they once were:

> For as a Jew, I was acquainted, as perhaps a Negro might be, with the alien and the divided aspect of life that passed from sight at the open approach, but lingered, available to thought, ready to reveal itself to anyone who would inquire softly. I had come to know a certain homelessness in the world, and took it for granted as part of nature; had seen in the family, and myself acquired, a sense of sadness from which both assurance and violence had forever vanished. We had accepted it unconsciously and without self-pity, as one might accept a sentence that had been passed generations ago, whose terms were still binding though its occasion had long been forgotten. The world is not entirely yours; and our reply is: very well then, not entirely. There were moments, however, when this minor world was more than universe enough; times such as when grandfather would be raised to nobility, or when the family, gathered of a holiday, would distil so rare and joyful a spirit that all the assurance which had been lacking would rush back in flood, and one could feel the presence of God in it, and one could cry, "This is reality, truth, beauty, freedom! What has the rest of the world to compare?" But then, this too would vanish, and I would ask, "What am I?" For as a Negro might ponder his outer body, asking himself why it should differ from other men's when inwardly he felt his common humanity, so I would

consider my skin, my eyes, my hair, and wonder why I should feel an inner difference when outwardly I was the same as other men.[47]

Here is the identification of the Jew with the Black man who accepts that he will never be recognized in the form that he knows himself; the embrace of homelessness as the condition of being-in-the-world; the double consciousness of the subject who sees himself simultaneously from the inside and the outside. The inner world radiates "nobility," joyfulness, self-assurance, "reality, truth, beauty, freedom," but since these qualities adhere to the Jewish atmosphere, not the boy, they are forfeited once he begins to move beyond it. It was Rosenfeld who famously defined the Jewish writer as "a specialist in alienation (the one international banking system the Jews actually control)."[48] Mark Shechner, who edited a collection of Rosenfeld's writing, calls alienation his leitmotif, "the irreducible condition of the emotions and the first principle of any defensible psychology or literature."[49] But Rosenfeld knew alienation was also a form of terminal adolescence, an unresolved conflict with father and society that inhibits a person from becoming a parental authority. Bernard and his author are irritated with themselves for not getting beyond their uncertainties.

BERNARD MALAMUD would appear to be the ideal American candidate for the Jewish canon. His old-world Jews with their Yiddish-inflected English and sorrowful sweetness are the conductors of such moral energy that, like the Brooklyn storekeeper Morris Bober, they have the power to convert Christians to their brand of religion. Frankie Alpine, the title character of *The Assistant* (1957), begins by robbing Bober and ends by assuming the Jew's life and responsibilities.[50] As in a fantastic Chagall, Alpine not only gives up his *goyish* ways and repents of having forced himself on Bober's daughter but has himself circumcised and, in densely symbolic language, *becomes* a Jew. Born and raised in Brooklyn, Malamud identified Jews with the capacity for suffering before they rise into wealth and prominence, but rather than channel this association into a passion for socialism, he sees in it the paradigm of Christianity. The Judaism to which Alpine converts is really a purer ethical form of his own Catholicism.

Ethnically, in the music of their speech and the herring aroma of their breath, Malamud's Jewish characters seem immediately familiar, as though they had stepped out of the world of Sholem Aleichem. But that step into modernity has rendered them fabulous, and they now seem to function as symbolic apparitions in the real America. Pinye Salzman, the marriage broker of Malamud's most famous story, "The Magic Barrel" (1954), resembles Tevye even to the point of being obsessed with the same themes, except that he surrenders to the ambiguities that Tevye tried to withstand. Salzman is contacted by an ardent rabbinical student, Leo Finkle, who, though once eager to find himself a bride, now almost despairs of the business after several disappointments. Negotiations between the matchmaker and client reach a mysterious turning point when a photograph of Salzman's daughter turns up among his prospective brides and captures the young man's heart on sight. Solicitous of his client, who represents the plain future of Judaism, Salzman tries to warn Finkle that his daughter will corrupt him as the condition of becoming his mate:

> "She is not for you. She is a wild one—wild, without shame. This is not a bride for a rabbi."
> "What do you mean wild?"
> "Like an animal. Like a dog. For her to be poor was a sin. This is why to me she is dead now."[51]

The father particularly indicts her revolt against poverty, hinting that it has cost her a too hard-won experience. The *yeshiva* student seems attracted equally by the erotic adventure and the redemptive possibility, though he is also tormented by the suspicion that the matchmaker planned what he feared would happen. Thus, the American happy ending is cast as a Jewish tragedy. As the lovers approach one another under a street lamp, the Jewish father intones the *Kaddish* over the meeting that he has brokered, in the name of his author who has written this remarkable elegy for Jewish life in America. In fact, once Malamud's heroes quit Brooklyn, they leave their Jewishness behind. His Jews dissolve into a fiction of enchantment or anonymity.

Jewish writing in America tended to treat Jewish civilization much as Irving Howe did in his social history, *The World of Our Fathers* (1976)—as a parental inheritance that, however precious, is no longer theirs to perpetuate:

We need not overvalue the immigrant Jewish experience in order to feel a lasting gratitude for having been part of it. A sense of
natural piety toward one's origins can live side by side with a spirit
of critical detachment. We take pleasure in having been related to
those self-educated workers, those sustaining women, those al-
most-forgotten writers and speakers devoted to excitements of
controversy and thought.[52]

Howe uses the construction "having been related" as though with the end
of immigrant poverty, the need for Jewishness had also come to an end.
Though no American Jewish writer did more than Howe to raise awareness of Yiddish culture, the parental world seemed valuable to him for the
very aspects that American Jews were determined to outgrow—Jewish socialism, Jewish Labor affiliation, Yiddish itself—and suspect for all that
Jews intended to achieve—national sovereignty for the Jewish people in
the Jewish homeland, prosperity in America, and a way of practicing the
Jewish religion in freedom. Delmore Schwartz mourned the artistic consequence of this progressive estrangement from the creative past. In one of
his stories, the son believes that he has been corrupted by distancing himself from family and community and that this withdrawal, really "self-con-
tempt and ignorance," is the reason his literary inspiration is drying up.[53]
Isaac Rosenfeld, Delmore Schwartz, Bernard Malamud, and the writers
who came to be known as the New York Intellectuals prolonged their filial
posture, alternately delighting in intellectual and artistic independence
and lamenting their alienation. It took the brilliant adolescent culture
many years to imagine itself in the role of a Jewish adult, a Jewish parent.

9

WRITING BEYOND ALIENATION

SAUL BELLOW, CYNTHIA OZICK, AND PHILIP ROTH

At times I feel like a socket that remembers its tooth.

SAUL BELLOW, *The Bellarosa Connection*[1]

I
N MAY 1949, the American Jewish writer Leslie Fiedler struck a brand-
new literary posture in a lead article in *Commentary* magazine asking,
"What Can We Do About Fagin?"[2] Citing the corrupter of youth in
Oliver Twist as the stereotype of the Jewish villain, Fiedler wondered how
Jews like himself could hope to inhabit and prosper in English literature.

> Made sensitive by Hitler and the collapse of the universalist
> dream, we re-examine our literary heritage as Jewish writers and
> readers of English—and we wince! Looking again at Lawrence or
> Pound, Shakespeare, Chaucer, Marlowe, Pope, Wordsworth, Scott
> or Dickens, T. S. Eliot, Charles Williams or Graham Greene,
> everywhere we come upon a myth of the Jew, central to our whole
> culture, before which as Jews we are embarrassed, dumb. Assured
> we are legitimate heirs, we enter into our supposed inheritance,
> only to find we are specifically excluded.[3]

The most remarkable feature of this polemical essay was Fiedler's use of
the first-person plural pronoun to designate "Jewish writers and readers of
English." During the previous decade young American Jews, the children
of immigrants educated in public schools and local colleges, had begun to
write about English and American literature in such numbers and with
such authority that they quickly became a force in the shaping of Ameri-

can culture. The cohort that would come to be known as the New York Intellectuals had been proving that they should be considered *American*. At age twenty-six Alfred Kazin completed his classic study of American prose literature, *On Native Ground* (1942), tracing what he called the emergence of American writing as a school in which American writers were learning from American novels and poems, America having become "its own tradition."⁴ In 1937 William Phillips (formerly Livinsky) and Philip Rahv (born Ivan Greenberg) resuscitated *Partisan Review*, the magazine they had founded three years earlier under Communist auspices, and turned it into the new intellectual pacesetter for American arts and letters. Lionel Trilling stormed the citadel of Columbia University with his study of Matthew Arnold to become its first Jewish tenured professor of English literature. Rahv defined typologies of American literature in "Paleface and Redskin." Clement Greenberg began his career as an art critic with a definitive article: "Avant-Garde and Kitsch." Robert Warshow expanded the range of serious criticism to include popular culture. These Jews showed no hesitation or ambivalence in becoming the purveyors of American culture. Norman Podhoretz, who was to become editor of the magazine that published Fiedler's article (and the ensuing debate over it), remarked that the at-homeness of this proliferating new literary "Family" in America was confirmed in the 1951 *Partisan Review* symposium "Our Country and Our Culture," "the pronoun by itself being as telling as anything the participants had to say."⁵

Fiedler, however, was inviting Jewish writers to do more than take possession of the literary tradition into which they were entering. His question "What response can we make to a culture in which so terrible and perilous a myth of ourselves is intextricably involved?"⁶ implied that they ought to be taking some responsibility for their Jewishness as well, first and foremost by passing critical judgment on that part of Anglo American literature that had so long pronounced its negative judgment on them.

Saul Bellow: *Mr. Sammler's Planet*

Saul Bellow's first novel answers Fiedler's call. One of the most famous depictions of the Jew in American literature was Ernest Hemingway's portrait of Robert Cohn in *The Sun Also Rises* (1926), a novel set in Europe following the First World War that set a tough new tone for American culture.

Robert Cohn figures in this book as the bothersome hanger-on, an excessively emotional, masochistic Jew who becomes the foil for the lean, masculine style that Hemingway was crafting. The opening paragraph of *Dangling Man* (1944) returns the compliment by drawing a bead on the Hemingway cult that asks you to strangle your inner life and to keep your feelings under tight rein. Bellow's narrator, Joseph, who is waiting for his induction notice during World War II, says provocatively, "Most serious matters are closed to the hard-boiled. They are unpracticed in introspection, and therefore badly equipped to deal with opponents whom they cannot shoot like big game or outdo in daring." Turning the tables on the tough guys, Joseph promises to talk openly about his difficulties, "and if I had as many mouths as Siva has arms and kept them going all the time, I still could not do myself justice."[7] Just as Isaac Babel had felt that an Odessan Jew could release untapped energies of Russian literature, Bellow knew he had something joyous to add to American literature by talking as demonstratively—as Semitically—as he knew how.

In this spirit of reinvigorating America, Bellow's main characters, who were almost always urban males his own age, remained boyish for many years. Joseph of *Dangling Man* seems prepared to go on waiting forever for his call-up into the army. Asa Leventhal in *The Victim* (1947) feels so forsaken during the absence of his wife over a long New York summer that we are not surprised when he becomes the victim of a character who claims to have been victimized by *him*. Bellow's most avowedly boyish character is Augie March, Chicago-born. As Cynthia Ozick phrased it, he erupted on the scene in 1953, "breaking through all restraints of language (mixing the lavish with the raffish) and of range: the barriers of inhibition kicked down, the freed writer exuberantly claiming authority over human and planetary organisms."[8] Augie was never meant to grow up. At the end of his long adventure novel, on the beaches of Normandy the *animal ridens* rises up in him and he looks out across the water with all the humor that Gatsby lacked, saying to himself, "Columbus too thought he was a flop, probably, when they sent him back in chains. Which didn't prove there was no America."[9] Then there was Tommy Wilhelm, forty-four years old when we catch up with him in *Seize the Day* (1956), still and forever the desperate son of an unloving father. Even when Bellow's heroes became husbands and fathers, just as he did, then divorced and remarried husbands with second families, they seem more intent on proving their freedom than on taking responsibility for the next generation. Henderson (*Henderson the Rain King*, 1959) leaves his family to follow his drumbeat—"I want! I want! I want!"—into the imaginary continent of Bellovian Africa. Herzog (1964), in whom I once thought I had located the prototype of the American *schlemiel*, makes fun of his own mental ambitions and Boy Scout meritoriousness, recognizing in himself the incorrigible adolescent: "He had a small foundation grant, and his twenty-thousand-dollar legacy from Father Herzog went into the country place." The earnings of the great intellectual are overshadowed by the rewards of the dutiful son.[10]

Artur Sammler was the first of Saul Bellow's major protagonists to outstrip him in age—by twenty years—and by experience, being a European Jewish survivor of the Second World War. With *Mr. Sammler's Planet* (1970), Bellow assumed for the first time the authority of a Jew, and the perspective of a disciplining parent. Sholem Aleichem broke with the literary convention of his day to write about the advent of modernity from the point of view of a traditional father, and Bellow defied American culture of the sixties by describing it from the point of view of a refugee from the Holocaust. Mr. Sammler is no longer a traditional Jew, yet he comes from Europe with a hard-won authority and with a moral confidence as powerful as Tevye's.

Sammler is slightly older than his century, a tall man with only one good eye. The only son of an assimilated Jewish family in Cracow, Poland, Sammler had gone to London as a journalist with his young wife in the 1930s and might have escaped the fate of continental Jews had his wife not decided to return to Poland to liquidate her father's estate. The couple saved their daughter Shula by placing her—as Slawa—in a Polish convent, but they themselves were consigned to a Jewish mass grave, from which the husband alone crawled out alive. After the war, Sammler is brought to New York with Shula-Slawa under the sponsorship of a wealthy nephew, Dr. Elya Gruner. There he serves as an avuncular authority, appreciated but rarely obeyed: in a reversal of the immigrant novel that brought Jews to America looking for salvation, *Mr. Sammler's Planet* imports a Jewish refugee from Europe with valuable hard-won wisdom to impart.

Despite Sammler's advanced age, the forty-eight hours of the novel are crammed with incident, including Sammler's confrontation with a pickpocket, an aborted speech at Columbia University, his daughter's theft of a manuscript and his attempt to return it to its owner, and several trips to the hospital to visit his dying nephew, where he argues with Gruner's two children, Angela and Wallace. Sammler is morally rugged. As though to ensure that the likes of François Mauriac would never mistake him for a risen Lazarus or Jesus, Sammler recalls—with unnerving satisfaction—how he had killed a disarmed German soldier in the Polish forests after he had joined a partisan group. When the Six-Day War breaks out in Israel, he leaves the safety of Manhattan to join much younger journalists in the Sinai. It is worth noting that Bellow never endowed any of his major protagonists with anything like his own magnificent Yiddish, his familiarity with Jewish practice, acquired in an Orthodox Jewish home, or his private preoccupation with the fate of the Jews and Israel.[11] Despite his survivor status, Sammler, too, is an attenuated Jew, different from Asa Leventhal, Augie March, Tommy Wilhelm, and Moses Herzog only in that his acculturation has been Polish and British rather than Anglo American. But Sammler is the first of Bellow's heroes to visit Israel, once to rescue his daughter from her abusive Russian Jewish husband, Eisen (his name means "iron"), and the second time, demonstratively, to be there in time of war. Sammler, who escaped the Jewish fate in Europe, does not want to escape the fate of being a Jew.

WHEN SAMMLER AWAKENS, like Joseph K., into a troubling day, his consciousness is in full control:

Shortly after dawn, or what would have been dawn in a normal sky, Mr. Artur Sammler with his bushy eye took in the books and papers of his West Side bedroom and suspected that they were the wrong books, the wrong papers. In a way it did not matter much to a man of seventy-plus, and at leisure. You had to be a crank to insist on being right. Being right was largely a matter of explanations. Intellectual man had become an explaining creature. Fathers to children, wives to husbands, lecturers to listeners, experts to laymen, colleagues to colleagues, doctors to patients, man to his own soul, explained. The roots of this, the causes of the other, the source of events, the history, the structure, the reasons why. For the most part, in one ear out the other. The soul wanted what it wanted. It had its own natural knowledge. It sat in superstructures of explanation, poor bird, not knowing which way to fly.[12]

This passage illustrates the standard features of Bellow's mature fiction: Sammler's heightened sense of the ordinary; the narrative's intimate trace of the character's thoughts, like an encephalogram that charts without controlling the state of the subject; suspicion of the intellectual mind to which we are confined; investiture of trust in that threatened modern species, the soul; the encompassing reach across all of society. Other elements, like Sammler's formality even in the privacy of his bedroom, are new to this novel. The formality signals a degree of separation between him and his society: "Like many people who had seen the world collapse once, Mr. Sammler entertained the possibility it might collapse twice. He did not agree with refugee friends that this doom was inevitable, but liberal beliefs did not seem capable of self defense, and you could smell decay."[13] Bellow's earlier heroes, like the four sons of the Passover Haggadah, had always been the ones asking the questions. In this book, however, the dynamic is reversed. For his definitive novel about the 1960s, whose youth took as their motto "Don't trust anyone over thirty," Bellow chose a man with the most dearly acquired moral authority of the century, a man who has fully earned—indeed, who must bear responsibility for—conservative wisdom.

Looking back from Sammler to Tevye, we see how far Jewish writing came in the twentieth century. The parent with whom we started out was also faced with revolutionary challenges from his children and their generation. In him, too, "laughter and trembling are so curiously mingled that it is not easy to determine the relations of the two," a definition which Bellow uses to describe literature that is characteristically Jewish.[14] It is even possible to suggest a literary connection between Feferl (Peppercorn), the revolutionary who marries Tevye's second daughter, and Lionel Feffer the frenetic *tummler*, who involves Mr. Sammler in his schemes. But Tevye, wearing millennia of tradition as lightly as his skin, was always looking to the future, expecting his children to bring him greater happiness than he had known. Sammler (*zamler* is Yiddish for collector), with his vast collection of languages, acquaintances, experiences, and knowledge, is always looking back, haunted by the knowledge of how bad things can get.

Mr. Sammler's lifetime of experience is at once the source of his authority as well as his fragility. In addition to having only one good eye, he has trouble with his heart, forcing him to rest periodically and to be cautious in his movements. No longer able to earn his living, Sammler is supported by his nephew, and he boards with his wife's niece Margot because he can't live on his own. The gap keeps widening throughout the book between the wrong that Sammler witnesses and the good he thinks he can do. Like Bellow's earlier hero Moses Herzog, who had helplessly witnessed the trial of a woman and her boyfriend who beat her child to death, Sammler cannot arrest the evil that he sees.

First, there is the Black pickpocket who plies his trade on what is also Sammler's habitual bus route on the Upper West Side. "As if watching open-heart surgery," he has seen the man lifting cash from his prey without rousing suspicion and also terrorizing an older passenger at the rear of the bus. In Queens, New York, the bystanders in the murder of Kitty Genovese had become a byword for civic indifference, but when Sammler takes the trouble to report a crime, the police are not grateful: "We haven't got a man to put on the bus. There are lots of buses, Art, and not enough men. Lots of conventions, banquets, and so on we have to cover, Art. VIP's and Brass. There are lots of ladies shopping at Lord and Taylor, Bonwit's, and Saks', leaving purses on chairs while they go to feel the goods."[15] Sammler's report to the police is child's play compared to his experience of evil under Hitler, yet he thinks that crime may be outstripping America's ability to stop it. He is not afraid of America, but *for* America.

Sammler's impotence is further exposed at the Columbia University seminar he has been invited to address on "The British scene in the thirties." The subject attracts him because he and his wife had come from Poland into that heady atmosphere of R. H. Tawney, Harold Laski, John Strachey, George Orwell, and H. G. Wells, with the last of whom he had even cultivated a slight friendship. Sammler is happy for the chance to recall his involvement with Wells's *Cosmopolis* project for a world state "based on the propagation of the sciences of biology, history, and sociology and the effective application of scientific principles to the enlargement of human life."[16] With the wisdom of hindsight, he feels "what a kindhearted, ingenuous, stupid scheme it had been" and what special prudence this failed utopianism should induce in his listeners were they to make the connection between democracy's will to innocence and tyranny's will to power. But Sammler is bringing his cautionary tale to the most wanton cohort in American history. When he quotes Orwell on the British radicals who were protected by the Royal Navy, he is choked off by a "thick-bearded" heckler:

> "Orwell was a fink. He was a sick counterrevolutionary. It's good he died when he did. And what you're saying is shit." Turning to the audience, extending violent arms and raising his palms like a Greek dancer, he said, "Why do you listen to this effete old shit? What has he got to tell you? His balls are dry. He can't come."[17]

In Europe, the storm troopers crushed the skulls of intellectuals; in America, the movement to arrest free speech is launched under the banner of free speech. Sammler is forced from the stage in the process of trying to fulfill the mandate of the university, there being no one in the university to offer him protection. Sammler's expansive consciousness takes in this brute speaker's Levantine charms, just as it acknowledges the physical grace of the silent criminal in the bus. Observations of this kind imply an invidious comparison with his own failing potency. He makes all the distinctions and considers all the refinements that his younger antagonists ignore. Yet no more than Tevye can he arrest or affect the actions of the young. Feffer the revolutionary entrepreneur unleashes a violence that he does not bother to control. We later see the mischief that Feffer foments when he tries to catch the pickpocket in the final chapter and is—again, as an accomplice—almost responsible for having him killed.

Stalking criminals and representing the European intellectual tradition against its would-be destroyers, Sammler is aware of a third, more threatening, layer of evil, one that derives from the very tradition he embodies. When Sammler tells his niece Margot about the incident in the bus, he feels himself drawn into the democratized version of twentieth-century philosophic debate. "It was her earnestness that gave the trouble—considering everything under the sun with such German wrongheadedness. As though to be Jewish weren't trouble enough, the poor woman was German too."[18] Since evil is the subject matter, Margot naturally wants to discuss with him Hannah Arendt's proposition about the "banality of evil," namely, that Nazi Germany produced no great spirit of evil but only ordinary administrators, banal bureaucrats, "small plants with shallow roots." And it is against this theory, rather than against the pickpocket, the police, or his Columbia host Lionel Feffer that Sammler strikes out hardest:

"The idea of making the century's great crime look dull is not banal. Politically, psychologically, the Germans had an idea of genius. The banality was only camouflage. What better way to get the curse out of murder than to make it look ordinary, boring, or trite? With horrible political insight they found a way to disguise the thing. Intellectuals do not understand. They get their notions about matters like this from literature. They expect a wicked hero like Richard III. But do you think the Nazis didn't know what murder was? Everybody (except certain bluestockings) knows what murder is. That is very old human knowledge. [. . .] Banality is the adopted disguise of a very powerful will to abolish conscience. Is such a project trivial? Only if human life is trivial. This woman professor's enemy is modern civilization itself. She is only using the Germans to attack the twentieth century—to denounce it in terms invented by the Germans. Making use of a tragic history to promote the foolish ideas of Weimar intellectuals."[19]

Arendt's thesis offends Sammler in much the same way it does Jean Améry, because its ambition to explain is greater than its moral outrage, because the engorged thesis forgets the "very old human knowledge" of Cain and Abel. Sammler presses the argument through form as well as content, refusing reason its claim over emotion. Provoked by the theorizing of one German Jewess, he lashes out at that other German Jewess who turned the Eichmann trial into an occasion for theorizing. He gets personal with the "woman professor" and "Weimar intellectual," because had he not undergone the compulsory education that was forced on him by Hitler, he might have sounded just like her. "Alert to the peril and disgrace of explanations, he was himself no mean explainer." Bellow transforms "dialectic into drama, casuistry into comedy," confining his book to the mind of an intellectual without falling prey to what he considers the intellectual's weakness.[20]

Mr. Sammler's impotence is certified at the end of the opening chapter when the Black pickpocket, who has seen Mr. Sammler watching him, follows him home and in the lobby of his apartment building wordlessly unzips his pants to exhibit his penis. The man is repeating with greater economy the Columbia student's warning that this is no country for old men. In all Sammler's encounters, and most emphatically in this one, we see that his awful knowledge cannot be put to use because he has no power, nor any access to power. As impotent as the novelist who can only draw attention to social distortions without being able to right them, Sammler has acquired his wisdom too late and at too great a distance to be able to repair what he deplores.

TEVYE RAISED HIS CHILDREN to follow in his ways. Mr. Sammler knows that he and his generation of liberal parents are implicated in the mess of their children's lives by having failed to teach them discipline. Gruner's daughter Angela is an advertisement for Eros: "It was all in [her] calves, in the cut of her blouses, in the motions of her finger tips, the musical brass of her whispers."[21] On a trip to Mexico she drew her boyfriend into a partner-switching sexual escapade that disgusted him, and enraged her father when he learned of it. Her brother Wallace is adrift in impractical schemes that he can only afford to indulge because they are being paid for by his father. Some of the eccentricities of Shula-Slawa, such as her suspension between Judaism and Christianity, may be attributed to her wartime sojourn in a Polish convent, but her theft of Dr. Lal's manuscript was enacted with apparent innocence as an attempt to *please* Sammler. Gruner accepts responsibility for Angela's "fucked-out eyes," Sammler for the sly childishness of the daughter over forty.

As already noted, Sammler is hardly an ideal Jew. On his first visit to Israel, he goes not to such topoi of Judaism and Zionism as the Western Wall, Mother Rachel's tomb in Hebron, the fortress Masada, or Herzl's tomb, but to Capernaum, where Jesus had preached.

> From afar, he saw the Mount of the Beatitudes. Two eyes would have been inadequate to the heaviness and smoothness of the color, parted with difficulty by fishing boats—the blue water, unusually dense, heavy, seemed sunk under the naked Syrian heights. Mr. Sammler's heart was very much torn by feelings as he stood under the short, leaf-streaming banana trees.

> *And did those feet in ancient time*
> *Walk upon . . .*

But those were England's mountains green. The mountains opposite, in serpentine nakedness, were not at all green; they were
ruddy, with smoky cavities and mysteries of inhuman power flaming above them.[22]

The reference is to Blake's preface to *Milton*, which reads:

> *And did those feet in ancient time*
> *Walk upon England's mountains green:*
> *And was the holy Lamb of God*
> *On England's pleasant pastures seen!*
>
> *And did the Countenance Divine*
> *Shine forth upon our clouded hills?*
> *And was Jerusalem builded here*
> *Among these dark Satanic Mills? [. . .]*
>
> *I will not cease from Mental Fight,*
> *Nor shall my Sword sleep in my hand:*
> *Till we have built Jerusalem*
> *In England's green & pleasant Land.*[23]

Approaching Zion from an altogether unexpected route—via Blake's
rather than Isaiah's vision of the new Jerusalem —uninformed by any standard expectations, Sammler takes in through his one good eye the splendid calm of Lake Kinneret, which is threatened by the menace above (the
heights were held by Syria before the Six-Day War, when Sammler paid
this visit) the natural landscape exalted by the "inhuman power flaming
above them." The threat of war that hangs over Israel supplants the Sa-
tanic Mills, the industrial threat to Blake's pastoral England. The reader accompanying Sammler is expected to complete the verse between the
opening and closing lines of Blake's poem and thereby have his own heart
torn by feelings as the glory of English poetry rejoins its ancient biblical
source in a country now restored to the living Jewish people but still
charged with great danger and divine inspiration. Sammler takes the foreign route home, through English literature.

The modern Jew's relation to force gives Bellow the most trouble of all in this novel. On the mundane level, Sammler first comes to Israel to rescue his daughter from abuse at the hands of her husband, Eisen, a Russian refugee who was lamed at Stalingrad. Eisen is a more brutally damaged version of Shula-Slawa, a "depressing fellow," according to Sammler, whose silk suits "might have made a satisfactory coffin lining." "Eisen certainly deserved to be cared for, and that was one of the uses of Israel, to gather in these cripples."[24] But when this angry man, fired with the ambition of becoming an artist, later comes to America to peddle his art and intervenes at Sammler's urging in a fight between the pickpocket and Feffer, who is trying to apprehend him, Sammler is horrified by the violence he invited. "What have I done! This is much worse! This is the worst thing yet." So he lets out his rage at Eisen. But the man retorts with definitive logic that when you hit a man, you must really hit him; otherwise, he will kill you. "We both fought in the war. You were a Partisan. You had a gun. So don't you know?"[25] Against this reasoning, Sammler has no defense. Of course, he sympathizes more with the wounded Black man than with the "homicidal maniac" from Haifa, but his exasperation incorporates disgust with himself. How is he to explain to Eisen that America is neither Stalingrad nor Israel and that the struggle for civilization here cannot be waged with the weapons of war? In this scene "laughter and trembling" are also commingled, but the slapstick breakdown in communication almost kills a man.

All in all, Sammler is like a Jewish spectator at the Roman games whose reluctant presence feeds the action. "They laughed so much. . . . Let us all be in the great fun fair, and do this droll morality with one another. Be entertainers of your near and dear. Treasure hunts, flying circuses, comical thefts, medallions, wigs and saris, beards. . . . Let us divert each other while we live!"[26] Sammler loathes the carnival. Yet neither is he attracted by the plan of the Indian scientist Dr. Govinda Lal to escape the earthly predicament by founding new colonies on the moon. Instead, Sammler takes as his unlikely model of the good man his nephew, Dr. Elya Gruner, who represents the very essence of middle-class morality, against which Bellow's generation of writers and intellectuals had rebelled. An ordinary Jew like Elya had exerted himself on behalf of his fellow Jews. Elya had located and brought his surviving relatives to America; he had supported his family, the state of Israel. Sammler admires the man who met his obligations.

When Gruner is struck with a fatal aneurysm, Sammler defends the dying man against his estranged daughter Angela. Although positioning himself thus endangers his relations with Angela, who will become his benefactress upon her father's death, he chooses to run the risk of offending her. What makes Sammler so reckless? Why does the survivor align himself with a dead man against the living on whom his living depends?

Sammler's final "mental whisper" at the bedside of the dead man hints at an answer. The soul we are introduced to at the start that sat unhappily "on superstructures of explanation, poor bird, not knowing which way to fly" now yields some of its "own natural knowledge":

> "Remember, God, the soul of Elya Gruner, who, as willingly as possible and as well as he was able, and even to an intolerable point, and even in suffocation and even as death was coming was eager, even childishly perhaps (may I be forgiven for this), even with a certain servility, to do what was required of him. At his best this man was much kinder than at my very best I have ever been or could ever be. He was aware that he must meet, and he did meet— through all the confusion and degraded clowning of this life through which we are speeding—he did meet the terms of his contract. The terms which, in his inmost heart, each man knows. As I know mine. As all know. For that is the truth of it—that we all know, God, that we know, that we know, we know, we know."[27]

Sammler can't sustain the liturgical cadences of real prayer. The rhythms of his thinking, like Tevye's, break the flow of his worship. Addressing the God toward whom he has been groping all along, he does not say the Kaddish but takes the measure of his benefactor and of himself. Sammler remains anthropocentric. What begins with "remember, God," ends in "we know, we know." He consigns Elya's soul to a higher power because he cannot bear to leave it at the mercy of his devouring children.

Indeed, Sammler's leave-taking offends the spirit of the sixties so deliberately that one might well believe, with Angela Gruner, that he intends to be insulting. It is not enough that he addresses the Divine Authority, that he eulogizes a "patriarchal" husband and father, not enough that he quits irony for declarative affirmation: Sammler insists that "we all" share his common moral intuition and expects us to recognize this "truth"! Given the proximity between character and creator, Saul Bellow must have known the danger he faced as a novelist once he began "lecturing" the young about their utopian schemes, reporting on Black intimidation of the intellectual class, and calling for a moratorium on sexual permissiveness. Subsequent attacks on the novel reflect to an uncanny degree the experiences of Sammler, as though Bellow had anticipated what it would mean to be caught in the act of "seeing" and scolding. He was accused of presenting a nasty caricature of campus radicalism, of giving no artistic credibility to the opposition.[28] Hannah Arendt's staunchest American defender, Alfred Kazin, dismissed Sammler as a prissy scold: "The unsatisfactory thing about Mr. Sammler is that he is always right while most other people are usually wrong."[29] Bellow's image of the Black pickpocket was treated as a manifestation of racial bigotry instead of as one of the book's many examples of America's social pathology. The implicit connection between Sammler and Bellow was brought eerily to life when the Black journalist Brent Staples stalked Saul Bellow in Chicago, dreaming revenge: "What would I do when I caught him? Perhaps I'd lift him bodily and pin him against a wall. Perhaps I'd corner him on the stairs and take up questions about . . . barbarous black pickpockets. I wanted to trophy his fear."[30] And *The New York Times Magazine* featured these violent fantasies as though they were a point of pride. Borrowing from the malevolent projections of Edward Said's *Orientalism*, academics ascribed to Bellow's novel their fixations with the Dark Other (a "direct symbol of anxiety about crime, more generally rooted in a larger ideology which renders blackness as the antithesis of civilization"),[31] then held Saul Bellow accountable for their monstrous scheme. "Nowadays we tend to forget what a bombshell it was," Hilton Kramer wrote of the book a quarter of a century after its publication.

> The first novel to give us a searing account of the moral collapse of the city (New York) and the class (the emancipated Jewish middle class) that were fundamental to our existence. It was also, among much else, a book about the failure of liberalism itself in the wake of the 60s rebellion, the sexual revolution, and the race war. It had taken the measure of the future of bourgeois urban life in America and pronounced it doomed.[32]

Mr. Sammler's Planet refuted the complaint, so often heard from writers in liberal democracies, that their work can never compete in impact with writing in repressive or totalitarian societies. This complaint ignores the hegemony of the liberal elites who sometimes control the democratic marketplace and try as viciously as repressive governments to silence and punish challengers and dissidents. Sammler's courage—and Bellow's—is to champion, against the flood of self-indulgence, all the unpopular virtues: restraint, civility, wisdom, obedience to the law, familial responsibility, honesty, modesty, and plain decency. Though he might have wrapped Mr. Sammler in the sympathic mantle of "Holocaust victim," Bellow does just the opposite, depreciating the enormity of suffering he has seen, and raising the ante of responsibility *because* of what such survival demands.

CONSIDERING THAT BELLOW might have drawn on his Yiddish—a language he speaks as masterfully as English—to create a Yiddish-speaking survivor, it is noteworthy that Bellow took Artur Sammler from his native Poland to Britain *before the war* to provide him with a credible intellectual level of English. Having once entered the tradition of English literature, Bellow seems never to have considered creating a Yiddish-thinking protagonist. He objected strenuously to critical confinement as an "American-Jewish" writer, wondering in a famous quip whether he, Philip Roth, and Bernard Malamud were not being treated as a high-class (Jewish) tailoring establishment, the "Hart Schaffner and Marx of our times."

> My joke is not broad enough to cover the contempt I feel for the opportunists, wise guys, and career types who impose such labels and trade upon them. In a century so disastrous to Jews, one hesitates to criticize those who believe that they are making the world safer by publicizing Jewish achievements. I myself doubt this publicity is effective.
>
> I did not go to the public library to read the Talmud but the novels and poems of Sherwood Anderson, Theodore Dreiser, Edgar Lee Masters, and Vachel Lindsay.[33]

This objection to being labeled Jewish seems to weigh in heavily against my inclusion of Bellow in the modern Jewish canon. But there is a difference between publicizing Jewish achievements by labeling writers Jewish, which appears to have provoked Bellow's ire, and recognizing the existence of a modern Jewish culture that perforce includes writers in non-Jewish languages. Bellow respected the autonomy of language. He understood language, rather than ethnicity or religion, to be the defining category of literature, and his artistic method of gliding into another man's consciousness required that he find someone who actually thought in his own literary tongue. However unfairly, by the late 1960s Yiddish was so powerfully associated with the kitsch of American Jewish culture that no novelist could have hoped to create in English a Yiddish intellectual authority of the kind that had actually flourished in that language between the wars. Isaac Bashevis Singer said the same about writing in Yiddish; because he, too, believed literature could only emerge from the natural sphere of its language, he confined his writing to the society of Yiddish-speaking immigrants while presenting to the English world in his public appearances an elfin persona that never took anything seriously. The Yiddish intonation that suited Malamud's shopkeepers and matchmakers could never have won the respect of Feffer, Angela, or Wallace; only by imagining Sammler as a thoroughly acculturated European, named by his mother for Artur Schopenhauer, was Bellow able to ascribe to him his own knowledge of Western literature and the slightly ceremonious diction needed for this particular hero. In literature more than in life, dignity is manifest in speech. Just as Tevye's confidence derives from his mastery of Yiddish, Mr. Sammler's inheres in his acquired and assimilated English, which contrasts with the slangier, sloppier usage of the young.

Even the greatest writer can't have everything. Writing in English, Bellow could endow this "doubly foreign, Polish-Oxonian" with his quality of mind, but not with his *yidishe neshome*, his Jewish soul. Which may be another reason why Sammler defers so genuinely to Elya Gruner, who, for all his flaws, tries to live as a decent Jew.

The Revisionism of Cynthia Ozick and Philip Roth

The Cannibal Galaxy *and* The Shawl

The return of parental authority to American Jewish literature signifies more than the aging of its writers. Sholem Aleichem created Motl the cantor's son as the last of his major heroes because he wanted a cheerful child to narrate the passage from Europe to America. Sixty years later, Saul Bellow responded to the excesses of American self-indulgence with a narrator who had been seasoned by Europe. This reversal called into question cherished assumptions about the moral as well as cultural development of America and its Jews. It recognized that the original constraints of a tight religious community had loosened to the point of disintegration, that children were more likely to want for parental guidance than to suffer its demands. Henry Roth and Saul Bellow were not alone in realizing that Jews in America might be in danger of vanishing, thanks to their growing popularity and waning distinctiveness. To be sure, the majority of Jews in English-speaking democracies protected their liberal image of acculturation as a romance that promised happiness ever after, with the husband lighting the Hannukah *menorah* and his wife the Christmas tree; they commemorated the Holocaust not like the Jews in postwar years, with determination never to let it happen again, but as though its horrors, if only advertised, would protect the Jews from being targeted anew. Most Jewish writers came from these liberal ranks and, like the American creators of *Fiddler on the Roof*, did not even know that they were traducing their Jewish sources when they traduced them. But a minority recognized that individualism had gone too far. "Make it the object of imitation to reach and release the high qualities," says Sammler in a critique of originality. "Make peace . . . with intermediacy and representations. Otherwise the individual must be the failure he now sees and knows himself to be."[34]

Cynthia Ozick was the first American-born Jewish writer to challenge the implicit harmony of such by now standard combinations as "modern Jew" and "modern Jewish writer." An avid student of American letters who took Henry James for her master and an observant Jew who took Moses for her teacher, Ozick probed the disjunction between her allegiance to the independence of Art and her allegiance to the supremacy of God. Neither imaginative literature nor Judaism could obey any absolutism but its own. If *modern* meant trust in human agency and *Jewish* meant following the commandments of Sinai, the Jew would have to mark his separation from the rest of society at the point that God's Sabbath and laws set the boundaries. Ozick's fiction disproves the liberal assumption that enlightened Jews can embrace secular modernity without forfeiting their moral strength. She is the master of the anti-romance, a New York Emily Dickinson whose gnarled protagonists convey through negative rather than positive affinities the author's anxieties, including that of being a Jewish writer in English.

The Cannibal Galaxy (1984) is an irritated book. Joseph Brill is a young Orthodox Parisian Jew who "crosses the Seine" from his parents' fish store on the Rue des Rosiers to the study of literature, and later astronomy, at the Sorbonne. When the Nazi roundup of Jews catches him unawares, Joseph, student of the stars, is hidden by nuns in the cellar of their convent school. All that he has with him, in a worn briefcase his teacher Rabbi Pult had given him as a parting gift, is a copy of the Talmudic treatise on fasts, *Ta'anit*, but in a priest's library that is also being concealed from the Nazis he discovers the work of fellow Jew Edmond Fleg. Fleg is the very paradigm of the modern Jewish writer who worked his way back from agnosticism to a passion for Jewishness and Jerusalem. Thus, experiencing the war as a battle of books, Joseph creates a synthesis that will determine his resumed life above ground. When survivor Brill later reaches America, he works his way up from impecunious Hebrew teacher to principal of the Edmond Fleg Primary School in the Midwest, and designs a dual curriculum for his American students that will combine the best of what he salvaged in the cellar—"Chumash, Gemara, Social Studies, French: the waters of Shiloh springing from the head of Western Civilization!"[35] The benefactress and parents of the school are delighted by his promise that Jewish children will receive the braided best of both traditions.

That promise is not fulfilled. Whether because he is too timid for so bold a project or because the concept of a dual curriculum is itself inauthentic, the novel seems to *mock* the solemn educator for failing both Jewish and Western ideals in his eagerness to amalgamate them. This is the more emphatic in that his nemesis is Hester Lilt, a mediocre student's brilliant mother (who bears more than passing resemblance to Cynthia Ozick in both the substance of her ideas and the tenor of her speech). Lilt demonstrates in the most exciting passage of the novel how the Jewish text can illumine modern understanding without compromising either. Analogically, respecting the separation of spheres, she uses an interpretive homily about the destruction of the Temple to teach that human striving should never "stop too soon." Her admonition implicitly targets the school psychologist, who reads her daughter's future from the flawed and preliminary evidence of a Rorschach test, and Principal Brill, who adopted the Latin motto *per aspera ad astra* (through hardship to the stars) but mistook precocity for true achievement. Lilt exposes not only the folly of trying to achieve greatness through a strategy of cultural compromise, but also the malignancy of educating for genius. Rabbi Pult had taught, "Always negate. Negate, negate," which Brill took as an admonition to separate yourself from the run of ordinary mortals.[36] He thinks this is what Hester Lilt does by turning the habitual inside out. But she is only accidentally different by virtue of staying true to her intuition. Her exceptionalism, like her idea of Judaism, is exceptional only because it remains true to itself.

One might expect Lilt, speaking for Ozick, to be the flawed principal's credible corrective. And so the book might be read. Brill is punished for his calculating pursuit of genius by a son who only wants to crunch numbers. Hester Lilt's daughter Beulah defies the prediction of Brill's school that she will remain ordinary and becomes a famous abstract painter. Indeed, the final image of Beulah laboring "without brooding in calculated and enameled forms out of which a flaming nimbus sometimes spread," would appear to cast a halo over the purely imaginative artist at the expense of the pedagogue whose curriculum she has forgotten. Yet Beulah's utter disregard for her Jewish past, which accompanies her genius, seems equally a reproof to the "imagistic linguistic logician" who is her mother. Hester Lilt lives without a husband, volunteers nothing about her daughter's father, and only reluctantly yields information about her European origins. "The more she delivered, the more she withheld. . . . She was all future; she cut the thread of genesis."[37] Whereas the principal struggles to reroot himself in America, Hester returns to Paris, where she may continue to live rootlessly. Her child may have become abstract in consequence of the mother's emotional reticence. Beulah has no use for the Jewishness that informs her mother's imagination. She has taken her mother's motto that a person should not "stop too soon" as leave to soar beyond the confines of Judaism entirely, mocking her mother just as her mother mocked Principal Brill. In this reading, the children stop both parents' projects in their tracks. Modern Jewish genius cuts off its roots; the Edmond Fleg Primary School turns into the uninspired Lakeside Grade School.

In contradistinction to so many of her artistic colleagues who invite us to like their Jewish characters rather than Judaism itself—and sometimes at the expense of Judaism itself—Ozick places a Jewish theme rather than Jewish characters at the center of her work. Through Lilt's writings and speeches she introduces Jewish teachings and demonstrates how they can penetrate the general culture, but she makes no claims for the woman who bears the message. In fact, Ozick's descriptions of American Jewry are uncommonly sour, with much to deride and little to admire. As Rabbi Pult instructed, she explores her subjects through negative example, which accounts for the slightly disagreeable two main characters and the book's resistance to romance. Ozick exploits the victim motif of the Holocaust even less than Bellow does: Brill's experience in the cellar may be formative, but it is certainly not redemptive and it may even explain some of his caution and coldness. At just the point that America began sentimentalizing the Holocaust, Ozick creates two survivors—the founder of a Jewish day school who consistently gets things wrong and is punished for his obtuseness, and the imaginative progenitor of an art that flagrantly denies its Jewish inheritance.

Ozick's story-and-novella *The Shawl* is an even bolder and more intricate work of revisionism. Two tales, one very short and the second somewhat longer (1980 and 1983), introduce Rosa, a mother who cannot shield her infant daughter Magda from the monstrous intentions of the Nazi Final Solution, and cannot thereafter recover her life. In the first story she sees her child hurled by a Nazi guard against the electric fence. We hear three of those "suppressed female voices" to which modern literary criticism ascribes such importance: the voice of eighteen-month-old Magda, who is murdered the first time she runs out into the open crying, "Maaaa——" to protest her deprivation; the stifled cry of the bereaved mother; and the unregistered shudder of Rosa's niece Stella, who provokes her cousin's cry by taking away the shawl in which she had been wrapped.

With the verbless opening sentence, "Stella cold, cold, the coldness of hell," the author puts into deep freeze any predictable sympathies for her subjects.[38] The exchange of hell's imagery of heat for a landscape of ice reorganizes our responses to the Nazi experiment and our thoughts and feelings about the people it trapped. The cold permeates fourteen-year-old Stella and Rosa, carrying the baby from one concentration camp to another on a forced winter march. It describes Stella's chilled body and soul and Rosa's attitude toward her niece, the competitor for her child's resources. Rosa is a brittle woman, her selfishness hardened but by no means begotten by the Nazis. She thinks that Stella is waiting for Magda to die "so she could put her teeth into the little thighs." Her shawl is the only tactile and symbolic alternative to the cold. It connects her cradling arms with her daughter, conceals, and even magically nurtures the infant. Stella seals her own fate as well as her cousin's when she takes the shawl away to cover herself, because Rosa can never forgive her niece for outliving her daughter. The triad of Rosa-Magda-Stella is a pitiless miniature of their pitiless universe. In Rosa's afterlife as a survivor, her shawl petrifies into an icon, the sacred shroud that eclipses all other human attachments, and stigmatizes Stella as the one who stole it to stay alive.

Concentrating the destruction of European Jewry in one emblematic narrative, *The Shawl* threatens to become an idolatrous work in the same way that the eponymous object does for Rosa. Hence, Ozick, who is forever concerned with the perverse potential of art, follows up her iconic story with a less chiseled novella that lets us get to know the unpleasant woman who survived the camps and now lives in Florida. But what is the connection between the horror so skillfully frozen in art and its sequel that locates Rosa thirty-nine years after she arrived in America? The literary scholar Hana Wirth-Nesher believes this to be the central question before the reader "not merely as a problem in aesthetics but as a moral problem in the representation of the Holocaust by an American author for an American audience."[39] When Jacob Glatstein eclipsed the reunion of the American Jewish poet with his family in Poland between Volumes One and Two of the Yash novels, he made that chasm the pivotal theme of the entire work. When Ozick moves from the cold narrative of the camp to the heat of Miami, she identifies a disjunction greater than the human mind can be expected to assimilate. Yet everyone must make the connection: Rosa, in order to live and not merely survive; Americans, who won the war against Hitler, so that they will remember why they fought; Jews, because it is theirs to forge a transition between the worst and the best diasporas they ever knew; and the Jewish artist, because the subject claims her. Ozick dares to fictionalize the Holocaust without having known it firsthand, warning through the uneven form of the two stories that it cannot be done by ordinary means.

Rosa Lublin comes from the same assimilated circles of Polish Jews as Artur Sammler, but she is more definitely anti-Jewish. She was engaged before the war to the son of her mother's closest friend, a converted Jew married to a Gentile, and although she insists that Magda was his child, not the consequence of rape by German soldiers, she is pleased with the child's un-Jewish appearance: "You could think she was one of *their* babies." By the time we are reintroduced to her, she has taken an axe to the secondhand furniture store she had owned in Brooklyn and moved down to Miami to live as "madwoman and scavenger." Rosa's snobbery is untamed by her circumstance. She conducts a passionate correspondence with Magda in her native and otherwise unused Polish, consigning to her imaginary grown daughter a scholar's life in the academy, the only accommodation she is prepared to make with America, even in her fantasy. Onto Stella, meanwhile, she projects the fullness of her loathing for the Jews, accepting without gratitude her financial support and dreaming cannibal dreams of boiling her tongue, her ears, her plump fingers, one at a time.

The man who tries to rescue Rosa from her exile-within-exile is just the sort of person she had always despised—a much-reduced version of Elya Gruner. When Persky, a retired button manufacturer with a Yiddish accent and a hospitalized wife, tries to cajole her out of her isolation, she is quick to warn him not to count on their common origins. "Your Warsaw isn't my Warsaw," she says, in negative paraphrase of the expression of loyalty that biblical Ruth gave to her Jewish mother-in-law Naomi. Persky is not dissuaded by her rudeness: "As long as your Miami, Florida, is my Miami, Florida."[40] She tells him that of her three lives—"the life before, the life during, and the life after"—it is the life before the war that "is our *real* life, at home, where we was born." He tries to persuade her to give the present a chance: "You went through it, now you owe yourself something."[41] No matter that his solicitude is born of loneliness, his compassion tainted by self-interest. His accented, imperfect English finally drives the spirit of Magda away. The simple need for companionship of this laundromat Romeo offers Rosa her best chance to come to terms with a flawed existence.

Ozick brings the Holocaust home to America but not like the museum curators. She tracks the damage Europe's hatred did to the Jews before, during, and since the war, the damage that America is powerless to remedy. Rosa and her interlocutors conduct a dialogue of the deaf. "Whatever I would say, you would be deaf," she tells Persky in response to his interest in her. Having despaired of getting Americans to understand what she experienced, she has learned to shame Americans by reminding them that they do not bear the stigmata of Hitler. But she falls prey, in turn, to a subtler contempt on the part of social scientists whose categories dehumanize the victims of dehumanization:

Survivor. Even when your bones get melted into the grains of the earth, still they'll forget *human being.* Survivor and survivor and survivor; always and always. Who made up these words, parasites on the throat of suffering![42]

A writer herself, Rosa is nevertheless helpless before the jargon of the "American Association of Clinical Social Pathology" that purports to explain her. That is where Cynthia Ozick comes in—to negotiate the no-man's-land between the life before, during, and after. Rosa's author is in no danger of either patronizing or sentimentalizing the reluctant Jewess. Just as Rosa's cultic worship of the shawl makes her cruel and violent, so too does the cult of the survivor threaten to numb its devotees. Rosa is the judgmental character of an even more judgmental author. But whereas Rosa insists that without assimilation life is unbearable, and that Hitler has made assimilation impossible, Ozick's novel ignores the second premise because it has never accepted the first.

Joseph Brill and Rosa Lublin, both European Jews, overestimate the value of Western culture, mistaking extrinsic features of life for its soul. Ozick does not accept their suffering under the Nazis as the mark of their identity. They are modern Jews, the same way Americans are modern Jews; their failure to become good parents is not attributable solely to the war, because even Rosa could have adopted her niece Stella had she not found it so hateful to raise a "Jewish" child. Ozick's fiction affirms Jewish trust in life by denying the Holocaust its primacy as the defining event of Jewish experience.

The Counterlife *and* American Pastoral

From the moment he surfaced with the short story collection *Goodbye Columbus* in 1960, Philip Roth assumed the role of the rebellious Jewish son, and as his popularity increased and his works proliferated, he seemed to fix American Jewish manhood in the image of the raunchy adolescent. From Ozzie Freedman, the *cheder* rebel who makes his rabbi admit that Jesus could have been born through immaculate conception, through the sexual liberationist Alexander Portnoy, to the prolific Nathan Zuckerman, Roth wrote from the angle of someone in the protective custody of a culture for which he assumes no adult responsibility. Roth's characteristic narrator was uneasily poised between the bourgeois Jewish family that

hemmed him in and the Christian cold shoulder that nudged him out—
but apart from the pantheon of American writers, it was never clear where
he thought he belonged or to what he owed allegiance.

Adolescents characteristically play around with identity, trying on different selves as they might different clothing. Roth had his most serious
fun with this device in *The Counterlife* (1987), which takes a major turn toward the postmodern by providing the main characters with alternative
plots. Nathan Zuckerman the author and his brother Henry the dentist
trade deaths and lives so that each has a chance to comment on the
choices of the other. In different versions of their lives, they also share the
same *shiksa* mistress, who absorbs their fantasies about sex and the Christian world. In one of Roth's earliest stories, "Eli the Fanatic," a suburban
lawyer had signaled his unhappiness with his comfortable existence by
donning the traditional Hasidic clothes of a Jewish refugee. In the later
novel, Roth endows the similarly dissatisfied Jewish dentist with no less
than an alternative life as an American Jewish settler in Judea. What Isaac
Rosenfeld defined as a Jewish propensity for yearning, Roth makes real by
splitting the character's existence so that he may both inhabit America and
settle in Israel. The novel is a masterpiece of controlled invention, but it is
arranged so that at the end Nathan is ready to put a lid on this discre-
tionary universe.

In his concluding metamorphosis, Zuckerman, in love with the Eng-
lishwoman Maria, learns that he is about to become a father and wants to
claim the child as an unambiguous Jew. Having discovered in England and
in Maria's family a good old-fashioned strain of antisemitism, he informs
her that he intends to circumcise their yet unborn son:

> Circumcision is startling, all right, particularly when performed
> by a garlicked old man upon the glory of a newborn body, but then
> maybe that's what the Jews had in mind and what makes the act
> seem quintessentially Jewish and the mark of their reality. Circum-
> cision makes it clear as can be that you are here and not there, that
> you are out and not in—also that you're mine and not theirs. There
> is no way around it: you enter history through my history and me.
> Circumcision is everything that the pastoral is not and, to my
> mind, reinforces what the world is about, which isn't strifeless
> unity.[43]

Zuckerman defines circumcision as the antidote to the charming inventiveness the author has been practicing. "The heavy hand of human values falls upon you right at the start, marking your genitals as its own. Inasmuch as one invents one's meanings, along with impersonating one's selves, this is the meaning I propose for that rite." In a leap across the boundaries of fiction that might have come from the pen of Philip Roth himself, the novelist and critic Mary McCarthy seemed to recognize herself in Maria, and piqued by Roth's "anti-antisemitism," she objected as a Christian to Roth's atavistic excitement about "making a child a Jew by taking a knife to him."[44] Roth defended his novel by pointing out that Zuckerman had also been influenced to raise his son a Jew by earlier arguments in the book for a strong Israel.

But if we turn back to the novel, Zuckerman's main attraction to circumcision is neither antisemitism nor the Jewish state. Nathan is keen to separate himself and his imagined progeny from what he calls the pastoral—the emotional, intellectual, and physical landscape that he associates with his British mistress—and though originally the source of his attraction to her, it is now the feature that impels him to mark his son a Jew. He deplores the "perfectly safe, charmingly simple and satisfying environment that is desire's homeland," the pastoral that "cannot admit contradiction or conflict."[45] Zuckerman considers the harmonious pastoral the denial of his own tragicomic complexity, and he resolves to stop it as the Jews did—with circumcision. The habit of opposition that Roth developed in his simultaneous combat against the Jewish tribe and the lures of Christianity has brought him paradoxically back to the cut that determined his life as a Jew. The complicated duality of Zuckerman's art derives from the existential contract that his father sealed on his flesh and that he resolves to seal on his son's.

The Counterlife situates Maria in Christendom, and Christendom in Gloucester, England. *American Pastoral* (1997), Roth's masterpiece of self-revision, brings home to America Zuckerman's resistance to the pastoral. The implied author Nathan Zuckerman is told the story of Seymour "Swede" Levov, a high school athlete he had idolized in his Newark youth and once the "household Apollo of the Weequahic Jews." When Zuckerman is invited to meet the Swede in 1995, he thinks he sees before him a simple and happy man. *"Swede Levov's life, for all I knew, had been most simple and most ordinary and therefore just great, right in the American grain."*[46] The still handsome Swede has three strapping sons (by a second marriage) and what looks like the realized American dream.

Himself the dutiful elder of two sons, Swede had taken over his immigrant father's glove factory in Newark and had done everything in his power to maintain its pride in highest-quality craftsmanship and decency in the workplace. He had contravened some of his father's wishes by marrying Miss New Jersey of 1949, but old Lou Levov was no Tevye. After a hilariously grueling interview that shows off Roth's brilliance as a satirist, the father yields to his prospective daughter-in-law: "I'LL GIVE YOU CHRISTMAS EVE AND I'LL GIVE YOU CHRISTMAS DAY AND I'LL GIVE YOU EASTER. BUT I'M NOT GIVING YOU THE STUFF WHERE THEY EAT HIM."[47] And so the Swede bought the house "he had been dreaming of since he was sixteen years old," and there, in genteel Old Rimrock, he had raised his daughter Merry with every expectation that his pleasure, his deep appreciation for America, would be passed on to her. *"He was totally wrong."* That sentence arrests the American dream the way Zuckerman in *The Counterlife* intended to "stop" the pastoral. Zuckerman was totally wrong in his assumptions about the Swede—"Never more mistaken about anyone in my life"—just as the Swede was fatally mistaken in his search for simplicity. Merry turns out to be an unhappy stammering teenager who in protest against the American way of life blows up people with homemade bombs—and, along with her victims, her parents' marriage and her father's innocence. The Swede whose story it is and Zuckerman, who makes it his story, both struggle to figure out why the fair life went so foul.

In previous Zuckerman novels, Roth had used multiple-choice scenarios as a postmodern technique for obscuring the need for moral choice. *American Pastoral* meets its moral obligations more squarely, asking how Dostoyevsky's "possessed," a generation of delinquent radicals, happened to surface in America among the Jews who had benefited so remarkably from its bounty. Jewish immigrants in their eagerness to satisfy America abandoned the Jewish strictures that made them such good immigrants in the first place. Levov senior could not keep his sons Jewish, and the Swede cannot keep his daughter civilized. The answers to what went wrong are to be sought in that progression. America had actually become to the Swede what Judaism was to Tevye the dairyman. He loved America. Loved being an American. "Just reciting the names of the forty-eight states used to thrill him back when he was a little kid."[48] But in Old Rimrock he had neglected to teach this love to his daughter. Jews had known that the discipline of Deuteronomy was all in repetition, in loving your God, yes, but in teaching His words diligently to your children, speaking them at home and on a journey, binding them as a sign on your hand and fore-head, inscribing them on your doorposts and gates. But Merry is the child of the American pastoral, which doesn't engender this kind of "primitive" reinforcement. Merry is a stammerer, like Moses, but instead of inspiring loving discipline, her infirmity inhibits her parents from teaching her any commandments.

Neither Ludwig Lewisohn nor Herman Wouk damns intermarriage as caustically as Roth does in the description of Thanksgiving, America's neutral de-religionized holiday

> when everybody gets to eat the same thing, nobody sneaking off to eat funny stuff—no kugel, no gefilte fish, no bitter herbs, just one colossal turkey for two hundred and fifty million people—one colossal turkey feeds all. A moratorium on funny foods and funny ways and religious exclusivity, a moratorium on the three-thou-sand-year-old nostalgia of the Jews, a moratorium on Christ and the cross and the crucifixion for the Christians, when everyone in New Jersey and elsewhere can be more passive about their irra-tionalities than they are the rest of the year. A moratorium on all the grievances and resentments . . . for everyone in America who is suspicious of everyone else. It is the American pastoral par excel-lence and it lasts twenty-four hours.[49]

The novel does not argue that the bargain between the Jew and Miss New Jersey *causes* an unmerry nihilism, but just as in *The Counterlife*, the arrange-ment of the book powerfully suggests such a connection.

In the book's final and climactic scene, Lou Levov is trying to get along with the Swede's neighbors and to ignore the undercurrents of desperation around the table. He does not yet know what his son knows, that his granddaughter, Swede's daughter, has killed three more innocent people, in addition to the one that sent her into hiding from the police. Lou is hu-moring the drunken wife of his daughter-in-law's lover, inquiring about drag hunting, an imitation of the British fox hunt where there are "a lot of good riders and everybody gets out there and bombs through those places and it's fun." The connection between one kind of bombing and another is not lost on readers. Swede, readying the barbecue, knows what his father is thinking without bothering to look up:

> Fun, his father was thinking, what *is* it with them and fun? What is this fun? What is so much *fun?* His father was wondering, as he had ever since his son had bought the house and the hundred acres forty miles west of Keer Avenue, Why does he want to live with these people? Forget the drinking. Sober's just as bad. They would bore me to death in two minutes.[50]

The son rehearses, in words almost identical to Sammler's, the qualms that his father passed on to him but that he set aside because he was so eager to join these Gentiles. Roth is to Saul Bellow as the Swede is to his father, reminded by the firm admonishment of his elder that through his negligence he has unwittingly unleashed the "fun fair." The Swede accepts the blame without understanding his crime. What is wrong with their life? "What on earth is less reprehensible than the life of the Levovs?" Are the Jews to be blamed for loving America too well? Roth has provided an indictment in search of its crime.

When American Jewish writers retrieve the image of the Jewish parent, they are not shoring up any kind of Jewish authority, because not one of these parents has any "Jewish" authority left to wield. Even those who do, like some of Ozick's protagonists, don't do it right. The parents stand rather as negative evidence of the un-Jewish children they brought into being. A literary tradition that began with high hopes for the integration of Jews into American culture produced its finest work in reaction to some of its guiding assumptions. American Jewish literature, written as it is for the general English reader, has not yet offered up many positive advertisements for Jewish life or teachings, but some of its most masterful work joins the Jewish canon in supplying the negative evidence of a community that has traduced its values and followed strange gods.

10

A CHAPTER IN THE MAKING

ISRAELI LITERATURE

The power of a language can scarcely be gauged. Language is
more than language. Within language lie concealed magic
forces of nature and history, lees of instinct and culture, a heritage of emotions, habits of thought, traditions of taste, inheri-
tances of will—the Imperative of the Past. It is impossible to
measure the power and influence of all this upon the soul,
upon the consciousness and upon its subterranean strata.

SHALOM SPIEGEL, 1930[1]

The Hebrew Revival

This book on modern Jewish fiction ends with Hebrew, which is by now
the dominant branch of modern Jewish literature and certain to become
even more so in the century ahead. When modern Jews determined to
change the course of their history by resuming their sovereign existence
in the Land of Israel, the revival of the Hebrew language was both the
means and the end of achieving political independence. Young people
began speaking Hebrew in revolt and reaffirmation: they defied the religious tradition that had relegated the language to the sanctified realms of
liturgy and learning, and they simultaneously demonstrated loyalty to the
unbroken chain of cultural transmission that began with the Hebrew
Bible. Reclaiming Hebrew was both a derivative form of European nationalism and a reaction against it. The Zionists who insisted on the exclusive use of Hebrew were emulating the zealots of other European
national movements who saw in language the essential expression of peoplehood, ethnicity, cohesion, and political resolve. Yet to elect Hebrew
over other European languages was part of a deliberate turn away from

Europe toward a new society in the Middle East. The Hebrew revival was both improbable and inevitable. The ideological Hebraists like Eliezer ben Yehuda (1858–1922) and Joseph Klausner (1874–1958), who broke off friendships unless they were conducted in Hebrew, remind us how much stubborn energy was required to bring an ancient language back into common use. Inside the Jewish settlement, the *yishuv*, in Palestine, the language war against Yiddish sometimes reached the point of violence. But most Jews who came to the Land of Israel understood instinctively that Hebrew was the only language uniting the Jewish people, hence the only credible national language of a Jewish state. The Jews had developed a uniquely supple attitude toward language as a result of their successive accommodation to sites in Asia, Europe, Africa, and the Americas; taking up Hebrew was yet another such feat of linguistic accommodation, this time to relocation in Eretz Israel.

Earlier generations considered the revival of Hebrew a miracle. Writing in New York in 1928–29, Shalom Spiegel delighted in the prank that history had played on the fathers of the Berlin enlightenment who had taken up Hebrew as a means of integrating the Jews into Europe.

> They wanted . . . to introduce them to the world of foreign values, through Hebrew; to spread, through Hebrew, the gospel of rationalism that discarded nationality. . . . They wanted, through Hebrew, to make their people hunger for other languages; and finally to pave the way, through Hebrew, for assimilation and absorption.[2]

But language has a logic of its own, and "once awakened to life," it spurred Jewish cultural and political renaissance. For Spiegel, as for A. M. Klein, the reawakening of Hebrew betokened the organic emergence of a modern Jewish nation.

Not that Jews are about to become a monolingual people. The religious civilization of the Jews has existed so long outside the Land of Israel that Jewish communities will almost certainly continue abroad, using different languages as before. Besides, today more than ever, overseas communities proliferate worldwide as continuing migrations create ethnic pockets far away from the nations that spawned them; the Jews are now only one of many peoples to sustain a diaspora outside the homeland. At the same time, Jewish demographics are changing and with them the national status of Hebrew: as the Jewish population concentrates in the Jewish state and as the Jewish birthrate in Israel grows while elsewhere it declines, Hebrew is becoming the vernacular of a majority of Jews. One hundred years ago, the tiny minority of writers in Hebrew felt like an embattled enclave within the Jewish world: Yosef Haim Brenner called his press Masada after the last Jewish desert fortress that held out against the Romans. Now approximately 350 Hebrew novels and 250 books of poetry are published annually in Israel. Israelis support their literary industry by buying almost 11 million books a year. Israel's 200 publishing houses put out over 4,000 new titles a year, one of the highest per capita outputs in the world. The Israel Institute for the Translation of Hebrew Literature helps to export the new literature; in a recent essay titled "The Boom in Contemporary Israeli Fiction," Alan Mintz suggests that Israeli literature may even be enjoying an "ironic loss of innocence," thanks to the anticipation of its writers that they may be translated into other languages.[3] In sum, with Hebrew in the ascendance, Jews may henceforth resemble other nations in having a national literature written largely in their national language.

Yet even if most Jews were now to write in Israel's national language, Jewish literature would not become synonymous with literature written in Hebrew. Yonatan Ratosh, who had emigrated to Eretz Yisrael from Warsaw in 1921, provoked this realization when he tried to force an ideological distinction between Judaism, the multilingual religious culture of the Diaspora, and Hebraism, the national culture of an autonomous country. In the 1940s, heading a small poetic movement of "Young Hebrews," who came to be known pejoratively as the "Canaanites," Ratosh declared his intention of winning national independence not only from the British and the Arabs but from the mentality of diasporism that had dominated the Jews for millennia. He tried to strip the Hebrew language of its semantic ties to Judaism and Zionism in order to quicken its attachment to the Levant, and without altogether discouraging the study of such European Hebrew writers as Bialik and Agnon, he wanted to have them treated as alien to the literature of Israel and to have the foreignness of their writing explored.[4] Although this radical Hebraism did not take root at the time, it did serve warning that henceforth some Israeli writers would not consider themselves "Jewish."

Four decades after Ratosh urged Hebrew writers to emancipate themselves from Jewishness, the Christian Arab Anton Shammas attracted critical attention for his Hebrew *Arabesques* (1986), a delicately patterned fictional autobiography that opened the prospect of a non-Jewish literature in a Jewish language, a reversal of the problem we have been investigating throughout this book.[5] The Jewish state of Israel is simultaneously the political state of its citizens, which means that its Hebrew vernacular is the language of citizenship and not the language of Judaism alone. Though Arab nationalism will probably inhibit most other Israeli Arabs from following Shammas's example (and Shammas himself no longer lives in Israel), other non-Jewish Israeli citizens are bound to become Hebrew writers. The institution of statehood that secures Hebrew also challenges its identification with Judaism and the Jews.

Literature derives from experience, which in the case of the Jews is both biologically settled and open to redefinition. A person is born Jewish or not, but since this is merely the beginning, not the end, of the matter, writers born in Israel will be as free as their counterparts elsewhere to speak as Jews, or not. The Israeli critic Barukh Kurzweil concluded regretfully that "our modern literature assumes, either consciously or unconsciously, 'a breach of the covenant with the unity of Jewish culture.'"[6] His contemporary Simon Halkin argued, to the contrary, that Hebrew writers were occupied, "at first less consciously, but ever more so as time went on" with the problem of "how the Jew can remain a Jew while bending so much of his energies to the modernization of his life."[7] Many a modern Hebrew novel could be cited as evidence for the two points of view, but this much is certain: the linguistic balance of power changed for the Jewish people once Hebrew became the national language of Israel. What happens within the literature only the writers will determine.

I HAVE CALLED THIS a chapter in the making because the canon formation of modern Israeli literature is only now beginning. Jewish literature in Israel today has what it never had before: the institutional support of schools and universities; a daily press and media in search of new subjects and personalities; a critical establishment of academics and intellectuals that awards prizes and confers ranking; a competitive publishing industry (which includes translation rights for foreign sales); and a large pool of budding writers who want to form or to define the next generation. Transposed into its own country, the Israeli counterpart of Warsaw's interwar Jewish Writers' Association now feeds off the energy of an entire society. In the preceding chapters I have tried to describe major trends of Jewish literature in a period and in places that did not confer such formal support. Israel will henceforth determine its canonical writings as all countries do, over the course of time.

In this it will be guided by exceptional teachers, scholars, and critics, all of whom play a key role in determining what should be published, taught, and valued. In 1972 Professor Gershon Shaked of the Hebrew University was commissioned to write a survey of Israeli literature as part of a series of books on Jewish literature through the ages. By 1998 he had published the fifth volume of this project.[8] Volume Five is devoted to the "new wave" of prose writers born in the thirties and forties, the literary generation to which Shaked himself belongs and which he introduced to the public; the book's cover photo of Amos Oz, A. B. Yehoshua, Aharon Appelfeld, and Amalia Kahana-Carmon represents his favorites from among the still-living members of that generation. Shaked's dynamic historical survey not only illumines the spectacular development of modern Hebrew literature once it rerooted itself in the Land of Israel but shapes the contours of a cultural narrative that culminates in his credo *"eyn makom akher"* (a phrase from Yosef Haim Brenner claiming that there is no Jewish alternative to the Land of Israel).[9] His chronicle of Hebrew literature is unassailable evidence of how Zionism nurtured the individual talent.

Shaked and his colleague and contemporary Dan Miron publish most of their criticism in the literary pages of the daily newspapers, some of which pay as much attention to literature as to sports, and precisely because the arguments over literature have been so competitive. In one of his books, Miron offers a moving description of what inspired his allegiance to the literary life. He recalls Professor Simon Halkin's course in Hebrew literature in the 1950s, taught at Terra Sancta when the Mount Scopus campus of the Hebrew University was under Jordanian occupation. Among Halkin's students were published poets and writers, critics just beginning to make their mark, veterans of the War of Independence (whose units had just been disbanded), and youngsters like himself. To impress upon his audience the challenge of Hebrew writing in the twentieth century, Halkin borrowed from Albert Thibaudet the concept of a "republic of letters" that "gives literature its atmosphere, its habits, its problems, its rhythms, its social status, its foreign relations."[10] Accounting for the decline of French belles lettres after 1789, Thibaudet contended that the literature of an epoch is normally sustained by a relatively small percentage of young people, namely, those who believe that it is interesting and important "what is made of literature," and that should this excitement over literature be forgotten or obscured for even a few years (as it was during the French Revolution), the generation in which this forgetting and obscuring occurs remains forever deprived.[11] Miron recognized in the vulnerable "Republic of Letters" his own call to destiny in that it granted the scholar-critic "a clear and defined place in the literary event."[12] He felt reassured that a principled young man like himself, citizen of a threatened and brand-new country, would not be shirking his duty by taking up the study of literature, because Thibaudet's image of the "Republic of Letters" endorsed a quasi-political entity that rivaled government in its importance to the nation. Miron became simultaneously a ferocious critic of what he considered Jewish chauvinism and an energetic proponent of the modern Hebrew canon. He provided that Republic with superb critical editions of the poets Haim Nahman Bialik and Uri Zvi Greenberg even as he inveighed against a nationalist approach to literature and the arts.

A third literary eminence emerged from the Hebrew University of the 1950s. Benjamin Hrushovski (now Harshav), one of the three graduate students in Yiddish literature when Dov Sadan inaugurated that program in 1951, was dissatisfied with the study of literature along national lines. A poet in both Yiddish and Hebrew as well as a literary scholar, Harshav wanted the study of literature to yield an *alternative* to the national obsessions of language, people, and polity, and he established the Department of Poetics and Comparative Literature at Tel Aviv University to embody that vision. Opposed, like Ratosh, to the presumption of Jewishness in Hebrew and Yiddish literature, he moved culturally in the opposite direction, in search of a transcendent, comprehensive theory of literature that concentrates on how meaning gets produced rather than on the meaning that is produced. In 1968 he founded *Hasifrut*, the first Hebrew periodical devoted to the study of literature, and eight years later, in English, *PTL: A Journal for Descriptive Poetics and Theory of Literature*, which was succeeded by *Poetics Today*.[13] Harshav and his former students investigated such problems as the history of rhyme, the structural principles of narrative, the anatomy of metaphor, and the theory and practice of rhythm in expressionist poetry. They read and tested the theories of the Russian formalists and later the European deconstructionists about the same time these became popular at Yale, where Harshav now teaches. The encompassing idea of literature as a discipline across national frontiers had the important benefit of bringing together the study of Hebrew and Yiddish, which had been ideologically riven by efforts to make Hebrew the national language of the Jewish state. Harshav's Tel Aviv colleague Itamar Even-Zohar came up with the influential concept of a cultural polysystem—"a network of interrelated textual genres and social and cultural institutions in a society, each one of which is a flexible system in its own right."[14] Harshav himself focused on the discontinuities of modern Jewish culture, the centrifugal influence of foreign cultures, the radical rebellions against tradition and religion, the schisms within individual authors and works. The "Tel Aviv school" stimulated local excitement over literature by joining an avant-garde international discourse, yet by undervaluing the ideational and national content of indigenous Jewish culture, it may have temporarily depleted the sources of Jewish creativity.[15] For a time, it quite overshadowed the diachronic study of a national corpus that was going on at the same university in the Department of Hebrew Literature.

More than any other branch of Israeli culture, Hebrew literature bridged the market and the academy. In 1994 there were over fifty teaching positions in Hebrew literature at the five major Israeli universities, in addition to the many posts in various teachers' colleges, as compared with the single professorship of Hebrew literature available at the single Hebrew university in 1948.[16] The first generation after statehood credited literature as the mainstay of national identity. Hebrew writers were given pride of place in the narrative of Zionism that restored the people to its land: Abraham Mapu, Mendele Moykher-Sforim, Ahad Ha'am, Micah Yosef Berdichevsky, Haim Nahman Bialik, Mordecai Ze'ev Feierberg, Uri Nissan Gnessin, Gershon Schoffman, Yosef Haim Brenner. A crystallizing genealogy identified the major writers of the mandate period, those born abroad whose work remained bound to the European experience from which they had emerged: I. D. Berkowitz, Dvora Baron, Shmuel Yosef Agnon, Asher Barash, Yehudah Burla, Haim Hazaz. Their successors were dubbed the "Palmach generation," after the *plugot makhatz*, or shock troops, of the Israel Defense Forces, signifying not their dedication to warfare but the fact that they and their writing were forged in the crucible of statehood. Either born in Palestine or having come with their parents at such an early age that Hebrew became their natural language, writers like S. Yizhar, Benjamin Tammuz, Aharon Megged, Moshe Shamir, Natan Shaham, David Shahar, Hanoch Bartov and Shulamith Hareven wrote in the emerging local idiom, of orange groves and olive trees rather than birch woods and evergreens. Yehuda Amichai and Haim Gouri, both poets, also wrote memorable fiction. Slightly younger authors, like Amos Oz, A. B. Yehoshua, and Aharon Appelfeld, gained international recognition for works that turned inward, toward private obsessions. The fame of others, like Amalia Kahana-Carmon and Yitzhak Ben Ner, remains homebound.

Compare the situation of Israeli prose writers—and I limit these remarks to prose writers only—with their Jewish counterparts in Poland (as described in Chapter Four), and you realize the transforming effect of sovereignty on the artistic as well as the political life of the Jewish people. Nevertheless, I do feel concern for the canonical impulse itself, which is becoming as threatened in Israel as it is elsewhere in the West. Traditional Jews always begin their study with the earliest sources, which are closest to the word of God. This religious-intellectual discipline not only preserved Judaism for thousands of years but ascribed power to words, which retain their influence over time. Moderns who put their faith in progress are prone to substitute the rage of the moment for yesterday's classic. Their disregard for permanence has the unfortunate consequence of weakening the status of literature by denying its relevance. Since literature is a valuable repository of experience, its evaporation prevents a people from knowing itself. A single pair of works may illustrate this point.

Mendele Moykher-Sforim: *The Mare*

In 1873, Sholem Yankev Abramovitch, who had become renowned under his pen name Mendele Moykher-Sforim, or Mendele the Book Peddler, published a novel in Yiddish, called *Di kliatshe* [The Mare] that he would later transpose into Hebrew and expand as *Susati* [My Steed]. As described in Chapter One, Abramovitch had created the persona of Mendele to negotiate the distance between himself, the highly critical enlightened Jewish intellectual, and the potential mass of Jewish readers, so that under the guise of bringing important manuscripts to the public, he could expose a whole run of social follies and abuses.[17] The gentler Mendele thus allowed the Swiftian author to indict Jewish beggary, stupidity, hypocrisy, superstition, cupidity, treachery, extortion, and child abandonment. His sense of urgency was heightened by the desperate conditions of Russian Jewry and by the prospects of real improvement through enlightenment and emancipation. But following the first pogrom in Odessa in 1871, Abramovitch experienced a change of heart. It was not that he looked any kindlier on Jewish society or felt any less eager to reform it, but the enmity he suddenly recognized in the tsarist regime and the Russian people revised his assessment of the underlying problem. Until then he had been convinced, or had tried to convince himself, that if the Jews were to demonstrate their willingness to become productive citizens, the Russian government would welcome their contribution to the common weal. He had even dedicated one of his satires to His Excellency, the governor of Odessa, as a "token of the author's deep esteem and devotion."[18] Now he perceived a more tangled causality that could only be portrayed by a new literary strategy. To expose the flaws of the polity as well as of the Jews would require him to portray the aggressors and to indict—under strict tsarist censorship—a hostile world he did not know. *The Mare* was his response to this artistic challenge.[19]

Mendele introduces this work in his habitual way by explaining how he came to acquire the manuscript in question, and then he turns the narrative over to the narrator-hero, Isrolik, a young man of twenty who is trying to become a *mentsh*. To become this genuine human being, "little Israel" knows he must defy his mother and the expectations of his reactionary society and go off to study medicine, the healing profession.

> Just as Noah in his ark was the only survivor of all the creatures in the world who were drowned in the Deluge, so I too, Israel son of Tsippe, was the only survivor in my little town, the only bachelor among all my friends, who because of that pestilential nuisance known as marriage-brokers, had become boy-husbands before their time and were up to their ears in poverty and squalor.[20]

Isrolik withstands the pressure of his mother and his community, but spared like Noah from the flood, he is left similarly stranded in an unfriendly world. When he tries to enter university, he is confounded by the requirement that he master Russian folklore, a requirement that seems designed to eliminate the Jewish student rather than test his ability to become a good physician. Isrolik finds it absurd that his attempt to escape the world of Jewish superstition should hinge on his mastery of Russian superstition! Exhausted by his efforts and terrified of remaining a *luftmentsh* all his life, he suffers the first of a series of mental breakdowns in a field outside his town. It is while lying there in a swoon that he sees the heroine of the novel. Young bullies are chasing a mare, pelting her with stones and commanding their dogs to harass and bite her. Shocked by this violence, Isrolik tries to come to her rescue, but in vain. The boys laugh him off and they only give up their sadistic sport once they have bloodied the horse to a pulp.

The aspirations of an enlightened intellectual are combined in Isrolik with the sensibility of a romantic. The dawn after a rain appears to him as a brilliant wedding scene, with the forest decked out like a bridegroom, the recently soiled and desolate earth sparkling like a bride, and the golden mother-sun beaming down on her child and its intended. In the Yiddish version, the scene is rendered homey in its description of a charming small-town wedding, whereas the Hebrew calls on loftier resources to send the majestic bridegroom-sun out to greet his earthly bride. Abramovitch never ceased to mourn the Jews' alienation from the natural world, which he considered to be partly the result of their socioeconomic predicament but also the consequence of Halakhic law, which he felt treated the members of the animal kingdom in too functional a manner, as creatures subject to the will of man. Isrolik first responds to the mare as a fellow creature and sets out, like the hero of a sentimental novel, to rescue the damsel in distress. His natural sympathies merge into support for natural law.

Isrolik's widowed mother is a staple of nineteenth-century Jewish literature, a harridan housewife who has been deformed by her burdens. In the allegorical figure of the scabby mare, the author offers a much more nuanced personification of the Jewish people, which despite the burdens of its material condition still bears traces of its aristocratic heritage and even a hint of its former beauty. The epigraph of the book (from *Song of Songs* 1:9) likens the beloved to the steed in Pharaoh's chariot ("*lesusati berikhvey faro dimitikh rayati*"). Since the rabbis had read the *Song of Songs* as the allegory of God's love for the people Israel, Abramovitch could expect readers to recognize in the mare his sympathetic image of the Jewish people. Thus, once the mare surprises Isrolik with the sound of her voice, she recounts the history of her metamorphosis from a proud prince (in the early centuries of Jewish self-government) into a beast of burden (through millennia of political dependency). Contradictory feelings beset our hero: "One moment, I felt as if my life were about to end out of pity for the poor, broken-down mare. The next moment, I was furious. How could she just lie in the mud, calmly, nonchalantly, as if she didn't grasp her awful situation!"[21] Torn between compassion and disgust for her passivity, Isrolik informs the mare that as a member of the Society for the Prevention of Cruelty to Animals he will ask its benefactors to come to her assistance. The SPCA symbolizes the St. Petersburg Society for the Promotion of Enlightenment among Jews, which had earlier subsidized Abramovitch's translation of a work on natural history. But when Isrolik writes to them requesting aid, they adopt the same attitude toward the mare that Abramovitch had formerly projected toward the Jews in his writing; that is, they promise to help the mare only on condition that she first improve herself.

Abramovitch does not spare himself in this revisionist critique. When Isrolik describes the benefits that will accrue to the mare once she has cleaned up and "learned to dance," she scoffs at him ("Rhetoric! Rhetoric!") and informs him that the dance cannot precede the food. The SPCA's sympathies are useless, and its advice misplaced. Reeling off her objections—that other horses are accorded acceptance without having to earn it; that, considered on its own terms, her breeding is at least a match for others; that she has proven herself much more useful than the breeding-farm horses that dare to judge her; and that the right to graze must be granted, not earned—the mare demands that the enlighteners stop sentimentalizing her condition and stop pretending that she is to blame for it. The mare cannot begin dancing until she is granted her right to live, until her persecutors stop their persecution. Isrolik can no more guarantee her safety than he could stop the hooligans from bloodying her up.

The mare's argument is unexpected. Who could have dreamed her capable of such oratory? And what is the hero to do once he recognizes the enormity of her condition? The Jew is often happiest demanding rights for others in the expectation that those can be attained, but the ferocity of antisemitism throughout the modern period has made it hardest of all to seek equal rights for the Jews. And hard as it is for Jews to face up to the apparently irrational hatred directed against them, the writer's problems are compounded by his inability to fathom the enemy who wishes him harm. I alluded to this problem in my discussion of Jewish writing of the Holocaust, whose authors had no access to the Nazi mind. Some of the Jewish writers in non-Jewish languages, such as Kafka, Babel, Rawicz, and Grynberg, were close enough to their detractors to represent them authentically. But what of the Jewish writer in a Jewish language who lacks imaginative access to those chiefly responsible for his fate? How could Abramovitch credibly represent the tsarist threat?

He found his way out of this dilemma by moving his venue from the earth to the atmosphere. When Isrolik, astonished by the mare's outburst, exclaims, "I think the devil's gotten into you!" the devil emerges in person and, pressing his bared knife against Isrolik's throat, invites him for a tour of the world beyond his ken. Isrolik feels the ground being pulled out from under him and falls—or perhaps rises—into the realm of the fantastic. This demonic figure, with analogical links to the folk mythology that his Russian examiners required him to study, evokes the despotism of the tsar without identifying it by name. The little humanist seemed fairly cocky as long he was addressing the mare, that is, offering his fellow Jews advice, but panic sets in with his realization that the Jewish fate lies in non-Jewish hands. The devil takes Isrolik on a voyage that defies the rational imagination. Asmodeus the devil and his entourage keep changing form and direction and argument as they venture into dark regions of politics and the soul. Flying in a formation of vampire bats, witches, and other evil apparitions, Isrolik is shown the munitions factories bringing industrial warfare to Europe and the special horrors that are visited on the Jews—pogrom mobs running wild, antisemites preparing vats of ink for their defamatory charges, judges ruling for the pogromists against their victims. The devil gloats, secure in the knowledge that he rules from above and below, from within and outside the Jewish community.

There does not seem to be any reasonable explanation for the devil's delight in torturing the Jews of Europe. When the ever-logical Isrolik asks his guide, "What do you have against us? What did we ever do to you?" the devil responds by quoting the midrash in which King Solomon captures the devil and imprisons him in chains. And when Isrolik then asks why that should be the Jews' fault ("Why should we have to pay for something that happened thousands of years ago?"), he echoes the incomprehension of Jews through the ages for the treatment meted out to them at Christian hands.[22] What Abramovitch captures best in the voice of the devil is the protean force and unbridled joy of antisemitism. The devil has taken over the heavens that once housed God, ridiculing the Jews' persistence in history. The demonic energy that whirls Isrolik aloft makes a mockery of his philosophic optimism. Thus, whereas the mare still uses rational persuasion to destroy Isrolik's faith in the enlightenment, his ride with the devil undermines his very trust in reason itself. He cannot save the mare, and he falls into madness.

Isrolik's final madness is morally induced. At the end of their journey the devil tries to prepare Isrolik for his return to earth by persuading him to "ride the mare." He asks Isrolik to accept a new Decalogue that will allow him to exploit his fellow Jews *under the pretext* of observing the commandments. When Isrolik refuses, he is precipitately dropped. He is last seen in bed, under his mother's care, having failed the entrance examinations to the university and fallen into such despondency that he had to be transported home. He wakes up attended by Jewish and Christian wonder-workers, who, in the book's final irony, diagnose his illness as the work of the devil.

No other work of modern fiction that I know offers so holistic a view of Jewish experience. Many aspects of *The Mare*, including the personification of the horse as an oppressed people, the demonic flight over Europe, and the intellectual's loss of reason, may have been borrowed from other works of Russian and European literature,[23] but Abramovitch evinces peerless clarity from his blend of allegory, fantasy, and sentimental realism. Through a succession of duets—Isrolik with his mother, with the mare, and with the despotic devil—the modern Jew is shown trapped between a defensive and decaying orthodoxy and an energetically antagonistic regime; he is stripped of his faith in divine intervention and, equally, of trust in positive political reform. *The Mare* appeals simultaneously to mind and heart, belongs simultaneously in Jewish and European literatures, and integrates the internal critique of the Jew with the story of his treatment as a subject minority. Isrolik collapses because, unlike Babel's Lyutov, he will not "learn how to ride" by betraying Jewish values. His insanity brings negative evidence of his integrity, akin to the insight that Lear finds in blindness.

NEITHER *THE MARE* nor any other work by Mendele Moykher-Sforim is currently taught in Israeli high schools, either in the religious or the secular stream. Although some of the most innovative Israeli literary criticism has been devoted to Abramovitch, who is credited with having laid the foundations of both modern Yiddish and Hebrew prose fiction, the difficulty of his work and his critical judgments of East European Jewish life are cited as reasons for his elimination from the curriculum.[24] To be sure, in order to fully understand Abramovitch-Mendele it is often necessary to know about such things as the history of the Jewish Pale of Settlement, the Crimean War, the introduction of conscription by Tsar Nicholas I, the administration of the meat tax within the Jewish community, and Chancellor Bismarck's decision to expel resident aliens from the German imperial state in 1880. To appreciate his wit it helps to know as much as he knew—the Bible by heart, the exegetical curriculum of Lithuanian *yeshivas*, and the then-contemporary works of Jewish and Russian literature. Well-intentioned pedagogues might be excused for their reluctance to expose Israeli schoolchildren to satire about the historical community most of which was destroyed under Hitler and Stalin. But in addition to neglecting a thrilling writer, their calculations obliterate a cultural trail.

Isrolik is a Jewish archetype, a fully conceptualized version of the heroes that dominate Hebrew literature from Abramovitch's day to this. Originally fugitives from Judaism ("banished from their father's tables"), they headed out for a brighter future but could not attain it in either the material or the spiritual sense. In the works of Micah Yosef Berdichevsky they are cast as tragic rebels, and in Yosef Haim Brenner as anti-heroes after the rebellion has failed. Gershon Shaked, who makes this distinction in a book appropriately called *Dead End*, calls the suicidal or deranged loner the typical hero of turn-of-the-century Hebrew literature, using the Hebrew term that has come to describe him—the *tolush*, or alienated man.[25] The *tolush* has abandoned the religious tradition that turned his author into a writer of Hebrew, but his formative past pursues the character in the medium through which the author tries to make his escape. Like Yehezkel

Hefetz of *Breakdown and Bereavement*, the *tolush* changes his place of residence without changing his luck; the internal damage is not amenable to geographical correction. Or else, a new political ambush is set for him in place of the old.

Yaakov Shabtai: *Past Continuous*

A century and a continent separate *The Mare* from *Past Continuous* (1977), the first novel of Yaakov Shabtai, and in many respects the distance between the two works confirms the cultural and political metamorphosis that occurred in between. Written in the form of one unbroken paragraph of 275 pages, with sentences that run on for longer than most reasonable paragraphs, Shabtai's novel tracks the friendship of three childhood friends, two known only by their first names (Israel and Caesar) and the other as Goldman, from the period before the founding of the state, when Tel Aviv was still emerging from the sand, to a winter in the 1970s, by which time these men are in their late thirties and early forties. The fluidity of Shabtai's narrative—so relatively soon after Abramovitch-Mendele invented an idiomatic Hebrew prose and Brenner used the halting stammer to represent authentic Hebrew patterns of speech—is evidence that a Jewish country now takes its language completely for granted. The prolonged paragraph replicates the exceptional intimacy of a society whose members are bound together by stronger-than-family ties and can hardly visit their parents or walk along the beach or drive to a funeral or an assignation without recalling who lived where and when or who had done what, where, and how.

Born in Tel Aviv in 1934, Shabtai had followed the high road of Labor Zionist ideology by joining a kibbutz after he did his army service. Labor Zionism was conceived as the antidote to the condition that had driven Isrolik mad. Zionism was to restore the Jews to their own land so that they would no longer be subject to the whims of hostile populations, and socialism's reorganization of an egalitarian society was to produce an unselfish individual, perforce a better Jew. The kibbutz was the jewel in the crown of Labor Zionism; the small, voluntary collective settlements of East European youth who produced the food that they ate by the sweat of their brow represented the wholesome antithesis to Abramovitch's peddler-and-beggar Jewry. Relatively few inhabitants chose this way of life, but its voluntary subordination of individual desire to the needs of the group and its promise of wholesome satisfaction became the ideal of the entire Jewish *yishuv*, which knew it had to pull together in order to survive. According to the forecast of the Zionist pioneers, joining a kibbutz ought to have liberated Shabtai from the burdens of Jewish history, cured him of the sickly individualism of capitalist society, and substituted for the psychology of guilt a bracing new confidence in himself, his country, and the future of the Jewish people. Much of that confidence and solidarity is manifest in the seamless unity of *Past Continuous*. And yet the novel, situated in his native city, also betrays an exhaustion that is uncannily reminiscent of Abramovitch's work. The protagonists feel even more crushed by parental pressure than Isrolik does by the demands of his mother. From an objective point of view, that is, by any comparative measure, the decades covered by the novel were the most vigorous in the history of the Jews, and perhaps in the life of any modern nation. During this period the Jewish inhabitants of Israel declared their political independence; fought four major wars; gathered in and resettled millions of refugees; developed cities, institutions, and the economy; and created a modern culture in the Hebrew language. Indeed, through Goldman's respect and awe for his Aunt Zipporah, the author expresses his gratitude to the emblematic founder "for all the help and kindness she had offered . . . without expecting anything in return, and without getting anything either."[26] But the young men in the foreground of the novel are as circumscribed as Isrolik in Russia's Pale of Settlement. If anything, Shabtai portrays a society even more hobbled by despair.

The Proustian title of Shabtai's book, *Zikhron devarim* (literally, "aide mémoire" or "remembrance of things"), draws attention to its obsession with the past—not with its recovery, however, but with the heavy shadow that it casts. The continuous paragraph that fuses all the characters into a claustrophobic narrative also grips them like a vise. The parent generation had once been exceedingly active: its members moved, whether enthusiastically or reluctantly, from Europe to Palestine. They married and raised families. They found ways of earning a living. We still see traces of the shacks they erected in Tel Aviv and the pioneering settlements they founded based on the ethic of labor. Some of them left the country, and some of those who left returned. Uncle Lazar, the younger brother of Goldman's father, abandoned his family to fight in the Spanish civil war and spent years in the Soviet Gulag as a consequence of his misplaced idealism. When he returns, humbled, he knows that

> although there was something in men which he called the "redemption instinct," his life experience had taught him that there was no single act in public or private life, however right or revolutionary, which was redemptive in the sense that from a certain point onward a new era would commence in which everything would be perfectly good and work out just the way people wanted it to and at the same time, despite this awareness, it was necessary to live as if redemption were possible and to strive for it. . . .[27]

After his radical removal from Zion, this Lazar "rises from the dead" and returns to the moral balance of the *Ethics of the Fathers*: "It is not thy duty to finish the work, but thou art not at liberty to neglect it."[28] But the three protagonists who occupy the foreground of the novel make no such meaningful decisions. They can neither meet the expectations of their elders nor strike out on their own.

The three friends are maimed in different ways. As the use of his patronymic suggests, Goldman, the oldest, is the yield of his family, a set of mismatched parents who detest one another, and of a sprawling clan whose history provides the Zionist texture of the novel. He still lives in his parents' home and has never moved out of his childhood bedroom except for his obligatory stints in the army and an aborted three-week marriage to "the beautiful Yemimah Chernov." As *his* name suggests, Caesar, "who was not prepared for any effort involving compromise or risk to himself," is the son of parents at least his equal in selfishness—a successful father who instructs his son in infidelity and lechery and a mother who is understandably afraid of being abandoned.[29] Caesar conducts three simultaneous love affairs and chases down every new available woman, while occasionally ministering to his former wife. His greatest passion, for his older half-sister Ruhama, is a misplaced bid for maternal affection, which helps explain why he cannot be a decent father to his two sons and which admits literal use of the term *incestuous* to describe the excessive intimacy of the novel. About Israel, this novel's Isrolik, the least is known. He lives without a profession for the duration of the book, absorbed in an existential trance, sleeping rent-free on a couch in Caesar's photographic studio, playing the piano, and occasionally practicing the organ in a Jaffa church. He is incapable of committing himself to Ella, a lonely woman for whom he seems to care; his treatment of her alternates between tenderness and cruelty, yet when he tells her to leave one day, he is almost surprised that she does. In the final pages of the book he follows her to Jerusalem, where she has relocated, by which time it is too late for them both. She gives birth to a son, apparently his, but when the hospital nurse tries to hand her the baby for feeding, she does not want to take it, ignoring the needs of the child just as Israel did hers. Inadvertently, he seems to have reproduced an infant as emotionally doomed as himself.

Does the book offer any clue to Israel's insensibility, the way Abramovitch supplies the transformative history of the mare? In the macabre opening sequence, Caesar and Israel are trying vainly to attend the funeral of Goldman's father, who, as it turns out, has been consigned to the wrong plot and must later be dug up and reinterred. The signature memory of the novel occurs during this comic misadventure, and it is summoned up from Israel's point of view: as a boy of ten, Israel had seen Goldman's father take the dog that belonged to their neighbor Kaminskaya, an animal provocatively named Nuit Sombre, tie the animal to the water pipe in their yard, and bludgeon it to death with a hammer, yelling, "Let him die! Let him die! He has to die!"[30] It is not yet clear to the reader, and certainly not to the boy at the scene, that Goldman's father had been provoked by Kaminskaya's indulgence of this animal and of her lovers at a time when the Jewish community of Palestine was rationing food and trying to create a voluntary ethic of responsibility for the collective.

> He and Hanoch Leviatan, Avinoam and Sonia's younger brother who had been in his class at school and had died two years later of pneumonia, hid behind the myrtle bushes in the shade of the big cypress trees which gave off a marvelous smell and watched the terrible thing happening a few feet away from them, Hanoch shaking like a leaf while he, Israel, stood turned to stone until Goldman's father disappeared with the dog's body, and then he vomited and vomited, and afterward he washed his mouth and face and went upstairs with all the strength drained out of him.[31]

The Leviatans are neighbors in the same courtyard, peripheral characters who are typically interwoven into Shabtai's narrative when they figure in the memory of an event. The brutal act that the two boys witness irrevocably transforms their redolent yard into a place of execution. Goldman's father considered the woman of loose morals his mortal enemy, for ostentatiously flaunting the national discipline. From the bludgeoner's point of view "[It] was the Second World War all over again," and Goldman's father, who had refused to exploit his connections or buy even a single grain of rice on the black market, pronounces sentence on this pet who has been fed the finest salami and Swiss cheese. If it were his own dog, the narrator informs us, Goldman's father would not have behaved any differently,

> because he was a Zionist and a Socialist and believed in plain living, hard work, morality, and progress, in the most elementary sense of the words, and hated right-wing nationalists, people who got rich or wasted money on luxuries, and people who told lies about Eretz Yisrael, and all this as part of a system of clear, fixed, uncompromising principles embracing every area of life and action, which he never doubted for an instant despite all the external changes and difficulties, and from which he saw no reason to deviate in the slightest degree.[32]

Shabtai's prose is no less punishing than Goldman's father. He brings down all his frustration with the founders in those furious hammer blows.

Goldman's father Ephraim (who is always referred to as his son's father, just as the son is always referred to as Goldman) is an extreme product of the Labor Zionism that governed Israel under David Ben Gurion, an "enforcer" in a society that did not yet have its own police. The crisis never stops for him, so he must redouble his vigilance once the formal wars are over. But according to Shabtai, this righteous demand for self-discipline and this certainty about moral values, "in the most elementary sense of the words," erupts in a deed of greater self-abandonment than Kaminskaya ever committed with her lovers and her indulged pet. The act of Goldman's father turns Israel "to stone" and leaves him "with all the strength drained out of him." Kaminskaya jumps to her death from her balcony shortly after the killing of her dog. From the associative pattern of the sentence it would appear that even the death of ten-year-old Hanoch two years later seems also to follow from his presence at the dog's execution. In the absence of any other explanation, this formative experience of paralysis, retching, and denial dominates the book right from the outset, the way it dominates the memory of those who witnessed it, and accounts for Israel's emotional dearth. It is not insignificant that the character who carries this memory also bears the name of the country.

The fatal connection between the generations is made explicit in the opening sentence of the novel:

> Goldman's father died on the first of April, whereas Goldman himself committed suicide on the first of January—just when it seemed to him that finally, thanks to the cultivation of detachment and withdrawal, he was about to enter a new era and rehabilitate himself by means of the "Bullworker" and a disciplined way of life, and especially by means of astronomy and the translation of the *Somnium*.[33]

The nine-month gestation period between the death of Goldman's father and the suicide of his only heir—his daughter Naomi having been killed years earlier in an ambiguous automobile accident—suggests that whereas some parents beget life, others beget death. Shabtai does not exactly blame Goldman's father for his son's suicide, since he shows the father himself to be the chief victim of his "devastating honesty,"[34] but the author has invented a syntactical device that without proving causality forges the links between the ideals of the parents and the suffering of the children. One reviewer of the book could not refrain from confirming in a personal footnote that "two-thirds of all the offspring of Labor Israel" will take the effects of its "emotional blackmail" (the phrase in English) with them to the grave: the options that the parents imposed on the children were so oppressive that they deprived the children of any possibility of choice.[35] If not an indictment of the founding fathers, Shabtai's novel certainly mourns their legacy. The collective security of the unbroken paragraph has smothered the life force of its young.

Like Abramovitch, Shabtai offers such an informed and exhaustive description of his society that he seems to be delivering two generations whole. Abramovitch concentrated on the socioeconomic picture, highlighting the ubiquitous beggar's pouch and tax man's collection box: the rapidly multiplying families of Jews of the Russian empire were trapped without adequate means of self-support; beggary and charity had become two sides of the same miserable *groschen*. Shabtai sees the loss of purpose that accompanies *improving* conditions. Sex is the preoccupation of a generation joined in common fate without common goals. Sex, not procreation. Sex, not love. The more tightly the characters are intertwined by the familial society, the harder they find it to form families of their own. When we take leave of Caesar, he has remarried and his wife is expecting a child, but his oldest son by the first marriage is dying of childhood leukemia. His friends hardly ask about the child, whose life seems to be seeping from him out of neglect. At the other end of the scale of "masculinity", Goldman and his three-week marriage to "the beautiful Yemimah Chernov" are alluded to again and again without ever being explained or accounted for. This concerned society that purports to know everything about everyone is too afraid of failure to inquire into its source.

Shabtai's novel is connected to the landscape, to the sounds and smells of his surroundings, to whatever was wrought by God and by man, with a possessive intimacy that Abramovitch could scarcely imagine. It is suffused with memory, not of ancient Jewish history but of the immediate past that brought it into being. And yet because of its greater temporal and cultural self-sufficiency, Shabtai's conception of his characters seems grimmer than Abramovitch's in two important ways. Isrolik may not find a way of restoring the mare to her former dignity, but she never loses confidence in her heritage. Shabtai's Tel Avivians find nothing in Jewishness to alleviate or mitigate their distress. "Among the many books cramming [Goldman's] bookcase were scattered books about Judaism and the Kabbala and rabbinic interpretations of the laws and prayer books, remnants of the period when he had made enthusiastic efforts, accompanied by great hopes, to return to the bosom of Judaism and to attain a religious frame of mind," but he finds no comfort in this "external intellectual sense of an acknowledgment of the necessity of faith and the desirability of God," a prescribed religion without belief that necessarily dwindles and dies.[36] Goldman's father has in his bookshelves the (mostly unread) books of Berl Katznelson, Ben Gurion, Bialik, Brenner, and Sholem Aleichem. The indifference to *Jewish* survival might not be as significant were Jewishness not the basis of their settlement in Israel. Given the demands that it makes on them, its failure to inspire must inspire their resentment.

Goldman seeks his salvation in translating the *Somnium* of Johannes Kepler into Hebrew, a putative autobiography in the form of a dream that incorporates Kepler's astronomical calculations about the moon. Kepler's *Somnium* in Shabtai's novel figures like the devil's journey in *The Mare*, that is, as a device for getting beyond the confines of the Jewish territory. But the translated passage that is discovered after Goldman's suicide suggests that his interest in the moon trip was not redemptive:

> "Worst of all is the initial shock of the acceleration, for he is flung and hurled upward as though in an explosion of gunpowder. He must therefore be prepared beforehand and dazed by the administration of narcotics. His arms and legs must be protected so that they will not be torn from his body . . . on a journey of this nature the body no doubt escapes and transcends the magnetic force of the earth and enters that of the moon, which from now on gains the upper hand . . ."[37]

Kepler used the dream to present scientific calculations that would have angered the authorities had they been published as science. Somewhat like Dr. Govinda Lal's journey to the moon in *Mr. Sammler's Planet*, his project holds out the promise of a new frontier. Whatever prompted Goldman to transcribe Kepler's journey into Hebrew, he uses it as a map, directing himself toward suicide.

The contrast between Shabtai's use of the *Somnium* and Abramovitch's flight with the devil also illuminates their contrasting views of the sources of Jewish impotence. Isrolik's horizons literally expand to the point that he sees all too clearly the encompassing powers inhibiting his freedom. Shabtai's main characters have fought off the Arab enemies, and Goldman does his annual army service during the course of the novel, but the *novel* does not address the lopsided war or how the war exacerbates the Israelis' sense of siege. All the anger here is turned inward; the real source of violence is suppressed. The war heightens Israel's claustrophobia in just the way that ghettoization increased internal tensions within Jewish communities of the Diaspora. Even generous Aunt Zipporah "couldn't bear it when anyone disparaged Eretz Yisrael in her presence or troubled her with endless talk of depression and illness and death"; she treats emigration as an act of treachery, much as religious Jews repudiated their children who married outside the faith. Because the novel itself takes no cognizance of the political offensive that is hammering away at the moral confidence of the *yishuv*, the despair felt by the characters seems more oppressive, self-induced.

Hence, Shabtai's most stunning, if inadvertent, achievement has been to reproduce artistically the solipsistic experience that he describes. He locks his community inside literary boundaries that evince the strain of its political encirclement. Many a long passage falls like an ironic sentence on those it describes. The housekeeping of Zina, Caesar's mother, declines to the point that she gives up all attempts to introduce order into the life of the house, "which was as shapeless and chaotic as a party on the point of dying and disintegrating."[38] A single ominous sentence that begins with Goldman's struggle with his own problems and the problems of the world, a description situated in the room where he imagines a life of liberation, boldness, and vitality, comes spiraling down to the death of his sister Naomi, "which had been a heavy blow to him and shocked him badly, besides causing an almost total breakdown of the family."[39] In a rare snippet of direct dialogue, the Jaques of the novel, a drunken cynic named Besh, foretells that the city of Tel Aviv will some day revert to sand. "[Don't] worry, one day the sand will bury this town. You can't mess around with sand."[40] Although the book does not echo this judgment, its circular form returns the future to the past.

SHABTAI'S SOLIPSISTIC RENDITION of Jewish society in Israel is uncannily reminiscent of the Abramovitch and Sholem Aleichem who used the flow of Jewish language to interpret and stave off a threatening world. Once again in modern Israel the artists of a beleaguered Jewish community have to deal with the problem of unearned enemies who try to settle Jewish destiny through the force of aggression, a problem that they lack both the means and inclination to represent in their fiction. The self-sufficiency of Jewish culture contrasts so painfully with the exposed position of Jewish politics that its writers are often tempted to obscure the latter by inflating the former, with the odd result that they corroborate the state of siege their writing tries to ignore. Jewish writers wanting to escape the confinement of their native communities might well resemble all other moderns in seeking greater personal freedom, but with this difference:

their communities are themselves being assaulted, and by much more dangerous powers than the ones oppressing them. Most of the works I have discussed in this book reflect this conundrum with varying degrees of sympathy or resentment, but the disappointment may fall hardest on Hebrew writers in Israel, who are born into the consequences of Zionism. Zionism fully intended to free its children from the condition of beleaguered Jews; it did not foresee that the Arab rulers and politicians would take up where the Europeans left off.

Shabtai's portraiture has many warm tones, veins of humor, sensations of piercing pleasure. But it is notable above all for the suppressed violence, in the form of depression, that burdens its characters. Amos Oz created a similar atmosphere in his early novel *My Michael*, the story of a Jerusalem woman, Hannah Gonen, with a "maddening desire to break loose from the trap of her own existence."[41] Hannah's husband Michael, an archaeologist, cannot penetrate the soul of his neurasthenic wife, which is possessed by erotic fantasies of Arab twins whom she imagines are stalking her as terrorists or rapists. The tension in Oz's novel (set in Jerusalem around 1966, when it was still a divided city), though much more palpable than in Shabtai's, takes the form of a paranoid fantasy, of internalized aggression rather than real attack. When Hannah finds herself pregnant in the closing pages of the novel, she might as well be Shabtai's Ella locked into terminal depression. The perpetuation of the disheartened or suicidal *tolush*, now also in its female form, unsettles the assumptions of early Zionism that the character's rootless and unhappy inner life was the consequence of the Jew's infirmity in exile. Modern Hebrew may be the most autochthonous branch of Jewish literature in that it represents political as well as cultural sovereignty, yet it is precisely in the political sphere that the experience of Israelis still resembles the fate of the Jews in exile. It should come as no surprise that the greatest works of Israeli literature attest to that similitude.

AUTHOR'S POSTSCRIPT

I N TAKING LEAVE OF MY SUBJECT let me reiterate that this book is only a signpost on an unfinished road. I myself am already in the position of the incredulous reader who will say, "How could you have failed to write about *that?!" That* is *Miriam* (1921), the culminating work of fiction of Micah Yosef Berdichevsky, one of the most innovative books in modern Hebrew prose by its fieriest rebel and boldest artist. I am comforted in this omission by Zipora Kagan's glorious critical edition of the novel and by the scholarship consecrated to this author by Avner Holtzman, which makes all his work accessible.[1] *That* is David Bergelson's Yiddish novel *Opgang* [Descent, 1920], recently reissued in Joseph Sherman's wonderful new translation by the Modern Language Association of America.[2] *That* is *Gates of Bronze* (1924, 1956, 1968), the politically engaged Hebrew novel by Haim Hazaz that dramatizes the vying Jewish ideas of messianism in a Russian town being taken over by the Bolsheviks.[3] Then there is Chaim Grade's incomparable two-volume *The Yeshiva* (1967–68), which is drawn from his own searing experiences in the Mussar movement of Lithuania and that delivers not only the social history of a lost community but the substance and emotional force of its ethical-intellectual debates.[4] Has any writer exerted greater influence on emerging Jewish literature than the enigma from Drohobycz, Bruno Schulz? In what must be the highest form of literary appreciation, the American Cynthia Ozick made a lost manuscript by Schulz the centerpiece of her novel *The Messiah of Stockholm* at almost the same time that the Israeli writer David Grossman animated his deathless spirit in the novel *See: Under Love.*[5] These authors do appear in the appendix of suggested further readings that I have added for the avid reader.

One of my favorite writers, Yitzhak Leybush Peretz, who is missing from this book because he did not write any sustained long work of fiction, liked run-on endings of three or four dots to signify a work or a thought still in progress. A book on the canon is by definition open-ended. Let readers take it as an invitation to set out on their own journeys through Jewish language and culture.

The canonical impulse that brought the Bible into being and encouraged civilization through an unbroken exegetical tradition faltered in the modern period when people either lost their faith in the moral power of inherited teaching or else assumed that human society could be improved without its ballast. Modern fiction attests to the preeminence of the individual both in its form and content: it swears no prior allegiance to anything but itself and bears witness to a world that functions without reference to Divine Authority. In the modern period, the God-intoxicated Jews became intoxicated with the world, and the result of their creative experimentation is registered in the diversity of this book. That a people should have entered the twentieth century speaking mostly one Jewish language and exited it speaking mostly another is proof of a remarkable—indeed, unprecedented—breach of cultural transmission and of an equally remarkable response to it. Nevertheless, the canonical impulse that forged Jewish civilization has also generated in individual works certain moral and cultural links to the tradition, and a modern Jewish canon has formed, like a new constellation, waiting to be discovered and studied and known.

Not all Jewish writers were inspired by their Jewishness—but many were. Not all Jewish writers comprehended the Jewish experience—but many did. Not all Jewish writers sought beauty in truth, but a surprising number created it. The writers discussed in this book have left as great a record of modern experience as any people could wish for. The rest is up to the readers, individually and through collective study and transmission. As with the Bible, the world will also value what the Jews find of value to themselves.

NOTES

Preface

1. "The Poetry of Abraham Sutzkever" (Folkways Records Album No. FL 9947). Reissued as cassette by Smithsonian Institution, Washington, D.C.

2. Susanne Klingenstein discusses this very incident within the larger context of how Jews entered the humanities departments of American universities. See her *Enlarging America: The Cultural Work of Jewish Literary Scholars, 1930–1990* (Syracuse, N.Y.: Syracuse University Press, 1998) and its predecessor *Jews in the American Academy 1900-1940: The Dynamics of Intellectual Assimilation* (New Haven, Conn.: Yale University Press, 1991).

3. See Max Weinreich, *History of Yiddish Language*, trans. Shlomo Noble with the assistance of Joshua A. Fishman (Chicago: University of Chicago Press, 1980): chapter 6.

4. Dov Sadan, *'Al sifrutenu. Masat-mavo* [On Our Literature. Introductory Essay] [Jerusalem: Youth and Halutziut Department of the Histadrut, 1950): See especially chapter two, 13–23.

5. Hana Wirth-Nesher, "Introduction," *What is Jewish Literature?* (Philadelphia: Jewish Publication Society, 1994): 4.

Introduction

1. *Tanakh: A New Translation of The Holy Scriptures According to the Traditional Hebrew Text* (Philadelphia: Jewish Publication Society, 1985): 284. The text has "serve as a symbol on your forehead" but offers the more traditional "frontlets" as an alternative.

2. Harold Bloom, *The Western Canon: The Books and School of the Ages* (New York: Harcourt Brace Company, 1994): 4.

3. Ibid.: 16.

4. Ibid.: 23, 65, 36.

5. Ibid.: 404.

6. The mention of Memmi reminds us that there is also a whole Sephardic side of modern Jewish culture, deriving from Jews of the Iberian peninsula and the Middle Eastern sphere of influence. Their literature is absent from this book, because I know this Sephardic culture only incidentally and haphazardly, having read certain works that came to my attention but without knowing just what there was to be read. Ladino did not generate anything like the Yiddish literature of Europe, but a Sephardic Jewish literature in French and Hebrew has been mushrooming since the Second World War, with Tunis, Baghdad, and Alexandria becoming the cities of Jewish memory, as Warsaw, Vilna, and Prague were for the Ashkenazim. As well, the descendants of European Jews who settled in

Latin and South America began to write in Spanish, just as their North American counterparts did in English; this hyphenated Jewish-Spanish literature is now also gaining strength and is represented by critics and scholars along with writers and poets. It is my hope that this book, which highlights Ashkenazic Jewish culture, will soon be complemented by those that present the Sephardic and Latin side of the Jewish canon. With Israel becoming the demographic center of Jewish life, many ethnic streams of Judaism are in the process of merging, and a common canon would help to reacquaint the various branches of the family.

7. Chaim Zhitlowsky, "The Jewish People and the Jewish Language," republished from *Der fraynt* (Petersburg, 1904)in *Geklibene verk* [Selected Works] (New York: CYCO, 1955): 112.

8. Piotr Rawicz, *Blood from the Sky*, trans. from the French by Peter Wiles (New York: Harcourt, Brace & World, 1964): 289-90.

9. Cynthia Ozick, "America: Toward Yavneh," *Judaism* (Summer 1970): 264-282. Quotations on pp. 274-5, 276. Republished in *Art & Ardor* (New York: Alfred A. Knopf, 1983): 151-177.

10. Ibid.: 280.

11. Dov Sadan, *A vort bashteyt* [The Word's the Thing], vol. 3 (Tel Aviv: I. L. Peretz Farlag, 1983): 145.

12. Ibid.: 147.

13. Ever the purist, Sadan adds that the favored dog in the anecdote may have been "imported" from a foreign source, since there are plenty of jokes in other languages about wealthy misers who leave their fortunes to dogs: 153.

14. Lionel Trilling, "Introduction," in *The Experience of Literature: A Reader with Commentaries* (New York: Doubleday & Company, 1967): x.

15. Mendel Beilis, *Di geshikhte fun mayne laydn* [The Story of My Trials] (New York: Mendel Beilis Publishing Co., 1925): 23–24, 30.

16. Bernard Malamud, *The Fixer* (New York: Farrar, Straus & Giroux,1966): 60.

17. Lionel Trilling, "1928," selected from his notebooks by Christopher Zinn, *Partisan Review 50th Anniversary Issue* (1984): 496.

18. Lionel Trilling, *Middle of the Journey* (New York: Harcourt Brace Jovanovich, 1975): 156.

19. Wallace Fowlie, *A Reading of Proust*, 2nd. ed.(Chicago: University of Chicago Press, 1975): 20.

20. See Marcel Proust, *A la recherche du temps perdu* (Paris: Robert Laffont, 1987): I,607.

21. Lucy Dawidowicz, *From That Place and Time: A Memoir 1938-1947* (New York: W. W. Norton & Co., 1989).

22. These distinctions among strata of Holocaust writing are delineated by David G. Roskies in his anthology *The Literature of Destruction: Jewish Responses to Catastrophe* (Philadelphia: The Jewish Publication Society, 1989).

23. Amos Oz, *Unto Death* [Ad mavet], trans. "Crusade" by Nicholas de Lange and Amos Oz (New York: Harcourt Brace Jovanovich, 1975).

24. See Sander Gilman, "To Quote Primo Levi: 'Redest keyn jiddisch, bist nit kejn jid [If you don't speak Yiddish, you're not a Jew],'" *Prooftexts* (September 1989): 139-160.

25. Isaac Rosenfeld, *Passage from Home*; Alfred Kazin, *Starting Out in the Thirties*; Bernard Malamud, *A New Life*; Norman Podhoretz, *Making It*.

26. Herbert Gold, *Fathers: A Novel in the Form of a Memoir* (New York: Random House, 1966): 15.

27. Symposium in *Commentary* (April 1961): 309–359. For further discussion of this issue see my article, "The Maturing of *Commentary* and of the Jewish Intellectual," *Jewish Social Studies* (Winter 1997): 29-41.

28. A. M. Klein, *The Second Scroll* (New York: Alfred A. Knopf, 1951): 107. Includes the quotation that follows in the text.

29. Meir Shalev, *The Blue Mountain [Roman Rusi]*, trans. Hillel Halkin (New York: Harper Collins, 1991): 274.

Chapter 1. The Comedy of Endurance

1. Letter to M. Spector in Warsaw, dated Kiev, 21 September 1894, and, according to the Hebrew calendar, the Fast of Gedalya (between Rosh Hashanah and Yom Kippur), 5655. The story's progress is discussed in letters of 26 September and 20 October. On November 4, Sholem Aleichem writes that he is still following the advice of his mentor, Mendele Moykher-Sforim, to "file, file, file" (to refine the writing by paring it down); three days later he sent off the first half of the story and on the 10th he announced that "Reb Tevye is done!" See *Briv fun sholem-aleykhem 1879-1916*, ed. Abraham Lis (Tel Aviv: Beit Sholem Aleichem and I. L. Peretz Farlag, 1995): 295 ff. For studies of Tevye's publication history, see Chone Shmeruk, "'Tevye der milkhiker': History of the Work" [in Hebrew] *Hasifrut* 26 (1978): 29-38; Ken Frieden, *A Century in the Life of Sholem Aleichem's Tevye*, The B. G. Rudolph Lectures in Judaic Studies, New Series, 1 (Syracuse, N.Y.: University of Syracuse Press, 1993-94).

2. See, especially, letter to the typesetters of *Hoyzfraynd* [Home Companion], 7 November 1894, *Briv*: 298.

3. Marie Waife-Goldberg, *My Father Sholem Aleichem* (New York: Simon & Schuster, 1968): 144–47. Nachman Meisel says that when he was in Boyarka in 1911, the local dairyman named Tevye told everyone he was famous, thanks to Sholem Aleichem. See *Our Sholem Aleichem* [in Yiddish] (Warsaw: Yiddish bukh, 1959): 57.

4. For an analysis of the persona in the works of these authors, see Dan Miron, *A Traveler Disguised: The Rise of Modern Yiddish Fiction in the Nineteenth Century*, 2nd ed. (Syracuse, N.Y.: Syracuse University Press, 1996); Miron, *Sholem Aleykhem: Person, Persona, Presence* (New York: YIVO, 1972).

5. Yosef Haim Brenner, "On Sholem Aleichem," from an essay written on Sholem Aleichem's death in 1916, *Kol kitvey Y. H. Brenner* [The Complete Works], vol. 3 (Tel Aviv, 1967): 106-8. Translated in *Prooftexts* 6: 1 (January 1986), quotation on p. 18.

6. *Hoyzfraynd* 4, (1895): 67.

7. Sholem Aleichem dropped the description of Tevye, along with Tevye's two-page "Letter to the Author," from the first collection of Tevye stories that he issued in 1903. The posthumous Folksfund edition of Sholem Aleichem's work, which became the model for all subsequent collected editions, restored Tevye's letter to the text, but neither the Hebrew translator I. D. Berkovitch nor the English translator Hillel Halkin included it.

8. Frank Kermode, *English Pastoral Poetry from the Beginnings to Marvell* (London: 1952): 37.

9. I. L. Peretz, "In the Mail Coach" (1893), trans. Golda Werman, in *The I. L. Peretz Reader*, ed. Ruth R. Wisse (New York: Schocken Books, 1990): 114.

10. Quoted by John D. Klier and Shlomo Lambroza, eds, *Pogroms: Anti-Jewish Violence in Modern Russian History* (Cambridge: Cambridge University Press, 1992): 41.

11. Aaron Lieberman, letter dated 23 November 1876, in *The Letters of Aaron Lieberman* [in Yiddish], with an introduction and notes by Kalman Marmor (New York: YIVO, 1950): 80.

12. Sholem Aleichem, *Gants tevye der milkhiker* in *Ale verk* [Selected Works] (New York: Tog-Morgn Zhurnal Edition on the Centenary of Sholem Aleichem, 1959), 1: 19. In the following notes, this Yiddish version is referred to as *Gants tevye*. For the English equivalent see Sholem Aleichem, *Tevye the Dairyman and The Railroad Stories*, trans. with an introduction by Hillel Halkin (New York: Schocken Books, 1987): 6, which is referred to in the following notes as *Tevye*. I occasionally slightly modify the translation to make it more literally faithful to the original.

13. I. I. Trunk, *Tevye and Menakhem Mendl as Expressions of Eternal Jewish Fate* [in Yiddish] (New York: Central Yiddish Culture Organization 1944): 38.

14. Frances Butwin, "Introduction" in *Tevye's Daughters* (New York: Crown, 1949): xv. Butwin later modified this notion of Tevye: her book, coauthored with her son, contends that "[each] of Tevye's locutions is controlled by his recognition of the paradoxical place of suffering in Jewish history." See Joseph Butwin and Frances Butwin, *Sholem Aleichem* (Boston: Twayne, 1977): 92. Tevye is funny the way musicians may be spontaneously musical. For a rich analysis of his verbal skill, see Michael Stern, "Tevye's Art of Quotation," *Prooftexts* 6 (1986): 79-96.

15. Rashi (1040–1105), called after the initial letters of his name *Rabbi Shlomo Yitzhaki*, is the foremost French exegete whose commentaries on the Bible and the Talmud are regularly printed together with the text.

16. Halkin, Introduction: xxiv-xxv.

17. *Gants tevye*: 30; *Tevye*: 14.

18. Y. Kh. Ravnitski, ed., *Yidishe vitsn* [Jewish Jokes], 2nd edition (Berlin: Moriah, 1923): 7-8.

19. *Gants tevye*: 32; *Tevye*: 15.

20. Sol Gittelman, *From Shtetl to Suburbia: The Family in Jewish Literary Imagination* (Boston: Beacon, 1978): 58.

21. A selection of Sholem Aleichem's Zionist writings appear in *Why Do the Jews Need a Land?*, translated from the Yiddish and Hebrew by Joseph Leftwich and Mordecai S. Chertof (New York: Cornwall Books, 1984).

22. *Stempenyu* (1888), trans. Joachim Neugroschel in *The Shtetl: A Creative Anthology of Jewish Life in Eastern Europe* (New York: Richard Marek, 1979): 287-375. *Yosele Solovey* (1889), trans. Aliza Shevrin as *The Nightingale, or The Saga of Yosele Solovey the Cantor* (New York: Putnam, 1985).

23. Harvey Mindess, *Laughter and Liberation* (Los Angeles: Nash, 1971): 23. Mindess considers Sholem Aleichem the most convincing exponent of "compassionate irony."

24. The Yiddish term for dairyman is *pakhter*, and as far as I can ascertain, Sholem Aleichem was the first to suggest *milkhiker* in its stead.

25. For biography see Chone Shmeruk, *Sholem Aleichem: His Life and Literary Work* [in Hebrew] (Tel Aviv: Porter Institute for Poetics and Semiotics, 1980); entry by Dan Miron in *Encyclopedia Judaica*, Vol. 14 (Jerusalem: Keter, 1971): 1271-1286; I. D. Berkowitz, *Our Pioneers: Memoiristic Stories About Sholem Aleichem and His Generation* [in Yiddish], 5 vols. (Tel Aviv: Hamenorah, 1966).

26. For a first-rate study of the development of *Menakhem-Mendl*, see Abraham Novershtern, "'Menakhem-Mendl' to Sholem Aleichem: From Textual History to Structural Analysis" [in Hebrew], *Tarbiz*, 54 (1985): 105-146.

27. Hillel Halkin's felicitous translation, *Tevye*: 27.

28. *Gants tevye*: 63; *Tevye*: 34–35.

29. Benjamin Harshav offers an analysis and diagramed study of Tevye's "chain of asso-

ciations" in *The Meaning of Yiddish* (Berkeley: University of California Press, 1990): 102–107.

30. Shmeruk: 29.

31. Sholem Aleichem, "Taybele," in *Ale verk*, 23: 14. My translation.

32. Sholem Aleichem, *Dos meserl*, ed. Chone Shmeruk (Jerusalem: 1983). Translated as "The Penknife," in *Some Laughter, Some Tears*, ed. Curt Leviant (New York: G. P. Putnam, 1968): 113–128. For other similar motifs see, e.g., "The Fiddle" (a boy gives up his instrument) in Sholem Aleichem, *Selected Stories*, intro. Alfred Kazin (New York, Modern Library, 1956): 307–323; "Visiting with King Ahasuerus" (a boy gives up acting with Purim players) in *Old Country Tales* trans. Curt Leviant (New York: Paragon Books, 1966): 51–64; "A Ruined Passover" (a boy's clothes are ordered oversized so he can grow into them) in *Holiday Tales*, trans. Aliza Shevrin (New York: Charles Scribner's Sons, 1979): 45–68.

33. Sigmund Freud, "Humour," in *Collected Papers*, vol. 5, ed. James Strachey (New York: Basic Books, 1959): 218–220. Hegel appears to be making a similar point in his distinction between tragedy and comedy: "In tragedy the individuals destroy themselves through the one-sidedness of their otherwise solid will and character, or they must resignedly accept what they had opposed even in a serious way. In comedy there comes before our contemplation, in the laughter in which the characters dissolve everything, including themselves, the victory of their own subjective personality which nevertheless persists self-assured." See G. W. F. Hegel, *Aesthetics: Lectures on Fine Art*, trans. T. M. Knox, II (Oxford, U.K.: Clarendon Press, 1974): 1199.

34. Halkin's translation reads, "Better my borscht without the universe than the universe without my borscht." *Tevye*: 73.

35. *Gants tevye*: 87; *Tevye*: 50.

36. *Gants tevye*: 98; *Tevye*: 55. The greeting by Tevye is translated by Halkin: "Hurry up or you'll be late for the wedding!"

37. *Gants tevye*: 118; *Teyve*: 69.

38. Letter to Y. Kh. Ravnitski, dated Lemberg, 16 April 1906, *Briv*: 453.

39. *Gants tevye*: 123–4; *Tevye*: 71.

40. *Gants tevye*: 126; *Tevye*: 72–73.

41. Letter to the children, dated St. Petersburg, 15 November 1904, *Briv*: 40.

42. *Gants tevye*: 138; *Tevye*: 81.

43. *Gants tevye*: 131; *Tevye*: 76.

44. *Gants tevye*: 138; *Tevye*: 81.

45. In this context, nothing is more ironic than Tevye's repeated protestation, whenever sentiment gets the better of him, that "Tevye is not a woman." Tevye's actual abiding concern, confided to Sholem Aleichem, is whether he has it in him to "be a man." "I'd give a lot to know if all males [*ale mansbiln*] are like me or if I'm the only madman of my kind. Once, for example . . . but do you promise not to laugh at me? Because I'm afraid you'll laugh . . ." *Gants tevye*: 139; *Tevye*: 82.

46. See, e.g., "Der fakishefter shnayder [The Haunted Tailor]," trans. Hillel Halkin, in *The Best of Sholem Aleichem*, ed. Irving Howe and Ruth R. Wisse (Washington, D.C.: New Republic Books, 1979): 2–36.

47. Waife-Goldberg, *My Father Sholem Aleichem*: 147.

48. *Gants tevye*: 160; *Tevye*, 95.

49. I. D. Berkowitz, *Our Pioneers*: 3: 199.

50. Letter to M. Ben Ami (Rabinovitz), dated Nervi, 21 March 1909, in *Briv*: 497.

51. *Gants tevye*: 175; *Tevye*: 103.

52. In the winter of 1914, Sholem Aleichem also wrote a dramatic version of the Tevye

stories, hoping that it would be a vehicle for the German actor Rudolph Schildkraut or for Jacob Adler of the American Yiddish stage. See Letters to David Pinski and Jacob Adler, *Briv*: 584–587.

53. *Gants tevye*: 200; *Tevye*: 116.

54. *Gants tevye*: 204; *Tevye*: 120.

55. Shmeruk: 37.

56. In the five years after the tsarist ukase of 17 April 1905, permitting converts to the Orthodox Church to return to their original faiths, 476 Jews returned to Judaism. See the discussion on East European Jewish converts in T. M. Endelman, "Memories of Jewishness," in *Jewish History and Jewish Memory: Essays in Honor of Yosef Hayim Yerushalmi*, ed. Elisheva Carlbach et al. (Hanover, N.H.: Brandeis University Press, 1998): 322–325.

57. Max Erik, "Menahem-Mendl: Character and Method" [in Yiddish], in *Shtern* [Star] (1935), 5 6: 180–202; 8: 82–90. This quotation is from a translation by David G. Roskies in *Prooftexts* 6: 1 (January 1986): 24–25.

58. Trunk, *Tevye and Menakhem-Mendl*: 82.

59. Jacob Glatstein, "Menakhem Mendl," in *In toykh genumen* [Sum and Substance] (New York: Farlag Matones, 1947): 483.

60. *Fiddler on the Roof* (New York: Limelight Editions, 1992): 150–51.

61. See Seth L. Wolitz, "The Americanization of Tevye or Boarding the Jewish *Mayflower*," *American Quarterly* 40 (1988): 514–36.

62. Jacob Weitzner, *Sholem Aleichem in the Theatre* (Madison, N.J.: Fairleigh Dickinson University Press, 1994): 83. See discussion of its performance history, pp. 74–110.

Chapter 2. The Logic of Language and the Trials of the Jews

1. Moses Hess, *Rome and Jerusalem*, trans. Meyer Waxman (New York: Bloch, 1943): 124–125.

2. Franz Kafka, entry for 13 September 1914, *Tagebucher*, ed. Hans-Gerd Koch, Michael Muller, and Malcolm Pasley (Frankfurt: S Fischer, 1990): 677. *The Diaries of Franz Kafka 1914–1923*, ed. Max Brod, trans. Joseph Kresh (New York: Schocken Books, 1965): 92. In the following notes the English diaries are referred to as D1 (1910–1913) and D2 (1914–1923).

3. *Tevye*: 122.

4. See Arnold J. Band, "Kafka and the Beilis Affair," *Comparative Literature* (1980): 176. Max Brod reports that among the papers Dora Dymant burned at Kafka's insistence was a story about the Beilis ritual murder trial. See Max Brod, *Franz Kafka: Eine Biographie* (Frankfurt: S. Fischer Verlag, 1954): 248.

5. Franz Kafka, "The Judgment," trans. Willa and Edwin Muir, in *The Complete Stories*, ed. Nahum N. Glatzer (New York: Schocken Books, 1976): 85.

6. Maurice Samuel, in his factual, highly readable account of the case: *Blood Accusation* (New York: Knopf, 1966): 4.

7. *Gants tevye*: 206; *Tevye*: 123.

8. *Tevye*: 131.

9. Hannah Arendt, *The Origins of Totalitarianism* (Cleveland: Meridian Books, 1958): 5.

10. Franz Kafka, *Der Prozess*, ed. Max Brod (Frankfurt: S. Fischer Verlag, 1979): 7. Though I developed a great fondness for the English translation by Willa and Edwin Muir, so smooth that it prompted Ronald Gray's article "But Kafka Wrote in German," the new English translation by Breon Mitchell, based on the definitive Fischer edition of Kafka's

collected works and designed to follow Kafka's unfinished text "with unusual fidelity," better suits my discussion of Kafka's anxiety over language. In the following notes, all references are to *The Trial*, trans. and with a preface by Breon Mitchell (New York: Schocken Books, 1998): 3.

11. "Translator's Preface": xix.

12. Hess, *Rome and Jerusalem*: 91–92.

13. Ezra Mendelsohn, *On Modern Jewish Politics* (New York: Oxford University Press, 1993): 38. See also his *The Jews of East Central Europe Between the Wars* (Bloomington: Indiana University Press, 1983): 132–139.

14. Paul Mendes-Flohr summarizes Buber's influence in *Divided Passions: Jewish Intellectuals and the Experience of Modernity* (Detroit: Wayne State University Press, 1991): 84–109.

15. Felix Weltsch, "The Rise and Fall of the Jewish-German Symbiosis: The Case of Franz Kafka," in *Leo Baeck Year Book*, vol. I (London: 1956): 259–261.

16. For ideas of nationalism that did attract Kafka, as opposed to Ahad Ha'am's and Martin Buber's, see Giuliano Baioni, *Kafka: Literatur und Judentum*, trans. from Italian by Gertrud Billen and Josef Billen (Stuttgart: J. B. Metzler, 1994): 34–41.

17. October 22, 1911, D1: 108.

18. November 1, 1911, D1: 125.

19. January 24, 1912, D1: 223

20. October 8, 1911, D1: 87.

21. Heinrich Heine, *On Poland* (1823), quoted from S. S. Prawer, *Heine's Jewish Comedy: A Study of his Portraits of Jews and Judaism* (Oxford: Clarendon Press, 1983): 61. The term *mauscheln* (to speak like Moses or, in Yiddish, Moyshe), defined by the *Langenscheidt German Dictionary* alternately as "to talk Yiddish" and "to jabber," associates Yiddish with the mangling of a language.

22. Franz Kafka, *Letters to Friends, Family, and Editors*, trans. Richard and Clara Winston (New York: Schocken Books, 1977): 122 mentioned henceforth in these notes as *Letters to Friends*.

23. January 6, 1912, D1: 215.

24. Apparently copied by hand from the original by Mrs. Elsa Brod, the German version can be found in Franz Kafka, *Nachgelassene Schriften und Fragmente* vol. I, ed. Malcolm Pasley (Frankfurt: S. Fischer, 1993): 188–193. I have modified the English translation by Ernst Kaiser and Eithne Wilkins in Franz Kafka, *Dearest Father: Stories and Other Writings* (New York: Schocken Books, 1954): 381–386.

25. Sander L. Gilman emphasizes Kafka's anxiety "about the inevitability of becoming that which he fears he must become." See *Franz Kafka, the Jewish Patient* (New York: Routledge, 1995): 8.

26. See, e.g., Walter H. Sokel, "Kafka's Poetics of the Inner Self," in *From Kafka and Dada to Brecht and Beyond*, ed. Reinhold Grimm et al., (Madison: University of Wisconsin Press, 1982): 7–9.

27. *Nachgelassene Schriften*: 192.

28. One can hardly overestimate the contribution of this linguistic symbiosis to the history of German–Jewish relations. The same Moses Mendelssohn who served both Jews and Christians as the Enlightenment ideal lobbied the Christian government against the corrupting influence of Yiddish, claiming that "this jargon has contributed to no small degree to the immorality of the common people." The political and social advantages that accrued to the speaker of German naturally helped to establish this hierarchical perception of German as the perfect version of an inferior Jewish. To identify with Yiddish as Kafka did was

to champion the most suspect sign of Jewishness and to reverse the most deeply held assumption about the relative standing of the two cultures.

29. October 24, 1911, D1: 111.

30. Marthe Robert, *As Lonely as Franz Kafka*, trans. Ralph Manheim (New York: Harcourt Brace Jovanovich, 1982): 56.

31. Erich Heller, "Kafka's True Will: An Introductory Essay," in Franz Kafka, *Letters to Felice*, ed. Erich Heller and Jurgen Born., trans. James Stern and Elisabeth Duckworth (New York: Schocken Books, 1973): xviii.

32. DI: 191.

33. *The Trial*: 201.

34. Ibid.: 91–92. I use the more standard spelling of the name Joseph K. in place of Mitchell's Josef.

35. Ibid.: 205–206.

36. Eric Marson, *Kafka's Trial: The Case Against Joseph K.* (Queensland: University of Queensland Press, 1975); Ritchie Robertson, *Kafka: Judaism, Politics, and Literature* (Oxford: Clarendon Press, 1985): 98.

37. *The Trial*: 6.

38. Ibid.: 9.

39. Ibid.: 6.

40. Ibid.: 11–12.

41. Aleksandr I. Solzhenitsyn, *The Gulag Archipelago 1918–1956: An Experiment in Literary Investigation*, vols. 1 & 2, trans. from the Russian by Thomas P. Whitney (New York: Harper & Row, 1973): 3.

42. *The Trial*: 87.

43. Laurent Cohen points out that Rudi Block, one of Kafka's few overtly Jewish figures, is also "the first literary portrait of the Western Jew that he so disparages." See *Variations Autour de K.: Pour une Lecture de Franz Kafka* (Paris: Intertextes, 1991): 30. I was most grateful to come across this intelligent book, which mediates between those who stress Kafka's alienation from Jewishness and those who exaggerate his Zionist and Jewish passions. We note that Block almost shares the patronymic and some of the unpleasant qualities of the only major full-fledged Jewish character in Marcel Proust's *A la recherche du temps perdu*.

44. *The Trial*: 195.

45. Ibid.: 217.

46. Ibid.: 225; "all-encompassing ambiguity" in Heinz Politzer, *Franz Kafka: Parable and Paradox*, 2nd ed. (Ithaca, N.Y.: Cornell University Press, 1966): 8.

47. *The Trial*: 231.

48. Letter of Franz Kafka to Max Brod (June 1921) in *Letters to Friends*: 286–289.

49. Michel Carrouges, *Kafka Versus Kafka*, trans. Emmett Parker (University, Ala., University of Alabama Press, 1968): 41.

50. December 25, 1911, D1: 191.

51. Gilles Deleuze and Félix Guattari, *Kafka: Toward a Minor Literature*, trans. Dana Polan (Minneapolis, Minn.: University of Minnesota Press, 1986): 16.

52. Ibid.: 27.

53. Stanley Corngold calls this theory "a kind of polemical ideolect aimed against high German literature." See "Kafka and the Dialect of Minor Literature," *College Literature* (February 1994): 89. My debt to Corngold as an interpreter of Kafka and his critics extends far beyond this reference.

54. Deleuze and Guattari: 22.

55. Kafka's pitiless dissection of liberal optimism makes it hard for us to imagine what he really thought of the work of those of his Jewish contemporaries who tried to use German to express the aspirations of a subject minority (e.g., his friend Max Brod's *Reubeni Prince of the Jews*). Brod was using German as a pan-European language to describe the development of a Jewish national redeemer on European soil. A later such "deterritorialized" novel was Franz Werfel's *The Forty Days of Musa Dagh*, a highly influential best-seller about the Armenian slaughter at the hands of the Turks, which obviously paralleled the situation of the Jews in Germany in 1933, the year it appeared. These two friends of Kafka's did sound their faith, as members of a "subject nation," in the ability of the German "oppressor" language to convey their liberal messages, unlike Kafka, who allowed the subject writer no escape.

56. Letter dated by the editors as early November 1923, in *Letters to Friends*: 395.

57. Yosef Haim Brenner, *Breakdown and Bereavement*, trans. Hillel Halkin (Ithaca, N.Y.: Cornell University Press, 1971).

58. Letter to Max Brod, dated by the recipient Berlin-Steglitz, postmarked on arrival as 25 October 1923 in *Letters to Friends*: 388. The final reference to the novel is in a letter to Robert Klopstock of 29 February 1924, (p. 409), where Kafka writes that a missing letter of Klopstock's turned up "in a Hebrew book in which I had kept it because I was reading a little in the book every day but hadn't opened it for a whole month."

59. Rabbi Benjamin (Joshua Feldman Radler), "Two Years: 1906–07," in *Yosef Haim Brenner* [In Hebrew] (Tel Aviv: Hakibbutz Hameuchad, 1944): 83.

60. Gershon Shaked, *Hebrew Narrative Fiction 1880–1970*, vol. 1: In Exile [in Hebrew] (Tel Aviv: Hakibbutz Hameuchad and Keter, 1977): 366.

61. Shalom Spiegel, *Hebrew Reborn*, 2nd ed. (New York: Meridian 1957): 376.

62. Barukh Kurzweil, "'Shikul vekishalon': Hatakhanah haakhronah shel kium ha-yehudi haabsurdi," introductory essay in *Shikul vekishalon* (Tel Aviv: Am Oved, 1972): 261–273.

63. *Breakdown and Bereavement*: 3

64. Ibid.: 13.

65. Ibid.: 77.

66. Ibid.: 33.

67. Ibid.: 123.

68. Robert Alter, *The Invention of Hebrew Prose: Modern Fiction and the Language of Realism* (Seattle: University of Washington Press, 1988): 49.

69. Gershon Shaked, *Dead End: Studies in J. H. Brenner, M. J. Berdichevsky, G. Shoffman, and U. N. Gnessin* [in Hebrew] (Tel Aviv: Hakibbutz Hameuchad, 1973): 99. Shaked's book contains a full study of this novel; see pp. 99–118.

70. *Breakdown and Bereavement*: 32.

71. Ibid.: 128–129.

72. Ibid.: 75.

73. Ibid.: 248.

74. Ibid.: 247.

75. Ibid.: 245.

76. *The Trial*: 166–167.

77. *Breakdown and Bereavement*: 174.

78. Yosef Haim Brenner, "On Sholem Aleichem," trans. David G. Roskies, *Prooftexts* 6: 1(January 1986): 18.

79. For a description and analysis of this method, see Boaz Arpali, *The Negative Principle: Ideology and Poetics in Two Stories by Y. H. Brenner* [in Hebrew]. (Tel Aviv: Hakibbutz Hameuchad and the Kats Research Institute for Hebrew Literature, 1992).

80. *Breakdown and Bereavement:* 251. I have slightly modified the translation for greater accuracy. The concluding phrase may be taken literally to mean that Palestine is not the place for such a plea for mercy.

81. *Breakdown and Bereavement:* 305.

Chapter 3. Literature of the Russian Revolution

1. Isaac Babel, *1920 Diary* (New Haven, Conn.: Yale University Press, 1995): 28.

2. Isaac Babel, "Odessa," in *You Must Know Everything: Stories 1915–1937*, ed. Natalie Babel, trans. Max Hayward (New York: Farrar, Straus & Giroux, 1966): 26.

3. *Ibid.:* 29.

4. The phrase itself comes from a manuscript that begins "Childhood. At Grandmother's," dated Saratov, 12 November 1915, and translated into English by Max Hayward in *You Must Know Everything:* (pp. 5–12). Though Babel's autobiographical stories reinvent rather than describe his childhood and adolescence, this account of the pressure to excel is borne out by independent sources.

5. Steven J. Zipperstein, *Elusive Prophet: Ahad Ha'am and the Origins of Zionism* (Berkeley: University of California Press, 1993): 71.

6. Renato Poggioli, *The Phoenix and the Spider* (Cambridge, Mass.: Harvard University Press, 1957): 230.

7. Alice Stone Nakhimovsky, *Russian-Jewish Literature and Identity: Jabotinsky, Babel, Grossman, Galich, Roziner* (Baltimore: The Johns Hopkins University Press, 1992): good comments on these books on 54–68.

8. See Efraim Sicher, *Jews in Russian Literature after the October Revolution* (Cambridge, U.K.: Cambridge University Press, 1995): 10–11.

9. Isaac Babel, "The Rebbe," in *Collected Stories,* ed. with notes by Efraim Sicher, trans. with introduction by David McDuff (London: Penguin, 1994): 124. This edition will be used throughout unless otherwise indicated.

10. Stone Nakhimovsky: 95. This curious reading does not detract from the value of Nakhimovsky's book as a whole.

11. Isaac Babel, "Shabbes Nakhamu," in *Collected Stories:* 13.

12. I. I. Trunk, *The Jolliest Jew in the World, or Hershele's Apprenticeship* [in Yiddish] (Buenos Aires: Yiddishbukh, 1953): xix.

13. Charles Rougle, "Isaac Babel and His Odyssey of War and Revolution," in his edition, *Red Cavalry: Critical Companion* (Evanston: Northwestern University Press, 1996): 27. Rougle confuses the narrator's "identity conflict" with his function as the prototypical "outsider" (p. 33) in an otherwise illuminating essay.

14. *1920 Diary:* entries of 5 June (July); 6 June (July); alternate months are indicated in parentheses because although Babel dated four entries by the roman numeral vi, historical evidence corresponding to internal descriptions suggests July as the probable date. Norman Davies, "Izaak Babel's 'Konarmiya' Stories and the Polish-Soviet War," *Modern Language Review* 67: 4 (October 1972): 847; Rougle: 58, n.13. The next two entries are of 16 July and 25 July.

15. "Babel Answers Questions about his Work," in *You Must Know Everything:* 216.

16. "Crossing the Zbrucz," *Collected Stories:* 91.

17. Efraim Sicher, *Style and Structure in the Prose of Isaak Babel* (Columbus, Ohio: Slavica, 1985): 32–34.

18. Carol Luplow says Babel uses contrastive juxtaposition of language to create "a romantic outlook." See *Isaac Babel's Red Cavalry* (Ann Arbor: Ardis, 1982): 10–11; 94–95.

19. Viktor Shklovsky, *A Sentimental Journey: Memoirs, 1917–1922*, trans. Richard Sheldon (Ithaca, N.Y.: Cornell University Press, 1970): 7.

20. Viktor Shklovsky, "Isaac Babel: A Critical Romance," reprinted in *Isaac Babel: Modern Critical Views*, ed. Harold Bloom (New York: Chelsea House, 1987): 9–14.

21. "Crossing the Zbrucz," *Collected Stories:* 91–92.

22. *Ibid.:* 92–93.

23. According to Rougle, Babel has the "wrong time, wrong river, wrong highway, wrong cities, wrong armies" in Rougle: 18, pass. James E. Falen, *Isaac Babel: Russian Master of the Short Story* (Knoxville: University of Tennessee, 1974): 137–141. Patricia Carden, *The Art of Isaac Babel* (Ithaca, N.Y.: Cornell University Press, 1972): 94–96.

24. David G. Roskies, ed., *The Literature of Destruction: Jewish Responses to Catastrophe* (Philadelphia: The Jewish Publication Society, 1989): 146. Excerpt from the Bialik poem: 162.

25. From Trilling's introduction to the first English translation (1955) of Isaac Babel's collected stories, reprinted as an appendix to *Collected Stories:* 340.

26. "Afonka Bida," *Collected Stories:* 170.

27. *Ibid.:* 175. The quotation below is also on this page.

28. "My First Goose," in *Collected Stories:* 123.

29. "Squadron Commander Trunov," *Collected Stories:* 182.

30. Ibid.: 188.

31. Nathalie Babel, introduction to *The Lonely Years: 1925–1939*, trans. Andrew R. MacAndrew and Max Hayward; ed. Nathalie Babel (Boston: David R. Godine, 1995) xii–xiii.

32. "The Rebbe's Son," *Collected Stories:* 226.

33. Shklovsky, "Isaac Babel: A Critical Romance": 9.

34. "The Rebbe's Son," in *Collected Stories:* 227.

35. See Semyon Budyonny, "An Open Letter to Maxim Gorky," originally in *Krasnaya Gazeta,* 26 October 1928. Translated by Max Hayward in *The Lonely Years:* 384–387.

36. "Argamak," *Collected Stories:* 228–229.

37. Ibid.: 233.

38. Ibid.: 233.

39. I discuss the political implications of this insight in *If I Am Not For Myself . . . The Liberal Betrayal of the Jews* (New York: Free Press, 1992): 162–164.

40. Isaac Babel, letter to his sister, Moscow, May 12, 1925, in *The Lonely Years:* 61.

41. Moyshe Kulbak, *Zelmenyaner I* in *Geklibene verk* [Selected Works] (New York: CYCO, 1953); *Zelmenyaner II* (Minsk: Melukhe farlag fun vaysrusland, 1935). An abbreviated translation of Part One by Nathan Halper is included in *Ashes out of Hope,* ed. Irving Howe and Eliezer Greenberg (New York: Schocken Books, 1977): 124–192. All translations here are my own.

42. Shmuel Niger, as quoted by Elkhonon Vogler, "Moyshe Kulbak the Poet of Raw Earth" [in Yiddish], *Di goldene keyt* 43(1962): 119.

43. *Zelmenyaner* I: 20.

44. Ibid: 79. Quoted from Moyshe Kulbak, "Di shtot [The City]," in *Memorial Book for A. Vayter* [pseud. Isaac-Meir Devenishski; in Yiddish] (Vilna: Rosenthal Pubs., 1920): Section for Belles Lettres and Criticism: 40.

45. *Zelmenyaner* II: 215–16.

46. The book is available in two English versions: *The Stormy Life of Lasik Roitschwantz*, trans. Leonid Borochowicz and Gertrude Flor (New York: Polyglot Library, 1960) and the much more readable *The Stormy Life of Laz Roitshvantz*, trans. Alec Brown (London: Elek Books, 1965). The following citations to the quotations here are from the latter: pp. 6, 46, 246.

47. Vasily Grossman, *Life and Fate*, trans. Robert Chandler (London: Collings Harvill, 1985): 94.

48. See Simon Markish, *Le Cas Grossman*, trans. Dominique Negrel (Jerusalem and Paris: Centre for Research and Documentation on East-European Jewry and Julliard/L'Age d'Homme, 1983); John Garrard and Carol Garrard, *The Bones of Berdichev: The Life and Fate of Vasily Grossman* (New York: Free Press, 1996).

49. See Vasily Grossman, "The Murder of Jews in Berdichev," in *The Black Book*, ed. Ilya Ehrenburg and Vasily Grossman, trans. John Glad and James S. Levine (New York: Holocaust Library, 1980): 3–24.

50. *Life and Fate*: 402.

51. Irving Howe, "Writing and the Holocaust," *The New Republic* (October 27, 1986): 29.

52. Vasily Grossman, *Life and Fate*: 348.

53. Ibid.: 230.

54. Ibid.: 546.

55. *The Bones of Berdichev*: 272.

56. See, among other emerging accounts based on Soviet secret files, Vitaly Shentalinsky, *Arrested Voices: Resurrecting the Disappeared Writers of the Soviet Regime*, trans. John Crowfoot, introduction by Robert Conquest (New York: Martin Kessler Books, The Free Press, 1993): 22–71. In one of many helpful notes, Shentalinsky reminds the reader that the Soviet secret police changed its title eight times: Cheka (1917–23), GPU (1922–23); OGPU (1923–34); NKVD (1934–43); NKGB (1943–46); MGB (1946–53); MVD (1953–54); and KGB from 1954.

57. Ibid.: 30–31.

58. "Babel Answers Questions about his Work," in *You Must Know Everything*: 221.

Chapter 4. Between the Wars

1. Melekh Ravitch, *Dos mayse-bukh fun mayn lebn* [The Storybook of My Life], vol. 3 (Tel Aviv: I. L. Peretz Publishing House, 1975): 20.

2. Isaac Bashevis (Singer) *Di familye mushkat*, 2 vols. (New York: Morris S. Sklarsky, 1950): 748. The translation is from *The Family Moskat* by A. H. Gross (New York: Noonday Press, 1950): 611. The passage ends the English version but not the Yiddish.

3. Isaac Bashevis Singer, *My Father's Court: Sequel Collection* [in Yiddish], selected with an introduction by Chone Shmeruk (Jerusalem: Magnes Press, 1996): 225. Originally in *Forverts*, 14 November 1955. My translation.

4. This confusing period is described with historical precision in Henry Abramson, *A Prayer for the Government: Ukrainians and Jews in Revolutionary Times, 1917–1920* (Cambridge, Mass.: Ukrainian Research Institute and Center for Jewish Studies, Harvard University, 1999).

5. Isaac Babel, *Collected Stories* trans. David McDuff (London: Penguin Books, 1994): 123.

6. Written after the Second World War by Antoni Slonimski, "Elegia Miastezek Zydowskich [Elegy on Jewish Shtetlakh]," in *Poezje Zebrane* [Collected Poems] (Warsaw: Panstwowy Instytut Wydawniczy, 1964): 495.

7. Ezra Mendelsohn, *The Jews of East Central Europe Between the World Wars* (Bloomington: Indiana University Press, 1983): 30.

8. Ravitch, *Dos mayse bukh fun mayn lebn* II: 520.

9. In much the same spirit, the Polish Jewish writer Alexander Wat recalled that his whole generation had reacted with spiritual joy to the "catastrophism" of war and revolution—because after the destruction of everything in an absolute earthquake, "here, precisely, something new could be built."

10. Yechiel Szeintuch, *Preliminary Inventory of Yiddish Dailies and Periodicals Published in Poland Between the Two World Wars* (Jerusalem: Hebrew University Center for Research on the History and Culture of Polish Jews, 1986).

11. This description of the "bourse" is in "Concerning Yiddish Literature in Poland" [in Yiddish], *Di zukunft* (August 1943): 468–475. For Singer's relations with women in the Club see Janet Hadda, *Isaac Bashevis Singer: A Life* (New York: Oxford University Press, 1997): 67–69. This connection between women and Tlomackie 13 figures prominently in the fictionalized memoir *The Writers' Club* [in Yiddish], published under the pseudonym Yitzhak Warshavski in weekly segments in *Forverts* beginning 13 January 1956. See also Isaac Bashevis, *Figures and Episodes from the Writers' Club* [in Yiddish], *Forverts* 28 June 1979 to 10 January 1980.

12. See Nathan Cohen, "The Jewish Literary and Journalistic Center in Warsaw 1920–1942 through the Prism of the Association of Jewish Writers and Journalists" (unpublished dissertation in Hebrew, Jerusalem, the Hebrew University, 1995): chap. 6.

13. Ravitch, *Dos mayse-bukh*, 3: 125. A file catalogue of these lectures can be found in the Melekh Ravitch Archive of the National Library in Jerusalem.

14 Reports on membership and this disrupted lecture are in *Literarishe bleter*, 10 January 1930, 7 February 1930.

15. For complete list of translations see David Neal Miller, *Bibliography of Isaac Bashevis Singer 1924–1949* (New York: Peter Land, 1983): 233–239.

16. For information about Esther Kreitman and her London circle, see Leonard Prager, *Yiddish Culture in Britain: A Guide* (Frankfurt: Peter Lang, 1990).

17. Magdalena Opalski, "Wiadomości Literackie: Polemics on the Jewish Question, 1924–1939," in *The Jews of Poland Between Two World Wars*, ed. Yisrael Gutman et al. (Hanover and London: Brandeis University Press and University Press of New England, 1989): 449.

18. Aleksander Wat, *My Century*, trans. Richard Lourie (Berkeley: University of California Press, 1988): 70.

19. Isaac Deutscher, *The Non-Jewish Jew and Other Essays*, ed. Tamara Deutscher (Boston: Alyson Publications, 1968): 40.

20. Evgenia Prokop-Janiec, *Interwar Polish-Jewish Literature as a Cultural and Artistic Phenomenon* [in Polish] (Krakow: Universitas, 1992), unpublished translation by Abe Shenitzer, with the editorial assistance of Hardy Grant.

21. Chone Shmeruk, "Hebrew-Yiddish-Polish: A Trilingual Jewish Culture," in *The Jews of Poland Between Two World Wars*: 285–311. The statistics on the Polish-Jewish press are from p. 306. The term *polysystem* is adapted from Itamar Even-Zohar (see p. 329). See also by Shmeruk, "Aspects of the History of Warsaw as a Yiddish Literary Center," *Polin* 3 (1988): 140–155; Michael C. Steinlauf, "The Polish-Jewish Daily Press," *Polin* 2 (1987): 219–245; and Andrzej Paczkowski, "The Jewish Press in the Political Life of the Second Republic," *Polin* 8 (1994): 176–193.

22. Daniel Singer, "Armed with a Pen," in *Isaac Deutscher: The Man and His Work*, ed. David Horowitz (London: Macdonald, 1971): 22–23.

23. I[srael] J[oshua] Singer, *Of a World That Is No More* [in Yiddish] (New York: Matones, 1946): 33; Janet Hadda *Isaac Bashevis Singer: A Life* (New York: Oxford University Press, 1997): 27.

24. I. J. Singer, *Erd-vey* [Earth-Woe, a drama in three scenes] (Warsaw: Kultur-Lige, 1922).

25. The stories are "Zamd" (1922) and "Altshtot" (1923), translated as "Sand" and "Old City," by Maurice Samuel in I. J. Singer, *The River Breaks Up* (New York: Vanguard Press,1938): 177–214; 3–24. For a complete bibliography and reliable study of the works of I. J. Singer, see Anita Norich, *The Homeless Imagination in the Fiction of Israel Joshua Singer* (Bloomington: Indiana University Press, 1991).

26. "A derklerung fun shriftshteler I.J.Zinger [A Statement by the Writer I. J. Singer]," *Folkstsaytung* (20 April 1928). Incident recounted by Norich: 21 and Ravitch, *Dos mayse-bukh*: 3: 169–173.

27. I. J. Singer, *"Di brider ashkenazi,"* *Forverts*, 1 December 1934–7 July, 1935, daily (excluding Sunday), dated by the author "Warsaw-New York, 1933–35," and published in book form by Bzoza (Warsaw), 1936; Max N. Maisel (New York), 1937; and Matones (New York), 1951. Translated as *The Brothers Ashkenazi* by Maurice Samuel (New York: Knopf, 1936) and by Joseph Singer (New York: Penguin, 1980). Quotations are from this latter edition.

28. The connection with Reymont was suggested by the title of a paper by Monika Adamczyk-Garbowska on the two authors.

29. Wladyslaw Reymont, *Ziemia obiecana*, [The Promised Land], trans. M. H. Dziewicki (New York: Alfred A. Knopf, 1927): vol. 1, 173. I have slightly modified the translation. Reymont won the Nobel Prize in 1924.

30. Ibid.: 293.

31. *The Brothers Ashkenazi*: 6.

32. This is the hypothesis of Jacob Katz, argued in *From Prejudice to Destruction: Antisemitism 1700–1933* (Cambridge, Mass.: Harvard University Press, 1980): 97–104.

33. *Di brider ashkenazi*: vol. 2, 88. This sentence is missing from the Singer translation. (The Yiddish novel was originally issued in three volumes.)

34. *The Brothers Ashkenazi*: 8.

35. Ibid: 3–4.

36. Ibid: 61.

37. Ibid.: 618.

38. *Di brider ashkenazi*: vol. 3, 215, my translation. Joseph Singer's translation heightens the irony by ending the chapter with this sentence; see *The Brothers Ashkenazi*: 402.

39. Sholem Asch, "In a karnivalnakht" [On a Carnival Night] (1909) in *From the shtetl to the Wide World* [in Yiddish], ed. Shmuel Rozhansky (Buenos Aires: Musterverk fun der yidisher literatur, 1972): 216–228.

40. *The Brothers Ashkenazi*: 360.

41. Esther Kreitman, "The New World," in *Yikhes, dertseylungen un skitsn* [Lineage, Stories and Sketches] (London: Narod Press, 1950): 25. A translation of this story by Barbara Harshav is in *Found Treasures:Stories by Yiddish Women Writers*, ed. Frieda Forman, Ethel Raicus, Sarah Silberstein Swartz, and Margie Wolfe (Toronto: Second Story Press, 1994): 77–82.

42. Kadya Molodovsky, "Froyen-lider:VI [Women-Poems]," trans. Kathryn Hellerstein, in *Paper Bridges:Selected Poems of Kadya Molodovsky*, ed. Kathryn Hellerstein (Detroit:Wayne State University Press, 1999): 79.

43. Rachel Korn, "I'm Soaked Through with You," trans. Ruth Whitman, from her *An-*

thology of Modern Yiddish Poetry: Bilingual Edition (Detroit: Wayne State University Press, 1995): 75.

44. Esther Kreitman, *Der sheydim-tants* [The Devils' Dance] (Warsaw: 1936). Translated as *Deborah* by Maurice Carr (London: W. and G. Foyle, 1946): 97. Quotations are from the latter edition.

45. *Deborah:* 27.

46. Ibid.: 216.

47. Esther Kreitman, *Briliantn* [Diamonds]. (London:W.& G. Foyle's Hebrew Department, 1944). An author's note indicates that the book was written 1936–1939.

48. *Deborah:* 293.

49. Esther Kreitman, *Deborah,* trans. Maurice Carr, with a new introduction by Clive Sinclair (London:Virago Press, 1983). The quotation is from the back cover.

50. Ibid.: 363.

51. Uri Zvi Greenberg, "In malkhes fun tseylem," in *Albatros,* vol. 1 (Warsaw: 1922):15–24. Reprinted in *Collected Yiddish Works,* vol. 2 (Jerusalem: Magnes Press, 1979): 470.

52. Gershom Scholem, *Sabbetai Sevi:The Mystical Messiah,* trans. by R. J. Zwi Werblowsky (Princeton, N.J.: Princeton University Press, 1973). In the course of his analysis, Scholem says that the characteristic feature of Polish kabbalism, its "unique fascination with the sphere of evil," finds its best expression in Bashevis Singer's stories: (pp. 82–83). Scholem's first published essay on the subject of Jewish messianism was "Redemption through Sin," [in Hebrew], *Keneset* 2 (1937): 347–92.

53. Isaac Bashevis Singer, *Der sotn in goray* (Warsaw: Library of the Yiddish PEN Club, 1935), translated as *Satan in Goray* by Jacob Sloan, with an introduction by Ruth R. Wisse (New York: Farrar, Straus, & Giroux, 1995): 3–4. This is the most reliable of Bashevis Singer's translations in its loyalty to the original text. All references are to this edition. The discussion of this book and some of the information in this chapter are based on my Introduction.

54. Hadda: 72–77.

55. Seth L. Wolitz, "*Satan in Goray* as Parable," *Prooftexts* (January 1989): 20. Wolitz suggests that Rechele-Rachel functions as an ambiguous redemptive figure who dies in childbirth so that the people Israel may be restored.

56. *Satan in Goray:* 147–48

57. Ibid.: 159.

58. Ibid.: 214.

59. Isaac Bashevis's circumscribed idea of the possibilities that lie open for the Yiddish writer is deftly and wittily set out in the essays "Concerning Yiddish Literature in Poland," [in Yiddish], *Di zukunft* 48(August 1943) and "Problems of Yiddish Prose in America," [in Yiddish] *Svive,* (March-April 1943), translated by Robert Wolf in *Prooftexts* (January 1989): 5–12.

60. Isaac Bashevis Singer, in interview with Joel Blocker and Richard Elman, *Commentary* (November 1963): 368.

61. This purism may have contributed to the prologued "writer's block" he experienced after coming to America. Bashevis's novels and stories that are set in America stay notably within the circles of Jewish survivors and new immigrants or else follow the author on speaking trips to South America or Israel.

62. *Satan in Goray:* 34. Singer had taken almost verbatim descriptions from the Jewish historical chronicles, but he situated his action in a clearly fictional place that lay "at the end of the world." See Nathan [Notah] Hanover, *Sefer yeven metsulah,* with notes by I. Halperin and an introduction by Y. Fichman (Tel Aviv: Hakibbutz Hameuchad, 1966):

31–32; translated as *Abyss of Despair* by Abraham J. Mesch (New Brunswick, N.J.: Transaction Books, 1983): 43.

63. The term is Dan Miron's. See "Passivity and Narration:The Spell of Bashevis Singer," trans. by Uriel Miron, *Judaism* 41:1 (Winter 1992): 6–17.

64. Isaac Bashevis, "A Few Words About Myself" [in Yiddish], *Svive* (May 1962): 17.

65. Aaron Zeitlin writes, "In today's Yiddish literature, which faithfully submits to the harness of proletarian 'requirements,' works like Bashevis's are a *splendid anachronism* [emphasis in the original]." See foreword to 1935 edition of *Der sotn in goray*:vi. The sentence was deleted from the two subsequent Yiddish editions of the book, published in New York, 1943, and in Jerusalem 1972.

Chapter 5. A Farewell to Poland

1. Jacob Glatstein, "Vegener [Wagons]," in *Gedenklider* [In Remembrance: Poems] (New York: Farlag Yidisher kemfer, 1943): 46. Translated by Chana Bloch in *The Penguin Book of Modern Yiddish Verse*, ed. Irving Howe, Ruth R. Wisse, and Chone Shmeruk (New York: Viking Penguin, 1987): 432–433.

2. Michael Andre Bernstein, *Foregone Conclusions: Against Apocalyptic History* (Berkeley: University of California Press, 1994). These phrases appear on pp. 95 and 2.

3. Thomas Mann, "The Making of *The Magic Mountain*" (1953), published as afterword to the novel in its reset edition (New York: Alfred. A. Knopf, 1955): 719–729.

4. Alfred Doblin, *Journey to Poland* [Reise in Polen], trans. Joachim Neugroschel, ed. Heinz Graber (London: I. B. Tauris & Co. Ltd., 1991); Walter Benjamin, *Moscow Diary* [Moskaver Tagebuch], trans. Richard Sieburth, ed. Gary Smith (Cambridge, Mass: Harvard University Press, 1986).

5. Shmuel Niger, "Concerning the Ethnonational Role of Yiddish and Yiddish Culture" [in Yiddish; 1950], reprinted in Joshua A. Fishman, ed., *Never Say Die! A Thousand Years of Yiddish in Jewish Life and Letters* (The Hague: Mouton, 1981): 137.

6. Jacob Glatstein, *Ven yash iz geforn* (New York: Farlag Inzikh, 1938). Translated as *Homeward Bound* by A. Zahaven (New York: Thomas Yoseloff, 1969); *Ven yash iz gekumen* (New York: Sklarsky, 1940), translated as *Homecoming at Twilight* by N. Guterman, with foreword by Maurice Samuel (New York: Thomas Yoseloff, 1962). References will be to *Yash* I and to *Homecoming*. Since the translation of *Yash* I is partial and not wholly reliable, I offer my own translations, sometimes based on Zahaven.

7. Dan Miron, Afterword to *Kesheyash nasah*, translation of *Ven yash iz goforn* (Tel Aviv: Hakibbutz Hameukhad and Sifre Siman Kriah, 1994): 210. Glatstein's sketch in dramatic form— "Nakhman Watchmaker," described as "a fragment of *Ven yash is tsurikgeforn* [When Yash Returned], the third part of the trilogy in preparation" in the Tel Aviv literary quarterly *Di Goldene Keyt* 30 (1958): 256–261—does not really indicate in which direction this third novel would have gone.

8. For a longer introduction to Glatstein, see my review article "Found in America," in *The New Republic* (September 18 & 25): 52–57; Janet R. Hadda, *Yankev Glatshteyn*, (Boston:Twayne Publishers 1980).

9. From the manifesto "Introspectivism" in *In zikh* (New York: Max Maisel, 1920): 7–8, translated by Benjamin and Barbara Harshav in their *American Yiddish Poetry:A Bilingual Anthology* (Berkeley: University of California Press, 1986): 776.

10. Benjamin Harshav, *Language in a Time of Revolution* (Berkeley: University of California Press, 1993): 17.

11. A. Leyeles, "More About the Spelling of Hebrew Words" [in Yiddish], *In zikh* (October 1940): 188–-89.

12. Some recent discussions of the aesthetics of Inzikh and Glatstein can be found in Yael S. Feldman, "Jewish Literary Modernism and Language Identity: The Case of In Zikh," *Yiddish* 6:1(1985): 44–54; Benjamin Harshav, *The Meaning of Yiddish* (Berkeley: University of California Press, 1990): 175–186; Abraham Novershtern, "The Young Glatstein and the Structure of His First Book of Poems," *Prooftexts* 6 (1986): 131–146; David G. Roskies, "The Achievement of American Yiddish Modernism," in *Go and Study: Essays in Honor of Alfred Jospe,* ed. Raphael Jospe and Samuel Z. Fishman (Washington, D.C: B'nai B'rith Hillel Foundations 1980): 353–368. The only book-length English study of the poet remains *Yankev Glatshteyn* by Janet R. Hadda.

13. Abraham Shulman, "Yankev glatshteyn's kritik [Glatstein's Criticism]," *Unzer Shtime* (4 January 1961): 3.

14. Marya Konopnicka, "A Yak Poszedl Krol . . .," in *Poezye,* ed. Jan Czubek (Warsaw: Gebethner and Wolff): vol. 3, 23.

15. I am indebted for this information about the link between Yash and Konopnicka's "O Janku Wedrowniczku" to Monika Adamczyk-Garbowska, whose research into Yiddish and Polish literature is opening a badly neglected area of comparative study.

16. Jacob Glatstein, "Ven yash iz geforn," *Inzikh* 6 (September–October 1934): 178. The quote below follows on this page.

17. I [saac] Bashevis, "Jacob Glatstein's *Ven yush iz geforn,*" *Tzukunft* (March 1939): 182.

18. *Yash* I: 37. The contraction God Abraham conveys the child's fused image.

19. Yankev Glatshteyn, "Zhurnalizm un poezye [Journalism and Poetry]," *Inzikh* 39 (October 1937): 71. The quoted phrase appears on p. 69.

20. *Yash* I:39.

21. Dan Miron draws attention to the connection between the author's golden ears and the mother's waxen ears in his Afterword, p. 217 ff. He also compares this novel with Agnon's and stresses the point I make about the absence of a homecoming scene.

22. *Yash* I: 222.

23. *Homecoming at Twilight:* 124–25.

24. Ibid.: 146.

25. Ibid.: 243.

26. Ibid.: 252.

27. Ibid.: 253.

28. See reference for the epigraph to this chapter.

29. Of the immense secondary literature on Agnon, I am particularly indebted to the essays on the novel by Shimon Halkin and Gershon Shaked, reprinted in *Sh. Y. Agnon babikoret haivrit,* Vol. 2: *Parshanut leromanim* [S. Y. Agnon, Critical Essays on His Writings, Vol. 2: Interpretations of the Novels] (Tel Aviv: Open University, 1992): 180–194, 195–227, and by Arnold Band, *Nostalgia and Nightmare: A Study in the Fiction of S. Y. Agnon* (Berkeley: 1968): 283–327, and to Dan Miron's discussion of the author in *Harofeh hamedumeh* [Le Medecin Imaginaire: Studies in Classical Jewish Fiction] (Tel Aviv: Hakibbutz Hameuchad, 1995): 161–343.

30. Shmuel Yosef Agnon, *Oreakh natah lalun* (Jerusalem: Schocken, Books, 1976): 7. All references are to this edition and to the English translation by Misha Louvish, *A Guest for the Night* (New York: Schocken Books, 1968): 1. The shortened titles *Oreakh* and *Guest* are used in the following notes.

31. See Anne Golomb Hoffman, *S. Y. Agnon and the Drama of Writing* (Albany: State Uni-

versity of New York, 1990): 78, and Barukh Kurzweil, *Masot al sipure Sh. Y. Agnon* [Essays on the Stories of S. Y. Agnon] (Jerusalem: Schocken Books, 1970): 51ff. Gershon Shaked suggests that the wordplay illustrates the author's ambivalence toward the town, but in *Guest for the Night*, unlike the works of Hebrew Enlightenment fiction that routinely parodied locations through invidious fictitious names, it is not clear how much of the spoilage is attributable to the Jewish inhabitants and how much to the damage that has been done to it by others. See Gershon Shaked, *Shmuel Yosef Agnon: A Revolutionary Traditionalist*, trans. Jeffrey M. Green (New York: New York University Press, 1989): 21.

32. *Oreakh*: 33; *Guest*: 30.

33. *Oreakh*: 8; *Guest*: 2.

34. Nitza Ben-Dov, *Agnon's Art of Indirection: Uncovering Latent Content in the Fiction of S. Y. Agnon* (Leiden, New York: E. J. Brill, 1993): 15.

35. *Guest*: 43.

36. For a full account of the visit, see Dan Laor, *S. Y.Agnon: New Perspectives* [in Hebrew]. (Tel Aviv: Sifriat Poalim, 1995): 154–174.

37. Shimon Halkin, on "Oreah Natah Lalun," [in Hebrew] in *S. Y. Agnon: Critical Essays on His Writings*, vol. 2 (Interpretation of his novels), ed. Avinoam Barshai (Tel Aviv: The Open University and Schocken Publishing House, 1992): 192.

38. Dan Miron points out that in this novel Agnon overcame his usual problems with closure. See his "Domesticating a Foreign Genre: Agnon's Transactions with the Novel," *Prooftexts* 7 (1987): 1–27.

39. *Oreakh*: 445; *Guest*: 477.

40. Agnon's version of the legend stands as the motto of *Polin*, the annual of studies in Polish Jewry begun in 1984.

41. The Book of Jeremiah 14: 7–8, *Tanakh: A New Translation of The Holy Scriptures According to the Traditional Hebrew Text* (Philadelphia: The Jewish Publication Society, 1985): 800–801.

42. *Oreakh*: 14; *Guest*: 8.

43. See *Oxford Universal English Dictionary*, 3rd ed., s. v. "Key." The Hebrew *Bibliography of Bibliographies* is called "The Key of Keys."

44. Yael Feldman, "The Latent and the Manifest: Freudianism in *A Guest for the Night*," *Prooftexts* (January 1987): 30.

45. Ibid.: 35.

46. Robert Alter, *The Invention of Hebrew Prose: Modern Fiction and the Language of Realism* (Seattle: University of Washington Press, 1988), 94–95.

47. *Guest*: 114.

48. *Oreakh*: 143; *Guest*: 149–50.

49. *Guest*: 136.

50. *Oreakh*: 383; *Guest*: 409.

51. Baruch Hochman arrives at this conclusion in his evocative memoir "An Afternoon with Agnon," *The American Scholar* (Winter 1988): 99.

Chapter 6. *Shoah, Khurbn,* Holocaust

1. Sh [merke] Kaczerginski, *The Destruction of Jewish Vilna* [in Yiddish] (New York: CYCO Publishers, 1947): 56–57.

2. Lawrence Langer writes, "Fifty years after the havoc, we have such an abundance of texts that Holocaust literature has grown into a genre of its own, needing neither excuse

nor vindication." He does not say what this "genre" comprises. See his *A Holocaust Anthology* (New York: Oxford University Press, 1995): 4.

3. Alexander Donat, *The Holocaust Kingdom* (New York: Holt, Rinehart, 1965). This book remains one of the clearest detailed eyewitness accounts of the Warsaw ghetto and the Maidanek death camp.

4. Rachel Auerbach, *Our Reckoning with the German People* [in Yiddish] (Tel Aviv: Hotsaat Hapoalim, 1952): 6.

5. Rachel Auerbach, *On the Fields of Treblinka* [in Yiddish] (Warsaw.: Central Jewish Historical Commission of Polish Jews, 1947): 29.

6. Auerbach cannot avoid the problem of aesthetics. The most experienced member of the investigative commission finds the skeleton of a child at the rim of a pit. A piece of skin is sticking to the bone. A second member of the commission, himself a survivor of Treblinka, lifts the remains and wraps it first in a newspaper, then in his coat, and holds it to his heart. "Maybe this is the foot of my little son that I brought here," he says. Auerbach comments: "The uncomfortable thing is that every one of us is similarly given to dramatic utterances (*melitsa*), which may either be appropriate or altogether superfluous, but can also be true, the plain factual truth." Ibid.: 107.

7. Jean Améry, *At the Mind's Limits: Contemplations by a Survivor on Auschwitz and its Realities,* trans. Sidney Rosenfeld and Stella P. Rosenfeld (Bloomington: Indiana University Press, 1980): 21–40.

8. *The Diary of Dawid Rubinowicz,* trans. from the Polish by Derek Bowman (Edmonds: Wash.: Creative Options 1982); *The Diary of Eva Heyman,* trans. Moshe M. Kohn (Jerusalem: Yad Vashem, 1971), based on the Hebrew translation from the Hungarian.

9. Yitskhok Rudashevski, *The Diary of the Vilna Ghetto, June 1941-April 1943,* translated from Yiddish by Percy Matenko (Tel Aviv: Ghetto Fighters' House and Hakibbutz Hameuchad, 1973): 30. Entry dated July 8, 1941.

10. David Weiss Halivni, *The Book and the Sword* (New York: Farrar, Straus & Giroux, 1996): 67–69. The author provides a gloss on the title: "The sword and the book came down from heaven tied to each other. Said the Almighty, "If you keep what is written in this book, you will be spared this sword; if not, you will be consumed by it." (Midrash Rabbah Deuteronomy 4: 2) "We clung to the book, yet we were consumed by the sword."

11. Jorge Semprun, *Life and Literature,* trans. from the French by Linda Coverdale (New York: Viking, 1997): 35–37. In this fascinating explanation for having made his friend Jewish, "because we wanted to liquidate all oppression and because the Jew—even passive, even resigned—was the intolerable embodiment of the oppressed," Semprun inadvertently shows the dangers of falsification in the name of such apparent homage. He goes on to describe a "quite real" Jew who is dying before his eyes in Buchenwald, and to prove his authentic memory, he describes this dying Jew chanting the Kaddish in Yiddish! Even supposing that the man was chanting the prayer for the dead over himself, the Kaddish is in Aramaic, not Yiddish.

12. Tadeusz Borowski, *This Way for the Gas, Ladies and Gentlemen and Other Stories,* trans. Barbara Vedder (New York: Viking Press, 1967): 64.

13. Ernst Wiechert, *Forest of the Dead* [Der Totenwald], trans. Ursula Stechow (New York: Greenberg Publisher, 1947): 72–73.

14. Romain Gary, *La Danse de Gengis Cohn* (Paris: Gallimard, 1967). Translated by Romain Gary with the assistance of Camille Sykes, *The Dance of Genghis Cohn* (New York: World, 1968).

15. Theodor W. Adorno, "Cultural Criticism and Society," in *Prisms,* trans. Samuel and Sherry Weber (Cambridge, Mass.: The MIT Press, 1981): 34.

16. George Steiner speaks of the "death of the German language" as a consequence of Nazi savagery in that language. "Everything forgets. But not a language. When it has been injected with falsehood, only the most drastic truth can cleanse it." In *Language and Silence: Essays on Language, Literature, and the Inhuman* (New York: Athenaum, 1967): 109.

17. Walter Benjamin, "Theses on the Philosophy of History," in *Illuminations*, edited and with an introduction by Hannah Arendt, trans. Harry Zohn (New York: Schocken Books, 1968): 256.

18. On Sutzkever's certainty that he owed his survival to his poetry, see my essay "The Last Great Yiddish Poet?" *Commentary* (November 1983): 41–48.

19. David G. Roskies, *Against the Apocalypse: Responses to Catastrophe in Modern Jewish Culture* (Cambridge, Mass.: Harvard University Press, 1984): 1–14.

20. With this question Judith Klein opens her inquiry *Literatur und Genozid: Darstellungen der nationalsozialistischen Massenvernichtung in der französischen Literatur* (Wien: Bohlau Verlag, 1992): 11.

21. Berel Lang, *Act and Idea in the Nazi Genocide* (Chicago: The University of Chicago Press, 1990): xxi. Lang evidently succumbed to the pressure of the term when he named his anthology of essays *Writing and the Holocaust* (New York: Holmes & Meier, 1988).

22. See the entry by Uriel Tal for *Holocaust* in *Encyclopedia of the Holocaust*, ed. Israel Gutman vol. 2, 681.

23. Dina Porat, *The Blue and the Yellow Stars of David: The Zionist Leadership in Palestine and the Holocaust 1939–45* (Cambridge, Mass.: Harvard University Press, 1990): 2. "[Shoah] was used at least as early as December 1938," at a meeting of the Mapai [Labor Party] leadership, discussing the events of Kristallnacht, November 9–10, 1938.

24. I realize that *khurbn* is usually transcribed phonetically as *khurbm*, following its pronunciation in Yiddish, but for those who recognize the term *khurban* (destruction), I prefer to suggest the Yiddish spelling rather than the pronunciation.

25. See Herman Kruk, *Diary of the Vilna Ghetto* [in Yiddish], ed. Mordecai Bernstein (New York: YIVO, 1961): 415–16. An annotated English translation of the Kruk diary is being prepared by Benjamin and Barbara Harshav for Yale University Press, but all translations here are mine. See also Zelig Kalmanovitch, *A Diary from the Ghetto in the Nazi Vilna* [in Hebrew], ed. Shalom Luria (Tel Aviv: Sifriat Poalim: 1977): 94; "A Diary of the Nazi Ghetto in Vilna," ed. Shlomo Noble, trans. Koppel S. Pinson, *YIVO Annual of Jewish Social Science* (New York: YIVO Scientific Institute, 1953): 9–81.

26. Ezra Mendelsohn, *Modern Jewish Politics* (New York: Oxford University Press, 1993): 43.

27. Mark Dworzecki, *The Struggle and Fall of Jerusalem of Lithuania: History of the Vilna Ghetto* [In Yiddish] (Paris: Union Populaire Juive, 1948): 66.

28. Kruk: 4.

29. Samuel David Kassow, "Vilna and Warsaw, Two Ghetto Diaries: Herman Kruk and Emanuel Ringelblum," in *Holocaust Chronicles: Individualizing the Holocaust through Diaries and Other Contemporaneous Personal Accounts*, ed. Robert Moses Shapiro (Hoboken, N.J.: Ktav, 1999): 192.

30. Kruk: 338.

31. Lucy S. Dawidowicz, *The War Against the Jews 1933–1945* (New York: Holt, Rinehart & Winston, 1975): 341.

32. For a description of the project, see Emanuel Ringelblum, "Oyneg Shabbes," trans. Elinor Robinson, in *The Literature of Destruction,*: 386–98.

33. Kruk: 51–55.

34. Kruk, entry of June 23, 1943: 578.

35. Kruk: 19.

36. Kruk, entry for January 17, 1942: 136.

37. Kalmanovitch: 51.

38. Moshe Flinker, *Young Moshe's Diary*, translated from the Hebrew by Shaul Esh (Jerusalem: Yad Vashem, 1965): 91, 108.

39. Dov Sadan, Foreword, in Hebrew version of Flinker's *Diary* (Jerusalem: Yad Vashem, 1958): 1–6.

40. For one such example, readers may wish to compare the Katsh translation of Chaim A. Kaplan's *Scroll of Agony* (cited in note 43) with the excerpt translated by Jeffrey Green in *The Literature of Destruction* (cited in note 32): 435–449. The editor David G. Roskies draws attention to this point.

41. Paul Fussell, *Thank God for the Atom Bomb* (New York: Summit Books, 1988): 75.

42. Ringelblum, "Oyneg Shabbes": 391.

43. *Scroll of Agony: The Warsaw Diary of Chaim A. Kaplan*, trans. and ed. Abraham I. Katsh (New York: Macmillan Co., 1965): 40. Entry of the evening of August 4, 1942.

44. See Reizl Korczak, *Flames in the Dust* [in Hebrew] (Moreshet: Beit Ahdut al shem Mordecai Anilewicz, 1965).

45. See Dworzecki, note 27; Abraham Sutzkever, *From the Vilna Ghetto* [in Yiddish]. (Moscow: Der Emes, 1946); Sz. Kaczerginski, *I Was a Partisan*, 2 vols. [in Yiddish] (Buenos Aires: Committee of the author's friends, 1952).

46. *Bleter vegn vilne* [Anthology of Materials About Vilna], ed. L. Ran and L. Koriski (Lodz: Organization of Vilna Jews in Poland, 1947): 11–12.

47. Elias Schulman, *The Holocaust in Yiddish Literature* (New York: Workmen's Circle, 1983): 5.

48. Dworzecki: 64.

49. Jerzy Kosinski, *The Painted Bird* (New York: Modern Library: 1983): 51.

50. Sidra DeKoven Ezrahi, *By Words Alone: The Holocaust in Literature* (Chicago: The University of Chicago Press, 1980): 152–53. She calls Nazism the "concentrationary universe," the "concentrationary civilization."

51. Alvin H. Rosenfeld, *A Double Dying: Reflections on Holocaust Literature* (Bloomington: Indiana University Press, 1980): 76.

52. *The Painted Bird*: 97.

53. James Park Sloan, *Jerzy Kosinski: A Biography* (New York: Dutton, 1996). Sloan goes so far as to say that his parents schooled their son in antisemitism, "the attribution to Jews of accent, habits, which, if absorbed by the unsuspecting child, will corrupt his opportunities" (pp. 20–21).

54. Sara R. Horowitz discusses this trope in *Voicing the Void: Muteness and Memory in Holocaust Fiction* (Albany: State University of New York Press, 1997): 85. She discusses how the boy "forfeits his power of speech as he forfeits his ability to define himself," without reference to the author's identical predicament.

55. Piotr Rawicz, *Le Sang Du Ciel* (Paris: Gallimard, 1961). Translated as *Blood from the Sky* by Peter Wiles (New York: Harcourt, Brace & World, 1964). This quotation is on p. 3.

56. Ibid.: 25

57. Ibid.: 27.

58. Ibid.: 155–56.

59. Ibid.: 284.

60. Ibid.: 316.

61. Horowitz: 102–103.

62. Rawicz: 34.

63. Alain Finkielkraut, *Le Juif imaginaire* (Paris: Editions du Seuil, 1980). Translated as *The Imaginary Jew* by Kevin O'Neill and David Suchoff (Lincoln: University of Nebraska Press, 1994): 12.

64. Elaine Marks, *Marrano as Metaphor: The Jewish Presence in French Writing* (New York: Columbia University Press, 1996): 153.

65. Elie Wiesel, *All Rivers Run to the Sea* (New York: Alfred A. Knopf, 1995). None of the growing body of Wiesel criticism seems to go beyond the biographical facts that he provides.

66. Eliezer Wiesel, . . . *un di velt hot geshvign* (Buenos Aires: Association of Polish Jews in Argentina, 1956); in French, *La Nuit* (Paris: Les Editions de Minuit, 1958), with a preface by François Mauriac; in English, *Night*, translated from the French by Stella Rodway with a foreword by François Mauriac (New York: Hill & Wang, 1960). Page references here are to the aforementioned editions and in English to the twenty-fifth anniversary edition, with a preface by Robert McAfee Brown (New York: Bantam Books, 1982).

67. Ellen S. Fine, *Legacy of Night: The Literary Universe of Elie Wiesel* (Albany: State University of New York Press, 1982): 11. Fine writes that this work defies all categories, but she analyzes it no differently from the rest of Wiesel's fiction.

68. . . . *un di velt hot geshvign:* 131–32.

69. Kapo, from the Italian *capo* for "boss," was the concentration camp term for inmates appointed by the Nazi S.S. to head the prisoner work gangs.

70. *Night:* 62.

71. *La Nuit:* 105.

72. . . . *un di velt hot geshvign:* 7.

73. Ibid.: 209.

74. Ibid.: 245.

75. Naomi Seidman, "Elie Wiesel and the Scandal of Jewish Rage," *Jewish Social Studies,* Second Series, 3: 1 (Fall 1996): 15.

76. Foreword by Francois Mauriac to *Night:* ix.

77. Seidman: 16.

78. Biographical information is summarized in Gila Ramras-Rauch, *Aharon Appelfeld: The Holocaust and Beyond* (Bloomington: Indiana University Press, 1994). Yigal Schwartz describes Appelfeld's artistic development in his devoted study of the author, *Individual Lament and Tribal Eternity* [in Hebrew] (Jerusalem: The Hebrew University, 1996).

79. Aharon Appelfeld, "Cold Spring," trans. J. Sloane, in *In the Wilderness* (Jerusalem: Achshav, 1965): 87. Some of this discussion is drawn from my article "Aharon Appelfeld, Survivor," in *Commentary* (August 1983): 73–76.

80. Aharon Appelfeld, *Tzili: The Story of a Life,* trans. Dalya Bilu (New York: E. P. Dutton, 1983): 182.

81. Aharon Appelfeld, *Badenheim 1939* [Badenhaim,ir nofesh], trans. Dalya Bilu (Boston: D. R. Godine, 1980):49.

82. Susan Suleiman, "On Reading Holocaust Memoirs," *Poetics Today* 17: 3 (Fall 1996): 643.

83. Levin's front page review appeared in *New York Times Book Review,* June 15, 1952. See also his earlier notice of the book in a review of John Hersey's *The Wall* in *Congress Weekly* (publication of the American Jewish Congress), November 13, 1950.

84. *The Diary of Anne Frank: The Critical Edition*, ed. David Barnouw and Gerrold Van Der Stroom (New York: Doubleday, 1986). The lengths to which the editors go in establishing the authenticity of this work, including handwriting analysis, collation of variant texts, and historical reconstruction, testify to the ferocity of Holocaust denial as well as to the stake of the Dutch government in the work.

85. Ibid.: 416. Entry for 8 November 1943.

86. Ibid.: 599–600.

87. Willy Lindwer, *The Last Seven Months of Anne Frank* (New York: Pantheon, 1991): 110.

88. The diaries and letters of Etty Hillesum, though culturally as firm as Anne Frank's writing, are written against the disturbing, less inviting background of Westerbork.

89. David Barnouw, "Attacks on the Authenticity of the Diary," in *The Diary of Anne Frank: The Critical Edition*. 84–101. It was in response to the Holocaust deniers that the Netherlands State Institute for War Documentation undertook to publish a variorum edition of the *Diary*, with a full critical apparatus to confirm Anne's authorship beyond the shadow of a doubt.

90. Quoted by Ralph Melnick, *The Stolen Legacy of Anne Frank: Meyer Levin, Lillian Hellman, and the Staging of the Diary* (New Haven, Conn.: Yale University Press, 1997): 115–16.

91. See especially Meyer Levin, *The Obsession* (New York: Simon & Schuster, 1973); Lawrence Graver, *An Obsession with Anne Frank* (Berkeley: University of California Press, 1995); and Ralph Melnick, *The Stolen Legacy of Anne Frank*.

92. David Denby, "The Humanist and the Holocaust," *The New Republic* (28 July 1986): 28.

93. H. Stuart Hughes, *Prisoners of Hope: The Silver Age of the Italian Jews 1924–1974* (Cambridge, Mass.: Harvard University Press, 1983): 74.

94. Primo Levi, *The Periodic Table*, trans. Raymond Rosenthal (New York: Schocken Books, 1984): 35.

95. Primo Levi, *If This Is a Man*, trans. Stuart Woolf, published with *The Truce* (New York: Penguin, 1979): 19.

96. Alvin Rosenfeld, *A Double Dying*: 29.

97. Primo Levi, *The Drowned and the Saved*, trans. Raymond Rosenthal (New York: Summit Books, 1988): 145.

98. *If This Is a Man*: 21.

99. Ibid.: 79–80.

100. Ibid.: 135–36.

101. Mirna Cicioni, *Primo Levi: Bridges of Knowledge* (Oxford, U.K.: Berg, 1995): 36.

102. Levi, *The Drowned and the Saved*: 146.

103. Levi, in "The Canto of Ulysses," *If This is a Man*: 119.

104. Primo Levi, *If Not Now, When?*, trans. William Weaver, introduction by Irving Howe. (New York: Summit Books, 1985).

105. Primo Levi, *The Collected Poems*, trans. Ruth Feldman and Brian Swann (London: The Menard Press, 1976), in Italian; p. 13; in English; p. 21. This poem is now routinely published with *If This Is a Man*.

106. Michael C. Steinlauf, *Bondage to the Dead: Poland and the Memory of the Holocaust* (Syracuse; N.Y.: Syracuse University Press, 1997): 52-54. Steinlauf's first three chapters offer a finely nuanced analysis of postwar relations.

107. Henryk Grynberg, *Child of the Shadows* [Zydowska Wojna], trans. Celina Wieniewska (London: Valentine, Mitchell & Co. 1969).

108. Ibid.: 66.

109. Ibid.: 77

110. Henry Grynberg, *The Victory* [Zwyciestwo], trans. Richard Lourie (Evanston, Ill.: Northwestern University Press, 1993): 3.

111. Ibid.: 74.

112. Ibid.: 73–74.

113. Ibid.: 107.

114. Abraham Sutzkever, "Unter dayne vayse shte [Beneath the Whiteness of Your Stars]," trans. Leonard Wolf, in *The Literature of Destruction: Jewish Responses to Catastrophe*: 499.

115. Kadya Molodowsky, "El khonen," [Merciful God]," in *Paper Bridges: Selected Poems*, trans. and ed. Kathryn Hellerstein (Detroit: Wayne State University Press, 1999): 352–355. See also the anthology she edited, *Poems of the Khurbn 1940-1945* [in Yiddish] (Tel Aviv: Peretz farlag, 1962): 152–153.

116. Aaron Zeitlin, "To Be a Jew [*Zayn a yid*]," trans. Robert Friend, in *The Penguin Book of Modern Yiddish Verse*, ed. Irving Howe, Ruth R. Wisse, and Chone Shmeruk (New York: Viking, 1987): 538–539.

117. Jacob Glatstein, "Without Jews [*On yidn*]," trans. Cynthia Ozick, in *The Penguin Book of Modern Yiddish Verse*: 434–437.

118. Z. Segalovitch, "For Whom Are You God?," in *Poems of the Khurbn 1940–1945* [in Yiddish]: 171.

119. Itsik Manger, "Eve and the Apple Tree [*Khave un der eplboym*]," trans. Leonard Wolf, in *The Penguin Book of Modern Yiddish Verse*: 562–565.

120. Chaim Grade, "Mayn krig mit hersh raseyner," *Der yidisher kemfer* (28 September 1951): 33–44, translated as "My Quarrel with Hersh Rasseyner" by Milton Himmelfarb, *Commentary* (November 1953): 428–441. Since Himmelfarb's translation, subsequently reprinted in Irving Howe and Eliezer Greenberg's influential *A Treasury of Yiddish Stories* (New York: Viking Press, 1954), was slightly abridged, Herbert Paper issued a private, unedited typescript of the story in February 1982, revising Himmelfarb according to the original.

121. Joshua Sobol, *Ghetto*, translated from the Hebrew by Miriam Shlesinger (Tel Aviv: Institute for the Translation of Hebrew Literature, 1986): 59–60.

Chapter 7. The Zionist Fate in English Hands

1. Arthur Koestler, *Thieves in the Night* (New York: Macmillan Co., 1946): 356.

2. Graham Handley, Introduction to *Daniel Deronda* (Oxford, U.K.: Oxford University Press, 1988): ix. Further references to this edition.

3. George Eliot, letter to Harriet Beecher Stowe, 29 October 1876, quoted in William Baker, *George Eliot and Judaism* (Salzburg: Institut fur Englische Sprache und Literatur, 1975): 92.

4. *Daniel Deronda*: 3.

5. Ibid.: 396.

6. Ibid.: 37.

7. The critic Irving Howe saw in the anatomy of the bad marriage between Gwendolen and Grandcourt "a system of dehumanized personal relations . . . the barbarism that civilization lightly coats and readily becomes." See Irving Howe, "George Eliot and Radical Evil," in *Selected Writings 1950–1990* (San Diego, New York, London: Harcourt Brace Jovanovich, 1990): 353.

8. *Daniel Deronda*: 540.

9. H. M. Daleski, "Owning and Disowning: The Unity of *Daniel Deronda*," shows how

the book's theme of the forsaken child combines with that of the long-suffering Jewish people and how the children in the Jewish section of the book reverse the familial paradigm by redeeming their parents. In Alice Shalvi, ed., *Daniel Deronda: A Century Symposium* (Jerusalem: Jerusalem Academic Press, 1976): 67-85.

10. *Daniel Deronda*: 688.

11. The phrase is James Baldwin's, and it is launched in protest against what he calls the virtuous sentimentality of "Everybody's Protest Novel." See *Partisan Review* (June 1949):578–585. It is interesting that while some Black nationalists resented Beecher Stowe's implicit condescension, Jewish nationalists felt no such ambivalence toward George Eliot. The criticism of Eliot has come rather from those who resent her championship of Jewish nationalism, from one of the first reviewers in the *Evening Post* to Edward Said, suggesting either that Eliot did the better job of representing her minority or that winning the support of English readers for Jewish nationhood is more difficult than winning their support for abolition.

12. Harriet Beecher Stowe, *Uncle Tom's Cabin: A Norton Critical Edition* ed. Elizabeth Ammons (New York: W.W. Norton & Co., 1994): 272.

13. *Daniel Deronda*: 453.

14. Shmuel Werses provides a valuable overview of Jewish reception history in "*Daniel Deronda* in the Hebrew Press and Literature," [in Hebrew] in *Milashon el lashon* [From Language to Language: Literary Works and their Transformation in Hebrew Literature] (Jerusalem: Magnes Press, 1996): 406–425. See also the 1976 centennial symposium at the Hebrew University that saluted Eliot's remarkable ability to "convey her prophetic vision of revived Jewish nationhood": Alice Shalvi, ed., *Daniel Deronda: A Centenary Symposium*: 2 (no pagination).

15. Nahum Sokolow, *History of Zionism 1600-1918*, 2 vols. (London: Longmans, Green & Company, 1919): vol. 1, 209.

16. F. R. Leavis cites Henry James's contention that "all the Jewish part is at bottom cold" as support for his own suggestion that the book should have been called *Gwendolyn Harleth*. Cited in "George Eliot's Zionist Novel," *Commentary* (October 1960): 317–325.

17. Stuart Gilbert, *James Joyce's Ulysses: A Study* (New York: Alfred A. Knopf, 1930): 143.

18. James Joyce, *Ulysses* (New York: The Modern Library, 1934): 60–61.

19. Ibid.: 628.

20. See, e.g., Marilyn Reizbaum, "A Nightmare of History: Ireland's Jews and Joyce's *Ulysses*," in *Between "Race" and Culture: Representations of "The Jew" in English and American Literature*, ed. Bryan Cheyette (Stanford, Calif.: Stanford University Press, 1996): 102-113.

21. Harold Fisch, *The Dual Image: The Figure of the Jew in English and American Literature* (London: World Jewish Library, 1971): 84. Ira B. Nadel dubs Joyce an honorary Jew for his rabbinic sanctification of the word and his Israelitish "exodus" from Ireland. In *Joyce and the Jews* (Gainesville: University of Florida Press, 1996): 9.

22. Henry Roth, *Mercy of a Rude Stream*, Vol. 2: *A Diving Rock on the Hudson* (New York: St. Martin's Press, 1995): 116. This is only a fraction of the extended rant.

23. For a different perspective on the subject, see Hani al-Rahab, *The Zionist Character in the English Novel* (London: Third World Center for Research and Publishing, 1985); Andrew Furman, *Israel through the Jewish-American Imagination 1928–1995* (Albany: State University of New York Press, 1997).

24. Alfred Kazin, *On Native Grounds: A Study of American Prose Literature from 1890 to the Present* (Garden City: Doubleday & Co. 1956): 204.

25. Long neglected, Lewisohn is the subject of a recent biography that is the most ex-

haustive ever accorded an American Jewish writer: Ralph Melnick, *The Life and Work of Ludwig Lewisohn*, 2 vols. (Detroit: Wayne State University Press, 1998).

26. Ludwig Lewisohn, *The Island Within* (New York: Harper & Brothers, 1928): 289.

27. Ibid.: 346.

28. Melnick: vol. 1, 468.

29. *The Island Within*:268.

30. Ibid.: 278.

31. Ibid.: 235–236.

32. Maurice Samuel, *The Gentleman and the Jew: Twenty-five Centuries of Conflict in Manners and Morals* (Philadelphia: Jewish Publication Society, 1950): 57.

33. Ibid.: 82.

34. Cynthia Ozick, Foreword in *The Worlds of Maurice Samuel: Selected Writings*, ed. Milton Hindus (Philadelphia: Jewish Publication Society, 1977): xix.

35. Maurice Samuel, *The Outsider* (Boston: The Stratford Co., 1929): 157.

36. Ronald Sanders, "Maurice Samuel: An Appreciation," *Midstream* (February 1973): 55.

37. *The Outsider*: 65.

38. Arthur Koestler, *Arrow in the Blue* (New York: Macmillan Co., 1962): 118–119.

39. Mark Levene, *Arthur Koestler* (London: Oswald Wolff, 1984): 96.

40. Arthur Koestler, *Thieves in the Night* (New York: Macmillan Co., 1946): 76.

41. Ibid.: 300.

42. David Cesarani, *Arthur Koestler: The Homeless Mind* (London: William Heineman, 1998): 247.

43. Despite their deep Zionist convictions, Meyer Levin and, later, Herman Wouk were more artistically convincing in their novels about American experience than in their novels promoting Zionism.

44. Leon Uris, *Exodus* (Garden City, N.Y.: Doubleday & Co., 1958): 4.

45. Ibid.: 55.

46. Ibid.: 625.

47. A. M. Klein, *Notebooks: Selections from the A. M. Klein Papers*, ed. Zailig Pollock and Usher Caplan (Toronto: University of Toronto Press, 1994): 131. Like every student of Klein, I am indebted to the excellent work of these two editors, to Usher Caplan also for his biographical study *Like One That Dreamed: A Portrait of A. M. Klein* (Toronto: McGraw-Hill Ryerson, 1982) and to Zailig Pollock especially for *A. M. Klein: The Story of the Poet* (Toronto: University of Toronto Press, 1994).

48. W. E. Collin, "The Spirit's Palestine," in *The White Savannahs* (Toronto: The Macmillan Company of Canada, 1936), reprinted in *A. M. Klein: Critical Views on Canadian Writers*, ed. Tom Marshall (Toronto: The Ryerson Press, 1970): 10.

49. Ludwig Lewisohn, foreword to A. M. Klein, *Hath Not a Jew: Poems* (New York: Behrman's Jewish Book House, 1940): v–viii. Lewisohn writes, "Only the poet who has a substance of his very own will be able to create a style of his very own. And so an apparent paradox becomes necessary truth. Abraham Klein, the most Jewish poet who has ever used the English tongue, is the only Jew who has ever contributed a new note of style, of expression, of creative enlargement to the poetry of that tongue."

50. A. M. Klein, *The Second Scroll* (New York: Alfred A. Knopf, 1951): 17–18.

51. Ibid.: 26.

52. A. M. Klein, "Notebook of a Journey," in *Beyond Sambation: Selected Essays and Editorials 1928–1955*, ed. M. W. Steinberg and Usher Caplan (Toronto: University of Toronto Press, 1982): 379.

53. *The Second Scroll:* 57.

54. Ibid.: 73–74.

55. Maurice Samuel, "The Book and the Miracle," in *Jewish Frontier* (November 1951): 11–15.

56. *The Second Scroll:* 4. Subsequent quotations in this paragraph are on pp. 8,20, 110.

57. Ibid.: 108–109. This includes the quote just following.

58. Ibid: 37–38.

Chapter 8. The Immigrant Phase

1. Henry Roth, *From Bondage,* vol. 3 of *Mercy of a Rude Stream* (New York: St. Martin's Press, 1996): 168.

2. Sholem Aleichem, *Motl peysi dem khazns,* edited and with an introduction by Chone Shmeruk (Jerusalem: Magnes Press, The Hebrew University, 1997): 15. The Motl episode under this title originally appeared as the second chapter in *Der amerikaner* [The American], New York, May 1907. Sholem Aleichem wrote the second series of Motl adventures when he was back in America in 1914, and he left the work unfinished at his death in 1915.

3. Sholem Aleichem, letter to Chaim Nahman Bialik, 18 August 1907. Quoted by Shmeruk in *Motl peysi dem khazns:* 317.

4. Mary Antin, *From Plotzk to Boston,* with a foreword by Israel Zangwill (Boston: W. B. Clarke, 1899). In a second edition, Antin explained that the printer had confused the Polish Plotzk (Plock) with her native Lithuanian city, Polotzk, but she let the error stand in the title.

5. Mary Antin, *The Promised Land,* with an introduction and notes by Werner Sollors (New York: Penguin, 1997): 1. This edition combines the best of everything, the photographs that accompanied the first edition of 1912, the corrections that were included in the second printing, an illuminating analysis of Antin's literary strategies, and an exemplary critical apparatus.

6. *Ibid.:* 191.

7. *Ibid.:* 164.

8. Naomi Sokoloff provides a useful overview of the literature on childhood narratives and penetrating studies of child heroes in Sholem Aleichem, Haim Nahman Bialik, Henry Roth, Aharon Appelfeld, and others in *Imagining the Child in Modern Jewish Fiction* (Baltimore: The Johns Hopkins University Press, 1992).

9. Ab[raham] Cahan, *Bleter fun mayn lebn* [Pages from My Life] (New York: Forward Association, 1928): vol. 4.

10. Abraham Cahan, *The Rise of David Levinsky,* Introduction by John Higham (New York: Harper Torchbooks, 1960): 86.

11. The protagonist of Herman Wouk's *Inside, Outside* (Boston: Little, Brown and Company, 1985) is one of the most confident and observant Jews in American fiction and a frank opponent of intermarriage.

12. Isaac Rosenfeld, "The Fall of David Levinsky," *Commentary* 14:2 (1952). Reprinted in Isaac Rosenfeld, *Preserving the Hunger: An Isaac Rosenfeld Reader,* ed. Mark Schechner, Foreword by Saul Bellow (Detroit: Wayne State, 1988): 155.

13. Ibid.: 155–156.

14. Werner Sollors, "Introduction" to *The Promised Land:* xvii–xxiv.

15. Anzia Yezierska, *Bread Givers* (New York: Doubleday, 1925). Quoted here from the

edition with a new introduction by Alice Kessler Harris (New York: Persea Books, 1975): 21.

16. Ibid.: 272.

17. Anzia Yezierska, *The Open Cage*, with an introduction by Alice Kessler-Harris and afterword by Louise Levitas Henriksen (New York: Persea Books, 1979): 245–251.

18. Michael Gold, *Jews Without Money* (New York: Carroll & Graf, 1984). The Introduction is dated New York, April 1935.

19. One of the most blatant examples of such accusation appears in Arthur Miller's *Focus*, a book that was presumably intended to defend the Jews against charges of antisemitism by proving that they are no different from everyone else. Hence, Newman, the antisemitic protagonist, is mistaken for a Jew when he has to start wearing glasses and is taught through this literary stratagem what it feels like to be mistreated as a Jew. But since Arthur Miller, like Michael Gold, feels that he must distinguish poor Jews from Jewish middlemen and exploiters who bring the hatred on themselves, he consigns one chapter to the Jewish candy store owner Finkelstein to have him figure out why money is at the root of the Jew's problem. The chapter has no natural function in the novel except to convey this message: "It was the pogrom that was inevitable, not its outcome. Its outcome only seemed inevitable because that money was in his house." See Arthur Miller, *Focus* (New York: Reynal and Hitchcock, 1945): chap. 15.

20. Budd Schulberg, *What Makes Sammy Run?* (New York: Random House, 1941). This quotation and those that follow are from the edition with a new afterword by the author (New York: Penguin Books, 1978): 20.

21. Ibid.: 50.

22. Ibid.: 247.

23. Mordecai Richler, *The Apprenticeship of Duddy Kravitz* (Don Mills, Ontario: Andre Deutsch, 1959).

24. Henry Roth, *Call It Sleep* (New York: Robert O. Ballou, 1934), reprinted (New York: Noonday Press/Farrar, Straus & Giroux: 1991), with an introduction by Alfred Kazin and an afterword by Hana Wirth-Nesher (the edition cited here). This section is adapted from my essay, "The Classic of Disinheritance," in *New Essays on Call It Sleep*, ed. Hana Wirth-Nesher (Cambridge, U.K.: Cambridge University Press, 1996): 61–74.

25. James Joyce, *A Portrait of the Artist as a Young Man*, with a commentary by Sean O'Faolain (New York: New American Library, 1954): 1.

26. *Call It Sleep*: 114.

27. Ibid.: 141.

28. Ibid.: 141.

29. Some of the finest studies of this novel concentrate on the author's narrative strategies in portraying a multilingual society. See Hana Wirth-Nesher, "Between Mother Tongue and Native Language in *Call It Sleep*," *Prooftexts* 10 (1990): 297–312. Reprinted as afterword in *Call It Sleep* (1991). See also Werner Sollors, "A world somewhere, somewhere else," in *New Essays on Call It Sleep*, pp. 127–188; Naomi Diamant, "Linguistic Universes in Henry Roth's *Call It Sleep*," *Contemporary Literature* 27:3 (1986):336–355.

30. Ibid.: 160.

31. Ibid.: 242.

32. Ibid.: 262.

33. Robert Alter writes, "Prose like this . . . was scarcely written in English before *Moby Dick*." See "Awakenings," *The New Republic* (25 January 1988):33–37.

34. *Call It Sleep*: 282.

35. Ibid.: 400.

36. Lamed Shapiro, "Shfoykh khamoskho [Pour Out Thy Wrath]," in *The Jewish Government and Other Stories*, ed. and trans. with an introduction by Curt Leviant (New York: Twayne, 1971): 144–151.

37. *Call It Sleep*: 405.

38. Ibid.: 419.

39. Ibid.: 437.

40. "The Most Neglected Books of the Past 25 Years," *The American Scholar* 25 (Autumn 1956): Fiedler, 178; Kazin, 486.

41. Henry Roth, *Shifting Landscape: A Composite, 1925–1987*, ed. with an introduction by Mario Materassi (Philadelphia: The Jewish Publication Society, 1987): xiii.

42. Ibid.: 50, 73.

43. Henry Roth, *From Bondage*: 210.

44. Ibid.: 73.

45. Ibid.: 75.

46. Saul Bellow discusses the poem in his introduction to Isaac Rosenfeld, *An Age of Enormity: Life and Writing in the Forties and Fifties*, ed. Theodore Solotaroff (Cleveland: World Publishing Co., 1962): 12–13. See also Chaim Raphael, "Yiddish or Hebrew, a Kasheh for Elijah," in *Jewish Chronicle Literary Supplement*, 6 June 1980; my "Language as Fate: Reflections on Jewish Literature in America," in *Literary Strategies: Jewish Texts and Contexts; Studies in Contemporary Jewry* (New York: Oxford University Press, 1996) vol. 12, ed. Ezra Mendelsohn: 129–131.

47. Isaac Rosenfeld, *Passage from Home* (New York: Meridian, 1961): 118.

48. Isaac Rosenfeld, "The Situation of the Jewish Writer," in *An Age of Enormity*: 69.

49. Mark Shechner, *After the Revolution: Studies in the Contemporary Jewish American Imagination* (Bloomington: Indiana University Press, 1987): 107.

50. Bernard Malamud, *The Assistant* (New York: Farrar, Straus & Cudahy, 1957).

51. Bernard Malamud, title story in *The Magic Barrel* (New York: Vintage, 1958): 212.

52. Irving Howe, *World of Our Fathers*, with the assistance of Kenneth Libo (New York: Harcourt Brace Jovanovich, 1976): 646.

53. Delmore Schwartz, "America! America!" in *The World Is a Wedding* (New York: New Directions, 1948): 128.

Chapter 9. Writing Beyond Alienation

1. Saul Bellow, *The Bellarosa Connection* (New York: Penguin, 1989): 79.

2. Leslie Fiedler, "What Can We Do About Fagin?" *Commentary* (May 1949): 411–418.

3. Ibid.: 412.

4. Alfred Kazin, *On Native Grounds: An Interpretation of Modern American Prose Literature*, abridged (Garden City, N.Y.: Doubleday & Co., 1956): 408.

5. Norman Podhoretz, *Making It* (New York: Random House, 1967): 123–124.

6. Fiedler: 416.

7. Saul Bellow, *Dangling Man* (New York: Vanguard Press, 1944): 9.

8. Cynthia Ozick, introduction to Saul Bellow, *Seize the Day* (New York: Penguin, 1996): xv.

9. Saul Bellow, *The Adventures of Augie March* (New York: Viking, 1953): 536.

10. Saul Bellow, *Herzog* (New York: Viking, 1964): 119–120. See also Ruth R. Wisse, *The Schlemiel as Modern Hero* (Chicago: University of Chicago Press, 1971): 104–105.

11. Bellow treated this subject directly in his nonfiction book *To Jerusalem and Back: A Personal Account* (New York: Viking, 1976).

12. Saul Bellow, *Mr. Sammler's Planet* (New York: Viking, 1970): 3.

13. Ibid.: 33.

14. Saul Bellow, introduction, *Great Jewish Short Stories* (New York: Dell, 1963): 12.

15. *Mr. Sammler's Planet*: 13.

16. Ibid.: 41.

17. Ibid.: 42.

18. Ibid.: 17.

19. Ibid.: 18.

20. Irving Howe, "Mr. Sammler's Planet," *Harpers* (February 1970): 112.

21. *Mr. Sammler's Planet*: 78.

22. Ibid.: 26.

23. *William Blake's Writings*, ed. G. E. Bentley, Jr. (Oxford: Clarendon Press, 1978): vol. 1, 318.

24. *Mr. Sammler's Planet*: 155.

25. Ibid.: 290–293.

26. Ibid.: 294.

27. Ibid.: 313.

28. Beverly Gross, "Dark Side of the Moon," *The Nation* (8 February 1970): 154.

29. Alfred Kazin, "Though He Slay Me," *New York Review of Books* (3 December 1970).

30. Brent Staples, "Into the Ivory Tower," *New York Times Magazine* (6 February 1994).

31. Ethan Goffman, "Between Guilt and Affluence: The Jewish Gaze and Black Thief in *Mr. Sammler's Planet*," *Contemporary Literature* (Winter 1997): 706.

32. Hilton Kramer, "Saul Bellow, Our Contemporary," *Commentary* (June 1994): 37.

33. Saul Bellow, "Starting Out in Chicago," *The American Scholar* 44: 1 (Winter 1974–75): 72–73.

34. *Mr. Sammler's Planet*: 149.

35. Cynthia Ozick, *The Cannibal Galaxy* (New York: Dutton, 1984) : 36.

36. Ibid: 81.

37. Ibid.: 92.

38. Cynthia Ozick, *The Shawl* (New York: Alfred A. Knopf, 1989): 3.

39. Hana Wirth-Nesher, "The Languages of Memory: Cynthia Ozick's *The Shawl*" in *Multilingual America: Transnationalism, Ethnicity, and the Languages of American Literature*, ed. Werner Sollors (New York: New York University Press, 1998): 315.

40. *The Shawl*: 19.

41. Ibid.: 58.

42. Ibid.: 36–7.

43. Philip Roth, *The Counterlife* (New York: Farrar, Straus & Giroux, 1987): 369–370.

44. Mary McCarthy and Philip Roth, "An Exchange," *The New Yorker* (28 December 1998 and 4 January 1999): 98–99.

45. *The Counterlife*: 368.

46. Philip Roth, *American Pastoral* (Boston: Houghton Mifflin Co., 1997): 31.

47. Ibid.: 398.

48. Ibid.: 206–207.

49. Ibid.: 402.

50. Ibid.: 331

Chapter 10. A Chapter in the Making

1. Shalom Spiegel, *Hebrew Reborn* (New York: Meridian Books, 1962): 21. First published by the Jewish Publication Society, 1930.

2. Spiegel: 20.

3. Alan Mintz, ed., *The Boom in Contemporary Israeli Fiction* (Hanover, N.H.: Brandeis University Press, 1977): 4.

4. See the sympathetic treatment of Dan Miron in *If There Is No Jerusalem . . . Essays on Hebrew Writing in a Cultural-Political Context* [in Hebrew] (Tel Aviv: Hakibbutz Hameuchad, 1987): 114–120; Yaacov Shavit, *The New Hebrew Nation: A Study in Israeli Heresy and Fantasy* (London: Frank Cass, 1987).

5. The translation of Anton Shammas's *Arabeskot* by Vivian Eden (New York: Harper & Row, 1988) was sponsored by Israel's Institute for the Translation of Hebrew Literature.

6. Barukh Kurzweil, *Our New Literature: Continuation or Revolution?* [in Hebrew] (Tel Aviv: Schocken Books, 1959): 15–16. Kurzweil cites as his source for the quoted phrase about "Judische Einheitskultur" Max Wiener, *Jöudische Religion im Zeitalter der Emanzipation* (Berlin, Philo Verlag, 1933): 5.

7. Shimon Halkin, *Modern Hebrew Literature: From the Enlightenment to the Birth of the State of Israel: Trends and Values*, 2nd ed. (New York: Schocken Books, 1970): 20.

8. Gershon Shaked, *Hebrew Narrative Fiction 1889–1980* [in Hebrew] vol. 5 (Tel Aviv: Jerusalem: Hakibbutz Hameuchad and Keter Publishing, 1998): 15.

9. Gershon Shaked, *No Other Place: On Literature and Society* [in Hebrew] (Tel Aviv: Hakibbutz Hameuchad, 1988).

10. Dan Miron, *When Loners Come Together: A Portrait of Hebrew Literature at the Turn of the Twentieth Century* [in Hebrew] (Tel Aviv: Am Oved, 1987): 9ff.

11. Albert Thibaudet, *Histoire de la littérature française de Chateaubriand à Valéry* (Paris: Librairie Stock, 1936): 3–5.

12. Miron: 14.

13. When Harshav writes, "Poetics is relevant to every scholar and student of literature, irrespective of the boundaries of language or specialization," he applies the word *relevance* to the academic discipline of literary studies rather than to the society or national community whose literature it may be. See "Poetics Plus" in *poetics today* 1: 1–2 (Autumn 1979): 5.

14. Benjamin Harshav, *Language in Time of Revolution* (Berkeley: University of California Press, 1993): 33. See Itamar Even-Zohar, "Aspects of the Hebrew-Yiddish Polysystem: A Case of a Multilingual Polysystem," in *Polysystem Studies*, ed. Even-Zohar (*poetics today*, vol. I,1): 121–130.

15. Alan Mintz raises a different set of questions in his balanced analysis "On the Tel Aviv School of Poetics," *Prooftexts* 4: 3 (September 1984): 215–234: "Poetics filters out the specific and particularistic: time, place, people, i.e., everything which comprises the Jewish content of Jewish literature. What is left? What *can* be left of Jewish literature once history and experience have been drained to expose the fundamental structures of literature?" (p. 232).

16. Arnold Band, "Modern Hebrew Literature," in *Report of the Task Force on Foreign Acquisitions: Israel*, supplement to Association for Jewish Studies *Newsletter* 44 (Summer 1994): 10.

17. From shortly after he began to use the pseudonym, Abramovitch was known as Mendele Moykher-Sforim, or just Mendele, in the same way that Sholem Rabinovitch was universally known as Sholem Aleichem. But since Dan Miron argued, in his influential thesis *A Traveler Disguised*, for the recognition of the author as distinct from his invented inter-

mediary, *Abramovitch* has been gaining the upper hand to allow for keener discussion of how fiction is made. There is a strong argument to be made for retaining *Mendele*, the name that continues to grace his books, but I will follow Miron here in using *Abramovitch* for the author and *Mendele* solely for the narrator–book peddler who appears in the work.

18. I. Nusinov, "From Book to Book" [in Yiddish], in *Tsaytshrift*, vols. 2–3 (Minsk: Institut far vaysruslendisher kultur, 1928): 431. The dedication in Russian explains that the author had heard the mayor, who was simultaneously governor of Odessa, say in an address to the Jewish delegation that Jews themselves would have to combat the abuses on the Meat-Tax, and that he permitted himself the dedication out of gratitude for those words.

19. I discussed this work more fully in "The Jewish Intellectual and the Jews: The Case of Di kliatshe by Mendele Mocher Sforim," Daniel E. Koshland Memorial Lecture, Congregation Emanu-El, San Francisco, 1992.

20. Mendele Mocher Sforim (Abramovitch), "The Mare," trans. Joachim Neugroschel in his edition *The Great Works of Jewish Fantasy and Occult* (Woodstock, N.Y.: The Overlook Press, 1986): 549. For Yiddish version see *Ale ksovim*, vol. 2: *Di kliatshe* (Odessa: A. Varshaver, 1889): 9. References here are to the English edition.

21. Ibid.: 560.

22. Ibid.: 626.

23. See Shmuel Werses, "Demonological Motifs in *The Mare*" [in Hebrew] in *From Mendele to Hazaz: Studies in the Development of Hebrew Prose* (Jerusalem: Magnes Press, 1987): 70–86.

24. Some of that innovative analysis, with a summary of the negative criticism, can be found in Menahem Perry, "Analogy and Its Role as a Structural Principle in the Novels of Mendele Mocher Sforim," *Hasifrut* 1: 1 (Spring 1968): 65–100. Perry does not include this work in his analysis.

25. Gershon Shaked, *Lelo motsa* [Dead End: Studies in J. H. Brenner, M. J. Berdichevsky, G. Shoffman and U. N. Gnessin] (Tel Aviv: Hakibbutz Hemeuchad, 1973): 58.

26. Yaakov Shabtai, *Zikhron devarim* (Tel Aviv: Siman kriyah, 1977), translated *Past Continuous* by Dalya Bilu (Philadelphia: Jewish Publication Society, 1985): 296.

27. Ibid.: 291.

28. Judah Goldin, ed., *The Living Talmud: The Wisdom of the Fathers* (New York: New American Library, 1957): 116.

29. *Past Continuous*: 88–89.

30. Ibid.: 13–14.

31. Ibid.: 16.

32. Ibid.: 18.

33. Ibid.: 3.

34. Ibid.: 212.

35. Nissim Calderon, "Until the 17th May 1977" [in Hebrew], *Siman Keriyah* 10 (1980): 433. The date in the title of the essay refers to the first defeat of the Labor party in the Israeli elections, which some of its adherents took to be the end of the country as they knew it.

36. *Past Continuous*: 169.

37. Ibid.: 383–384. For complete translation see *Kepler's Dream* by John Lear, with the full text and notes of Kepler's *Somnium, Sive Astronomia Lunaris*, translated by Patricia Frueh Kirkwood (Berkeley: University of California Press, 1965): 106–107.

38. *Past Continuous*: 96.

39. Ibid.: 58–59.

40. Ibid.: 145.

41. Robert Alter, "Fiction in a State of Siege," in *Defenses of the Imagination: Jewish Writers and Modern Historical Crisis* (Philadelphia: The Jewish Publication Society, 1977): 223.

Author's Postscript

1. See *A Completed Novel: M. Y. Berdyczewski's Miriam—a Novel of Two Townships*, annotated with an introduction by Zipora Kagan [in Hebrew] (Haifa: The University of Haifa, 1997). English: *Miriam: A Novel about Life in Two Townships*, trans. A. S.Super (Tel Aviv: Hakibbutz Hameuchad: Institute for the Translation of Hebrew Literature, 1983). Avner Holtzman, *Hakarat panim* [in Hebrew; Essays on Micah Josef Berdyczewski] (Tel Aviv: Cultural Department of the Holon Municipality, 1994).

2. David Bergelson, *Descent*, ed. and trans. Joseph Sherman (New York: The Modern Language Association of America, 1999). This work is also featured under the title *Departing* in Golda Werman, *The Stories of David Bergelson* (Syracuse: Syracuse University Press, 1996): 25–154.

3. Haim Hazaz, *Delatot nekhoshet*, trans. *Gates of Bronze* by S. Gershon Levi (Philadelphia. Jewish Publication Society, 1975).

4. Chaim Grade, *Tsemakh atlas* trans. *The Yeshiva*, 2 vols. by Curt Leviant (New York and Indianapolis, Bobbs-Merrill Co., 1976–77).

5. Cynthia Ozick, *The Messiah of Stockholm* (New York, Alfred A. Knopf, 1987). David Grossman, *Ayen erekh 'ahava.'* English:. *See: Under Love*, trans. Betsy Rosenberg (New York: Farrar, Straus & Giroux, 1986).

Suggested Reading from the Modern Jewish Canon

THE FOLLOWING MODEST LIST is meant to serve as a reference guide for those readers who want to conduct their own journey through twentieth-century Jewish fiction. It includes only works that are available in English, translated from Ashkenazic-European and Jewish languages. Instead of separating them according to their original languages, I have grouped the books chronologically to encourage consideration of how language informs literature that was written around the same time and from many different perspectives. The list is confined to works of fiction and a tiny number of memoirs, some of which are discussed at length in this book. Furthermore, I have listed only one major book by each author, although of course other works by many of these authors might be included as well. If nothing else, I sincerely hope that readers will take this list as an invitation to investigate the modern Jewish canon and then propose their own nominees from among the ample pool.

From Modern to Modernist Literature

Mendele Moykher-Sforim, *The Mare*. Yiddish/Hebrew (1873–1909)
Sholem Aleichem, *Tevye the Dairyman*. Yiddish (1895–1914)
Franz Kafka, *The Trial*. German (1914, 1925)
Abraham Cahan, *The Rise of David Levinsky*. English/American (1917)
David Bergelson, *Descent*. Yiddish (1920)
Yosef Haim Brenner, *Breakdown and Bereavement*. Hebrew (1920)
Micah Yosef Berdichevsky, *Miriam*. Hebrew (1921)

Jewish Literature of War and Revolution

Isaac Babel, *Red Cavalry*. Russian (1926)
Vladimir Ze'ev Jabotinsky, *Samson*. Russian (1926)
Moyshe Kulbak, *Zelmenyaner*. Yiddish (1928)
Israel Rabon, *The Street*. Yiddish (1928)
Avigdor Hameiri, *The Great Madness*. Hebrew (1930)
Joseph Roth, *Job*. German (1930)
Sholem Asch, *Three Cities*. Yiddish (1929–1931)
Nadezhda Mandelstam, *Hope Against Hope*. Russian (1970)

Jewish Literature of the Thirties

Bruno Schulz, *The Street of Crocodiles*. Polish (1934)
Henry Roth, *Call It Sleep*. English/American (1934)
Isaac Bashevis Singer, *Satan in Goray*. Yiddish (1935)
Israel Joshua Singer, *The Brothers Ashkenazi*. Yiddish (1936)
Esther Kreitman, *Deborah*. Yiddish (1936)
Jacob Glatstein, *Homecoming at Twilight*. Yiddish (1938)
Der Nister (Pinhas Kahanovitch), *The Family Mashber*. Yiddish (1939, 1943)
S. Y. Agnon, *A Guest for the Night*. Hebrew (1939)

Literature of the Holocaust (*Shoah, Khurbn*)

Anne Frank, *Diary of Anne Frank*. Dutch (1942–1944, 1947)
Primo Levi, *If This Is a Man*. Italian (1946)
Elie Wiesel, *Night*. Yiddish (1956) French (1958)
Vasili Grossman, *Life and Fate*. Russian (1960; 1980)
Piotr Rawicz, *Blood from the Sky*. French (1961)
Henryk Grynberg, *The Victory*. Polish (1969)
Chava Rosenfarb, *The Tree of Life*. Yiddish (1972)
Aharon Appelfeld, *Badenheim 1939*. Hebrew (1974)
The wartime diaries of Etty Hillesum, Moshe Flinker, Abraham Lewin, Zelig Kalmanovitch, Chaim Kaplan, Yitzchak Katzenelson, Janusz Korchak, Herman Kruk, Emanuel Ringelblum, Hannah Senesh, and others, occupy a privileged place as literary testimony in this section of Jewish literature.

Jewish Literature of Mid-Century

Arthur Koestler, *Thieves in the Night*. English/British (1945)

Abraham Moses Klein, *The Second Scroll*. English/Canadian (1951)
Albert Memmi, *Pillar of Salt*. French (1953)
Bernard Malamud, *The Magic Barrel*. English/American (1958)
Yehuda Amichai, *Not of This Time, Not of This Place*. Hebrew (1963)
Chaim Grade, *The Yeshiva*. Yiddish (1967–1968)
Haim Hazaz, *Gates of Bronze*. Hebrew (1924–1968)
Albert Cohen, *Belle du seigneur*. French (1968)
Shulamith Hareven, *City of Many Days*. Hebrew (1972)

From Modernism to Postmodernism

Saul Bellow, *Mr. Sammler's Planet*. English/American (1969)
Yaakov Shabtai, *Past Continuous*. Hebrew (1970)
Cynthia Ozick, *The Pagan Rabbi and Other Stories*. English/American (1971)
Adele Wiseman, *Crackpot*. English/Canadian (1974)
Amos Oz, *The Hill of Evil Counsel*. Hebrew (1976)
A. B. Yehoshua, *Mr. Mani*. Hebrew (1990)
Philip Roth, *American Pastoral*. English/American (1997)

INDEX